CW01676664

بِسْمِ اللَّهِ الرَّحْمَٰنِ الرَّحِيمِ

In the name of Allah, the Most Beneficent, the Most Merciful

ASALET®

ASALET®

The Name of Book	THE MESSIAH Isa Son of Maryam the Complete Truth
Author	Dr. Ali Mohammad al-Sallabi
Publication Number	26
Editor	Recep Songül
Translator	Alai Mohammad Awwad
Translation Editor	Anas Altikriti
Graphics and Design	AsaletAjans
ISBN No	978-605-7721-00-6
Certificate Number	40687
Printing	1st Edition, İstanbul, March 2020
Print and Cover	StepAjans Matbaa Ltd. Şti. Göztepe Mh. Bosna Cd. No:11 Bağcılar / İST. Certificate Number: 45522
Publishers	Asalet Eğitim Danışmanlık Yayın Hizmetleri İç ve Dış Ticaret
Publisher Address	Balaban Ağa Mh. Büyük Reşit Paşa Cd. Yümni İş Hanı, 16B/16 (Vezneciler) Fatih / İSTANBUL-TÜRKİYE 0090 212 511 85 47 www.asaletyayinlari.com asaletyayinlari@gmail.com

© 2020 Asalet Publications

This book is in copyright. Subject to statutory exception and to the provisions of relevant collective licensing agreements, no reproduction of an part may take place without the written permission of the publisher.

THE MESSIAH

Isa Son of Maryam
the Complete Truth

Dr. Ali Mohammad al-Sallabi

ASALET®

The views and opinions expressed in this book are those of the author and not necessarily those of the publisher. The publisher is not responsible for the accuracy of the information presented.

Table of Contents

Chapter Two

Isa (pbuh) in the Holy Qur'an

CHAPTER III

The Miracles of Prophet Isa (pbuh) and Raising him to the Heavens

Chapter IV

Najran's Nasraanis – from Arguing to Mubahala

Introductory words for "*Isa son of Maryam, the Complete Truth*"

By Professor Ali al-Qaradaghi

Secretary General of the International Association of Muslim Scholars

These words are part of a new book entitled, "*The Messiah Isa son of Maryam – the Complete Truth*" by learned scholar and friend, his excellency Dr Ali Mohammed al-Sallabi who has delved into a topic considered among the most complex and controversial, even for Nasraanis themselves. Yet, with the Grace of God, Dr al-Sallabi was able to find that which he sought in the Holy Qur'an, which God descended as cure and mercy for all. The Qur'an was descended to reveal the truth about disagreements that occurred among past nations and the facts which past and present scholars have also disagreed upon. God Says in Surat al-Nahl (39): {In order that He may manifest to them the truth of that wherein they differ, and that the rejecters of Truth may realise that they had indeed (surrendered to) Falsehood}.

Dealing with such complex and grand topics is not something alien to the writer who has coexisted with the Holy Qur'an in all its facets as both his Master's and Doctorate dissertations were on subjective interpretation; this is in addition to his many useful writings on Prophet Mohammad's life and on historical benchmarks which have aided him in completing this book – Nay, this great project!

When the honour of scientific knowledge is due to the nobility of its topics, this book has earned two great honours, i.e. the subject matter of the book that gives prominence to one of the greatest prophets and messengers the world has witnessed. This prophet is none other than our master Isa son of Maryam Peace be upon him, who is also one of the five prophets of Inflexible Purpose, and one whose followers form the largest percentage among heavenly religions at almost 31%.

The second honour is that the Holy Qur'an is the source from which the author utilised the proofs for his book; this Book that has given unsurmountable prominence to all which is related to Prophet Isa to the extent that the third Surah in the Qur'an was named Aal-Imran (Imran's Folk). Then another Surah is named after his mother, Maryam (Peace be upon her) and a third is entitled al-Maa'idah (the Repast) which Isa's followers requested God to descend upon them. This is in addition to other holy verses mentioned in the Qur'an on the children of Israel and the family of Isa (Peace be upon him).

The kind author has invested his historical specialisation in exemplifying the historical benchmarks of the homeland in which Prophet Isa was born, i.e. Palestine, and allocated information thereof in its first chapter along with the political, social and intellectual norms at the time. In the second chapter, the author exhausted all instances of the Qur'an's mention of Prophet Isa and deducted many bright and blessed conclusions therefrom. He also explained everything in well laid out format and organisation that gives an independent and inclusive image of Prophet Isa (pbuh).

I can say with conviction that not a single verse about or related to Isa or his near or distant family has not been mentioned and explained by the author, as well as having mentioned all opinions and meanings these may carry with total objectivity. The book's third chapter then covers all miracles performed by Prophet Isa (pbuh).

Chapter Four of the book complements the most important aspects related to Prophet Isa's followers as it details the debate that occurred between Najran's Nasraanis and Prophet Mohammad (pbuh). The chapter also discusses the dialogue among the four Bibles on an objective-scientific level and utilises hundreds of sources and references that have enriched the book with much insight.

The Book is a Comprehensive Truth

All who read this great work shall reach an unembellished truth that it has provided a cohesive, inclusive and balanced image of Prophet Isa (pbuh) in accordance with the Jurisprudence of Balances. This is because it relied on proofs from the Holy Qur'an which: {No falsehood can approach it from before or behind it: It is sent down by One Full of Wisdom, Worthy of all Praise} (Surat Fussilat: 42), and on the words of Prophet Mohammad (pbuh) who God Says of them: {Nor does he say (aught) of (his own) Desire. It is no less than inspiration sent down to him} (Surat Fussilat: 3-4).

Accordingly, the Holy Qur'an, along with its interpretation, has revealed the complete truth about our Prophet Isa son of Maryam (pbuh) so as to clear any disagreements about that truth. The verifying author states that the most important conclusion his investigative book has achieved is: "There exists no Book on Earth that has given the Messiah (pbuh), his Virgin Mother and her family such honouring and reverence more than the Holy Qur'an. This reverence undoubtedly surpasses that of the currently existing Torah and gospels. In addition to this honouring, the Holy Qur'an corrected mistakes, accusations and baseless allegations that were directed at Prophet Isa and his pure mother by Jews and even Christians themselves." The author was able to identify the meticulous and detailed Qur'anic information considered "among the miraculous facets of informing, accounting for, educating and scientifically detailing the many incidents of renewal in the life of God's prophet and servant, Isa son of Maryam (Peace be upon them).

The author also based his book on the understanding of Qur'anic imagery from the confirmed Sunnah of Prophet Mohammad;

this is in addition to the acknowledged sources of *Tafseer* (interpretation), explanation, investigation of meanings, auditing of linguistic usage and the facets of textual miracles.

The Jurisprudence of Balances

That revealed in the Holy Qur'an about Prophet Isa and his mother Maryam is based on Qur'anic balances concerning the Creator and His creations which reveal facts that agree with common sense and righteous minds. The jurisprudence balance of The Almighty Creator is that He exists and is not created, enacted, born, in need of anyone, eats, drinks, excretes or the like. The balance of God's creations is that mankind is a creature enacted through God's Will from a void, who is born and in need, and for who He set a meticulous system to follow.

Hence, we notice how the Holy Qur'an has focused of these balances and described the creation of Prophet Isa from its onset. The Qur'an first mentions how Imran's wife made a vow: {Behold! a woman of Imran said: "O my Lord! I do dedicate unto Thee what is in my womb for Thy special service: So accept this of me: For Thou hearest and knowest all things."} (Surat Aal-Imran: 35). This holy verse shows that Isa (pbuh) is a creation born of his mother Maryam, who was in turn born out of her mother, as means of emphasising that Isa is no different from any other man except in two matters:

First: A breath from God created Isa without a father's seed.

Second: That Isa was a messenger of God, created through God's Word (be!), was blessed with the ability to perform great physical miracles and who was described by the Almighty as possessing great traits. The wording of the Qur'anic verse on Maryam, above, shows that she was a created being and in need, and that her mother had beseeched God that Maryam and her offspring be saved from Satan. The words on how Zakariya then looked after her, along with all the blessings God bestowed upon her are to emphasise that Maryam was a creation and not a god. As the mother was definitely not a god, the Qur'an brings forward conclusive intellectual proofs that her son too was not a god. Accordingly, the Holy Qur'an accentuates Isa as the son of Maryam, a born creation, not a creator nor a god in any facet of creation or divinity. Qur'anic proofs clarify this through the instance when the angels conveyed the blessed news to Maryam: {Behold! the angels said: "O Mary! Allah giveth thee glad tidings of a Word from Him: his name will be Christ Jesus, the son of Mary} (Surat Aal-Imran: 45). Hence, the Creator is of mandated existentialism, ancient and preceded by neither person nor matter.

If there exists any abnormality in that Isa has no father, the Almighty has shown that this was due to His Ability of doing much more than that, for if God wants anything to exist, He would Order it to (be!) so and it would materialise.

The fact that Prophet Isa was born out of no seed from a physical father, and that he is a Word from God, in no way means that Isa is a god as such a fatherless creation does not deny him being a creation. Also, describing Isa (pbuh) as "God's Word" or "A Word from God" is meant to show that God created Isa by merely uttering His Wish without the existence of the natural reasons for creation, i.e. the seed created by male semen and female ovary. Accordingly, the creation of Isa was similar to that of Adam who God created from dirt without the presence of a father or even a mother for that matter. God says (p5&6). Hence, God is Able to create anything or anyone He wishes from a complete void, rendering the creation of a man without a physical fatherly seed so much easier. God Says: {The similitude of Jesus before Allah is as that of Adam; He created him from dust, then said to him: "Be". And he was.} (Surat Aal-Imran: 59). When God is able to create from nothingness, it is much easier for Him to create a man without a father. God Says: {It is He Who begins (the process of) creation; then repeats it; and for Him it is most easy} (Surat al-Roum: 27). Also, Prophet Isa was a foetus in his mother's womb, a child in cradle, a young man and then a mature man. He was persecuted and tortured by the Jews and others, lived a turbulent life of humans who are influenced by events and who influence others, whose circumstances changed with the temporal changes surrounding him, and who transformed from young age to an older one. All of these are conclusive proofs agreeable to the mind and eye that Isa was a creation affected by events, not a god as claimed by the vast majority of Nasraanis.

Based on the above, the claim by the majority of Nasraanis that Isa is a god or the son of a god within the Trinity contradicts with intellect and proofs, and a claim where each of the three contradicts with the other. Christians acknowledge that Maryam was pregnant with Isa, that he had a childhood and was tortured, and that he was even crucified and killed – which the Holy Qur'an refuted – so how can such a "man" be a god?!

Most Nasraanis, except those Unitarians among them, deem that the god of the Trinity is but one, i.e. the Father who is creator and owner of all, the son born of and equal to the Father in essence, and the Holy Spirit. They consider that these three are united in essence and will but that they do not form one self, but rather three selves and a trinity where each is a completely independent god. On this premise, Isa (pbuh) is a god in the form of a man but who is also a god. Accordingly, the scales here have become misguided, confused and utterly contradictory.

Many scholars and intellectuals have refuted these claims and stated that such a notion was one of the Roman civilisation and that recognised gospels do not distinctly reference the Trinity. Some scripture in these gospels states that when Prophet Isa performed a miracle, he would first pray to the Almighty via supplication, praise and then thank The Almighty for His grace. The gospel of Mark (2:28) states that (Jesus Christ) was a man and son of a man. The gospel of Luke (2:52) states that he was a man who was born and raised. The gospels of Luke (7:34-35 & 6:12) and Mark (1:35) state that he ate and drank like all humans, prayed and supplicated most of the day and night. The gospel of Luke (4:42-43) states that he was sent as a prophet, messenger and teacher to the children of Israel.

In this regard, Clyde Tarns states, "The name the Messiah called himself by was (the son of man), and all that which the Bible reported to us of him was that he was a man who lived like one and who had all physical traits of one. The Messiah grew up, felt physical pain, cried, slept and died. All these trials testify to Jesus's humanity."

The Old Testament (Torah) clearly indicates that prophets were not gods and that they had no ability to perform miracles except through the Will of the Almighty.

The verses in the Holy Qur'an on Maryam and Isa (pbut) are proof of the balance of miracles that is based on exceeding norms and reason through The Almighty's Ability.

It is also clear that the balance of Divine revelation is not influenced by that which occurs within the prophet's psychology and his followers. Despite the presence of a struggle between them and Nasraanis, and all the disagreement and doubts Prophet Mohammad (pbuh) received from most of them, the Holy Qur'an still spoke of Prophet Isa, his mother and grandmother with much kindness, and attributed to them many great traits.

So these are many clear proofs that the Holy Qur'an was descended by The Almighty God; not from the Prophet, whose human feelings would have otherwise been reflected in its verses.

In conclusion, this book "Isa Peace be upon him – the Complete Truth" is a great endeavour that truly brings forward the complete truth about our prophet Isa (pbuh) and his truthful mother Maryam through the holy source, i.e. the Qur'an. It is a comprehensive and inclusive book that is greatly beneficial and insightful for Muslims, Christians and all other truth seekers as it answers those questions which have torn apart the fabric of Christian unity – since the Nicaean Council of 325 AD. The author has listed all verses of the Holy Qur'an related to Prophet Isa, his mother and her family in a framework that is based on scientific balances and deep understanding of jurisprudence.

Accordingly, I strongly recommend that this book be published at the widest scale possible and translated into the world's most important languages so that all people, especially Nasraanis, may learn of the Holy Qur'an's stance regarding the truth about our great prophet, Isa (pbuh).

Introduction

All thanks and gratitude be to Allah, The Almighty God, through whose guidance I have been able to complete this work.

{O ye who believe! Fear Allah as He should be feared and die not except in a state of Islam}[1] (Surat Aal-Imran: 102).

{O mankind! reverence your Guardian-Lord, who created you from a single person, created, of like nature, His mate, and from them twain scattered (like seeds) countless men and women; reverence Allah, through whom ye demand your mutual (rights), and (reverence) the wombs (That bore you): for Allah ever watches over you} (Surat al-Nisaa': 01).

{O ye who believe! Fear Allah, and (always) say a word directed to the Right: That He may make your conduct whole and sound and forgive you your sins: He that obeys Allah and His Messenger, has already attained the highest Achievement} (Surat al-Ahzaab: 70-71).

On 29.4.2015, and while on a trip to Italy as a guest of the Saint Aguido civil society organisation, God's Will had its own way in causing me to embark on this book. I was accompanied by colleagues Atif BuKarra and Waleed al-Lafi al-Farjani al-Tarhouni on a mission of peace and reconciliation among the warring parties in Libya. Those who attended from the organisation's side were:

- Father Angelo Romano
- Mr Andrea Trintinni
- Interpreter, Mrs Angela al-Rayyis.

The meeting took place in a Vatican owned church in Rome and during it I spoke of God's Holy Names, including that of Peace,

[1] Translator's note: Translations of Qur'anic verses in this book are taken from Yusuf Ali's translation of the Holy Quran.

and how our prayers start with (God is Greatest) and end with the word "Peace", in addition to the fact that one of Heaven's names is also "The House of Peace".

I then spoke of Islam's stance on Prophet Isa and his virgin mother and began by reciting the verse: {Relate in the Book (the story of) Mary, when she withdrew from her family to a place in the East} (Surat Maryam: 16).

Then when I began explaining the verses: {"O sister of Aaron! Thy father was not a man of evil, nor thy mother a woman unchaste!" But she pointed to the baby. They said: "How can we talk to one who is a child in the cradle?" He said: "I am indeed a servant of Allah. He hath given me revelation and made me a prophet; And He hath made me blessed wheresoever I be, and hath enjoined on me Prayer and Charity as long as I live} (Surat Maryam: 28-31), the interpreter began crying and her eyes filled up with tears. It was this incident that the idea came to me – most probably as a revelation from God – that we needed to highlight the verses of the Holy Qur'an which speak of Prophet Isa's life, and that of his mother, and phrase them in an intellectually modern book that is in line with the current era and modern human discourse. Such a book would be based upon the Words of God, first and foremost, and which would revel the truth about Prophet Isa (pbuh)[2] in an intellectually logical manner that resonates with human instinct's yearning for understanding the truth about the Messiah Isa son of Maryam.

Accordingly, I embarked on collecting and purchasing all books related to Prophet Isa and read all information about Christian sects and their origins, the history of churches, the old and new testaments, the gospels of Luke, Matthew, John, Mark and Barnabas, university dissertations on these topics, persecution which Unitarian Nasraanis suffered throughout history, as well

[2] Peace Be Upon Him - Her

as dialogues and arguments between Islamic scholars and their Christian counterparts in both old and modern times.

I also studied Qur'anic verses in a subjective interpretive way, which is what I had specialised in as my Master's dissertation was on "Moderation in the Holy Qur'an" while my PhD dissertation was on "Empowerment in the Holy Qur'an."

I referred to scholars' interpretation of the Holy verses relating to Prophet Isa and his mother, including his message and status among prophets and messengers. That was when I realised how ignorant I was regarding such a blessed life and thought to myself that my life is worthy of being spent in researching and bringing to the masses all information regarding such messengers and prophets of Inflexible Purpose who The Almighty had appointed as leaders, icons of nations and humanity and truth-seekers throughout history.

This book is considered the onset of a grand civilisation project in introducing mankind to the lives and messages of prophets and messengers via the Holy Qur'an which contains all truths. It is the tip of the iceberg in explaining their ethics, messages, and the origins of that which they were entrusted with through the confirmed Hadeeths of Prophet Mohammad and the words of renowned scholars, in a modern wording that suits the phase in which humanity is experiencing wretchedness by alienating itself from Divine Guidance.

I thank God The Almighty that He has guided me toward catering to these topics and I beseech Him to aid me in carrying them out them purely for His sake. I pray for ease of printing, publishing, acceptance by the masses, a means for guiding many lost souls towards the path of righteousness; that these words may be well received by minds, instincts, hearts and souls; and that they may be a beacon that fills with light the darkened paths marred with satanic lusts. I pray that it would be reason for me, and for all who assisted and partook in publishing this book, towards an afterlife in the company of prophets, martyrs and the righteous.

I have named this book **"The Messiah Isa son of Maryam, the Complete Truth"** and divided it into a number of chapters. **Chapter One** is on the historical roots of the nation in which Isa (pbuh) was born where I wrote about the history of Palestine; the eras of Israelites' reign – jurists', kings' and the era of division, and their political, social and intellectual life; the impact of the Greek civilisation and the Romans on Palestine and the Levant; the Jewish groups prevalent during the emergence of the Messiah such as the Samarians, Sadducees, Pharisees, Qumranians, Asanians, the Temple and men of religion, as well as their dogmas and beliefs; and meanings of important words in this book such as Nasraaniism and Christianity, why Isa was dubbed the Messiah, and the difference between Christians and Nasraanis.

I titled the **Chapter Two**: (Isa (pbuh) in the Holy Qur'an). In it, I registered all instances that mentioned Isa (pbuh) and his mother. I also traced from the Qur'an all instances that mentioned his maternal grandmother, the clan of Imran, why they were mentioned in Surat Aal-Imran, who the clan of Imran are and why God selected them from among all others.

I discussed Maryam from the Qur'an's point of view and showed that the meaning of her name is she who worships and serves God. I also shed light on the supplication of Imran's wife to The Almighty, her beseeching of Him and submittal to His Will through calling Him by His Names of Greatness, i.e. The One God, The All-Hearing, The All-Knowing, and how He accepted her prayers and requests and took care of her daughter (and provided her with a good upbringing). The verse states the soundness of her growth and the completeness of her natural figure through pure Heavenly care. It also states how The Almighty had Zakariya commit to caring for Maryam (pbuh) and to her raising. I also wrote about the dignifying of Maryam as God provided her with her means of sustenance without having to toil for it, how Zakariya supplicated to The Almighty that He grant him good and righteous children after having reached an old age, and how The Almighty granted him his prayers. I also spoke about Zakariya's soft prayer to God and his beautiful prelude to the supplication, God's good news to Zakariya as he was in the praying space, the traits of Yahya (pbuh) that were mentioned in the Qur'an and showed the lesson and reason for mentioning the stories of Yahya and Zakariya when speaking about Maryam's life. When The Almighty spoke of the story of Yahya's birth of an barren woman and old man – which is a supernatural matter – He followed it with the birth of Isa without the presence of a father as a matter of much more awe and greatness.

I also wrote about God's choosing of Maryam as the purest among mankind at the time, whether she was a Siddeeqah (a conveyor of Truth) or a prophet, her prayers and supplications late at night, the angels' glad tiding to her about the birth of Isa and informing her of a number of his traits such as being of great importance in life and the Afterlife, close to God, speaks to people as an infant and a young man and one who is righteous, along with Maryam's response to this news.

I have also discussed the dialogue that occurred between the angel Jibreel (pbuh) and Maryam which is stated in Surat Maryam, and explained its meanings, values and lessons as per the words of *Tafseer*[3] jurists. I clarified what it means that Isa is God's Word and a Spirit from Him, the nature of this Spirit, its meanings in the Holy Qur'an and the explanation thereof.

I described the birth of Isa (pbuh) through the Qur'anic verses which expressed this great event, and the physical and psychological distress which Maryam (pbuh) experienced to the point that she

[3] Qur'an interpreters.

wished for death, as well as all Divine blessings and gifts accompanying that.

I mentioned Isa's (pbuh) ability to speak while still in the cradle in defence of his mother against the accusations attributed to her, through the Holy verses: "I am indeed a servant of Allah. He hath given me revelation and made me a prophet; And He hath made me blessed wheresoever I be, and hath enjoined on me Prayer and Charity as long as I live; (He) hath made me kind to my mother, and not overbearing or miserable; "So peace is on me the day I was born, the day that I die, and the day that I shall be raised up to life (again)" (Surat Maryam 30-33).

I shed light on the deep meanings of Qur'anic verses explaining the truth about Isa (pbuh), and conveyed the stance of king of Abyssinia, al-Najaashi, upon hearing the verses from Surat Maryam when read to him by Ja'afar bin Abu Talib. I also explained the great role Maryam played in human history, being a school of honesty with her God, self and religion, in chastity, piety, patience, worship, prayer and dependence upon Him.

I wrote exhaustively on Isa's message to the Israelites, his humanity, the need to believe he is a servant of God and His messenger, and believe in his message of Monotheism (Tawheed). Also, that the Holy Qur'an has openly expressed these facts through sound deduction, clear logic and unequivocal proof. God Says: {The similitude of Jesus before Allah is as that of Adam; He created him from dust, then said to him: "Be". And he was} (Surat Aal-Imran: 59)

Also in: {It is not (possible) that a man, to whom is given the Book, and Wisdom, and the prophetic office, should say to people: "Be ye my worshippers rather than Allah's": on the contrary (He would say) "Be ye worshippers of Him Who is truly the Cherisher of all: For ye have taught the Book and ye have studied it earnestly} (Surat Aal-Imran: 79)

And in: {O People of the Book! Commit no excesses in your religion: Nor say of Allah aught but the truth. Christ Jesus the son of Mary was (no more than) a messenger of Allah, and His Word, which He bestowed on Mary, and a spirit proceeding from Him: so believe in Allah and His messengers. Say not "Trinity": desist: it will be better for you: for Allah is one Allah. Glory be to Him: (far exalted is He) above having a son. To Him belong all things in the heavens and on earth. And enough is Allah as a Disposer of affairs. Christ disdaineth nor to serve and worship Allah, nor do the angels, those nearest (to Allah: those who disdain His worship and are arrogant,-He will gather them all together unto Himself to (answer)} (Surat al-Nisaa': 171-172).

And in: {They do blaspheme who say: "(Allah) is Christ the son of Mary." But said Christ: "O Children of Israel! worship Allah, my Lord and your Lord." Whoever joins other gods with Allah, Allah will forbid him the garden, and the Fire will be his abode. There will for the wrong-doers be no one to help. They do blaspheme who say: Allah is one of three in a Trinity: for there is no god except One Allah. If they desist not from their word (of blasphemy), verily a grievous penalty will befall the blasphemers among them. Why turn they not to Allah, and seek His forgiveness? For Allah is Oft- forgiving, Most Merciful. Christ the son of Mary was no more than a messenger; many were the messengers that passed away before him. His mother was a woman of truth. They had both to eat their (daily) food. See how Allah doth make His signs clear to them; yet see in what ways they are deluded away from the truth! Say: "Will ye worship, besides Allah, something which hath no power either to harm or benefit you? But Allah,- He it is that heareth and knoweth all things." Say: "O people of the Book! exceed not in your religion the bounds (of what is proper), trespassing beyond the truth, nor follow the vain desires of people who went wrong in times gone by, who misled many, and strayed (themselves) from the even way} (Surat al-Maa'idah: 72-77).

And in: {And behold! Allah will say: "O Jesus the son of Mary! Didst thou say unto men, worship me and my mother as gods in derogation of Allah?" He will say: "Glory to Thee! never could I say what I had no right (to say). Had I said such a thing, thou wouldst indeed have known it. Thou knowest what is in my heart, Thou I know not what is in Thine. For Thou knowest in full all that is hidden. "Never said I to them aught except what Thou didst command me to say, to wit, 'worship Allah, my Lord and your Lord'; and I was a witness over them whilst I dwelt amongst them; when Thou didst take me up Thou wast the Watcher over them, and Thou art a witness to all things. "If Thou dost punish them, they are Thy servant: If Thou dost forgive them, Thou art the Exalted in power, the Wise." Allah will say: "This is a day on which the truthful will profit from their truth: theirs are gardens, with rivers flowing beneath, their eternal Home: Allah well-pleased with them, and they with Allah. That is the great salvation, (the fulfilment of all desires). To Allah doth belong the dominion of the heavens and the earth, and all that is therein, and it is He Who hath power over all things.} (Surat al-Maa'idah: 116-120).

This is in addition to other Holy verses on the truth, calling and humanity of Prophet Isa (pbuh).

I also explained the status of Isa among prophets and messengers, that the source of his teachings is from The Almighty God and that he is among those of Inflexible Purpose, as per the following verse: {The same religion has He established for you as that which He enjoined on Noah - the which We have sent by inspiration to thee - and that which We enjoined on Abraham, Moses, and Jesus: Namely, that ye should remain steadfast in religion, and make no divisions therein: to those who worship other things than Allah, hard is the (way) to which thou callest them. Allah chooses to Himself those whom He pleases, and guides to Himself those who turn (to Him)} (Surat al-Shourah: 13).

Also through the verses of the Holy Qur'an, I explained the origins of laws he called for; those of belief, ethics and virtues; differences among messengers, and emphasised the important truth that the religion of prophets and messengers is Islam and mentioned the proofs thereof since the times of Noah, Ibrahim and henceforth till the time of Prophet Mohammad (pbut)[4].

I mentioned the affirmation by Isa of the Torah, how the Holy Qur'an describes it and the alteration it underwent; as well as of that of the Injeel after God raised Isa to the Heavens.

I also mentioned the most important studies on this topic, and the conclusions I reached regarding the gospels:

• (Distortion and Contradiction in the Four Gospels), a study by Dr Sarah Hamid Mohammad al-Abbaadi – scientific article in a book.

• (Methodology of Collecting al-Sunnah and the Gospels), a comparative study by Dr Aziyyah Ali Taha – scientific article in a book.

• (Sources of Nasraaniism), a study and critique by Dr Abdul-Razzak Abdul-Majeed – scientific article in a book.

I also listed the traits of Prophet Mohammad (pbuh) as mentioned in the Torah and Bible, as well as the good news received by Prophet Isa as per the holy verse: {And remember, Jesus, the son of Mary, said: "O Children of Israel! I am the messenger of Allah (sent) to you, confirming the Law (which came) before me, and giving Glad Tidings of a Messenger to come after me, whose name shall be Ahmad." But when he came to them with Clear Signs, they said, "this is evident sorcery!" Who doth greater wrong than one who invents falsehood against Allah, even as he is being invited to Islam? And Allah guides not those who do wrong} (Surat al-Saff: 06-07). In addition, I mentioned those schol-

[4] Peace Be Upon Them.

ars among people of the Book who embraced Islam due to these glad tidings.

Chapter Three discusses the following:

- Miracles of Isa (pbuh), the Hawaaris, his ascension to the Heavens, miracles' conditions, difference between Miracles and Graces, the miracles of Isa that are mentioned in the Qur'an like his fatherless birth, granting him the assistance of the Holy Spirit, teaching him the Word of God, curing the born blind and lepers, resurrecting the dead, creating bird-like figurines from clay and breathing life into them, informing Isa about concealed matters from mankind as all miracles were granted to Prophet Isa from the One God to support him in the delivery of God's message of testifying to His Singularity and worshipping and submitting to God's Will.

- The Hawaaris and how they responded to the calling of Isa (pbuh) and supported him, the descending of the Repast, God's inquisition of Isa witnessed by all on Judgment Day as per the verse in the holy Qur'an: {And behold! Allah will say: "O Jesus the son of Mary! Didst thou say unto men, worship me and my mother as gods in derogation of Allah?" He will say: "Glory to Thee! never could I say what I had no right (to say). Had I said such a thing, thou wouldst indeed have known it. Thou knowest what is in my heart, Thou I know not what is in Thine. For Thou knowest in full all that is hidden. Never said I to them aught except what Thou didst command me to say, to wit, 'worship Allah, my Lord and your Lord'; and I was a witness over them whilst I dwelt amongst them; when Thou didst take me up Thou wast the Watcher over them, and Thou art a witness to all things. If Thou dost punish them, they are Thy servant: If Thou dost forgive them, Thou art the Exalted in power, the Wise"} (Surat al-Maa'idah: 116-118).

- The Israelites' treachery of Isa, God's protection of him, raising him to the Heavens, God's emphasis that Prophet Isa was neither killed nor crucified as per the holy verse: {They killed him not, nor crucified him, but so it was made to appear to them} (Surat al-Nisaa': 157).

- The proceedings on the night the lookalike was captured, the sequence of that night's events as mentioned by grand historian and interpreter Ibn Katheer, the verses on denying the killing and crucifixion of Isa as it was the lookalike who died, opinions of well-founded scholars on the matter, confusion among the gospels in the events leading to the death of the lookalike where the closest is that of Barnaba's, Crucifixion and Sacrifice to Nasraanis, the descending of Prophet Isa in the future and proofs thereof from the Qur'an and well-sequenced narrations of Sunnah, the reason why he will be descended, according to what he will rule, his most important actions and how long he will remain on Earth prior to his death.

Chapter Four covers the following:

- Najran's Nasraanis and their arguing of Prophet Mohammad (pbuh), their stance of Mohammad's calling when they went to see him and how they were dressed when they arrived there, councils of arguing and debate, the most important matters argued upon and holy verses on them, calling for but fearing to go through with Mubahala as they knew of Prophet Mohammad's honesty and the truth of his prophethood, their proven admission that the advent of Mohammad was foreseen in their holy books, requesting a truce with Prophet Mohammad (pbuh) and the latter's approval thereof.

The book concludes with:

- Calling for the reigning of the righteousness which The Almighty God ordered, as per the holy verse: {Say: "O People of the Book! come to common terms as between us and you: That we worship none but Allah. that we associate no partners with Him; that we erect not, from among ourselves, Lords and patrons other than Allah." If then they turn back, say ye: "Bear witness that we (at least) are Muslims (bowing to Allah's Will)} (Surat Aal-Imran: 64).

- That prophets and messengers have called for Monotheism and the worship of The Almighty, informed mankind of their Great Creator and of the facts of the universe, life and death, heaven and hell, devils and angels and the nature of Man through Divine Revelation descended upon all prophets by Allah.

- The life stories of the prophets, histories, and origins of their callings as preserved in the Holy Qur'an, the life of Prophet Isa (pbuh) and that of his mother.

- God's description of Himself with traits of perfection and that only He possesses them, that He is One with no other, needing of none and needed by all as per the holy verse: {Say: He is Allah, the One and Only; Allah, the Eternal, Absolute; He begetteth not, nor is He begotten; And there is none like unto Him} (Surat al-Ikhlaas: 01-04)

Through this book, I have attempted to clarify the Complete Truth about Prophet Isa (pbuh) through objective interpretation of verses from the Holy Qur'an.

The writing of this book was concluded on Monday 25th February, 2019 in Istanbul, at 5:40pm.

All thanks and gratitude be to Allah The Almighty God Who I beseech to accept from me this humble effort well.

God Says: {"O my Lord! so order me that I may be grateful for Thy favours, which thou hast bestowed on me and on my parents, and that I may work the righteousness that will please Thee: And admit me, by Thy Grace, to the ranks of Thy righteous Servants"} (Surat al-Naml: 19).

Ali Mohammad al-Sallabi

February 25th, 2019

Chapter One

Historical roots of Prophet Isa's homeland

Prophet Isa (pbuh) was born in the land of Galilee, Palestine or the "Galilee of Nations" as Israelis later named it, as it was an open territory for all Eastern and Western nations, i.e. in Bethlehem, which is about 100 km south of Jerusalem.

It is therefore important to introduce the geography of this area and the events that took place there prior to the calling of Isa (pbuh). Galilee in Hebrew means "the circle", which they mean as the circumference because it has absorbed many of those who are unable to stay in other areas of Palestine, especially the south where Judaism reigns[5].

Galilee is located in the northern part of Palestine between the Mediterranean Sea and Lake Tiberias, south of what is known as Lebanon. Tiberias was the political capital of this region, and its villages that are acclaimed in the Bible are Kafr Nahum, Nazareth – where Jesus was raised – Nayn and Majdal[6].

First: The history of Palestine

The history of Palestine is rich; in the third millennium BC, groups of Arab tribes migrated to this region, which was later called Palestine. These included the Phoenicians, a Semite people whose origin is still not precisely known. They were the first group to migrate to this area and found a good place to settle at the Mediterranean Sea's shores in the northwest of Palestine where they established their most important cities of Sidon and Tyre.

---

5 Basma Ahmad Jastinyeh, "Altering the Messiah's Message throughout History: Reasons and Consequences", al-Qalam House, Damascus, 1st Ed., 2000, p.21.

6 Ibid. See also: Henry S. Abboudi, "Dictionary of Semitic Civilisations", Lebanon, Grus Press, 1st Ed., 1990, p. 320-835.

To the south of the Phoenicians, Arab tribes descended and settled on the west bank of the Mediterranean Sea in the central region of Palestine, and the area became known as "the land of Canaan." The area encompassed several cities, most notably Samaria, which around 880 BC became the capital of the Kingdom of Israel[7].

In 1200 BC, groups from Crete Island, known as "Filisteen" tribes, descended to the coast overlooking the Mediterranean between Jaffa and Gaza and Canaanites mingled with them and later called them "Palestinians". The whole area then became known as Palestine.[8]

Palestine is within the region which people of the book state that Ibrahim al-Khalil (pbuh) migrated to, although not having mentioned that he did so because the harm he had received from his people and their attempts to kill him when he called upon them to worship God. While in Palestine, his children Ismail and Isaac were born, and his son Isaac had Yacoub to who the Israelites are attributed[9].

The Israelites, sons of Jacob bin Ishak (pbut), remained roaming the land of Palestine like shepherds and lived the life of Bedouins, as The Almighty Said of Yusuf (pbuh): {He was indeed good to me when He took me out of prison and brought you (all here) out of the desert} (Surat Yusuf: 100).

---

7 Ibid, p.454.

8 "Altering the Messiah's Message throughout History: Reasons and Consequences", Ibid, p.22.

9 Israel: Compound noun: Isr & Ael: Strength & the god (God). Also means God's Might. Islamically: God's purest or God's servant. The Holy Qur'an attributes both as names of Yacoub (pbuh). Also name of Palestine's Northern kingdom. See: Abdel Shakour Mohammad Aman, "The Israelites and their stance of God and the prophets", PhD dissertation, Um al-Qura Univ., Saudi, 1402h, p129. See also: Al-Shawkaani, "Fath al-Qadeer", Ibn Katheer House/Al-Kalim al-Tayyib House, Damascus, Beirut, 1st Ed., 1414h, 1/73-84. And: "Dictionary of Semitic Civilisations", p.78.

They continued as such until they moved to Egypt in which they settled during the life of Yusuf and which they then exited a long after that with Mousa (pbuh) after God sent the Revelation: {By inspiration we told Moses: "Travel by night with my servants; for surely ye shall be pursued"} (Surat al-Shu'araa': 52) Afterwards, God decreed they wander the lands as punishment for having refused to combat the people of the Holy Land[10].

Mousa reached the land of Moab east of Jordan, went up to the top of a mountain across from Jericho, gazed upon the land which he told the Israelites to enter, yet he died on the land of Moab and did not enter the Holy Land[11].

Mousa was succeeded by Yasoo'a – as dubbed by people of the Book – "Joshua son of Nun" whom Mousa had chosen before his death to lead the Israelites. It was Joshua who took the Israelites to the land of Canaan - Palestine – as their wandering ended around the thirteenth century BC, marking the first settlement of the Israelites, and the colonisation of Palestine[12].

Second: Israelites' Eras

Israelites' existence in Palestine underwent three distinct periods:

1. Era of Judges:

In this period, Jewish rulers were judges from among their rabbis, and no Israelites were kings in those days. History has marked this period in the gospel of Judges.

---

10 Saud bin Abdul-Aziz al-Khalaf, "Studies on Judaism and Nasraaniism", Adwaa' al-Salaf Library, Riyadh, Saudi, 1st Ed., 1997, p.32-33.

11 Al-Maqreezi, "History of the Copts", Ver. By Abdul-Majeed Diyab, al-Fadeelah House, copy of al-Tawfeeq Press, Egypt, 1898, p.43.

12 "Altering the Messiah's Message throughout History: Reasons and Consequences", Ibid, p.24.

2. Era of Kings:

This is when ruling became a monarchy, and God has provided us with information on their first king: {Hast thou not Turned thy vision to the Chiefs of the Children of Israel after (the time of) Moses? they said to a prophet (That was) among them: "Appoint for us a king, that we May fight in the cause of Allah"} (Surat al-Baqarah: 246). So God appointed Talout as king – in their books named Saul – who was succeeded by Dawoud (pbuh). Jerusalem became the capital of the monarchy and Suleiman (pbuh) ascended the throne after his father, and their eras were the most flourishing in the history of the Israelites.

3. Era of Division "Demise of Israelites' Kingship":

This was the era after that of Suleiman (pbuh) where his kingdom was divided into two, i.e. Judah in the south with Jerusalem as its capital, and Israel in the north with its capital Nablus in the Galilee. The two entities were at war with one another, but fought together when both their borders were threatened by their neighbours. Their rulers and people also worshipped figurines in many periods throughout their history[13].

They were then overcome by their enemies and their rule demised at the hands of the Assyrians who seized and destroyed the State of Israel in 722 BC. Judah then fell to the Pharaohs around 603 BC. Then the ruler of Babel, Chaldean Bakhtanasr, regained al-Sham and Palestine regions and expelled the Pharaohs therefrom. He then marched again against the state of Judah which had rebelled against him, and destroyed it and the Temple of Yerushalayim and marched its people on foot to Babylon. This is what is

[13] Ahmad Shalabi, "Judaism", al-Nahda al-Masriyah Library, Cairo, 8th Ed., 1988, p.69-70. See also: Mohammad Abdul-Haleem Mustafa Abu al-Sa'ad, "Analytical Study of Mark's Gospel: Historically and Objectively", al-Jablaawi Press, Egypt, 1st Ed., 1404, p.49.

known in history as the Babylonian Captivity which occurred at the demise of the state of Judah around the year 586 BC.

Then the State of Babel fell into the hands of the Persians during the reign of their king Cyrus in 538 BC, who allowed the Jews to return to Jerusalem and build their temple, and appointed a ruler on them from among them.

The Persians continued to rule from 538-332 BC until Greek Alexander the Macedonian overran the Levant and Palestine, extracted the Persians and ruled over Jewish areas from late 400 BC to mid 100 BC. Then in 63 BC, Roman leader Pompey marched hither and unseeded the Greeks, rendering the Jews under Roman control. It was during that time that Prophet Isa (pbuh) was born[14].

Third: Political and social situation

Palestine had been under Roman rule since 13 BC and initially adopted a system of protection whereby a local Jewish king held pictorial authority so as to ensure his loyalty.

It should be noted that some Jews welcomed Roman rule and cooperated with them in ruling the country, but others considered their presence worthy of resisting. Groups from these people emerged and contributed to the development of Nasraaniism.

During the reign of Roman emperor Augustus (died 14 AD), the Roman Empire encircled the entire Mediterranean Sea, European countries west of the Rhine to the Black Sea, Anatolia "Turkey", Mesopotamia, the Levant, Egypt and all of North Africa. Hence, the cradle of Nasraaniism was where both East and West worlds met, Semites and Romans, Greeks and Jews and non-Jews[15].

---

[14] "Altering the Messiah's Message throughout History: Reasons and Consequences", Ibid, p.25.

[15] John Lorimer, "Church's History in Early Eras", al-Thaqaafah House, Cairo, D. T., p.3.

A reckless man, Herod the Great, ruled over Palestine during 4 – 37 AD, and as of 6 AD, the entire region became subject to Rome's direct rule with Jewish districts of the south and Samaria in the centre united in one state[16].

After the death of Herod the Great, his three sons succeeded him in ruling Palestine and were approved by the Roman government. Antipas (4 BC - 39 AD), one of Herod the Great's sons, retained control of his district that included the Galilee in northern Palestine, whose capital was Tiberias near Nazareth, where Prophet Isa (pbuh) grew up. The outskirts of the Levant were ruled by Philip (4 BC - 34 AD)[17].

Judea and Samaria fell under the rule of Archelaus (4 BC – 6 AD) – which included the area of Jerusalem. Roman Tiberius then ruled over the Roman Empire after Augustus and his reign lasted two years and twenty days. Palestine and its surrounding region underwent many disturbances under the rule of so many men. The masses did not like Herod Sr. because of his submission to the Romans on the one hand and his tyranny on the other. Jewish clergy continued to regard him as the pagan lover of Hellenism in whose era the temple built by the Jews during the time of Ezra was destroyed, and which Ezra then rebuilt it on its same foundations from the time of Solomon. Herod was known for his violence and ferocity, who did not hesitate to kill anyone he suspected of posing a threat to the regime. He hideously persecuted Sanhedrin members for merely sensing they had some power[18].

Upon Herod's death, his kingdom was socially and economically devastated and politically divided among his three sons. This contributed to igniting revolutions and unrests after his death; and

---

[16] "Altering the Messiah's Message throughout History: Reasons and Consequences", Ibid, p.26.

[17] Ibid.

[18] Ibid, p.27.

various alliances, factions and sects among the Jews arose, from the extremist to the moderate. All of this contributed in the destruction of Yerushalayim in 70 AD.

The reign of Archelaus over Jews was so bad that many of them complained about him to the Roman emperor, where the latter deposed him and appointed Pilates the Pontius in his stead. Roman-born Pilates ruled over the Jews for 10 years as of 26 AD before being deposed as well. At the time, the Galilee was under the rule of Antipas who was even more fierce than his brother, and it was he who killed Yahya son of Zakariya (pbuh)[19] after the latter issued a fatwa that Antipas's marriage of a certain woman was prohibited. The New Testament states that Prophet Isa had dubbed him the Fox due to his intelligence.[20]

Many Jews of the time forfeited their previous values and became influenced by the Jews who integrated into the nations under the empire, as well as by those who came to Palestine and Jerusalem on pilgrimage. Even their own religious leaders forfeited their posts and values which beckoned the Pharisees to call for reembracing olden values and increased Asanians' anticipation for the arrival of the awaited Messiah.[21]

Several clashes occurred between the Romans and the pilgrims coming from Jerusalem, which spread to many areas, especially between the two authorities and a group called the Jealous who were characterised by national fanaticism in rejecting the foreign coloniser and paying land tax, coupled with religious fanaticism, in an attempt to purge the Temple of non-Jews[22].

---

19 Ibn al-'Ibri Gregarious al-Maalti, "Tareekh Mukhtasar al-Duwal", Catholic Press, Beirut, Lebanon, D.T., p.26.

20 Rev. Faheem Azeez, "Introduction to the New Testament", al-Thaqaafah House, Cairo, D.T., p.27.

21 Rev. Hanna al-Khadri, "History of Christian Thought", al-Thaqaafah House, Cairo, 1st Ed., D.T., p.101-110.

22 Ibid, p.110-112, 216.

The region of Palestine was in a state of revolt against the Roman Empire, as most scholars agree, especially in the era of Cyparios; whereas other scholars feel otherwise.

With the exception of the Sadducees who collaborated with the Roman Empire (Roman Colonisation), other parties were in constant and violent struggle against the Romans[23]. As a result of these disturbances, the idea of awaiting the advent of the promised Redeemer became more entrenched; a matter that intensified the persecution between them and the Romans[24].

Prophet Isa (pbuh) was born at the end of Herod Sr's reign, and witnessed the eras of his sons afterwards.

The political situation in Palestine in the era of the Messiah was horrific, and the social situation was even more dire as power that was wielded by its rulers superseded the rule of law. There was great disparity between rulers and the people where the former had wealth, luxury and ruled tyrannically, while the latter were poor and hapless. The taxes levied on behalf of Rome constituted yet further suffering and the goal of the clergy became limited to collecting money. The community became void of cohesion and harmony, tribalism spread among people and class divisions emerged[25].

Fourth: Intellectual Life:

It is logical when we begin to talk about Isa (pbuh) that we discuss the era in which he lived, along with its events, because the Prophet's message was meant to reform them. All messengers are sent so as to rectify matters of dogma but then differ qualitatively

---

23 Ibid, p.213-215.

24 "Altering the Messiah's Message throughout History: Reasons and Consequences", Ibid, p.28.

25 "Altering the Messiah's Message throughout History: Reasons and Consequences", Ibid, p.28.

according to the social diseases which infest every nation – a matter that varied from one society to another[26].

Many scholars have studied the environment in which Jesus emerged and grew up in so that they may prove that he was influenced by it and by the ideas therein, and that, accordingly, his teachings came as a product of the ideas and prevalent beliefs of his time. This view indicates the humanity of Prophet Isa (pbuh) and that he did not receive these teachings via Divine Revelation. The following two main factors are in support of this idea:

Factor I: The Divine teachings of Prophet Isa were suitable for this environment and would remedy its problems. When physical wants prevailed in that society, the teachings of the Messiah were spiritual and of a higher order to solve that self indulgence[27].

Factor II: No doubt that the ideas and beliefs prevailing in and around that region had a great impact on the Christian faith after Prophet Isa. Therefore, it was necessary to study the age or environment in which he appeared because it nourished Christianity with new ideas and philosophies that polluted it in different ways. Three conflicting matters were at play there: the (Greek civilisation) that shaped man's thinking, (the Roman state) which defined its institutions and (the Jewish religion) which Christianity had originally come to reform after it had become subversive of the mind and of life[28].

---

26 Abdel Ghani Abboud, "The Messiah, Christianity and Islam", al-Fikr al-Arabi House, Cairo, 1st Ed., 1984, p.18. See also: Mohammad Ali Abdel Mu'ti Ahmad, "Paganism in People of the Book's Dogmas", al-Azhar Univ., Islamic Da'awa Faculty, 2006, p.264.

27 Mohammad Ahmad al-Haaj, "Nasraaniism: From Unitarianism to the Trinity", al-Qalam House, al-Shaamiyeh House, Beirut, 1413h, p.35.

28 "Paganism in People of the Book's Dogmas", p.365.

1. Greek civilisation:

It is one of the Mediterranean Basin's civilisations which includes those of Egypt, Mesopotamia, i.e. between the Tigris and the Euphrates, the Greeks and the Romans[29].

The wielders of these civilisations were the Greeks who represented a nation of great importance among others, and were called (the Greeks) due to their civilisation's entrenchment and influence among members of Jewish groups in Egypt, Burqa, Syria, Asia Minor and Palestine, which continued throughout the Roman period[30] - as shall come, further down.

It is well known that the Greek civilisation started later than those of the Mediterranean basin, but its strategic location in the Mediterranean region had a significant impact on connecting with countries of ancient civilisations in this sea (in the north of Palestine) specifically. They also connected with eastern and southern civilisations of the sea basin and gained much from them; the most beneficial of which to them was the ancient Egyptian civilisation[31].

They took from it much of their religious, philosophical and scientific knowledge, such as astronomy, medicine, agriculture, engineering, fine arts, architecture, sculpture and photography, as well as other matters dubbed Applied Arts that were related to everyday life, and even to politics at times.[32]

Many famous Greek philosophers (e.g. Plato) were educated at Egypt's universities. Many Greek famous scholars like Pythagoras and Democritus also visited Egypt, but still, Greece was able to surpass the other countries from which it took their civilisation, especially in the field of philosophy. This is due to the fact that these countries were not ruled by long-standing states and no

---

[29] Ibid, p.365.

[30] Ibid, p.365.

[31] Ibid, p.366.

[32] Taha Hussein, "Future of Culture in Egypt", al-Ma'aarif House, Cairo, 1996, p17.

priest-state was entrenched alongside it that passed on the secrets of knowledge and research in the origins of creation and life, or in divine matters by which priests and men of religion are influenced.[33]

It is untrue that which some people perceive, out of ignorance or ill-intention, that the life of the Greeks developed and prospered because they alienated religion from their public life, unlike groups that preceded them, and then lagged behind them on the same path. They elevated the status of intellect and painted their teachings with a civic brush.[34]

Perhaps it is right that which Will Durant felt about the Greek civilisation having been a religious one, like others that preceded and came after it, where Greek laws considered abstaining from worshiping the Greek gods as a capital offense punishable by death. This was the same law that condemned Socrates to death.[35]

Accordingly, with Will Durant, we find that life in Greek lands was not a worldly one as described by historians, but rather that religion was of major importance throughout Greece. Yet it was of individual character, not nationalistic, in the sense that the state did not possess an official religion regarded by all or any fixed doctrines. Religion was not the recognition of certain doctrines, but rather the participation in official rites, and anyone was able to believe in whatever he wished on the condition that he did not curse or desecrate the city's gods.[36]

It was this religious individualism and subsequent religious chaos, due to the Greeks' mingling with the East and being influenced by religious concepts prevailing there, that precipitated

33 "Paganism in People of the Book's Dogmas", Ibid, p.367.

34 "Paganism in People of the Book's Dogmas", Ibid, p.367.

35 Wil Durant, "The Story of Civilisation", presented by Muhyi Eddine Sabir, Trans. Zaki Najeeb Mahmoud, ALECSO, Tunis, al-Jeel Publishing, Printing and Distribution House, Beirut, D.T., 5/91.

36 "Paganism in People of the Book's Dogmas", Ibid, p.368.

the dismantling of the Greek society and led to its fast toppling under the blows of the Romans. Nonetheless, the Greeks left behind them that which was effective in shaping the form of life in the Roman Empire itself, and that which had great influence on Christianity as well[37]. This can be summarised in the following:

- The disintegration of the one human entity by elevating some of the gifts God granted mankind and degrading others. The Greeks, for example, elevated the importance of mind over body, degraded manual labour and caring only about financial enrichment. They held high regard for political warriors and farmers, and prohibited slaves and other craftsmen of citizenship rights and from enjoying democracy[38].

- As a result, blatant distinction between Greeks and non-Greeks was evident within and outside the Greek society. On the inside, Aristotle considered slaves to be human machines and believed that slavery was going to persist until the day self-sustainable machines will be able to carry out all degrading jobs. Outside its borders, the humanistic spirit for Greeks was a matter of nationalist pride, and they were therefore first-class colonialists. They were aided in this task through their international trade which led to their emergence and that of their civilisation to which history has attested.[39]

- Pure Materialism: There was inclination towards embodying abstracts despite delving on philosophy, and then they accepted the physical explanation of existence and of mankind. This materialistic pagan notion was mirrored by the Greek notion of divinity as "no religion draws its gods closer to humans that do the Greeks' gods."[40] The Greeks believed that their gods ate, drank,

---

[37] Ibid.

[38] George Sol, "Grand Economic Facets", Trans. Rashid al-Baraawi, al-Nahda al-Masriyah Library and the Franklin Est. for Publishing and Distribution, Cairo-New York, p.18-19.

[39] "The Story of Civilisation", Ibid, 2/68.

[40] "Paganism in People of the Book's Dogmas", Ibid, p.370.

played, fought battles, won or lost, felt pain and joy, spewed wrath on all who angered them and whose vengeance was harsh. This is why Socrates died as a martyr of truth when he was ordered to drink poison because he revealed mysteries of the gods and the immortality of the spirit. They deemed him an infidel of the gods as they believed that Earth was where Greek gods dwelled, not in the heavens.[41]

This is the reason they worshiped various gods like those of crafts, various professions, war, nature, the two main symbols of male and female fertility, some animals and the dead.[42]

2. The Roman State:

All diseases of civilisation that usually result from its decadence and imminent demise ravaged Athens as all factors of collapse infested Greek society. But at that same, factors of development and prosperity were pounding in the young adjacent body of the Roman society which was at its highest point during the age of Isa (pbuh). The entire known world was under its rule except for the Far East, and its peoples were of different races, languages and creeds. All known religions of the time were present in Rome, Alexandria, Nablus and Jerusalem. Roman land (Italy nowadays) was adjacent to that of the Greeks (Greece today) on the same northern coast of the Mediterranean and almost the same latitude. Such closeness of proximity formed an easy passage for transferring the religion of the Greeks to the Romans, yet the latter's schools of religion were based on ethics. Although the Greeks elevated ethics and virtues to the status of divinity, Roman's religion was extreme in this facet as it knew of no specific god nor acknowledged the existence of one or another. The Romans only focused on instilling ethics and virtues in their children, and hence

---

[41] Ibid.

[42] Ibid.

one can claim that the philosophy of Roman religion was born out of its Greek counterpart.[43]

Notion of Religion: Religious individualism which we witnessed was not a trait of religious life for the Greeks – it had never suited the Romans. It suited the Greeks as thinkers, but not the Romans as warriors as the former demand freedom while the warriors demand a group along with them on whose behalf they can fight.[44]

The family then held a rank in Roman religious thought which remained throughout the ages as it was that which connected between people and objects on the one hand, and the gods on the other. It was the heart from which the veins of religion, creation, order, economy and the state emanated. It was also the source from which it drew all these concepts. [45]

Notion of Divinity: This was a tangible notion to the Greeks, while to the Romans, it was pure intangibles like Health or Youth. The Romans believed that some gods impersonated sacred animals like horses, slaughtered animals or sacred geese.[46] Rome (Italy) utilised a system of stable priesthood with the father in the level of priest in his household, yet public prayers were headed by groups of priests, with a vicar at their helm.

Before the advent of Christianity: Emperors had begun finding a place for them in this Roman religious thought. In religious ceremonies, the emperor presided over celebrations and was the chief priest of the state's religion.

Under Emperor Augustus's rule in the first century BC, the Roman religion took on another important form in the personal

---

[43] Mohammad Fu'ad al-Hashimi, "Religions in the Balance", al-Hurriyah House for Journalism, Printing and Publishing, 1986, p.33.

[44] "Paganism in People of the Book's Dogmas", Ibid, p.371.

[45] "The Story of Civilisation", Ibid, 1/122.

[46] "Paganism in People of the Book's Dogmas", Ibid, p.370.

worship of the emperor himself. Augustus, according to Will Durant, was one of the greatest rivals of his gods. Caesar was an icon of such rivalry as his senate acknowledged the divinity of Caesar two years after his death, and his worship spread throughout the empire soon after.[47]

Hence, both the Greeks and the Romans left behind the notion of the divinity of Man, in addition to institutions, structures and organisations that regulated Roman religious life, which transferred to that of Christianity, yet with the great and dangerous deviation from the Nasraaniism which God sent Isa (pbuh) to deliver.

Fifth: Jewish sects at the advent of Prophet Isa

According to contemporary scholars, the most important Jewish groups during the period of Prophet Isa (pbuh) were the Samarians, Sadducees, Pharisees, Qumranians and the Asanians.[48]

All but the Samarians emerged in the intermediate period after the Babylonian Captivity. Some writers believe that most Jewish groups which emerged in ancient times and later periods had become extinct without having left many written traces for later peoples to know exact details about them. A few details were known about two groups from among them, i.e. the Pharisees and the Qumranians.

As for the Pharisees, knowledge of them came about by rabbis who preserved a lot of information about them, particularly in the books of the Talmud. Knowledge of the Qumranians was due to the discovery of the Dead Sea Scrolls and accordingly became among known Jewish groups after having remained obscure for almost a millennium.

Each of the above-mentioned Jewish sects had its own opinion on recognising Old Testament books, or the oral statements

[47] Ibid, p.372.

[48] Josephus, "Jewish History", Christian Books Library, Beirut, 1872, p.264-286.

they claim to be attributed to Prophet Mousa (pbuh) in the Talmud. They also deny some of the above, reject to adopt the teachings of each and every group had its own belief on awaiting the promised Messiah.[49]

The following is a presentation of these groups[50], what is known about each and their general beliefs during the time of Prophet Isa:

1. The Samarians:

Samarians are named after Samaria region in Palestine. Al-Samirah was the capital of the Kingdom of Israel and its people became known as Samarians. It is the oldest of the groups mentioned above and is dubbed the Northern Group as its followers were in northern Palestine – a mixture of Jews and Assyrians who lived in the ancient kingdom of Israel.

The Jews of Judah considered the Samarians a division beyond Judaism.[51] The most important characteristics of the Samarian faith are:

- Believing in Mousa (pbuh) and denial of any other Israelite prophet.

- Recognition of only the Torah and the gospel of Joshua bin Nun (pbuh), and denial of any other books attributed by the Jews to prophets and others, as well as their non-belief in the Talmud.

- The belief that the holy mountain is that of (Jerzim), and this was among the most important points of difference between Jews and Samarians.

---

[49] Al-Saxi, "Al-Burhaan fi Ma'arifat 'Aaqaa'id Ahl al-Adyaan", al-Manar Library, Jordan, 2nd Ed., 1417h, p.89-90.

[50] "Altering the Messiah's Message throughout History: Reasons and Consequences", p.34. See: Ahmad Shalabi, "Judaism", p.215-218. See: Abdul-Majeed al-Sharafi, "Islamic Thought in Responding to Nasraanis", Tunisian Publishing House, Tunis, National Book Institute, Algeria, 1986, p.25-28. Mohammad Shaheen, "Nasraaniism", p.20.

[51] Mohammad Shaheen, "Nasraaniism", Ibid, p.35.

It is also said that Samarians held some hidden beliefs which they prohibited telling others. This is an important observation because Nasraani texts state that discreet Nasraani sects, called Gnostic sects, came from the Samarians who claimed to follow Prophet Isa (pbuh), as per Dr Omar al-Farouq.[52]

They believe in spiritual salvation at the hands of the Awaited Messiah and believe they had found them worthy of the name "Israelis" as they are of Yacoub (pbuh). Samarians continue till this day, although only a small group in Palestine[53].

2. Sadducees:

They are the followers of Saddouq, who people of the book say he was head priest during the reign of Suleiman (pbuh). They are among the strongest groups of Jews after the Babylonian Captivity, economically and politically, due to their influence at the Temple.

Their relation with ruling Persian and Roman countries was one of the best, and they took into account the interests of foreign rulers in many matters. They were among Palestine's most influenced Jews by Hellenic philosophy to the extent that Sadducee priest Jason (175 BC - 172 BC), who was a priest during the Seleucid kingdom, wanted to convert Jerusalem into a Hellenistic city and name it Jerusalem's Antakya where he would establish Hellenic institutes and schools.

Sadducees were a small group in terms of number of followers, but large in terms of its members' wealth and influence on economy and politics.

As for their doctrines, some scholars noticed a similarity between theirs and those of the Samarians, yet the Sadducees were

---

52 "Altering the Messiah's Message throughout History: Reasons and Consequences", p.35.

53 Mohammad Shaheen, "Nasraaniism", Ibid, p.19.

very interested in the Temple and rites that were held there as they were supervisors thereof. Also, among the similarities was that Sadducees rejected the books of prophets who came after Mousa, said that only the Torah was the source of Judaism and did not recognise the Talmud nor the oral narratives told by others. They also do not believe in Resurrection, the Hereafter or reward therein. They were known for the leniency of their laws and although they rejected the oral accounts of Jews and books of prophets, they possessed a private book in which they transcribed their fatwas, cases and provisions, and exhibited distrust in stories about the End of Days and all matters related to Isa (pbuh). Then when God sent Isa as prophet, the Sadducees called him a liar and were among the most fierce enemies of Isa, like Hananiah and Qayaf[54].

3. The Pharisees:

Pharisees are among the most important Jewish groups as they relate to late Judaism of the rabbis which most Jews after the Messiah have followed.

Pharisees is Aramaic and means those who have splintered from the group and were not in the top tier of priests, although the opposite was also claimed[55]. Some researchers believe that the Pharisees were part of the Hasidic sect but then splintered from it.[56]

They held positions of influence in the Council of the Seventy which headed the affairs of Jews and Judaism from the Babylonian Captivity and until the destruction of the temple in 70 AD. This explains their influence before the advent of Isa (pbuh) that was due to the important positions they assumed.

---

[54] Ibid, p.13-14.

[55] "Altering the Messiah's Message throughout History: Reasons and Consequences", Ibid, p.37.

[56] Abel Mun'im Hafni, "Critical Encyclopaedia of Jewish Philosophy", al-Seerah House, 1st Ed., 1400h, p.95.

Their influence endured without interruption. When the Messiah was born, Pharisees were among the most powerful of the Council of Seventy, and their influence increased greatly during Roman rule when they did not participate in the Great Revolution against the Romans which occurred between 66-70 AD.

After the failure of the Jews and the destruction of the Temple, they approached the Romans and requested their permission to establish a Pharisee institute for teaching Judaism in southern Palestine. This institute became one of the most important centres of Judaism after the destruction of the temple, and one of the most important scientific establishments. Some claimed that Pharisees were the intellectual leaders of the Jewish people in the time of Isa (pbuh) although some researchers believe that none among its members was at par with presidents or dignitaries.[57]

They believed in later prophets and messengers who came after Mousa and Haroun (pbut) and in angels, demons, resurrection, judgment and punishment.[58] But they disagreed on matters of destiny and fate, and held a position similar to that of the Mu'tazila Muslims.

They believed in oral narratives attributed to Mousa (pbuh), like the Talmud, yet still believed that the Pharisees' version of events was the correct one and which the Jews must adopt. They mandated that all Jews must imitate the rabbis who reported this version, decreed rabbis as the most knowledgeable on Judaism and granted them a status higher than that of priests. In doing so, they were awaiting the Isa (pbuh) in spirituality, i.e. one of no state authority.[59]

---

[57] "Nasraaniism", Ibid, p.13-14.

[58] Boutros Abdel Malik et. al, "Dictionary of the Holy Book", al-Thaqaafah House, Cairo, D.T., p.15.

[59] "Nasraaniism", Ibid, p.15.

Pharisees did not reject the Temple, but rather made it a secondary order in Judaism and among the non-necessities. This was not meant to belittle it, but they felt that the preparation for the arrival of the Messiah was only in study, worship and applying God's Law in their daily lives. This is why they refused to accept certain groups as there was a necessity for toiling as a premise for preparing to meet Isa (pbuh).

In the age of Isa, they were divided into two groups; one following wiseman (Hallel) who came to Palestine from Babel, and the other group followed wiseman (Shamay) who had almost splintered from the group to the extent of rejecting the entry of other willing people into Judaism. They also rejected Hellenism, and even to the contrary, had been open to the doctrines of Persian dualism, reincarnation of souls, speaking to the dead, and the science of the afterlife.[60] Paul is noted to have exhibited such influence later as he was one of them.

The enmity between Pharisees and early Nasraanis was fierce, and they were among the most prominent Jewish groups who proclaimed their staunch opposition to the calling of Isa (pbuh).

4. Qumranians (Wadi Qumran group):

This group was found in Qumran valley on the north-western shore of the Dead Sea and is the closest area of the Dead Sea to "al-Quds al-Sharif".

This group claims itself as being God's battalion or His steadfast soldiers. They believe in Mousa and Joshua Bin Nun (pbut) and are in constant readiness for Jihad (exerting an effort) in the name of God. They await the End of Days' prophet who will lead them to defeating all nations.

---

60 "Altering the Messiah's Message throughout History: Reasons and Consequences", Ibid, p.39.

They also sometimes call themselves the Poor; accordingly, some researchers claimed that the community of Wadi Qumran is the Abion group which was a Jewish community during the era of Isa (pbuh).[61]

One has reservation on such matters as Jewish sects from the second century BC until the destruction of the Second Temple in the year 70 AD were many, varied and in conflict with one another; a matter which prevents us from confirming their belonging to the groups mentioned by researchers, particularly since no books of Asanians have been discovered to act as a baseline.

The sanctity of Moses' law was of great importance to them, and they mandated that all must study it meticulously and correctly at the hands of their priests. They believe in angels, destiny, fate, resurrection and Judgment. They also concur with all the righteous and good deeds for which prophets and messengers have called; a matter that exemplifies their superiority over other Jewish groups and their likes in Wadi Qumran.

It seems that they had - through their texts - many followers in Jerusalem and in all other Jewish cities in Palestine at that time.

Some researchers went on to say that the first Nasraani group that was in Jerusalem under the leadership of Jacob the Just, Peter, and John the Apostle - since Jesus was raised around 64 H - had close ties to the people of Qumran Valley and were similar to the first Nasraani group in the Palestine-Jordan region and the extended Levant.

Some researchers have noted the similarity between Jacob the Just (Nasraaniism's first priest) after the raising of Isa and the Just Guide as mentioned in their scrolls. It is important to note that the Qumran Valley group considered its presence in the desert as a facet of accepting the Messiah (pbuh) and the End of Days' prophet

[61] Abel Mun'im Hafni, "Critical Encyclopaedia of Jewish Philosophy", Ibid, p.43.

who will come to them from there; a matter they state they follow as per the words of Prophet Isaiah.[62]

5. The Asanians:

Some researchers believe that this group was among the most prominent and most active Jewish groups when Prophet Isa came to be, to the extent that any who write on Judaism at the emergence of Nasraaniism always mention it.

But information on this group is shrouded in mystery, due to the scarcity of ancients writing about them, as it does not exceed 20 paragraphs by historian Josephus, as is the case for ancient Nasraani writings.[63]

Scholars believe the word is (Asanians) means doctors and that its Aramaic origin is (Aseeya), meaning the doctor and healer, as per the Arabic (Asee), yet others say differently.[64]

Most researchers tend to associate Asanians as doctors with Isa and his miracles, and seem to have not divulged to the outside world much about themselves.

It seems that they had a religious and moral philosophy influenced by foreign non-Jewish currents, including Pythagorean philosophy, Persian Magian religious faction based on sanctifying light and its connection to goodness, residues and remnants of Egyptian Pharaonic beliefs, particularly those related to the sanctification of the sun as well as beliefs emanating from holy Jewish books of course.[65]

So these were the most important Jewish groups during the emergence of the Messiah (pbuh).

---

62 Hassan Thatha, "Jewish Religious Thought: Facets and Sects", al-Qalam House, Damascus / Science and Culture House, Beirut, 1407h, p.221.

63 Ibid.

64 Ibid.

65 "Jewish Religious Thought: Facets and Sects", Ibid, p.221-235. See also: Mohammad Shaheen, "Nasraaniism", p.15.

Dr Basma Ahmad Jastinyeh pointed out that those who devoted themselves to the cloak and the servitude of God were not an organised sect, but were singular individuals scattered apart and who multiplied before the birth of the Messiah. This coincided with the end of the fourth millennium since the beginning of creation according to the Hebrew calendar, i.e. the awaited date for the emergence of the awaited prophet. Prophet Yahya (pbuh) was considered one of their elite members.[66]

These devotees were people of goodness and a powerful force in the era of Isa (pbuh), particularly as they believe they are the pioneers of the call to embrace Isa (pbuh) and who await his appearance without being bound by a certain sect or limited doctrine.[67]

6. The Temple and the clergy:

The temple is that built by Suleiman (pbuh) as a centre for worship. Four thousand years later the Babylonians demolished it. Then Persian (Cyrus) ordered it rebuilt in 536 AD. Five centuries later, King (Herod) renewed its construction and it was concluded in the age of Prophet Isa.

As for the status of the Temple and that of the priests in the age of Prophet Isa, they had a higher class of clergy and a lower class of scribes or jurisprudence scholars. The former ensured the carrying out of regular prayers at the temple and supervised the provision of sacrifices, but did not study or teach laws of the religion as their main tasks were to memorise scripture and perform religious rites – particularly annual events when many pilgrims came to Jerusalem. They were careful in ensuring they influenced the people, yet at the same time were subject to Roman rule.[68]

---

[66] "Altering the Messiah's Message throughout History: Reasons and Consequences", Ibid, p.42.

[67] Ibid, p.43.

[68] "Nasraaniism", Ibid, p.20-21.

The scribes or the scholars of law transcribed religious poems to those who requested them and delved on explaining the holy book, yet were not immune to influence from the dual doctrines and Greek theories of god, the universe and man.[69]

Some writers even say that they were responsible for the meticulous interpretations of the Torah. These scribes did not hold any temple posts and were all Pharisees. They recognised modern books and relied on them in acts of worship and transactions, and at the time of the birth of Isa, Temple functions were entrusted to the Assembly of Sanhedrin.[70]

In the era of Isa (pbuh), this assembly confiscated the right to rule over major crimes. Its rulings were pending the decision of the Roman ruler, and they did not welcome the anticipated emergence of Isa as it would in turn mean that the entire universe was corrupt, insinuating their own culpability as well.[71]

Sixth: Definition of key words:

1. Nasraanis:

Nasraanis are those who embraced, vindicated and defended Prophet Isa (pbuh) and his calling. Nasraaniism was the religion that Isa son of Maryam brought forward and called for following.

Imam al-Shihristani says, "Nasraanis are the nation of Isa son of Mary, God's Messenger and a Word from Him, and he is the true messenger after Mousa (pbuh)."

---

[69] "Altering the Messiah's Message throughout History: Reasons and Consequences", Ibid, p.43.

[70] Original Greek: A gathering or court. Named after Jews' court. Its members are Sadducees and grand priests. Pharisees joined them later. At the onset of the birth, its members numbered 71. Most famous among them was Gamaliel – Paul's mentor. See: "Dictionary of Semitic Civilisations", p.495. See also: Mohammad Shaheen, "Nasraaniism", p.21.

[71] "Altering the Messiah's Message throughout History: Reasons and Consequences", Ibid, p.44.

A Nasraani is one who follows Nasraaniism. They were called as such in reference to the village of Nasirah (Nazareth) in Palestine from the land of Galilee in which Isa was sent and from which he transmitted the religion of God to the people. He was then dubbed the Messiah Isa of Nazareth.

Others say they were called Nasraanis because they supported, embraced and vindicated Isa. Al-Alusi says, "Nasraanis is the name of Prophet Isa's companions who were called as such either because they supported him or one another."[72] (The Arabic base of the word (Nasr) means victory.)[73]

They were originally twelve men called the Hawaaris, and they will be discussed later.

The traditional definition of Nasraanis: They are the followers of the religion brought forth by Isa son of Maryam, whether they merely adhered to their religion or did so in excess.[74]

The Qur'an and Sunnah refer to Prophet Isa's followers as *Nasaara*. God Says: {Those who believe (in the Qur'an), and those who follow the Jewish (scriptures), and the Nasaara[75] and the Sabians,- any who believe in Allah and the Last Day, and work righteousness, shall have their reward with their Lord; on them shall be no fear, nor shall they grieve} (Surat al-Baqarah: 62).

In the Sunnah, Prophet Mohammad (pbuh) says, "Every child is born to instinct, where his/her parents raise him/her a Jew, Nasraani or Magian."[76]

---

72 "Paganism in People of the Book's Dogmas", Ibid, p.88.

73 Added by Translator.

74 Suleiman bin Abdullah bin Salih al-Rumi, "Muslims call on Nasraanis to embrace Islam during the Crusades", al-Rushd Library – Publishers, Riyadh, 1st Ed., 2007, 1/17.

75 Corrected by Translator.

76 Verified by al-Bukhari, "Kitaab al-Janaa'iz", no. 1385.

2. Christianity:

Nasraanis call themselves Christians in reference to Christ (pbuh), and their religion as Christianity. This name (in Arabic)[77] is not stated in the Qur'an or Sunnah. It is said to first been heard of in the 3rd Century AD or earlier, around 42 AD in Antakya. Some scholars feel it was meant to demean them.[78]

Therefore, they are a group opposing the society in which Isa (pbuh) and his followers appeared, where pagan Romans ruled and Jews exhibited great hostility towards them and even sought Roman assistance to kill him. Therefore, it is more prudent that they are named by that which the Qur'an ascribed them, i.e. Nasaara (Nasraanis).[79]

3. Why Jesus was named the Messiah:

When God Willed to create Isa (pbuh), He sent the angel Jibreel to Maryam (pbuh) to deliver the glad tidings. Jibreel told her that God will have her give birth to a son named Isa, who God dubbed the Messiah, and he mentioned to her some of Isa's traits prior to breathing life into her which led to her pregnancy. God Says: {Behold! the angels said: "O Mary! Allah giveth thee glad tidings of a Word from Him: his name will be the Messiah Isa, the son of Mary, held in honour in this world and the Hereafter and of (the company of) those nearest to Allah. He shall speak to the people in childhood and in maturity. And he shall be (of the company) of the righteous"} Surat Aal-Imran: 45-46). Therefore, his name is Isa and his title the Messiah, and that he is the son of Maryam.

"Isa" is a foreign proper noun and is substituted by Nasraanis with Jesus, which to them means the Saviour. But we use the name God gave him, mentioned in the Qur'an, with his title as the Mes-

---

77 Translator's addition.

78 "Muslims call on Nasraanis to embrace Islam during the Crusades", Ibid, 1/17.

79 Ibid, 1/18.

siah. This title was mentioned 11 times in the Holy Qur'an, and we shall see now why Isa was given it and whether it refers to being in the Active Participle or Passive Participle.[80]

Imam al-Raghib al-Asfahaani said that "to wipe" (the Arabic meaning of Maseeh – Messiah)[81] is to pass the hand along a surface and remove any marks from it.[82] Some say he was called the Messiah as he wanders through the lands, while others say because Isa would wipe his hand on an imperfection and that part would heal.[83]

Others said it is because forces of bad influence were stripped from his traits, like ignorance, gluttony and all others.[84]

So if "al-Maseeh" is in Active Participle form, it is because he wanders and surveys the lands, or that he would wipe his hand on an ill person who would then heal. But if the title is meant to be in Passive Participle form, it means that God has wiped Isa with His Blessing.[85]

Hence, Prophet Isa was Wiped and Blessed, and we note that his title was in both Active Participle and Passive Participle form.

- Another meaning of "Wiped" is one who has a flatfoot that contains no internal cavity.

- A further meaning is "one who is blessed with beauty" as Prophet Mohammad said of Jareer bin Abdullah.[86]

---

80 Salah al-Khalidi, "Mawaaqif al-Anbiyaa' min al-Qur'an", al-Qalam House, Damascus, 1st Ed., 2010, p.377.

81 Translator's addition.

82 Al-Raghib al-Asfahaani, "Al-Mufradaat fi Ghareeb al-Qur'an", ver. Safwan Adnan al-Dawdi, al-Qalam House, Damascus / al-Shaamiyeh House, Beirut, 1st Ed., 1412h, p.767-768.

83 "Mawaaqif al-Anbiyaa' min al-Qur'an", Ibid, p.378.

84 "Al-Mufradaat fi Ghareeb al-Qur'an", Ibid, p.767-768.

85 "Mawaaqif al-Anbiyaa' min al-Qur'an", Ibid, p.378.

86 Al-Bukhari, no. 3183. See also: Muslim, no. 245.

- The meaning of "al-Maseeh" to Nasraanis is he who is dedicated to servitude and sacrifice. "He was named Jesus the Messiah as he was revered and dedicated to servitude and sacrifice, and promised his return immediately after the fall."[87]

Isa (pbuh) was called in connection to his mother Maryam, as he was fatherless, in order to rebuff Nasraanis' claims of Isa's divinity. They say "Jesus is the son of God", but the Qur'an calls them out as liars and states that they know he is the son of Maryam, who they know well, and hence how can he be the son of God![88]

4. Difference between Christians and Nasraanis:

When viewing books written by Nasraani and Christianity scholars, it becomes evident that there exists a consensus on the existence of a fundamental difference between the followers of each. But the difference between these begins at specifying the name that truly describes the followers of Isa. The matter is limited to two stances:

• Those who embrace **Stance I** feel that "Nasraanis are the true followers of Isa (pbuh) and utilise the testimony of the Qur'an as God Says: {Behold! the angels said: "O Mary! Allah giveth thee glad tidings of a Word from Him: his name will be the Messiah Isa, the son of Mary, held in honour in this world and the Hereafter and of (the company of) those nearest to Allah. He shall speak to the people in childhood and in maturity. And he shall be (of the company) of the righteous} (Surat Aal-Imran: 45-46).

In the above verse, the Qur'an calls those who have embraced the call of Isa, supported and vindicated him as al-Nasaara (Nasraanis).[89]

[87] "Dictionary of the Holy Book", Ibid, p.860.

[88] "Mawaaqif al-Anbiyaa' min al-Qur'an", p. 379.

[89] Dr Nour Eddine Adil, "Mujadalat Ahl al-Kitaab fi al-Qur'an al-Kareem wal Sunnah al-Nabawiyyah", al-Rushd Library, Riyadh, 1st Ed., 2007, p.88.

To strengthen their stance, these scholars point out an important matter being that followers of the Injeel prefer to be dubbed Nasraanis than Christians, to the extent that one can barely find one text that calls the followers of Jesus as Christians. The only mention is of Nasraanis as they represent Prophet Isa's true supporters and followers.[90]

Then there are those who adopt **Stance II** who deduct that Christians are the true followers of Jesus from the semantics of the word "Messiah". The word "Maseehi" in Arabic – a Christian – means one of the Messiah (pbuh). A group of priests also prefers the name Maseehi over Nasraani. Reverend Hamo'el Mashriki stated that among life's hardships for Christians is that since the Islamic Conquest they have been dubbed Nasaara, contrary to truth. He then stated that "Nasaara" was a name of a group of Jews who believed in Isa as being the awaited prophet, not the awaited Messiah. He adds that Christians are those who believe Isa to be God or a god.[91]

The true name is "Nasraaniyah" as it is that brought forward to us in the Holy Qur'an. God has called the followers of Prophet Isa as:

• Hawariyeen: {As said Jesus the son of Mary, to the Disciples (Hawariyeen), "Who will be my helpers to (the work of) Allah." Said the disciples (Hawariyoun)[92], "We are Allah's helpers!"} (Surat al-Saff: 14).

• Believers from among Nasraanis: God Says: {Strongest among men in enmity to the believers wilt thou find the Jews and Pagans; and nearest among them in love to the believers wilt thou find those who say, "We are Nasaara": because amongst

---

[90] Ibid.

[91] Ibid, p.90.

[92] Translator's note: *Hawariyeen is in object position and Hawariyoun in subject position. Hence the discrepancy.*

these are men devoted to learning and men who have renounced the world, and they are not arrogant. And when they listen to the revelation received by the Messenger, thou wilt see their eyes overflowing with tears, for they recognise the truth: they pray: "Our Lord! we believe; write us down among the witnesses} (Surat al-Maa'idah: 82-83).

Chapter Two

Isa (pbuh) in the Holy Qur'an

Isa (pbuh) is God's prophet and is among the five prophets of Inflexible Purpose. In himself, Isa is a miracle from the day his virgin mother Maryam bore him and throughout his entire life. His birth was a miracle of God and he was sent as mercy for all mankind. Some people have strayed from the path of righteousness and deviated from God's path and the dogma of unifying the One God, the All-Mighty Allah. They gave Isa (pbuh) divine traits that are neither appropriate nor fitting of his modest status and humility to God. One time they say that he is God, then they say he is the son of God and yet a third they say he is one of three. This is why the Holy Qur'an mentioned Isa (pbuh) in many instances.

One may wonder, regardless of creed or following, how it is that we deem the Qur'an and its complementing Sunnah the source of correct information about Prophet Isa when a Book was descended upon him as was the Qur'an upon Mohammad (pbuh).

There are many reasons that highlight and justify this; the following are but some:

1. That God The All-Mighty described the Qur'an as one that gives credit to previous holy Books and which is supreme to all. God Says: {To thee We sent the Scripture in truth, confirming the scripture that came before it, and guarding it} (Surat al-Maa'idah: 48). Then of Prophet Mohammad (pbuh), God Says: {Nor does he say (aught) of (his own) Desire. It is no less than inspiration sent down to him} (Surat al-Najm: 03-04).

2. History does not provide us with necessary verified information about the Messiah's calling due to many reasons like the long timespan since the time of Isa, as well as conflicting historical accounts. It is almost certain that a human element played a role

in this meddling of events, rendering it difficult to distinguish the good from the wrong and the righteous from the unjustifiable.

3. The Injeel that was descended upon Prophet Isa does not exist nowadays, even among Nasraanis; hence how can we deviate from the Heavenly Revelation of the Holy Qur'an to embrace human compositions branded in our times as gospels?

4. The Holy Qur'an and the correct Sunnah of Prophet Mohammad (pbuh) are in reality the only sources, both scientifically and historically, that have given us a high quality and accurate depiction of Heavenly Messages' history from the first thereof, Adam (pbuh) till the last, Mohammad (pbuh). There does not exist, whatsoever, a Divine Book or an earthly one that possesses scientific reverence based on preserving and cascading its scripture from one generation to the next as does the Holy Qur'an.[93]

As for the gospels which Nasraanis acknowledge nowadays, they are neither historically trustworthy nor scientifically well-regarded due to their differences, contradictions and scientific and historical mistakes. Examples on each will be discussed further down.

5. These gospels received much severe criticism, both in past and present, from Nasraanis who converted to Islam or those who remained faithful to Nasraaniism and embraced no other. Among the first group is French orientalist (Alfonse Etan Denieh)[94] who said, "As Allah has revealed the Injeel to Isa in his and his people's language, the undisputed fact is that that Injeel was lost, has no trace or that it was destroyed."[95]

Among the second group is (Dr Nathmi Luqa) who says, "When I say Christianity, I mean that which Isa (pbuh) brought

[93] Mitwalli Yusuf Shalabi, "Adwaa' 'Aala al-Maseehiyah", Kuwaiti printing and Publishing House, Kuwait, 1sr Ed., 1968, p.17.

[94] Alfonse Etan Denieh: French painter and orientalist; embraced Islam while in Algeria in 1913 and became known as Nasser Eddine Denieh; died in 1929.

[95] Nasser Eddine Denieh, "Rays of Islam's Light", al-Maktab al-Fanni, 1960, p.51.

forth of his words, not that alteration that was added to them and to his life by others."[96]

6. We see that the Holy Qur'an holds a solid scientific position, even among Nasraanis, who admit – even though they admonish the Qur'an – that it is of authentic origin, detailed in information, cascading from generation to another without fault and void of all contradictions, mistakes, changes, replacements, additions and deletions that mar their gospels.

Emil Derminghem[97] says, "The Messiah holds an elevated status in the Qur'an as his birth was not like that of other people and he was the Messenger of God who spoke to God out loud of his intentions. The Qur'an means true Nasraaniism when it states that Isa is God's Word or God's Spirit which He sent to Maryam, and that he is human. The Qur'an also denounces those who say that Christ is of one nature, and those stating that he is divine among other beliefs held by blasphemous Nasraani sects, not true Nasraaniism."[98]

Based on the above, we come to an undeniable scientific truth that no source other than the Holy Qur'an, and the proven Sunnah – can be accepted to deal with the matter at hand.

As for confused historical accounts, whether within gospels or beyond them, they cannot be taken into account or based upon for this purpose. This has been emphasised by some non-Muslim historians who state that the phenomenon of Isa (pbuh) did not draw the attention of his contemporary historians. Accordingly, and from a historical point of view, any story of his life that is written about him is deemed a marginal collection of contradicto-

96 Nathmi Luqa, "Mohammad the Message and the Messenger", Modern Books House, Cairo, 1st Ed., p.58.

97 Emil Derminghem: French orientalist; was administrator of Algiers Library for a while and has written many works.

98 Emil Derminghem, "The Life of Mohammad Peace be upon Him", ver. By 'Aal Zu'aaiter, Arab World House, 3rd Ed., 2016, p.131-132.

ry events and inputs surrounded by a void barely inhabited by an elusive shadow.[99]

It is worth noting that the Qur'anic verses on Nasraaniism, its Prophet and its Book are no more than 220 verses, i.e. 3.5% of the Qur'an, in contradiction to what many Nasraani writers imagine that the Qur'an's main purpose is to attack Nasraani dogmas or mislead them. These 220 verses were mentioned in only 28 chapters of the Qur'an, some of which contain one or two verses and where others mirror each other.[100]

7. Instances of mentioning Isa and Maryam (pbut) in the Qur'an: Not a single book on Earth has granted the Messiah (pbuh), his virgin mother and his kind family more honour and glorification than the Holy Qur'an. It actually surpasses that existing in the current Torah and Bible. The Holy Qur'an also sets straight all mistakes, accusations and false allegations that were directed to the Messiah and his pure mother by Jews and even Christians themselves.

In the Holy Qur'an there exists Surat Aal-Imran, which is the name of Prophet Isa's family who were kind and honourable, as "Aal" is a wording given to such people, and it is the second longest Surah in the Qur'an. Another Surah is entitled "Maryam", the name of the Virgin Mother of the Messiah (pbuh); whereas no Surah exists in the Holy Qur'an entitled by the family name of Prophet Mohammad (pbuh) – Bani Hashem or Bani Abdul-Muttalib – nor another named after the Prophet's mother (Amina bint Wahb).[101]

The Holy Qur'an is the only historically renowned and credible document that contains no ambiguity or alteration and which

---

[99] "Islamic Thought in Responding to Nasraanis", Ibid, p.23.

[100] Abdul-Razzak Abdul-Majeed, "Sources of Nasraaniism: Study and Critique", al-Tawheed Publishing House, Riyadh, 1st Ed., 2007, p.49-53.

[101] Bassam 'Aajk, "Islamic-Christian Dialogue: Principles, History, Topics, Goals", Qutaibah Printing House, Damascus, 1998, p.72.

enjoys absolute integrity regarding the clarity and truthfulness of Prophet Isa, and that of his mother, family, creed, calling, supporters and people.

The proof-supported scientific details, below, will reveal all facets of the Qur'an's miraculous reporting, scientific and educational detailing of a number of occurrences in the life of Prophet Isa (pbuh).

The detailing of these events testifies to the Holy Qur'an's Divinity and Prophet Mohammad's truthfulness in that he could not have drawn these facts from the Old and New Testaments due to the immense difference between the latter and the true embodiment of the righteous Isa (pbuh). Furthermore, the Qur'an details incidents that were not mentioned in either of these two Testaments.

As examples on the above, we note the miracle of Isa (pbuh) speaking to others while still an infant in the cradle where he pronounced total submission to Allah. Then there is the miracle of the Table (Repast) which God descended to the Hawaaris from the Heavens in response to their request and the supplication of Prophet Isa thereof. Furthermore is the miracle of saving Isa from the hands of the Jews in which Allah did not allow them to either torture, humiliate or desecrate his dignity as current gospels describe. The Holy Qur'an emphasises that The Almighty Allah raised Prophet Isa to the Heavens until he later returns to Earth to break the cross, kill the pig and lead Muslims in prayers, as prophet Mohammad (pbuh) was informed.[102] This is a form of informative and historical miracle which we find only in the Qur'an.[103]

The name of Prophet Isa was mentioned 25 times in the Qur'an and his mother's, Maryam, was mentioned 24 times.

---

[102] Al-Bukhari, "Kitaab al-Mathaalim", no. 2476.

[103] Zaghlool al-Najjar, "Al-'Ijaaz al-Tareekhi wal Inbaa'i fil Qur'an al-Kareem", al-Ma'arifah House, Beirut, 1st Ed., 2013, 2/894.

Occurrences of the name "Maryam" (pbuh) in the Holy Qur'an:

The name of Prophet Isa's mother, Maryam, was mentioned – devoid of Isa – six times in Surat Aal-Imran when speaking of her birth, Zakariya caring for her, the angels speaking to her and when bringing her glad tidings of giving birth to Isa (pbuh).

Her name was also mentioned – on its own – in Surat al-Nisaa' when denouncing the Jews for their blasphemy, accusation of Maryam and in deciding on the truth of Isa as being God's Word which The Almighty bestowed upon Maryam.

Surat Maryam, which bears her name, speaks in detail of the glad tidings sent her way announcing her pregnancy with Isa. Her name was mentioned twice here at the onset of presenting her story upon approaching her people carrying her child.

Her name was also mentioned once in Surat al-Tahreem when relating her to her father (Maryam daughter of Imran) and praising her for her believing and piety.

Surat Aal-Imran details the entire story of Maryam since her mother bore her and vowed that her unborn child shall be for Allah's sake, where He received her well and looked after her. Men of righteousness disagreed on who would cater to her needs as a child, and so they cast their pencils in a draw. Zakariya (pbuh), her brother in-law, won the draw and raised Maryam as a believing and righteous girl where God continually provided her with sustenance. Zakariya was astonished as to where the food came from and she answered that it was sent by Allah. He then prayed to God to be graced with a male child. This is mentioned in verses (35-38) of the same Surah and shall be later explained.

The Surah's verses then speak of the glad tiding brought to Maryam by the angels that God has selected her from among all women and that she must be pious, kneel and pray to Him. They also gave her the good news that God will grant her a son, i.e. Isa (pbuh), and shall make him a prophet and messenger. When Maryam found that strange, the angels told her that such is God's Will and that He does whatever He Wills. This is mentioned in verses (42-48) of the same Surah.

Surat Maryam detailed her pregnancy of Isa (pbuh) where the verses begin with at the scene where she went eastwards from her people. Then when she was alone, God sent Jibreel (pbuh) to her in the appearance of a man. He told her that he was a messenger from God so as to grant her a good boy. When finding the matter strange and asking how she, the pious virgin girl, would be able to do so, he said that such is God's Will. So Jibreel breathed life into her and she was pregnant with Isa who she then gave birth to under a palm tree. Then Jibreel instructed her to eat dates, drink water and not speak to anyone for three days. She then carried her son and went to her people who were surprised to see her child. When they asked about him, she pointed to him as he had the answer. They were even more astonished as they heard him speak and introduce himself as Allah's servant and future messenger. This is mentioned in verses (16-34) of the Surah.

Other instances of mentioning Maryam in the Qur'an are but quick flashes as the gist of her story lies in Surat Aal-Imran and Surat Maryam.[104]

Occurrences of the name "Isa" (pbuh) in the Holy Qur'an:

The story of Prophet Isa son of Maryam (pbuh) was mentioned in the following Surahs: Maryam, Aal-Imran, al-Maa'idah, al-Nisaa', al-Saff, al-Hadeed, al-Zukhruf.

- His story and that of his mother intertwine in Surat Maryam as if both stories were one, as per verses (16-34) thereof. The vers-

[104] Salah al-Khalidi, "Al-Qasas al-Qur'ani: Presentation and Analysis of Events", Ibid, 4/164.

es after these added the determination of God's Oneness, and that He has neither a wife nor a son, as per verses (34-40).

- Surat Aal-Imran mentions Isa's name five times, where his and his mother's stories also intertwine. The angels gave glad tidings of Isa to Maryam, some of his traits and message to the Israelites were mentioned as well as some of his miracles. When the Israelites branded him a liar, his Hawaari followers believed in him. Then when Isa was in danger, God protected him and raised him to the Heavens. The above are mentioned in verses (48-57). The verses after that speak of Nasraanis' argument and proving them wrong and teaching Prophet Mohammad (pbuh) what to say to them to disprove their argument, as per that mentioned in verses (58-74).

- The verses of Surat al-Maa'idah are on arguing with Nasraanis regarding Prophet Isa. In discussing the story of Isa, the Surah presents the Repast scene when God descended it upon Isa and his Hawaaris, as per verses (112-115). Then a scene from Judgment Day is presented where Isa absolves himself from Nasraanis' worship of him, as in verses (109, 111, 116, 120).[105] The name of Prophet Isa is mentioned six times in this Surah.

- Surat al-Nisaa' details the Jews' stance of Isa (pbuh) as they said lies about his mother and wanted to kill him. The Holy verses state that God protected him and that they neither killed nor crucified him as they did so to his lookalike, while Isa was raised to the Heavens. The verses then state that people of the Book will believe in him prior to his death and praise the believers among people of the Book following Prophet Mohammad (pbuh). This information is in verses (156-162) and Isa's name is mentioned three times in the Surah.

- Surat al-Saff makes reference to Isa twice; once upon delivering God's Message to the Israelites when they called him a liar in

[105] Salah al-Khalidi, "Al-Qasas al-Qur'ani: Presentation and Analysis of Events", Ibid, 4/166.

verse (6), and when the Hawaaris supported him and his religion in verse (14).

- Surat al-Hadeed speaks of the message of Prophet Isa and how priests invented the Priesthood after him, in verse (27).

- Surat al-Zukhruf speaks of Isa's prophethood and worshipping him, and reprimands Nasraanis for this worship, in verses (57-65).

Other instances of mentioning Prophet Isa (pbuh) is in passing as one among other prophets, or his doctrine and message. He is mentioned three times in Surat al-Baqarah, and once in each of al-An'aam, al-Ahzaab and al-Shourah.

The Qur'an mentions the description of Isa at times, i.e. al-Maseeh (The Messiah), sometimes alone and in others connected to that of his mother, i.e. al-Maseeh son of Maryam. The Qur'an mentions the word "al-Maseeh" 11 times:

- Surat Aal-Imran (once)
- Surat al-Nisaa' (3 times)
- Surat al-Maa'idah (5 times)
- Surat al-Tawbah (twice)

First: The family of the Messiah (pbuh) in the Holy Qur'an:

1. Who are Aal-Imran and why were they mentioned in the Surah?

Maryam is Imran's daughter as per the Holy verse: {And Mary the daughter of ʹImran, who guarded her chastity} (Surat al-Tahreem: 12). The name (Imran) was mentioned three times in the Qur'an:

- In Surat Aal-Imran, verses (33-34): {Allah did choose Adam and Noah, the family of Abraham, and the family of 'Imran above all people. Offspring, one of the other: And Allah heareth and knoweth all things}.

- Imran's wife and Maryam's mother in Surat Aal-Imran, verse (35): {Behold! a woman of 'Imran said: "O my Lord! I do dedicate unto Thee what is in my womb for Thy special service"}.

- Imran's daughter in Surat al-Tahreem, verse (12): {And Mary the daughter of 'Imran, who guarded her chastity}.

So who are Imran's clan who are mentioned in the third Surah of the Qur'an, which is also entitled with their name?

2. Who are Imran I and Imran II?

They are two Israelites many centuries apart from one another.

Imran I: He is the father of prophets Mousa and Haroun (pbut).

The proof that Mousa's father is named Imran is that verified by al-Hakim of Anas bin Malik that Prophet Mohammad (pbuh) said, "Mousa son of Imran is God's pure one."[106] Also, that verified by Muslim of Ibn Abbas that Prophet Mohammad said, "On the night I was raised to the Heavens, I came across Mousa bin Imran (pbuh)."[107]

The Holy Qur'an referred to the clan of Imran I: His wife, her reaction when she gave birth to Mousa, his daughter who she ordered to keep watch of her brother Mousa's coffin and Haroun, Mousa's brother. So these five righteous ones are Imran's family, and we do not know if he had children other than the ones mentioned in the Qur'an.

Imran II: He is the father of Maryam (pbuh). The Qur'an noted his wife's pregnancy of Maryam and vowing her to God's servitude, and to Maryam's brother (Haroun) – not that of Mousa's brother. More details on him shall ensue later in this book. Prophet Mohammad (pbuh) mentioned that Isa and Yahya (pbut) are cousins

---

[106] Reported by al-Haakim in "Al-Mustadrak", 2/576.

[107] Reported by Muslim, no. 165. See also: "Al-Ahaadeeth al-Saheeha", no. 182.

from the mother's side, meaning that Zakariya (pbuh) was married to Maryam's sister.

Accordingly, Imran II's family mentioned in the Qur'an and Hadeeth also consisted of five members, three of who we know – Imran, his son Haroun, his daughter Maryam – yet his wife's and other daughter's names were not revealed by the Qur'an.

Imran I lived in Egypt during the Pharaohs' era, at the onset of Israelites' history, while Imran II lived in the area of Palestine-Jordan during the last days of Israelites' history, with many centuries apart.[108]

3. Who were the family of Imran who God chose as purest from among all mankind?

Some scholars state that the offspring of Imran's sons, Mousa and Haroun, are the ones meant by this statement as from them emanated most prophets sent to the Israelites.

Other scholars believe that the family of Imran are Maryam, her son Isa (pbuh), her mother and her brother (pbut).

- God Says: {Allah did choose Adam and Noah, the family of Abraham, and the family of 'Imran above all people. Offspring, one of the other: And Allah heareth and knoweth all things} (Surat Aal-Imran: 33-34).

Imam Ibn Katheer says, "Allah informs us that He chose these families from among all mankind. He chose Adam (pbuh); created him with His hands and breathed life into him from His own. He then ordered all His angels to kneel for him, taught him the names of all, made Heaven his abode, then removed him from it to Earth due to His wisdom. God also chose Nouh (pbuh) and made him the first prophet to mankind on Earth. God chose the family of Ibrahim, including the last and concluding Prophet Mohammad (pbuh).

[108] "Al-Qasas al-Qur'ani: Presentation and Analysis of Events", Ibid, 4/168.

God also chose the family of Imran, i.e. the father of Maryam, mother of Isa (pbuh).[109]

Although Imran's clan originates from Ibrahim's, they were mentioned individually so as to honour and dignify them.

Imran led prayers of the Israelites at the time, was a good man and had a good wife who was pure, pious, faithful to her husband and to God. As a result of this blessed union, God dignified them with Maryam (pbuh).[110]

- "Among all Mankind": God chose each according to those living at that time. God gave them higher status due to sending them as prophets and messengers. God gave Maryam higher status through her pregnancy and birth as a virgin, due to dedicating herself to prayer and being provided with sustenance when it was not in season, as well as choosing her as the mother of Isa who God Willed that he be borne without a father's seed.[111]

- "Offspring, one of the other, and Allah is All-Hearing and All-Knowing": Offspring one similar to the other in goodness, virtue, good intent, good deeds, dedication and affirming the Oneness of God are all reasons why they were chosen from among all others. It is this offspring that God stated in the context of speaking of Ibrahim: {We gave him Isaac and Jacob: all (three) we guided: and before him, We guided Noah, and among his progeny, David, Solomon, Job, Joseph, Moses, and Aaron: thus do We reward those who do good: And Zakariya and Yahya and Jesus and Elias: all in the ranks of the righteous: And Ismaeel and Elisha, and Jonas, and Lot: and to all We gave favour above the nations: (To them) and to their fathers, and progeny

---

[109] Mohammad Abu Zahra, "Zahrat al-Tafaseer", al-Fikr al-Arabi House, Cairo, 2008, 4/597

[110] Ahmad al-Sharqaawi, "Al-Mar'ah fil Qasas al-Qur'ani", Ibid, 2/597.

[111] Abdullah Shahatah, "Tafseer al-Qur'an al-Kareem", Ghareeb Publishing and Printing House, Cairo, 200, 2/1557.

and brethren: We chose them, and we guided them to a straight way} (Surat al-An'aam: 84-87).[112]

- "And Allah is All-Hearing, All-Knowing": This means that God hears all of what mankind utters, has insight into their consciences and deeds, and it is He who chooses from among them who He knows are righteous. He is All-Hearing and answers supplications of goodness and honest beseeching; He is All-Knowing of the affairs of mankind as He sees what's in their hearts. The two verses are guidance towards the necessity of following prophets, considering them icons to follow and following in their footsteps.[113]

4. The birth of Maryam (pbuh):

God Says, {Behold! a woman of ´Imran said: "O my Lord! I do dedicate unto Thee what is in my womb for Thy special service: So accept this of me: For Thou hearest and knowest all things." When she was delivered, she said: "O my Lord! Behold! I am delivered of a female child!"- and Allah knew best what she brought forth - "And no wise is the male like the female. I have named her Mary"} (Surat Aal-Imran: 35-36).

Allah mentions the upbringing of Isa through that of his mother as a declaration to contradict that which Nasraanis hold as believing he is the son of God. The Qur'an's method in dismantling a belief is to show its origin, then its error, upon which its aftermath is debunked. Accordingly, arguing on matters whose origins are baseless cannot reach truth. They claim that Isa is the son of God when he has a mother named Maryam, who in turn has a father and mother, who in turn have mothers and fathers from Adam. So from where did God's paternity of him come?

This is the reason God mentions the marital relationship between Imran and his wife. God Says: (Behold! a woman of

[112] Ibid, 2/1557.

[113] "Al-Mar'ah fil Qasas al-Qur'ani", Ibid, 2/599.

´Imran said) in reference to the paternity and maternity of Maryam. God mentions the name "Maryam", but not that of her mother as Isa's lineage goes from his mother to her father, as is the case throughout human history. Maryam's mother was Hannah, and so Isa (pbuh) is the son of Maryam daughter of Imran, not Isa son of Maryam daughter of Hannah. Maryam was mentioned since Prophet Isa's lineage was connected to her in the absence of a father, but since Maryam (pbuh) had a father, Hannah was let go and Imran was instead mentioned. Since Maryam's mother is non-existent in Prophet Isa's lineage, God Says (a woman of Imran).[114]

God states the circumstances when the Virgin Maryam was borne by her mother, her birth and her upbringing. Worship and supplication shadowed her as a foetus in her mother's womb and until she became of age when The Almighty chose her from among all women for a matter of utter importance and sanctity. While her mother was pregnant with her, she – the mother – vowed that her child – Maryam – would be in the total servitude of The Almighty and of all in the Holy Land.

Imran's wife wished that the child she bore be dedicated to the servitude of God, liberated from all that binds it in this life so that it may instil true freedom by liberating it from the chains of humiliation and moral enslavement, not restrained by lusts and pleasures, nor by worldly matters. She wanted her child to work only in the path God mandated and appointed her with, and to rise above all restrictions that impeded her worship.

If a believer is as such, he is the free and liberated one to pursue God's Will; otherwise, he is a slave of worldly life, lust and necessity.[115]

---

[114] Abdel-Aziz al-Tareefi, "Al-Tafseer wal Bayan Li Ahkaam al-Qur'an", Dar al-Minhaaj Library, Riyadh, 1st Ed., 2017, 2/582.

[115] "Al-Qasas al-Qur'ani: Presentation and Analysis of Events", Ibid, 4/175.

The story about Prophet Isa's grandmother, from his mother's side, reveals to us the heart of (Imran's wife) Maryam's mother and how it was filled with belief by forsaking her most precious asset to the servitude of The Almighty, i.e. her foetus, liberated from all bindings except for God. It is an expression of absolute submission where one seeks comfort and safety only in God, as any other form is merely faking the truth even if it reflects the false image of freedom.

Mankind cannot be free when owing a debt to any but God, whether within himself, throughout his life, in any facets of this life, or when adhering to laws controlling this life that are not drawn from God. The only means for being liberated is to forfeit all for the sake of God – as expressed by Isa's grandmother through her supplication and prayers.

{"O my Lord! I do dedicate unto Thee what is in my womb for Thy special service: So accept this of me: For Thou hearest and knowest all things"}[116].

- "Thou hearest and knowest all things": Hearer of all words, Who answers all supplication of goodness and Who is aware of all intentions and actions.[117]

- "Thou hearest" – my beseeching, supplication and call.

- "Knowest" – that which lies within my conscience, heart and intention.

- "Thou hearest" – all audible matters including my beseeching and prayer.

- "Knowest" – all information including that which is in my conscience.[118]

---

[116] Sayyid Qutb, "Fi Thilaal al-Qur'an", al-Shurouq Printing House, Cairo, 32nd Ed., 2003, 1/392.

[117] "Al-Mar'ah fil Qasas al-Qur'ani", Ibid, 2/601.

[118] Ibid.

5. Imran's wife's delivery of a female:

God says: {When she was delivered, she said: "O my Lord! Behold! I am delivered of a female child!"- and Allah knew best what she brought forth - "And no wise is the male like the female. I have named her Mary, and I commend her and her offspring to Thy protection from the Evil One, the Rejected"} (Surat Aal-Imran: 36).

She had been anticipating a boy as vowing to dedicate one for worship was only akin of males, so that they may serve the Temple and dedicate themselves to celibacy and prayer. But as she gives birth to a female, she supplicates sadly to God by saying (O my Lord! Behold! I am delivered of a female child!- and Allah knew best what she brought forth) as if apologising for not having had a son to take up the mission.

- (And no wise is the male like the female): The female cannot undertake that which a male does in this facet. (I have named her Maryam): She speaks to God as if to herself, in a soft and self-expressive manner as is the case of those chosen subjects with their God. She prays to Him as if He were near her, in a direct and friendly manner that relieves her burdened soul, without complication, to an All-Hearing and close God.[119]

Scholars have discussed deep meanings of the previous verses:

- (Allah knew best what she brought forth): The purpose of this sentence is to emphasise God's prior knowledge of what she brought forward as He knew what lay in her womb when she made the vow; He had already known what she would bear and give birth to before either had occurred.

It is God who preordained that she bear a female for a lesson which He chose as He is the All-Knowing of occurrences before they happen, and who creates them according to His will. Accord-

[119] "Fi Thilaal al-Qur'an", Ibid, 1/393.

ingly, the meaning of this part of the verse is that God knew of the child she gave birth to, that it is female and was not as her mother expected or wanted.[120]

- (And no wise is the male like the female): This was said by God, not Imran's wife. It is a truth God wanted to express on this topic. The phrase is specific to the context of vowing that that which was in her womb was meant to be dedicated to worship and servitude.

The meaning of this holy phrase is that the servitude of the house of God and only worshipping Him requires more effort, strength, perseverance and endurance than a female can undertake. The female will not be able to do this well as a male is stronger and more able-bodied than a female.

But we do not feel this phrase (And no wise is the male like the female) should be generalised to cover all facets of male-female lives, nor do we feel it indicates absolute preference of men over women in everything.

There exists no clear text in preferring men over women. In fact, the Holy Qur'an is clear in deeming piety as the basis for preference, favouring and exaltation. God Says: {O mankind! We created you from a single (pair) of a male and a female, and made you into nations and tribes, that ye may know each other (not that ye may despise (each other). Verily the most honoured of you in the sight of Allah is (he who is) the most righteous of you} (Surat al-Hujuraat: 13). Whether male or female, the most honoured are the most righteous.

The meaning of (male) is based on harshness, strength and rigidity; (female) is based on softness and mellowness. God is Wise in His creation of both male and female; He did not create them bearing the same traits in everything. God created males stronger

---

[120] "Al-Qasas al-Qur'ani: Presentation and Analysis of Events", Ibid, 4/176.

than females so that they may perform their message in life, and created females softer and more tender so that they may carry out their duty in life and be wanted and yearned for. Truest is The Almighty in saying (And no wise is the male like the female).[121]

- (I have named her) and (Maryam) is the only proper name of a female present in the Qur'an. All other women are mentioned as per their pseudonyms lie (Mousa's mother), (Haroun's sister), (Pharaoh's wife) and the like.[122]

The meaning of (Maryam) in their language is the worshipper. She wishes that her baby becomes a worshipping and humbled female to The Almighty. Having named her this upon her birth shows her awareness of the purpose she wants her daughter to fulfil, and accordingly hastened in naming her out of optimism and hope.[123]

By such a name, she indicated her decision to fulfil her vow and prayed that God would accept it although she turned out a female. If she cannot be a curator of Bayt al-Maqdis, then one of the worshippers at it.[124]

- (And I commend her and her offspring to Thy protection from the Evil One, the Rejected): This is said by Imran's woman who prayers to The Almighty that He accepts her baby girl and protects her from Satan. God is The Saviour and the Most Merciful, and Imran's wife probably made this supplication so that Maryam may grow up and have offspring, and God granted that to her.[125]

The verses which record Imran's wife's supplication denote the purity of her spirit, greatness of belief and warm connection to The Almighty. God Says: {"O my Lord! I do dedicate unto Thee what

[121] "Al-Qasas al-Qur'ani: Presentation and Analysis of Events", Ibid, 4/176.

[122] Ibid, 4/178.

[123] Farouq Hamadah, "Aabaa' wa Abnaa': Malaamih Tarbawiyah fil Qur'an al-Kareem", al-Qalam House, Damascus, 1st Ed., 1997, p.235.

[124] "Al-Mar'ah fil Qasas al-Qur'ani", Ibid, 2/607.

[125] Ibid.

is in my womb for Thy special service}. God Says: {"And I commend her and her offspring to Thy protection from the Evil One, the Rejected"}. The offspring of Maryam was limited to Isa (pbuh) as the Qur'anic context shows she did not marry and had Isa only through a Word from God. Isa was raised to the Heavens and did not get married, so he has no offspring.

Our Prophet Mohammad (pbuh) stated that God answered the prayers of Imran's wife and saved Maryam and Prophet Isa from the devil's misdeeds, from the time each of them was born.[126]

Abu Hurayrah stated that Prophet Mohammad (pbuh) said, "Not a single human is not touched by the devil upon his birth, which is why they cry, except for Maryam and her son." Abu Hurayrah then added the holy verse, "And I commend her and her offspring to Thy protection from the Evil One, the Rejected.[127]"

Prophet Mohammad (pbuh) guided us to fortify our offspring from Satan. Accordingly, one says when his family come to visit after the birth of a child, "Dear God, save me from Satan and what You have granted me from him as well.[128]"

6. God's acceptance of Maryam and rooting her well:

God knew the sincerity of Imran's wife's call to Him as she said "O Lord!". She requested God's aid in raising Maryam well from her cradle till her death. Although sad she had given birth to a female, God mended her heart and accepted her vows, upon which that female became more complete and perfect that most males, and through her occurred more determinations than can be mentioned.[129]

---

126 Ibid, 4/180.

127 Al-Bukhari, no. 3431. See also: Muslim, no. 2366.

128 Al-Bukhari, no. 3283.

129 Al-Sa'adi, "Tafseer al-Sa'adi Tayseer al-Kareem al-Rahman fi Tafseer Kalam al-Mannaan", ver. By Abdul-Rahman bin Mu'aalla al-Luwayhiq, al-Risalah Est., Beirut, Lebanon, 1st Ed., 200, 1/218.

God then inspired Zakariya (pbuh) to accept the new-born Maryam within Bayt al-Maqdis, as no other female had had that honour before her, so that she may serve His Will and dedicate herself to His worship. This was God's answering the prayers of Imran's wife that Maryam accompany the righteous.

God allowed for Maryam's upbringing to be the best in body and form as she was blessed with a beautiful and cheerful demeanour. Since her early childhood, she was surrounded by righteous men and women and evil had no hold on her.

The Holy verse of Surat Aal-Imran (37): {Right graciously did her Lord accept her: He made her grow in purity and beauty} is a rule in Qur'anic upbringing of children and of protecting them during that fragile time so that belief and good deeds may be instilled in them. Then when evil encroaches upon them, it will find no crack in their spirits to seep through.

In order to cement her good upbringing, God made Zakariya (pbuh) her guardian as he was also the husband of her maternal aunt, most probably, or of her sister as mentioned in the Hadeeth on the incident of Israa' and Mi'raaj (Prophet Mohammad's ascension to the Heavens): "And then I saw the son of the maternal aunt Isa son of Maryam and Yahya son of Zakariya."[130]

Imam Malik and others stated that Maryam's mother handed her to them after her breastfeeding period had finished – a matter which the majority of interpretation scholars have favoured. They agree that her mother wrapped her with a cloth and took her to the temple where she handed Maryam to the worshippers living there. As Maryam was the daughter of their supreme priest, they argued on who would be blessed more than the rest with caring for baby Maryam that would bring them God's favour. This quarrel was also due to the fact that Maryam is connected to

[130] Al-Bukhari, "Ahadeeth al-Anbiyaa'", 6/467.

a blessed family and that Divine Revelation was the reason she was being handed to them in Bayt al-Maqdis. They then concluded it by making a draw, as God Says: {This is part of the tidings of the things unseen, which We reveal unto thee (O Messenger.) by inspiration: Thou wast not with them when they cast lots with straws, as to which of them should be charged with the care of Mary: Nor wast thou with them when they disputed (the point).} {Surat Aal-Imran: 44)

God's Destiny for Maryam was that she be under the guardianship of Prophet Zakariya, her maternal aunt's husband. In conjunction with the Hadeeth, "A maternal aunt is like a mother,"[131] God intended for Maryam's aunt to cater to her feminine needs, and for Zakariya to cater to her righteousness and absolute safety. This is a lesson for fathers that they choose for their children guardians and teachers who are competent and righteous.

As for Imran's wife's wish to bear a male, the Holy verses on Imran's wife show us the path of the good and righteous who ready their children for grand and supreme tasks; foremost of which is servitude of religion and informing the masses of God's Message so that it may be instilled within them and persist. Then when she gave birth to a female, Imran's wife neither complained nor was incensed. She was accepting of her fate as acceptance is not about subsiding an ill that has befallen you, but rather not objecting to one's destiny.

The verses also tell us that we must be careful to choose names of righteousness for our children so that they may live their lives to their grey years knowing the purpose for which they were meant.

Arabs used to name their children (Sakhr – rock, Harb – war) and the like. They used to name their servants (Nafi' – useful, Aflih – hardworking, Barakah – blessing), and when asked why,

[131] Al-Bukhari, "Kitaab al-Sulh", 5/304.

they would say: "Our sons are for our enemies and our servants are for us."

She then extended her hands in prayer for her son and offspring, and we know that the supplications of parents are held in high regard by God.

These Divine Directives have also taught us to be as careful as possible in rooting goodness within our children and to hold fast to this day and night.[132]

God Says, {Right graciously did her Lord accept her} (Surat Aal-Imran: 37). "Acceptance" means to take a matter happily; "Graciously" means a matter above good that will be noted in Maryam's upbringing. It is not any acceptance, but rather one done graciously. This is why God Says: {He made her grow in purity and beauty: To the care of Zakariya was she assigned} (Surat Aal-Imran: 37).

Growing in Purity was manifested in two manners in the life of Maryam (pbuh):

First, that she was under God's watch as a foetus, just as a farmer caters for the growth of his crops.

Second, God gratifying Imran's wife's prayers with acceptance was a sign of her devotion as He granted Maryam righteous upbringing and made Zakariya her guardian.[133]

God accepted the supplication of Maryam's mother immediately as He is close to the hearts of all believers and fulfils their requests. God Says, {When My servants ask thee concerning Me, I am indeed close (to them): I listen to the prayer of every supplicant when he calleth on Me: Let them also, with a will, Listen to My call, and believe in Me: That they may walk in the right way}

[132] "Aabaa' wa Abnaa': Malaamih Tarbawiyah fil Qur'an al-Kareem", Ibid, p.241.

[133] Mohammad Mitwalli al-Sha'araawi, "Maryam and al-Maseeh", compiled and prepared by Abdul-Qadir Ahmad 'Aata, Islamic Heritage Library, Cairo, D.T., p.52.

(Surat al-Baqarah: 186) – and – {And your Lord says: "Call on Me; I will answer your (Prayer)} (Surat Ghaafir: 60).[134]

The holy verse {He made her grow in purity and beauty} while also being well accepted by God as He had blessed her with such growth. Ibn Katheer explained that God made her look nice and pleasing[135] and that He granted her good upbringing through worship and obedience to Him.[136]

7. Zakariya's patronage of Maryam (pbuh):

Having accepted Maryam and granted her good upbringing, God allocated for her he who would cater to her needs and care about her righteousness in the form of Prophet Zakariya (pbuh). Hence, such patronage of her was a blessing from God {To the care of Zakariya was she assigned} (Surat Aal-Imran: 37). But how did such patronage and caretaking manifest itself?

It was achieved through the Grace of The Almighty after priests had fought among themselves as to who would be her patron, each hoping that he would have the honour of such position as Maryam was the daughter of their leader and Teacher Imran (pbuh), the honest and righteous man who had died before seeing his daughter. Hence, in order to embrace such an honour, and in gratitude and loyalty to their master, each of the priests competed fiercely with his peers so as to win such an honour of raising Maryam, to the extent that they fought and argued fiercely among one another.

God Says, {This is part of the tidings of the things unseen, which We reveal unto thee (O Messenger) by inspiration: Thou wast not with them when they cast lots with arrows, as to which of them should be charged with the care of Mary: Nor wast thou with them when they disputed (the point)} (Surat Aal-Imran: 44).

---

134 "Al-Mar'ah fil Qasas al-Qur'ani", Ibid, 2/608.

135 "Tafseer Ibn Katheer", 1/359.

136 "Al-Mar'ah fil Qasas al-Qur'ani", Ibid, 2/610.

Each of Imran's followers was extremely keen on looking after the orphaned girl, yet when none of them conceded to the other this honour nor granted it to Zakariya as they should have, they decided to draw lots and see who wins.

God Says, {Thou wast not with them when they cast lots with arrows, as to which of them should be charged with the care of Mary}. Ibn Abbas explains the drawing of lots as having thrown their pencils in water and that that of Zakariya was floating highest among the others and hence he won the draw.[137] Ibn Hajar concurs with this explanation.[138]

But regardless of the manner in which the draw was conducted, Zakariya won it and became the man charged with Maryam's schooling and upbringing.[139]

The holy phrase {He assigned her} is indicative of God having determined that Maryam was to be assigned to Zakariya and that he won the draw only because of God's Will.[140]

At the time, Zakariya was head of the Jewish Temple as the caretaking of it was entrusted to him as a descendant of Haroun.[141]

Zakariya was a kind prophet and who Maryam, throughout her childhood and youth, gained much knowledge from on sciences, worship, prayers, demeanour and manners as he was her icon to follow. Accordingly, she was brought up in righteousness and good belief, and was connected to The Almighty through her prayers and supplication throughout her formative and early youth, until becoming a grown and mature young lady.[142]

---

137 Ibn Hajar al-'Asqalaani, "Fath al-Baari Sharh Saheeh al-Bukhari", ver. & corrected by Mohammad Fuad Abdul-Baaqi & Muhib Eddine al-Khateeb, al-Ma'arifah House, Beirut, 1379h, 5/345.

138 "Al-Mar'ah fil Qasas al-Qur'ani", Ibid, 2/612.

139 Ibid.

140 Ibid.

141 "Fi Thilaal al-Qur'an", Ibid, 1/393.

142 "Al-Qasas al-Qur'ani: Presentation and Analysis of Events", Ibid, 4/185

8. Dignifying Maryam (pbuh):

God Says, {Every time that Zakariya entered (Her) chamber to see her, he found her supplied with sustenance. He said: "O Mary! Whence (comes) this to you?" She said: "From Allah; for Allah Provides sustenance to whom He pleases without measure} (Surat Aal-Imran: 37).

Upon becoming her guardian and allowing her to reside at Bayt al-Maqdis, Zakariya made Maryam's abode in a chamber at the temple's most honoured locale, i.e. its Mihrab.[143]

God granted Maryam grace and dignity by providing her with sustenance as she was reciting prayers at the Mihrab. Zakariya (pbuh) witnessed this as evidenced in the holy verse: {Every time that Zakariya entered (Her) chamber to see her, he found her supplied with sustenance. He said: "O Mary! Whence (comes) this to you?" She said: "From Allah. for Allah Provides sustenance to whom He pleases without measure}.

The word "Every-time" indicates repetition, which means that whenever Zakariya came to the Mihrab and found Maryam there praying or supplicating to God, he saw food near her; a matter that was out of the ordinary and special. Zakariya knew that someone else had provided her with that food as he, her caretaker, had not brought it to her.

Zakariya knew that such special food had not been provided to her by a human, and that it was from God, but he asked her the question so that she would pronounce the miracle herself.

Maryam answered him frankly by saying (It is from The Almighty) Who delivered it to the Mihrab without toil.

Al-Hassan al-Basri said, "Whenever Zakariya entered her chamber at the Mihrab he would find sustenance near her that originated from the Heavens, not from people. Had Zakariya

[143] "Al-Mar'ah fil Qasas al-Qur'ani", Ibid, 2/613.

known such sustenance to be of earthly origin, he would not have questioned her about it."[144]

After this holy phrase, God comments on Maryam's response by reminding all of the truth that {Allah Provides sustenance to whom He pleases without measure}.

God does not "measure" what He provides to His subjects as it does not in any way deplete His abundance of goodness. One who does so is mankind who is fearful that depletion of resources may occur.[145]

As Maryam was not a prophet, her provision with such sustenance in a miraculous manner was a miracle in itself. When such occurs for non prophets, it is dubbed a "Dignity" as evidenced in the Qur'an for having been granted to others before Maryam like that to the Sleepers of the Cave. We affirm such "dignities" being provided to certain righteous people of olden times, and do not deny their occurrence as do some individuals, as this contradicts with the Words of God and that of Prophet Mohammad (pbuh).

The (sustenance) received by Maryam included all food and drink that she needed, yet the Qur'an does not mention the types of those foods – a matter which we should not argue about what kinds of vegetables, meats, drinks, etc. as there exists no proof thereof.[146]

What does matter to us, though, is knowing that she was blessed with plentiful sustenance that wowed her caretaker prophet to the extent that he questioned her about where she had amounted it from.

The mention of such unknown phenomenon of God providing Maryam with sustenance directly from Him is a prelude to the

144 "Al-Qasas al-Qur'ani: Presentation and Analysis of Events", Ibid, 4/186.

145 "Al-Qasas al-Qur'ani: Presentation and Analysis of Events", Ibid, 4/187.

146 Ibid.

wonders that shall come after it like the birth of Yahya and Isa. It was then that the old Zakariya, who had never had any children, began yearning for children of his own so that his paternal instinct would be satisfied and that life after him would continue on his path.[147]

Second: Zakariya prays to The Almighty to be blessed with righteous progeny:

God Says: {There did Zakariya pray to his Lord, saying: "O my Lord! Grant unto me from Thee a progeny that is pure: for Thou art He that heareth prayer} (Surat Aal-Imran: 38).

The explanation of the verse, above, is that when Zakariya saw the dignities being provided to Maryam, he called upon God that He grant him a son of blessed nature despite him being of old age and having a sterile wife.

The supplication of Zakariya (pbuh) in Surat Aal-Imran was a general one, yet it was somewhat specific at the beginning of Surat Maryam: {Kaf. Ha. Ya.´Ain. Sad. (This is) a recital of the Mercy of thy Lord to His servant Zakariya. Behold! he cried to his Lord in secret, Praying: "O my Lord! Infirm indeed are my bones, and the hair of my head doth glisten with grey: but never am I unblest, O my Lord, in my prayer to Thee! Now I fear (what) my relatives (and colleagues) (will do) after me: but my wife is barren: so give me an heir as from Thyself - (One that) will (truly) represent me, and represent the posterity of Jacob; and make him, O my Lord! one with whom Thou art well-pleased!} (Surat Maryam: 1-6).

God's description of Zakariya as His servant is meant to honour and dignify him as the status of being a servant of God is the most elevated and honourable of all.[148]

---

[147] "Fi Thilaal al-Qur'an", Ibid, 1/393.

[148] "Al-Qasas al-Qur'ani: Presentation and Analysis of Events", Ibid, 1/114-115.

Servitude to God is an honourable and elevated status by which close ones are described as it grants richness and worthiness. Yet servitude to any other is humiliation and demeaning, like when one is servant to Satan, one's lusts, money, office and authority through which one forfeits religion and principles.[149]

1. Zakariya beseeches God in secret:

{Behold! he cried to his Lord in secret} (Surat Maryam: 3).

Zakariya called upon God away from people's eyes and ears, in solitude, in order to offload that which weighed on his chest, and then says: {O my Lord! infirm indeed are my bones, and the hair of my head doth glisten with grey}. As God is Merciful and All-Knowing of mankind's instincts, He responds by telling them to invoke His Name whenever they are overburdened: {And your Lord says: "Call on Me; I will answer your (Prayers)} (Surat Ghafir: 60) so that they may feel relief and their hearts be at peace having complained of them to the Mightier and the More Capable.[150]

2. Beautiful prelude to a supplication:

{"O my Lord! infirm indeed are my bones, and the hair of my head doth glisten with grey: but never am I unblest, O my Lord, in my prayer to Thee! Now I fear (what) my relatives (and colleagues) (will do) after me: but my wife is barren: so give me an heir as from Thyself - (One that) will (truly) represent me, and represent the posterity of Jacob; and make him, O my Lord! one with whom Thou art well-pleased!" (His prayer was answered): "O Zakariya! We give thee good news of a son: His name shall be Yahya: on none by that name have We conferred distinction before"} (Surat Maryam: 4-7).

---

[149] Adel Ahmad Sabir al-Rawini, "Ta'ammulaat fi Surat Maryam", al-Nawaadir House, Syria, 2011, p.

[150] "Fi Thilaal al-Qur'an", Ibid, 4/2302.

When bones have gone frail, it means that the entire body is even more so. Then the metaphor of hair alight with greyness is indicative that all black strands have disappeared rendering Zakariya an old man as he prays to The Almighty for a son.

Zakariya then adds: {but never am I unblest, O my Lord, in my prayer to Thee!} as he acknowledges that God has blessed him with answering his prayers when he does so. As an old man now, Zakariya is all hope that God will answer his prayers so that a son may succeed him, after his demise, and continue on the path of guiding the Israelites along the path of righteousness. Having been one of the Israelites most prominent prophets, and the caretaker of Maryam as she served the Mihrab which he curated, he fears that his legacy will not be upheld by his people unless God Grants him a son, and accordingly he beseeches God.[151]

In explaining the above, Imam Ibn Katheer says:

- First: Zakariya feared that his followers would deviate from his message once dead, and hence prayed for a son who would be a prophet to lead them; and God answered his prayers.

Zakariya did not fear for whatever earthly possessions he would leave behind after his death as he was of higher status than to worry about such insignificant matters.

- Second: It was never stated that Zakariya possessed any money as he was a carpenter who made money through his sweat, and such a man – particularly a prophet – does not accumulate money as prophets are utterly altruistic.

- Third: Zakariya did not leave behind any money as it is prohibited for prophets' belongings to be inherited. If they had left money behind after their death, it would be deemed charity. Evidence on this is the Hadeeth reported by al-Bukhari and Muslim

[151] "Fi Thilaal al-Qur'an", Ibid, 4/2302.

of Aisha that the Prophet (pbuh) said, "We cannot be inherited, and whatever we leave behind is charity."[152]

Zakariya wished that his prophethood be inherited as per {"(One that) will (truly) represent me, and represent the posterity of Jacob"}, similar to that reported by God of Dawoud inheriting prophethood from his father Suleiman (pbut): {And Solomon was David´s heir} (Surat al-Naml: 16).

Scholars state that the legacy of Zakariya was knowledge, not money, and as he was a descendant of Yacoub, he wished for his son to inherit him in prophethood.[153]

Hence, Zakariya (pbuh) wished that God grant him a son who would inherit him in knowledge and prophethood, and who would in turn inherit the prophets of the Yacoub clan.[154]

3. {And make him, O my Lord! one with whom Thou art well-pleased!}:

Ibn Katheer says this means Zakariya requests from God that the son He grants him be accepted by God and embraced by people.[155]

Zakariya wanted to ensure that his heir will be neither arrogant nor greedy.[156] He also wished that his character be moulded upon acceptance, pleasure and happiness so that his relationships with others may be based on the same.

Acceptance is neither strict, nervous, judgmental, sad nor miserable, but rather open minded, patient and of good manners.[157]

---

152 Al-Bukhari, no. 6730. See: Muslim, no. 1758.

153 "Tafseer Ibn Katheer", 3/109.

154 "Al-Qasas al-Qur'ani: Presentation and Analysis of Events", Ibid, 4/119.

155 Ibid.

156 "Fi Thilaal al-Qur'an", Ibid, 4/2302.

157 "Al-Qasas al-Qur'ani: Presentation and Analysis of Events", Ibid, 4/119.

4. Zakariya's wife: From barren to pregnant:

God was just as gracious as Zakariya had expected and granted him a son through His mercy. But it was a miracle in itself as his wife was barren, yet who became pregnant from Zakariya as it was God's Will that it so be.

This truth was echoed in verses 89-90 of Surat al-Anbiyaa': {And (remember) Zakariya, when he cried to his Lord: "O my Lord! leave me not without offspring, though thou art the best of inheritors." So We listened to him: and We granted him Yahya: We cured his wife's (Barrenness) for him}. The inheritance meant here is that of prophethood and knowledge through which Zakariya intended for his son to continue performing after he passes away.

God fulfilled Zakariya's wish and gave him Yahya after having made the former's wife biologically fertile, and this was also a miracle.

In the Qur'an, when Zakariya's wife was barren, she was called his (woman), but then when she became fertile it changed to (wife). This is indicative that Qur'anic terminology is extremely specific as that not all words of similar meaning are fully synonymous.

The Holy Qur'an calls a man's Halal female partner a "woman" if there is any disharmony between them for any tangible or intangible reason. So if she can bear children or is barren, she is a (wife) or a (woman) respectively. The same applies if she is Muslim or non-believer. The Qur'an states: Noah's woman, Lot's woman, Pharaoh's woman, but if the relationship between the two is a harmonious one, the female partner is called (wife) as marriage is based on harmony.

So when God made Zakariya's woman fertile, she was no longer considered only a woman, but a wife who can fulfil her marital role (biologically) in bearing a child.[158]

[158] "Al-Qasas al-Qur'ani: Presentation and Analysis of Events", Ibid, 4/124.

5. God's glad tidings to Zakariya as he was at the Mihrab:

God Says: {While he was standing in prayer in the chamber, the angels called unto him: "(Allah) doth give thee glad tidings of Yahya, witnessing the truth of a Word from Allah, and (be besides) noble, chaste, and a prophet - of the (goodly) company of the righteous." He said: "O my Lord! How shall I have son, seeing I am very old, and my wife is barren?" "Thus," was the answer, "Doth God accomplish what He willeth"} (Surat Aal-Imran: 39-40).

The supplication was answered favourably by God and the angels brought glad tidings to Zakariya informing him of a male child named by God prior to his birth. His traits were also described as a generous master, abstaining from physical lusts, has a hold on himself, a believer of a Word coming to him from God and a righteous prophet like many righteous ones before him.

The acceptance of the prayers and the glad tidings he received from the angels surprised Zakariya – for he is merely a man – and was very keen on God informing him how such a miracle in mankind's calculations can become a reality. God reports him saying: {"O my Lord! How shall I have son, seeing I am very old, and my wife is barren?"} {"Thus," was the answer, "Doth God accomplish what He willeth"}.

In God's realm, there are neither familiar matters nor strange ones for He Wills any matter and it occurs without restraints like those to which we humans are accustomed.

6. Zakariya requests a sign from God:

Zakariya (pbuh) was so much in anticipation of the glad tidings materialising when God informed him that he shall be unable to utter a single word to people for three days, and that he must spend that time in prayer and supplication. God Says: {He said: "O my Lord! Give me a Sign!" "Thy Sign," was the answer, "Shall be that thou shalt speak to no man for three days but with signals. Then celebrate the praises of thy Lord again and again, and glorify Him in the evening and in the morning"} (Surat Aal-Imran: 41).

The sign and actual miracle was that the people of Zakariya knew that he could speak eloquently, with high linguistic quality and that he suffered no ill of gab. Yet after being given glad tidings of a son, they were surprised of him communicating with them only via signals and hand movements – a matter which persisted for three days and nights.

During these three days, Zakariya was in one state or another:

- First: When he was alone and nobody could hear him, his tongue was eloquent in prayer and supplication to The Almighty, and he was able to hear his own words.

- Second: When he would see his people and wished to speak to them, he was unable to do so as his tongue would be miraculously restrained from movement, and he would then communicate with them via signals.

This made Zakariya's people in awe and shock as to what may be the reason behind his tongue being restrained. But it was God's Will that caused this, and it had nothing to do with Zakariya himself.

The holy verse brings together these two states as Zakariya experienced God's miracle in these three days: {"Thy Sign," was the answer, "Shall be that thou shalt speak to no man for three days but with signals. Then celebrate the praises of thy Lord again and again, and glorify Him in the evening and in the morning"} (Surat Aal-Imran: 41).

God ordered Zakariya to pray profusely to Him in these three days and told him He would not hold his tongue from moving when he does so. The verse states that Zakariya must pray to God from the afternoon till sunset and from dawn till day break.[159]

---

[159] "Al-Qasas al-Qur'ani: Presentation and Analysis of Events", Ibid, 4/140.

Although his tongue was restrained when wanting to speak to his people, Zakariya continues to speak of God's goodness by signalling this to his people. He was blessed with silence as it relieves oneself and also grants him serenity. Prophet Mohammad (pbuh) said, "Two phrases are easy to say and weigh heavily in God's scale: Subhan Allah and through His Grace, Subhan Allah the Greatest."[160]

God Says of Zakariya's signalling to his people of God's Grace and their need to praise Him at all times when his tongue is restrained from speaking: {So Zakariya came out to his people from him chamber: He told them by signs to celebrate Allah's praises in the morning and in the evening} (Surat Maryam: 11).[161]

7. The traits of Yahiya (pbuh) as stated in the Holy Qur'an:

Once the three days had lapsed, Zakariya informed his people that it was God who had restrained his tongue while in their presence and that He would release it when he was away from them. He also told them that this was a sign from God as a prelude to another miracle in the form of the son God will be granting him.

Upon learning of the miracle to come, the belief of Zakariya's people, in God and in His ability to do away with norms, increased. God then fulfilled Zakariya's miracle as his barren woman became impregnated by him. She then gave birth nine months later to the child who his father named (Yahya) in fulfilment of God's order.[162]

God then mentions some of Yahya's traits: {"(Allah) doth give thee glad tidings of Yahya, witnessing the truth of a Word from Allah, and (be besides) noble, chaste, and a prophet - of the (goodly) company of the righteous"} (Surat Aal-Imran: 39).

---

160 Reported by al-Bukhari, "Kitaab al-Da'awaat", no. 6406.

161 "Al-Mar'ah fil Qasas al-Qur'ani", Ibid, 2/641.

162 "Al-Qasas al-Qur'ani: Presentation and Analysis of Events", 4/143.

- Meaning of (Yahya – *of Life*[163]): He was named as such because God gave him the life of belief and prophethood. Some scholars say that he was named as such because God revived people's righteousness through him, or because God revived his mother's womb through him.[164]

- Meaning of (His name shall be Yahya: on none by that name have We conferred distinction before): Never before have We – God – given such a name to anyone and never have barren women given birth to such a boy.[165]

a. (Witnessing the truth of a Word from Allah):

Tafseer scholars have two opinions on the meaning of (a Word from God that Yahya is true to): First, that it is Word that reaches him from God as he is a prophet, and God grants His prophets whatever Words and Books He wishes. So this Word may be in the form of a Holy Book which God descends upon him containing provisions that he abides by, believes in and commits to. Second, that the Word from God is Isa son of Maryam (pbuh) as the Holy Qur'an has stated that Isa is a *Word from God*.

God Says: {Behold! the angels said: "O Mary! Allah giveth thee glad tidings of a *Word from Him*: his name will be Christ Jesus, the son of Mary"} (Surat Aal-Imran: 45). Prophet Isa lived while Yahya was also alive, and each was a prophet. When God sent Isa as Messenger, Yahya was the first to believe in him and concur to his prophethood. He testified that Isa was the servant and messenger of God who had sent him as a prophet. Yet both statements are not contradictory to one another as they actually complement one another for Yahya was an honourable prophet upon who God sent His Words, and he was the first to believe in and follow them.

[163] Translator's addition.

[164] "Al-Qasas al-Qur'ani: Presentation and Analysis of Events", Ibid, 4/129

[165] Ibid, 4/131.

b. (Master):

God made him an honourable master and nobleman among his people as a prophet with knowledge, worship and patience – as explained by Prophet Mohammad's companions and by those who followed in their footsteps.

Scholars have explained the word (Master) in varied forms, such as:

- Patient and God-fearing
- Of knowledge and worship
- Of generosity
- Patient and unbecoming of anger
- Knowledgeable and scholarly
- A Sharif[166]

None of these explanations are contradictory to one another and all were embodied in Yahya (pbuh).

c. (Chaste):

Meaning one who perseveres in not being driven by lust.[167] Yahya willingly decided to be celibate and not lust for women due to his own sense of chastity; not because of any physical short-comings as this was a matter of inferiority which prophets did not possess.[168]

d. (A righteous prophet):

The holy verse {… and a prophet - of the (goodly) company of the righteous} states Yahya's prophethood and that God shall also make him among the righteous.

This was another glad tiding for Zakariya (pbuh), and greater than that which preceded it of being granted a child.

166 "Tafseer Ibn Katheer", 3/341.

167 "Al-Mufradaat fi Ghareeb al-Qur'an", Ibid, p.238-239.

168 "Al-Qasas al-Qur'ani: Presentation and Analysis of Events", Ibid, 4/145.

When Zakariya's wife was pregnant with a child, he knew that it was a boy and that he would become a prophet. These are the four traits of Yahya that are mentioned in Surat Aal-Imran.[169]

- Yahya (pbuh) as a young man: God informs us in Surat Maryam of Yahya after having come of age and becoming a prophet. God Says: {"O Yahya! take hold of the Book with might: and We gave him Wisdom even as a youth, And piety (for all creatures) as from Us, and purity: He was devout, And kind to his parents, and he was not overbearing or rebellious. So Peace on him the day he was born, the day that he dies, and the day that he will be raised up to life (again)!"} (Surat Maryam: 12-15).

This is considered the first instance of Yahya being deputised to bearing the great responsibility.

e. (O Yahya! take hold of the Book with might):

That meant by (the Book) is the Torah which God descended upon Mousa (pbuh) as God had preserved it as a Book for the Israelites after the death of Mousa. God ordered Yahya to hold strongly onto that book and to implement its commandments with moral might and determination. So that meant here is not physical strength, but a moral one of understanding, knowledge, discipline, performance, action and dissemination of calling.

f. (We gave him Wisdom even as a youth):

Yahya (pbuh) was not a ruler of the Israelites, but rather a young man, prior to puberty, of great understanding, knowledge, insistence and good doing.[170]

g. (And piety (for all creatures) as from Us):

God has been gracious towards Yahya by granting him piety for all creatures from within Him. It came as God's favourable

[169] "Al-Qasas al-Qur'ani: Presentation and Analysis of Events", Ibid, 4/146-147.

[170] Ibid, 4/148.

acceptance of Zakariya's prayers when he requested his son be one of good disposition.

God responded favourably to his father's prayers and granted Yahya tenderness of heart, mercy and empathy towards others. This was a great blessing which God bestowed on Yahya.

h. (And purity)

That meant by "purity" is from guilts and wrongdoing; purity of soul; and embracing of obedience and worship of God.[171]

Accordingly, God graced Yahya with purity, chastity and cleanliness of heart and demeanour to aid him in purifying the ills of mankind's hearts and souls.[172]

i. (He was devout)

Yahya (pbuh) was devout to God, worshipped Him, feared Him, performed His rites, avoided His prohibitions and was fast in obeying Him. As God had granted Yahya all traits of knowledge, understanding, ruling, tenderness, mercy and empathy, among others, he became devout, connected to The Almighty and prayed to Him day and night.[173]

j. (And kind to his parents):

As Yahya's parents were of old age, and having had him in that old age, he was kind to them and treated them with all tenderness.

This kind treatment is the greatest of blessings that God bestows upon old parents.

k. (And he was not overbearing or rebellious):

God here describes Yahya with two positive traits that negate two negative ones. "He was neither overbearing nor rebellious."

---

[171] Ibid, 4/150.

[172] "Fi Thilaal al-Qur'an", Ibid, 4/2304.

[173] "Al-Qasas al-Qur'ani: Presentation and Analysis of Events", Ibid, 4/151.

Yahya was not overbearing or domineering in that he did not disdain others nor feel superior to them in any way that would do them injustice, demean or oppress them.

He was also not one of wrongdoing.

Verses 12-14 of Surat Maryam clearly show the correlation of the traits granted to Yahya: {We gave him Wisdom even as a youth, And piety (for all creatures) as from Us, and purity: He was devout, And kind to his parents, and he was not overbearing or rebellious}.

l. (So Peace on him the day he was born, the day that he dies, and the day that he will be raised up to life (again)!):

God here informs us of the peace he added to Yahya's traits in that it fills his soul throughout all stages of his life.

Yahya will be overcome with peace on the day he was born, and hence the devil was unable to harm him; then on the day he dies in that he will be well cared for in his grave and no punishment shall befall him; and finally upon his resurrection on Judgment Day as he will not suffer from the fear or torture that shall befall others on that day.

These three phases are the most lonely in mankind's life as one is born – exiting that which he has been used to, then dying – seeing unfamiliar peoples, and then resurrected – finding oneself in a vast area packed with people. Therefore, God bestowed His grace on Yahya (pbuh) by saving him from the horrors of these three periods.[174]

Prophet Mohammad (pbuh) spoke of the great status of Yahya and Zakariya (pbut). Al-Tirmithi reported of Abu Sa'eed al-Khudrii that Prophet Mohammad said: "Al-Hassan and al-Hussein will be the masters of Heaven's youth, except for the two maternal cousins Isa son of Maryam and Yahya son of Zakariya; and Fatima

[174] "Al-Qasas al-Qur'ani: Presentation and Analysis of Events", Ibid, 4/153.

shall be the lady of Heaven's women, except for that from Maryam daughter of Imran."[175]

Prophet Mohammad (pbuh) considered Yahya and Isa (pbut) the masters of Heaven's youth as Isa was raised to the Heavens as a young man – as shall come further down. It seems that Yahya had died as a young man as well. Prophet Mohammad reported that he had seen the two maternal cousins – Isa and Yahya – when he was raised to the Heavens on al-Mi'raaj night, and that they were awaiting to welcome him as he arrived at the second tier of the Heavens.

In the long Hadeeth concerning al-Israa' and al-Mi'raaj, reported by Anas bin Malik: "... We were then raised to the second sky and Jibreel was first to enter it. It was said: Who are you? He said: Jibreel. It was said: Who is with you? He said: Mohammad. It was said: He was summoned? He said: He was summoned. So the gates opened for us, and I saw the two maternal cousins Isa son of Maryam and Yahya son of Zakariya, peace be upon them, and they welcomed me and wished me well ..."[176]

Hence, Zakariya and Yahya (pbut) were among the last prophets of the Israelites and only Isa son of Maryam was sent to them afterwards.[177]

8. Reason for mentioning Yahya son of Zakariya (pbut):

God had stated the story of Yahiya's birth from a barren old lady and an older man as something out of the ordinary in Earthly terms, as a prelude to something much greater of a miracle by speaking of the birth of Isa (pbuh) without a father.[178]

---

175 "Sunan al-Tirmithi", no. 3768. See also: "Al-Ahaadeeth al-Saheeha", no. 68.

176 Muslim, "Kitaab al-Iman", no. 162.

177 "Al-Qasas al-Qur'ani: Presentation and Analysis of Events", Ibid, 4/160.

178 Mohammad al-Hajjaar, "Min Qisas al-Tanzeel", al-Bashaa'ir al-Islamiyah House, Beirut, 1st Ed., 1999, p.504.

Third: God's choosing of Maryam from among all other women on Earth:

God Says: {Behold! the angels said: "O Mary! Allah hath chosen thee and purified thee - chosen thee above the women of all nations. O Mary! worship Thy Lord devoutly: Prostrate thyself, and bow down (in prayer) with those who bow down"} (Surat Aal-Imran: 42-43).

God speaks of Imran's clan and how He chose them from among all nations. He speaks of Imran's woman and how He fulfilled her prayers and vows. God then speaks of Maryam, her righteous upbringing, Zakariya's patronage of her – a matter that was a blessing for her and for Zakariya who prayed to God that He grant him a son after having seen all the riches God bestowed on Maryam; a matter which God fulfilled for him and granted him Yahya – and then the context reverts to Maryam once again.

1. (Behold! the angels said: "O Mary! Allah hath chosen thee"):

This means that God has chosen her for this supreme status, giving her descendance from a good home, accepting her well, raising her well, having Zakariya as her caretaker, providing her with sustenance and being kind to her. The angels here are informing Maryam that God had ordered them to let her know that He had chosen her from among all women due to her worship, altruism, honour and purity. In truth, God chose Maryam for:

- Accepting her dedication for serving the temple although being female as this had never been granted to a female before her,

- The sustenance she received from God,

- God's dedication of her for His worship, thus providing her with kindness, guidance and chastity,

- Allowing the angels to speak to her directly,[179] as per the holy verse: (Behold! the angels said: "O Mary!).

This is a reminder for Prophet Mohammad (pbuh) and for all mankind of Maryam's story, God's choosing of her, purifying her and her devotion in worshipping Him from the purest of sources, i.e. the Holy Qur'an. God had also done the same with Zakariya when the angels gave him glad tidings of the soon to be son of his, Yahya: {While he was standing in prayer in the chamber, the angels called unto him: "(Allah) doth give thee glad tidings of Yahya"} (Surat Aal-Imran: 39).

It is not a wonderous matter that the angels have spoken directly to Maryam although she was not a prophet as it was by order from God. God may order angels to speak directly with righteous men and women as they did with Ibrahim's woman allaying her questioning of bearing Ishak while she was a barren and old lady.

What matters is that Maryam (pbuh) saw angels in front of her, probably after they transformed from their angelic form into human ones.[180]

2. ("And purified thee"):

This means that God has purified Maryam from ill manners, distress, vices and gave her traits of beauty.[181]

Purity is of four levels: Purity of exterior, soul and heart that all mankind may possess, and purity that which is concealed which only prophets and chosen ones may possess.[182]

The purity of Maryam is in her great belief in God, obeying Him, being saved from blasphemy and insurrection, having pu-

179 "Al-Mar'ah fil Qasas al-Qur'ani", Ibid, 2/641.

180 "Al-Qasas al-Qur'ani: Presentation and Analysis of Events", Ibid, 4/189.

181 Ibn Katheer, "Qasas al-Anbiyaa'", al-Ma'arifah House, Beirut, Lebanon, 1st Ed., 2000, p.553.

182 Al-Ghazaali, "Ihyaa' 'Uloum al-Deen", al-Ma'arifah House, Beirut, Lebanon, 1st Ed., D.T., 1/251.

rity of good manners that shield her from ill ones, chastity and innocence from accusations of the Israelites as was spoken by Isa (pbuh) while an infant in the cradle.[183]

3. ("Chosen thee above the women of all nations"):

The "choosing" by God of Maryam was twofold: First, He chose and selected her from among all other women in order to fulfil His Will. Second, as a result of the first, He made her the most preferable among all other women on Earth.

The graces that God bestowed on Maryam had not occurred to any woman before her, regardless of how pious and righteous any of those were – hence the first choosing based on selection. Having done so, God then purified and rid her of flaws and impurities. God chose Maryam from among all women so that she may bear a child without a father's seed; a miracle which she alone had the honour of bearing.[184]

a. The Holy Qur'an is God's Words:

This testimony for Maryam was stated in the Holy Qur'an although Prophet Mohammad (pbuh) was in a fierce intellectual battle with Nasraanis, as proof that the Qur'an is God's Words and an aspect of fairness and justice in Islam. The mentioning of "purity" here is symbolic because of the doubts that surrounded Isa's birth which the Israelites hurried to accuse the Pure Maryam of wrongdoing as, in their belief, no such birth may occur in the world of the living without a father. Hence, they claimed that a dishonourable secret was what caused her pregnancy.

Thus the greatness of Islam, as the Messenger of Islam Mohammad (pbuh) was suffering all sorts of torment and disbelief by people of the Book, including Nasraanis. Mohammad is told the

---

183 "Al-Mar'ah fil Qasas al-Qur'ani", Ibid, 2/150.

184 "Al-Qasas al-Qur'ani: Presentation and Analysis of Events", Ibid, 4/192.

truth of Maryam's greatness by The Almighty and how He gave her preferential treatment from among all other women on Earth. In such a debate between our Prophet (pbuh) and those who held Maryam in high regard – who utilised this as an excuse for not believing in Mohammad – we find the Qur'an revealed to Mohammad glorifying her.

The honest Prophet Mohammad receives the truth about Maryam from God and pronounces it to all. Had he not been a messenger sent by God, he would have never uttered these words of truth.[185]

b. Maryam, the best among all women:

The Holy Qur'an and the Hadeeths by Prophet Mohammad state that Maryam was the best among all women since Eve till the last woman on Judgment Day, followed by Fatima bint Mohammad (pbuh), then Khadija bint Khuwailid, then Asiya bint Muzahim.

The Hadeeths of Prophet Mohammad (pbuh) on Maryam are as follows:

- "The best among all women is Maryam bint Imran, then Khadija bint Khuwailid, then Fatima bint Mohammad, then Pharaoh's woman Asiya."[186]

- "Allah has made many men complete; yet among women, He made complete only Maryam bint Imran and Asiya, the woman of Pharaoh. The goodness Aishah has given to women is like that of al-Thareed to all other types of food."[187]

Although these four women were elevated in status to completeness, none of them reached the level of prophethood.

[185] "Fi Thilaal al-Qur'an", Ibid, 1/359-396.

[186] Reported by al-Haakim in "Al-Mustadrak", 2/595.

[187] Al-Bukhari, no. 3411.

The meaning of "Complete" in the above is possessing unlimited virtues of goodness, piety and charity, among other high morals and traits.

Prophethood was not meant for women as it entailed public speaking and calling on and mingling with the masses to embrace God's Will. Women needed to be detached from the masses so as to reach the level of a Siddeeqah, which is a great level just beneath prophethood.[188]

In the Hadeeth, above, the Prophet (pbuh) acknowledged Maryam's "completeness", sound mind and that which the Holy Qur'an stated of her most elevated status in virtue among all other women.[189]

- **Was Maryam a Siddeeqah or a Prophet?**

The truth of the matter is that she was a Siddeeqah, not a prophet as evidenced through the following:

- {Nor did We send before thee (as messengers) any but men, whom we did inspire - (men) living in human habitations. Do they not travel through the earth, and see what was the end of those before them? But the home of the Hereafter is best, for those who do right. Will ye not then understand?} (Surat Yusuf: 109).

- {Before thee, also, the messengers We sent were but men, to whom We granted inspiration: If ye realise this not, ask of those who possess the Message} (Surat al-Anbiyaa': 07).

- {And before thee also the messengers We sent were but men, to whom We granted inspiration: if ye realise this not, ask of those who possess the Message.} (Surat al-Nahl: 43).

As prophethood was a heavy physical burden and difficult delegation to carry out, God allocated it only to males – a matter

[188] "Min Qisas al-Tanzeel", Ibid, p.514.

[189] Omar Suleiman al-Ashqar, "Qisas al-Tawraah wal Injeel fi Daw' al-Qur'an wal Sunnah", al-Nafaa'is House, Beirut, Lebanon, 1st Ed., 2011, p.325.

which women's biological and psychological composition cannot handle. Hence, all prophets were men as this entailed toil, perseverance, travel, fighting battles and bearing hardships[190].

Nowhere in the Holy Qur'an or in the Prophet's Sunnah was Maryam described as a prophet. Rather, she was described as bearing traits of righteousness and purity. God Says: {Christ the son of Mary was no more than a messenger; many were the messengers that passed away before him. His mother was a woman of truth. They had both to eat their (daily) food} (Surat al-Maa'idah: 75). She was called a Siddeeqah as she was an ardent believer of God's omens, of what her son told her and of her delivery of Isa.

The purpose for calling her a Siddeeqah is to negate having had a description of higher status than that, i.e. of divinity, so as to countenance those who say that God is one of three – rendering Maryam the third thereof. So this is to refute Isa's and his mother's divinity as both were humans who ate and drank, and of course who then naturally excreted stool and urine.[191]

She was described as a Siddeeqah due to the perfection of her devotion and submittal to God's Will both externally and internally.

4. Maryam's submittal to prostrating and bowing down in prayer:

God Says: {"O Mary! worship Thy Lord devoutly: Prostrate thyself, and bow down (in prayer) with those who bow down"} (Surat Aal-Imran: 43).

Having graced her with such elevated status, God orders Maryam – via the angels who delivered His Message – that she toil in worshipping Him to thank Him for such graces He

---

[190] Ali al-Sallabi, "Al-Iman bil Rusul wal Risalaat", al-Asriyah Printing & Publishing House, Beirut, 2011, p.54.

[191] Ibn Katheer House, Damascus, 1st Ed., 2018, p.619.

bestowed upon her and so that she may persist on the path of righteousness.[192]

The repetition of the calling "O' Mary" denotes attention and reference to the importance of the commands that lie within. It means: You who is named Maryam, you must toil in your worship of The Almighty.

The holy verse orders Maryam (pbuh) to toil in worship, persist in her obedience of Him, prostrate herself more in prayers and bow down with those who do the same so that she may be drawn closer to God as it is prayer that does so.

Prophet Mohammad (pbuh) said, "A subject is closest to God when he is prostrating, so supplicate plenty."[193] Hence, the life of Maryam (pbuh) was one of obedience, worship, submissiveness, bowing in prayer and connected to God in preparation for the great occurrence.[194]

5. (This is of the tidings of things unseen, which We reveal unto thee by inspiration):

God Says: {This is part of the tidings of the things unseen, which We reveal unto thee (O Messenger) by inspiration: Thou wast not with them when they cast lots with arrows, as to which of them should be charged with the care of Mary: Nor wast thou with them when they disputed (the point)} (Surat Aal-Imran: 44).

This is in reference to all the information mentioned in previous verses on how Imran's woman vowed that the child she bore would be devoted to God, as well as the birth of Maryam, Zakariya's caring for her, the good tidings he received of Yahya and the angels speaking to Maryam.

---

[192] "Al-Mar'ah fil Qasas al-Qur'ani", Ibid, 2/659.

[193] Al-Nawawi, "Al-Minhaaj Sharh Saheeh Muslim bin al-Hajjaaj", Ihyaa' al-Turath al-Arabi House, Beirut, 2nd Ed., 1392h, 4/200.

[194] "Fi Thilaal al-Qur'an", Ibid, 1/396.

The verse considered these pieces of news among the things unseen as they had occurred in the ancient past, centuries prior to the prophethood of Mohammad (pbuh). Having not witnessed them in person, they were unseen matters for him. But God revealed these occurrences to Mohammad – a matter which proves the truth of his prophethood. People of the Book from among the Israelites and the Nasraanis knew that Prophet Mohammad was unlettered, who could neither read nor write – a matter which necessitates that he did not learn this information from books. He also had no friends from among priests of Nasraanis nor Israelites. So how did he become aware of such concealed information that only a few priests knew?

It was God who revealed this information to Mohammad (pbuh) as he was His messenger.[195] God Tells Mohammad: (Thou wast not with them when they cast lots with arrows, as to which of them should be charged with the care of Mary: Nor wast thou with them when they disputed (the point)).

This is in reference to the incident when her mother brought her to the Temple in fulfilment of her vow to God to do so; an incident which was neither mentioned in the Old Testament nor the New Testament. Yet the incident of casting lots must have been known by Temple and Nasraani priests.

The Qur'an does not detail this event as it was probably known to those who heard it or maybe because it does not add anything to the truth's origin which it wishes to present to future generations. We are only to understand that they agreed upon a specific means – via casting arrows – that would determine who would care for her. Some say that they cast their arrows in the River Jordan and that they were taken along by the current, except that of Zakariya, and that this was the sign upon which they granted him that honour.

---

195 "Al-Qasas al-Qur'ani: Presentation and Analysis of Events", Ibid, 4/182.

All of these events were among the matters unseen to Prophet Mohammad as he was not present when they did so, nor had he heard of it as it may have been among the Temple's secrets which are not announced to the public. But the Qur'an detailed these events so as to confront the high priests of the Book at the time as evidence that God had revealed such to His honest messenger. The Qur'an does not state that they had refuted such information for had it been a point of argument, they would have done so, as arguing was the main reason for which they had approached Prophet Mohammad.[196]

Accordingly, the Holy Qur'an gives the true image of Prophet Isa's minute details, his upbringing and details about his mother. This aids truth seekers in knowing the real story of Isa (pbuh) unlike the gospels which Nasraanis believe in – which are contradictory and in contrast to one another. Some of these gospels concur with Jews' accusations against Maryam as in those of Luke and Matthew. All gospels agree on the real ancestry of Isa and claim him to be the son of Yusuf the Carpenter who was engaged to Maryam prior to the birth of Prophet Isa, and that he then married her and the couple gave birth to other children who became sort of Prophet Isa's siblings. Yet the Holy Qur'an has given Maryam her true due in a manner that none of the gospels have, and stated the elevated status God granted her, as well as her purity, honourable bloodline and selecting her from among all other women.[197]

The stories on Isa and his virgin mother Maryam in all gospels are conflicting, contradictory and far from the truth to the extent that those who interpreted them were very confused and made many mistakes while explaining these gospels. The story of Yusuf

---

[196] "Fi Thilaal al-Qur'an", Ibid, 1/396.

[197] "Al-Mar'ah fil Qasas al-Qur'ani", Ibid, 2/664.

the Carpenter was planted in the gospels and is not related to the virgin Maryam (pbuh) in any way whatsoever.[198]

Prophet Isa (pbuh) had no brothers or sisters, and anything to the contrary is historically baseless. He was born from the virgin Maryam who was not married.[199]

This discrepancy between that mentioned in the gospels and in the Holy Qur'an on Maryam's upbringing, purity, chastity and bearing of Isa (pbuh) without the presence of a father refutes the claims of Orientalists that much of the Qur'an's stories is taken from the books of Jews and Nasraanis; the Holy Qur'an is a Book which is supreme to all the above and which is void of manipulation and distortion.[200]

- God Says: {This is the true account: There is no god except Allah. He is indeed the Exalted in Power, the Wise} (Surat Aal-Imran: 62).

- God Says: {We have, without doubt, sent down the Message; and We will assuredly guard it (from corruption)} (Surat al-Hijr: 09).

- God Says: {Do they not consider the Qur´an (with care)? Had it been from other than Allah, they would surely have found therein Much discrepancy} (Surat al-Nisaa': 82).

God informed Prophet Mohammad (pbuh) that the virgin Maryam, mother of Isa (pbuh), was the best among women and that He chose and considered her preferentially among all others. The Prophet expressed this to all, and all instances in the Holy Qur'an of mentioning Maryam and her preferential status, as well as the story of Isa, are proof that the Holy Qur'an is God's Words.

Surah (19) of the Holy Qur'an is entitled, "Maryam", in recognition and honouring of the chaste mother of Isa (pbuh). Such hon-

---

[198] Ibid, 2/665.

[199] Mohammad Ali al-Baar, "Modern Studies in the New Testament and Nasraani Dogmas", al-Qalam House, Damascus, 1st Ed., 2006, p.101.

[200] "Al-Mar'ah fil Qasas al-Qur'ani", Ibid, 2/665.

our was never bestowed on her in the gospels of Christians, and even if we go through all 66 Protestant gospels and the 73 gospels of Roman Catholics, no part of any of them has her name as title. One can find gospels entitled Matthew, Mark, Luke, John, Peter, Paul and persons of less importance, yet none is entitled "Isa" or "Maryam".

Had Mohammad (pbuh) been the author of the Qur'an, he could have easily introduced the name of his mother, Aminah, along with those of Maryam or Isa (pbut). Then again, he could have introduced the name of his faithful wife, Khadijah, or that of his beloved daughter, Fatima! But No! The Qur'an is the Words of God, not Prophet Mohammad's![201]

6. The Angels' ushering of glad tidings to Maryam of giving birth to Isa, and a number of his traits:

God Says: {Behold! the angels said: "O Mary! Allah giveth thee glad tidings of a Word from Him: his name will be Christ Jesus, the son of Mary, held in honour in this world and the Hereafter and of (the company of) those nearest to Allah. He shall speak to the people in childhood and in maturity. And he shall be (of the company) of the righteous"} (Surat Aal-Imran: 45-46).

Once God had chosen Maryam (pbuh), purified her and directed her to toil in worship, obedience, sincerity and submission to His Will, Maryam was ready for the grand miracle of bearing Isa without the presence of a father.

It was to be as the angels had informed her of the glad tidings that not only was she chosen to be the purest among women, but also that she was chosen to bear Isa (pbuh).[202]

[201] Ahmed Didat, "The Messiah in Islam", Trans. & ver. By Mohammad Mukhtaar, al-Fadeelah Publishing House, Riyadh, Saudi, 1988, p.27.

[202] "Al-Mar'ah fil Qasas al-Qur'ani", Ibid, 2/667.

a. (Behold! the angels said: "O Mary!):

A group of angels brought forth the glad tidings to Maryam, and Surat Maryam, verse 19, speaks of how the angel Jibreel (pbuh) came to her and said: {"Nay, I am only a messenger from thy Lord, (to announce) to thee the gift of a holy son"}. The group of angels, including Jibreel, first gave her the glad tidings, then Jibreel took a human form and repeated the news to pacify her as she was in awe as to how such an event could occur.[203]

b. (Allah giveth thee glad tidings of a Word from Him):

God Himself was the one who named Isa and Who dubbed him as "His Word." Isa was the Word from God as He had created him via uttering the word "Be!" so that he may be created directly. Isa was thus created and came to "be" just as God created all other matter in the universe. God Says in verse 82 of Surat Yaseen: {Verily, when He intends a thing, His Command is, "be", and it is!}. God created Isa with this word, hence dubbing him His Word, just as He did when He created Adam (pbut) with the same "Be!".[204]

The Holy Qur'an draws the attention of those bewildered by the way Isa was created to Adam who was created in the same manner without neither father nor mother. God Says: {The similitude of Jesus before Allah is as that of Adam; He created him from dust, then said to him: "Be". And he was} (Surat Aal-Imran: 59).

God's Word, which He bestowed on Maryam, is Isa son of Maryam (His name is the Messiah son of Maryam)[205] who existed through God's Word – Be! – as he was fatherless; unlike the offspring of Adam who were born of mother and father. Hence, Isa

[203] Ibid, 2/668.

[204] Al-Sameen al-Halabi, "Al-Durr al-Masoon, fi 'Uloum al-Kitaab al-Maknoon", ver. by Ahmad Mohammad al-Kharraat, al-Qalam House, Damascus, 3rd Ed., 2011, 2/173.

[205] "Al-Qasas al-Qur'ani: Presentation and Analysis of Events", Ibid, 4/202.

is the creation by God's Word, which describes the miracle of his existence more fully.[206]

c. (His name will be Christ Jesus, the son of Mary):

Jesus (the Messiah) is a title, "Isa" is a name, "Son of Maryam" is a description and Isa's title is the Messiah. This title was mentioned 11 times in the Holy Qur'an in both subject and object forms. In the former, he would "pass"[207] his hand over the ill and cure them, and in the latter God would have wiped or passed His hand over Isa to bless him. So being the Messiah incorporates both meanings and usages. To Nasraanis, the word means he who has dedicated himself to servitude and sacrifice.[208]

"Isa" in Arabic means the "Master". Some say that it is derived from al-Eess" which means the white coloured camels untainted by dark colours and that Isa was named as such as his complexion was reddish white.[209] As the word "Isa" is that which is pure and which originates from one source, untainted by another, he was born of only his mother without the presence of another, i.e. having been conceived without a father's seed like the rest of mankind.[210]

The title "Son of Maryam" of Prophet Isa (pbuh) was mentioned 23 times in the Holy Qur'an and was done so intentionally so as to emphasise his humanity through these three words – Isa, son (of), Maryam – due to the miracles that accompanied his creation, birth and life. It was also intended so as to counter Nasraanis' claims

---

[206] Al-Aloosi, "Rouh al-Ma'aani fi Tafseer al-Qur'an al-'Aatheem wal Sab'a al-Mathaani", ver. by Ali Abdul-Baari Atiyyah, al-Kutub al-'Ilmiyyah House, Beirut, 1st Ed., 1415h, 3/160.

[207] Translator's note: "Messiah" in Arabic can mean to wipe or to pass one's hand over something in subject form, and to be blessed in object form.

[208] "Al-Qasas al-Qur'ani: Presentation and Analysis of Events", Ibid, 4/203-204.

[209] "Al-Mar'ah fil Qasas al-Qur'ani", Ibid, 2/670.

[210] Abdul-Majeed al-'Aarabli, "Uhibbuka Ayyuha al-Maseeh", Yafa Scientific Publishing House, Jordan, 1st Ed., 2009, p.22.

about Isa's divinity and that he was the son of God. Hence, the Qur'an expresses that he was the son of Maryam, who they knew for certain, and accordingly he cannot be the son of God as well.[211]

The birth of Isa without the seed of a father clearly shows God's Greatness and that He does whatever He wishes. God is not bound by Earthly laws in His creation as He is Supreme to them as the Creator of all beings.

God's Creation of Isa without a father's seed is an announcement of His Ability in a world that has been overtaken by the physical aspects of life and in an age of philosophy based on the so-called big bang theory. The creation of Isa is a sign of the timeless Ability of the Creator.

The creation of Isa (pbuh) without a father's seed is a complementary cycle of four other aspects which stand witness to God's Greatness. These are:

- **First Aspect:** Creation from Nothingness as per the creation of Adam (pbuh) as father of humanity from earth. This was one unrepeated example of creation.

- **Second Aspect:** Creating a female from a male without the presence of a mother as per the creation of Adam's wife. This, too, was one unrepeated example of creation.

- **Third Aspect:** Creating a male from a female without the presence of a father as per the creation of Isa son of Maryam (pbut) when Maryam was a celibate virgin. This was also an unrepeated example of creation.

- **Fourth Aspect:** The creation of sons and daughters from a male and female couple, which is a repetitive aspect and is God's Will in creation.[212]

---

[211] "Al-Qasas al-Qur'ani: Presentation and Analysis of Events", Ibid, 4/205.

[212] Mohammad Abdul-Majeed Lasheen, "Anbaa' al-Risalaat al-Samawiyyah", al-Afaaq al-Arabiyyah House, Cairo, 1st Ed., 2009, p.326.

d. (Held in honour in this world and the Hereafter):

This means that Prophet Isa will have an elevated status coupled with high honour and dignity in life – as God had protected and saved him from his enemies – and in the Hereafter in the most elevated level of Heaven along with his fellow prophets, and appreciated by all.[213]

The attacks and persecution Isa had suffered at the hands of the Israelites neither demeaned nor belittled his honourable status. Prophets are the most honourable of God's creations, and even when persecuted by mankind, it only made them more so as they believed in the messages with which God had entrusted them.[214]

e. (And of (the company of) those nearest to Allah)

Isa (pbuh) is among those nearest to God, who He elevated in status. They shall precede all mankind in entering Heaven.[215]

f. (He shall speak to the people in childhood and in maturity):

Prophet Isa (pbuh) spoke to people while still an infant in the cradle. He spoke to them as soon as he was born as his people became suspicious of Maryam when they saw her carrying him forth. God gave him the ability to speak when only hours old so as to introduce himself to them and to exonerate his mother from any accusations.[216] The miracle of him speaking at that age was proof of his mother's innocence from any claim, a sign of his prophethood and of his caring for his mother. Isa also stated at that same instance that he was neither oppressive nor totalitarian.[217]

Isa would also speak to them in maturity, i.e. in his forties or even at the age of 33 as some have stated. "Maturity" is the de-

---

213 "Al-Qasas al-Qur'ani: Presentation and Analysis of Events", Ibid, 4/205.

214 "Al-Mar'ah fil Qasas al-Qur'ani", Ibid, 2/670.

215 Al-Khalidi, Ibid, 4/205.

216 Ibid, 4/206.

217 Ibid, 2/672.

scription given to one whose youth and strength have completed their formulation. Others say it is meant to show the eloquence of his speaking ability in both infancy and adulthood. Another opinion is in reference to that he will be elevated to the Heavens then brought down to Earth at the End of Days and speak to the masses. Among the benefits of his ability to speak in adulthood is also to guide people towards that which leads to good religious and worldly lives.[218]

g. (And he shall be (of the company) of the righteous):

The people among who Isa (pbuh) belongs are "the Righteous."[219] A righteous person is one whose life is led in such a way till the day he/she dies, and it is that with which God concluded the traits of Isa.[220]

Maryam (pbuh) was informed of Isa's traits prior to giving birth to him; mentioning them in the Qur'an emphasises Isa's humanity.[221]

From the day Prophet Isa was born and until his adulthood, he was influenced by events and changed according to them. He transformed from youth to manhood, and therefore, had he been a god or son of God as non-believing Nasraanis claimed, this would not have occurred. God described Prophet Isa's changing states, like those of mankind from their young years till older ones, yet God made an exception only for Isa that allowed him to speak as an infant due to his prophethood, and so that mankind may realise God's Might.[222]

---

218 Ibid.

219 "Fi Thilaal al-Qur'an", Ibid, 1/398.

220 Mohammad Saleh al-Munjid, "Tafseer al-Zahrawayn al-Baqarah wa Aal-Imran", al-Obaikan Library, Riyadh, 1st Ed., 2016, p.557.

221 Al-Khalidi, Ibid, 4/206.

222 Ibid, 4/207.

7. Maryam's response to these glad tidings:

God Says: {She said: "O my Lord! How shall I have a son when no man hath touched me?" He said: "Even so: Allah createth what He willeth: When He hath decreed a plan, He but saith to it, 'Be', and it is!"} (Surat Aal-Imran: 47).

Maryam was surprised and astonished when she heard of the glad tiding from Jibreel (pbuh) that she will be giving birth to Isa as she was a celibate virgin. She expressed this astonishment to Jibreel: (She said: How shall I have a son when no man hath touched me?), then directed her speech to God by asking Him the same in the sense of how may such a matter occur when I, Maryam, have never been touched by a man, am not married nor do I plan on doing so?[223]

She received the response of the simple truth, to which mankind is oblivious due to their clinging onto the argument of Causes and Effects:

- (He said: "Even so: Allah createth what He willeth: When He hath decreed a plan, He but saith to it, 'Be', and it is!").

When this primal truth is understood, no more is there any confusion and the heart feels at ease. Hence is the Qur'an in creating the Islamic view of these grand truths in such ease that is void of suspicions and which are accepted by both mind and heart.[224]

- (He said: "Even so: Allah createth what He willeth):

Meaning that such creation which you, Maryam, feel is unlikely – as you have never been touched by a man – is but the brilliance of God's creation. This phrase denotes a number of matters:

• Such a form of creation is a matter within God's reach as He is The Creator and His powers are not new to mankind. It is He

[223] "Tafseer al-Zahrawayn al-Baqarah wa Aal-Imran", Ibid, p.558.

[224] "Fi Thilaal al-Qur'an", Ibid, 1/398.

who created the first man and the cosmos, and it is He who is capable of changing them.

• The creation of Isa was an order given by God, and he is but one of God's creations. God made Isa out of nothingness similar to His creation of other creatures, and hence Isa is neither a god nor son of one.

• God creates according to His Will; hence the reason behind which He created Isa without a father's seed. God Says: (To Him is due the primal origin of the heavens and the earth: How can He have a son?).

This is a scientific response to believers in tangible philosophy that states the universe was created by the primal mind. Then God speaks of His Great Ability:[225] ("When He hath decreed a plan, He but saith to it, 'Be!' and it is!").

This statement is evidence to the simplicity of creation to God, a representation of His wholesome ability, the ease in which He creates and the implementation of His Will. Accordingly, God's response to Maryam's bewilderment was: {He said: "So (it will be): Thy Lord saith, ´that is easy for Me: and (We wish) to appoint him as a Sign unto men and a Mercy from Us´: It is a matter (so) decreed"} (Surat Maryam: 21).

So, Maryam received the glad tidings from the angel Jibreel (pbut) and became certain that God will grant her a boy, and that all which remained was the fulfilment of the matter.[226]

The verses in Surat Aal-Imran then proceed to detail how the masses received Prophet Isa's calling. Maryam is also mentioned elsewhere, and in "Surat Maryam" in particular, which was named so as to honour her. The following details the story of Maryam through this Surah.[227]

---

[225] Mohammad Abu Zahra, "Zahrat al-Tafaaseer", 3/1225.

[226] "Al-Qasas al-Qur'ani: Presentation and Analysis of Events", Ibid, 4/211

[227] "Al-Mar'ah fil Qasas al-Qur'ani", Ibid, 2/673.

8. Dialogue between Jibreel and Maryam prior to the bestowing of breath:

God Says: {Relate in the Book (the story of) Mary, when she withdrew from her family to a place in the East. She placed a screen (to screen herself) from them; then We sent her Our Spirit, and he appeared before her as a man in all respects. She said: "I seek refuge from thee to Allah Most Gracious: (come not near) if thou dost fear Allah." He said: "Nay, I am only a messenger from thy Lord, (to announce) to thee the gift of a holy son." She said: "How shall I have a son, seeing that no man has touched me, and I am not unchaste?" He said: "So it is: Thy Lord saith, 'that is easy for Me: and (We wish) to appoint him as a Sign unto men and a Mercy from Us': It is a matter (so) decreed"} (Surat Maryam: 16-21).

In the verses above, God tells Prophet Mohammad (pbuh): (Relate in the Book (the story of) Mary), to mean: "State O' Mohammad from the Qur'an which We, God, have descended upon you, the story of Maryam and giving birth to Isa, to the masses so that they may all know.

"Mentioning these verses is proof that you are God's Messenger as it is God who descended them upon you. Had the matter not been so, you would not have known of such events as you are unlettered and learnt none of this information from anyone; this information is also not present in the books of Nasraanis." Such discourse is proof of Mohammad's prophethood and in determining the truth that the Qur'an is the Words of God.[228]

a. Maryam's location when Jibreel presented himself in human form:

God Says: (Relate in the Book (the story of) Mary, when she withdrew from her family to a place in the East). Maryam had left her family's abode and went away from them towards the East,

[228] "Al-Qasas al-Qur'ani: Presentation and Analysis of Events", Ibid, 4/213.

i.e. East of Bayt al-Maqdis. She probably went there to worship in solitude as it draws one closer to God.[229]

The angel Jibreel came to her while she was at this blessed and pure location.[230]

b. (She placed a screen (to screen herself) from them):

Maryam put up a screen to shield herself from her family and all others so that nothing will distract her from worship.

c. (Then We sent her Our Spirit):

This was the angel Jibreel (pbuh) who God sent to Maryam while she was at that eastern location to relay to her the glad tidings regarding Isa (pbuh). After having veiled herself from her people, and after Jibreel informed her of God's decision, He realised it for her.[231]

The Arabic word in the Qur'an referring to Jibreel is "Rouh", meaning "Spirit". That God sent His "Rouh"[232] to Maryam is direct reference to the angel Jibreel who was mentioned using the same word in the Qur'an in many instances such as in the following verses:

In Surat al-Shu'araa', verses 192-194, God Says: {Verily this is a Revelation from the Lord of the Worlds: With it came down the **Spirit** of Faith and Truth - To thy heart and mind, that thou mayest admonish}.

In Surat al-Qadr, verses 3-4, God says: {The Night of Power is better than a thousand Months. Therein come down the angels and the **Spirit** by Allah's permission, on every errand}.

In Surat al-Nahl, verses 101-102, God Says: {When We substitute one revelation for another, and Allah knows best what He

229 "Al-Mar'ah fil Qasas al-Qur'ani", Ibid, 2/677.

230 Ibid.

231 "Al-Qasas al-Qur'ani: Presentation and Analysis of Events", Ibid, 4/218.

232 "Al-Mar'ah fil Qasas al-Qur'ani", Ibid, 2/677.

reveals (in stages), they say, "Thou art but a forger": but most of them understand not. Say, the Holy **Spirit** has brought the revelation from thy Lord in Truth, in order to strengthen those who believe, and as a Guide and Glad Tidings to Muslims}.

God gives Jibreel much reverence and honour by calling Jibreel (Our Spirit), similar to when He Says the same about Prophet Mohammad (pbuh) as per verse 19 from Surat al-Maa'idah: {O People of the Book! Now hath come unto you, making (things) clear unto you, **Our Messenger**, after the break in (the series of) Our messengers, lest ye should say: "There came unto us no bringer of glad tidings and no warner (from evil)": But now hath come unto you a bringer of glad tidings and a warner (from evil). And Allah hath power over all things}. That meant by (Our Messenger) is Prophet Mohammad (pbuh).[233]

d. (And he appeared before her as a man in all respects):

The angel Jibreel (pbuh) transformed as a man of pleasant looks to Maryam so that she would not feel intimidated by him and so that she may understand his words, for had she seen him in his original form, she may have not been able to comprehend what was happening.[234]

The angel Jibreel's transformation into a man is proof of angels' ability to take human form, that they do so with the Permission and Will of God, and that when their missions are over, they revert to their original angelic forms.

When they transform into human beings, angels are always male, as per those who approached prophets Ibrahim and Lot (pbut). Their non-transformation into females is deemed to refute unbelievers' claims that angels are God's daughters.[235]

---

233 "Al-Qasas al-Qur'ani: Presentation and Analysis of Events", Ibid, 4/219.

234 "Al-Mar'ah fil Qasas al-Qur'ani", Ibid, 2/678.

235 "Al-Qasas al-Qur'ani: Presentation and Analysis of Events", Ibid, 4/220.

e. (She said: I seek refuge from thee to Allah Most Gracious: (Come not near) if thou dost fear Allah):

As Maryam was in her seclusion, she was startled by the presence of a man: (Then We sent our Spirit, and he appeared before her as a man in all respects), and responded as does a young virgin girl by beseeching The Almighty and appeasing to the man's senses of piety: ("I seek refuge from thee to Allah Most Gracious: (come not near) if thou dost fear Allah"). A pious person's being is shaken at the mention of God's Name in a manner that repels lust and removes evilness.

As she was chaste, pure and pious, Maryam sought refuge in God from that complete man she saw before her so that He would save her from the man she considered foreign to her.[236]

This is a sign that seeking refuge in God to be saved from the ill ways of the devil is a trait of believers who do so whenever they embark on any action so that they are not led astray.[237]

f. Maryam's astonishment of Jibreel's purpose and mission:

As Maryam was beseeching the man to fear God, the angel Jibreel caused her an even greater shock when he informed her of his mission. God Says: {He said: "Nay, I am only a messenger from thy Lord, (to announce) to thee the gift of a holy son} (Surat Maryam: 19).

Although she had already known of the matter, her extreme fear of the man, coupled with her coyness of seeing this stranger in front of her, she forgot that she knew and was overcome with fear, anxiety and worry. Also, as he was forthright in telling her that he shall be granting her a blessed boy who is free of all guilt and inadequacies, she needed to be on the same level with him

[236] Mohammad Mustafa al-Zuhayli, "Shri'aat Allah Lil Anbiyaa' fil Qur'an al-Kareem, Ibid, p.606.

[237] Ibid, p.606.

despite her embarrassment as a celibate virgin as such a stance requires frankness.[238]

g. Maryam's astonishment upon hearing the glad tidings:

God says: {She said: "How shall I have a son, seeing that no man has touched me, and I am not unchaste?"} (Surat Maryam: 20).

Maryam was certain that the glad tidings were true and that that in front of her was an angel sent by God, yet she still wondered how such an unlikely matter could occur as it is customary that pregnancy happens when copulating with a man, either legitimately or illegitimately, while she had never been even touched by a man and was in no way a prostitute.[239]

h. Jibreel's response to Maryam's question:

God Says: {He said: "So it is: Thy Lord saith, ´that is easy for Me: and (We wish) to appoint him as a Sign unto men and a Mercy from Us´: It is a matter (so) decreed"} (Surat Maryam: 21).

The explanation of the verse above is that God Says He concurs with Maryam that she is neither married nor a prostitute. But God is Able, Unbound by worldly norms and His Will is realised no matter what for He created Adam from no father or mother and created Eve from one of Adam's ribs. Accordingly, He can create Isa from a mother without the seed of a father.

God created Isa in such a manner so as to make him a sign for mankind that God's Ability is absolute.

God created Isa as mercy from Him for mankind, and that Isa will be a prophet and messenger.

Finally, Jibreel – in the form of a man – informed Maryam of the matter's details and allayed her astonishment as the verse con-

---

[238] "Al-Qasas al-Qur'ani: Presentation and Analysis of Events", Ibid, 4/222.

[239] "Al-Mar'ah fil Qasas al-Qur'ani", Ibid, 2/682.

cluded with: (It is a matter so decreed), i.e. that the creation of Isa is a matter that shall occur.[240]

As such, the dialogue between the Honest Spirit Jibreel and the virgin Maryam ended. The holy verses do not describe how Jibreel breathed life into Maryam that she became pregnant with Isa as this is an unseen matter beyond the comprehension of our minds. It is as if the phrase (And it is a matter so decreed) calls upon us not to delve into how the breathing of life into Maryam occurred and to move forward after the event towards the later scenes. There also exist other holy verses that speak of Jibreel breathing life into Maryam that caused her pregnancy of Isa (pbut), yet no details of the matter are present.[241]

9. Breathing life into Maryam (pbuh):

Once Maryam (pbuh) became pacified, accepted God's Will and realised it was His Will and Wisdom, the Sacred Spirit was breathed into her and she became pregnant with Isa (pbuh).

This breathing of life was mentioned in both Surat Maryam and Surat al-Tahreem as a sign of the Holy Qur'an's unity where each verse has a context that is aligned with those which precede and follow it. As all verses covering the same subject come together, we behold a unique mosaic, solid structure and comprehensive topic.[242]

God says: {A. L. R. (This is) a Book, with verses basic or fundamental (of established meaning), further explained in detail, from One Who is Wise and Well-acquainted (with all things)} (Surat Hud: 01).

God says: {Allah has revealed (from time to time) the most beautiful Message in the form of a Book, consistent with itself,

[240] "Al-Qasas al-Qur'ani: Presentation and Analysis of Events", Ibid, 4/225.

[241] Ibid, 4/226.

[242] "Al-Mar'ah fil Qasas al-Qur'ani", Ibid, 2/685.

(yet) repeating (its teaching in various aspects): the skins of those who fear their Lord tremble thereat; then their skins and their hearts do soften to the celebration of Allah's praises. Such is the guidance of Allah. He guides therewith whom He pleases, but such as Allah leaves to stray, can have none to guide} (Surat al-Zumar: 23).

God says: {And (remember) her who guarded her chastity: We breathed into her of Our spirit, ...} (Surat al-Anbiyaa': 91). God, here, informs us that Jibreel (pbuh) breathed into Maryam of God's Spirit and she became pregnant with Isa (pbuh). This was said in the context of praising Maryam for her chastity.

The praise allayed upon Maryam for having guarded her chastity, coupled with God's Testament to her purity, is meant to dispel the lies of Jews who accused her of having borne a child illegitimately. This Testament of Maryam by God is also proof that the Qur'an is God's Words and that Mohammad (pbuh) is God's Messenger.[243]

In Surat al-Tahreem, verse 12, God Says: {And Mary the daughter of Imran, who guarded her chastity; and We breathed into (her body) of Our spirit; and she testified to the truth of the words of her Lord and of His Revelations, and was one of the devout (Servants)}.

Surat al-Tahreem deals with certain matters that occurred among the prophets' wives where God clarifies that being related to one does not replace religious affiliation as what matters is belief and good deeds. The Surah speaks of the wives of Noah and Lot who were unbelievers, and the believing wife of Pharaoh and Maryam daughter of Imran. Despite the status of the two prophets, their wives were promised Hell. Yet the blasphemy of Pharaoh changed nothing of his wife's status as she was a believ-

[243] "Al-Qasas al-Qur'ani: Presentation and Analysis of Events", Ibid, 4/229.

ing worshipper who was honest and who persevered. Maryam (pbuh) was raised in a good home and was chaste and honest, and accordingly, God chose her to be, along with her son, a Sign for all mankind. God Says: {And Mary the daughter of Imran, who guarded her chastity; and We breathed into (her body) of Our spirit; and she testified to the truth of the words of her Lord and of His Revelations, and was one of the devout (Servants).} (Surat al-Tahreem: 12).[244]

- Correlation between masculine and feminine form of the Arabic (it) in relation to the breathing of life into Maryam:

God sent His Spirit Jibreel (pbuh) to fulfil His promise and breathe life into Maryam so that she may bear Prophet Isa. God Says in Surat al-Anbiyaa': (She who protected her virginity and so We breathed of Our Spirit into **her**), and used the feminine pronoun in reference to Maryam.

Then in Surat al-Tahreem God Says: (She who guarded her chastity; and We breathed into **it** (her body) of Our spirit), with the Arabic (it) in the masculine form as referring to her vagina, which is also in masculine form.

Some say that (it) is in reference to the slit in Maryam's dress, not her vagina, and that it was that which she guarded, not her actual body part. They claim that Jibreel breathed into the slit in her dress and that that gust of air seeped into her body upon which Maryam became pregnant with Isa (pbut).

The majority of scholars believe that the angel Jibreel breathed into her vagina and that that breath flowed into her womb, yet as it is a matter of the unseen, and we shall not delve into it as the masculine and feminine forms of the pronouns are non-contradictory.[245]

---

[244] "Al-Mar'ah fil Qasas al-Qur'ani", Ibid, 2/686.

[245] "Al-Qasas al-Qur'ani: Presentation and Analysis of Events", Ibid, 4/231.

Hence, after having informed Maryam of the glad tidings that Isa shall be born by God's Will and without a father's seed, the angel Jibreel breathed the Spirit into Maryam so as to fulfil the miracle.[246]

10. Meaning of Isa being (God's Word and Spirit from Him):

a. The Qur'an's description of Isa as being (His Word which He Bestowed on Maryam and a Spirit from Him):

Nasraanis have clung to these descriptions in justifying their beliefs. They claimed that the Word by which the Messiah was described is God Himself, and misconstrued God's Words (And a Spirit from Him) to mean part of God's Spirit which was transferred to Isa. This is one of the most contentious matters between Muslims and Nasraanis, and hence, we feel it is of utmost importance to show the real intention of the Qur'an's description of Isa (pbuh). We begin with specifying the meanings of the (Word) and the (Spirit) as per the Holy Qur'an where grand scholar al-Razi finds that (Word) carries five possibilities:

- That he was created through God's Word (Be!) without a father and that that meant by it is Creation. It is a word that exhibits God's Will and that Isa (pbuh) was accordingly created; an explanation to which the majority of scholars ascribe.

- That he spoke when only a few hours old and that God provided him with the Book at that young age. Hence, as one who spoke at that early age, Isa is deemed a Word.

- The Word also means Explanations and Facts as Isa would guide people towards grasping divine facts and secrets.

- Holy Books of past prophets had spoken of his arrival, then when he did appear, the people said: He is the Word.

246 "Al-Mar'ah fil Qasas al-Qur'ani", Ibid, 2/689.

- One may be named FadlAllah, or LutfAllah, and accordingly Isa is named Kalimat[247] Allah.[248]

As for "Word" in the holy verse (and His Word, which He bestowed on Mary), it is the same Word with which God created all creatures, i.e. (Be!)[249]. God Bestowed this Word upon Maryam and created Isa in her womb without a father's seed. It is the Word which creates everything from nothingness and hence it is not a strange thing for it to create Isa from the Breath expressed by God in (and a Spirit from Him).[250]

b. What is the Spirit?:

In the holy verse (We breathed into her of Our spirit), the word "Spirit" was expressed in the Holy Qur'an in different meanings, among which are the following:

- **"Spirit" meaning "Inspiration"** as per the following verses from the Holy Qur'an:

{And thus have We, by Our Command, sent **inspiration** to thee: thou knewest not (before) what was Revelation, and what was Faith; but We have made the (Qur'an) a Light, wherewith We guide such of Our servants as We will} (Surat al-Shourah: 52).

{He doth send down His angels with **inspiration** of His Command, to such of His servants as He pleaseth, (saying): "Warn (Man) that there is no god but I: so do your duty unto Me"} (Surat al-Nahl: 02).

{Raised high above ranks (or degrees), (He is) the Lord of the Throne (of Authority): by His Command doth He send the Spirit

[247] Translator's note: "Kalimah" in Arabic means "Word". When a word comes after it, it becomes "Kalimat".

[248] Abdul-Qadir Bakhoush, "Adyaan al-'Aalam al-Muqaarin", al-Diyaa' Publishing House, Kuwait, 1st Ed., 2014, p.195.

[249] "Al-Qasas al-Qur'ani: Presentation and Analysis of Events", Ibid, 4/235.

[250] Ibn Taymiyah, "Al-Jawaab al-Saheeh Liman Baddal Deen al-Maseeh", ver. by Ali bin Hassan bin Nasser & Abdul-Aziz bin Ibrahim al-'Aaskar & Hamdan bin Mohammad al-Hamdan, al-'Aasimah Publishing House, Riyadh, Saudi, 2nd Ed., 1999, 1/270.

(of **inspiration**) to any of His servants he pleases, that it may warn (men) of the Day of Mutual Meeting} (Surat Ghafir: 15).

Inspiration is called **Spirit** as it revives the heart and soul.

- "**Spirit**" meaning Strength, Steadfastness and Victory which God Bestows upon whomsoever He wishes of His believing subjects:

God Says: {For such He has written Faith in their hearts, and strengthened them with a **Spirit** from Himself} (Surat al-Mujadilah: 22).

- "**Spirit**" refers to the angel **Jibreel** (pbuh) who is charged with delivering revelation and one of the four supreme angels:

God Says: {Verily this is a Revelation from the Lord of the Worlds: With it came down the **Spirit** of Faith and Truth – To thy heart and mind, that thou mayest admonish} (Surat al-Shu'araa': 192-194).

God Says: {We sent her our **Angel**[251], and he appeared before her as a man in all respects} (Surat Maryam: 17).

- God naming **Jibreel** as (the Holy Spirit):

God Says: {Say, the **Holy Spirit** has brought the revelation from thy Lord in Truth, in order to strengthen those who believe, and as a Guide and Glad Tidings to Muslims} (Surat al-Nahl: 102).

God Says: {We gave Jesus the son of Mary Clear (Signs) and strengthened him with the **Holy Spirit**} (Surat al-Baqarah: 87).

- "**Spirit**" meaning a Great Angel who rises on Judgment Day with the other angels.

God Says: {The Day that the **Spirit** and the angels will stand forth in ranks, none shall speak except any who is permitted by Allah Most Gracious, and He will say what is right} (Surat al-Naba': 38).

[251] Translator's note: The Arabic word in the Qur'an is *Rouh, i.e. Spirit.*

God Says: {Therein come down the angels and the **Spirit** by Allah's permission, on every errand} (Surat al-Qadr: 04).

God Says: {The angels and the **Spirit** ascend unto him in a Day the measure whereof is (as) fifty thousand years} (Surat al-Ma'aarij: 04).

- "**Spirit**" meaning Mercy and God's Ability and Judgment, as per the following verse:

God Says: {And never give up hope of Allah's Soothing **Mercy**[252]: truly no one despairs of Allah's Soothing **Mercy**, except those who have no faith} (Surat Yusuf: 87).

- "**Spirit**" meaning Rest, Satisfaction or Forgiveness:

God says: {Thus, then, if he be of those Nearest to Allah, (There is for him) **Rest and Satisfaction**, and a Garden of Delights} (Surat al-Waaqi'ah: 88-89).

- "**Spirit**" may also mean that through which grants life, i.e. the secret of life and connecting the word to God as an honour:

God Says: {But He fashioned him in due proportion, and breathed into him something of His **Spirit**} (Surat al-Sajdah: 09).

God Says: {"When I have fashioned him (in due proportion) and breathed into him of My **Spirit**, fall ye down in obeisance unto him"} (Surat al-Hijr: 29).[253]

The Spirit is also known as being a specificity of God. When the Israelites asked Prophet Mohammad (pbuh) about it, God descended the following, found in Surat al-Israa', verse 85: {They ask thee concerning the Spirit (of inspiration). Say: "The Spirit (cometh) by command of my Lord: of knowledge it is only a little

252 Translator's note: Here and in the line below, the Arabic word in the Qur'an is *Rouh, i.e. Spirit.*

253 Consult. Mohammad Izzat al-Tahtaawi, "Al-Meezan fi Muqaranat al-Adyaan: Facts and Documents", al-Qalam House Damascus, al-Durar al-Shaamiyah Beirut, 1st Ed., 1993, p.185-187.

that is communicated to you, (O men!)"}. Hence, this power that enacts creation and life is one that only God is aware of, and only He bestows it on whomsoever He wishes.[254]

c. (And a Spirit from Him):

The word (from) is not meant to extract as God's Spirit does not break up into sums, nor does it disintegrate into parts. That meant by (from) is that its source is The Almighty.

A dialogue on the above occurred between a Nasraani and Ali bin al-Hussein bin Waqid al-Maroozi. The Nasraani said: "The Qur'an itself contains that which testifies that Isa is part of God," and he recited (And a Spirit from Him). Ibn Waqid countered his claim by reciting verse 13 of Surat al-Jaathiyah: {And He has subjected to you, **as of Him**, all that is in the heavens and on earth: Behold, in that are Signs indeed for those who reflect}. He then told the Nasraani, "Had your claim been correct, then all these things in the Heavens and on Earth would have to be of God, which is impossible." And so, the Nasraani was silent and then pronounced Shahadah and became Muslim.

This similitude between the creation of Isa (pbuh) and that of Adam (pbuh) is the same. God Says: {The similitude of Jesus before Allah is as that of Adam; He created him from dust, then said to him: "Be". And he was} (Surat Aal-Imran: 59).

God Says of the creation of Adam: {Behold, thy Lord said to the angels: "I am about to create man from clay: "When I have fashioned him (in due proportion) and breathed into him of My spirit, fall ye down in obeisance unto him"}. Nobody claimed Adam to be a god when The Almighty breathed into him of His Spirit.[255]

---

[254] Ahmad Shalabi, "Muqaranat al-Adyaan", al-Nahda al-Masriyyah Library, Cairo, 8th Ed., 1984, p.44.

[255] "Al-Mar'ah fil Qasas al-Qur'ani", Ibid, 2/739.

(A Spirit from Him) connects the Spirit to God but does not merge it with Him. It is the addition of a creation to its Creator; a fabricated matter to its Maker. But in this sense, it is meant as a charitable Spirit that obeys God.[256]

The Holy Qur'an did not connect only Isa (pbuh) to God; rather, it did the same with many others as a form of honouring them:

- The Spirit of Adam (pbuh) as in the following account informing angels about him:

God Says: {Behold! thy Lord said to the angels: "I am about to create man, from sounding clay from mud moulded into shape; When I have fashioned him (in due proportion) and breathed into him of My spirit, fall ye down in obeisance unto him"} (Surat al-Hijr: 28-29).

- The she-camel that was the miracle of Prophet Saleh (pbuh) for his people of Thamud:

God Says: {The Thamud (people) rejected (their prophet) through their inordinate wrongdoing, Behold, the most wicked man among them was deputed (for impiety). But the Messenger of Allah said to them: "It is a She-camel of Allah. And (bar her not from) having her drink!"} (Surat al-Shams: 11-13).

- The area of Kaaba:

God Says: {We covenanted with Abraham and Ismaeel, that they should sanctify My House for those who compass it round, or use it as a retreat, or bow, or prostrate themselves (therein) (in prayer)} (Surat al-Baqarah: 125).

- God's Devotee:

God Says: {"Yet when the Devotee of Allah stands forth to invoke Him, they just make round him a dense crowd"} (Surat al-Jinn: 19).

---

256 "Al-Meezan fi Muqaranat al-Adyaan: Facts and Documents", Ibid, p.184.

- That which God provided for mankind of the sky and land:

God Says: {And He has subjected to you, as of Him, all that is in the heavens and on earth: Behold, in that are Signs indeed for those who reflect} (Surat al-Jaathiyah: 13).[257]

Accordingly, that which is meant by the "Spirit" is contrary to what Nasraanis believe. God's order (Be!) created Isa via the breathing conducted by the angel dubbed (The Spirit). The event was not a specificity of Isa (pbuh) – as Nasraanis claim – that would elevate him to the status of divinity. God Says: {The similitude of Jesus before Allah is as that of Adam; He created him from dust, then said to him: "Be". And he was} (Surat Aal-Imran: 59).[258]

It would have been unbecoming of Isa (pbuh) to tell his people that they should worship him along with God or other individuals after God had chosen him as a man from among mankind to deliver His message to the Israelites. It would be unbecoming of him to do so after God gave him the Book that guides mankind to worshipping God, wisdom and prophethood void of errors. Instead, Isa tells his people to be well-informed in knowledge and action as they shall study the Book and teach it to people – who should follow and not deviate from it.

It is also wrong of them to deem the angels, including the Holy Spirit Jibreel, and prophets as gods. It would have been unbecoming of Isa – a Godsent prophet – to order his people to commit blasphemy if they are loyal and obedient to God. This only happened because they mixed truths with untruths and manipulated the verses of the Torah and Injeel in an evil manner.[259]

In reprimanding them for doing so, God Says: {It is not (possible) that a man, to whom is given the Book, and Wisdom, and the prophetic office, should say to people: "Be ye my worship-

---

[257] Ibid, p.185.

[258] "Adyaan al-'Aalam al-Muqaarin", Ibid, p.196.

[259] "Al-Meezan fi Muqaranat al-Adyaan: Facts and Documents", Ibid, p.173.

pers rather than Allah's": on the contrary (He would say) "Be ye worshippers of Him Who is truly the Cherisher of all: For ye have taught the Book and ye have studied it earnestly. Nor would he instruct you to take angels and prophets for Lords and patrons. What! would he bid you to unbelief after ye have bowed your will (To Allah in Islam), i.e. in submission to God[260]? (Surat Aal-Imran: 79-80).

Relating the Spirit to God in (and a Spirit from Him) is meant to grant honour and preference, and as among its meanings are mercy and blessing from God towards his servants, so was the Messiah to his people as he guided them to that which pleased them in life and the Hereafter, and was so dubbed a Spirit from God.[261]

God Says: {Christ Jesus the son of Mary was (no more than) a messenger of Allah, and His Word, which He bestowed on Mary, and a **spirit** proceeding from Him} (Surat al-Nisaa': 171).

11. Maryam gives birth to Isa (pbut):

Jibreel met with Maryam as she was towards the East away from her family and breathed into her, by order from God, a breath which contained the word (Be!) and a spirit from God. God Willed that a foetus is created in her womb due to that breath and she became pregnant with Isa (pbut).

The Holy Qur'an speaks briefly of the virgin Maryam giving birth to her son Isa (pbut). God Says: {So she conceived him, and she retired with him to a remote place. And the pains of childbirth drove her to the trunk of a palm-tree: She cried (in her anguish): "Ah! would that I had died before this! would that I had been a thing forgotten and out of sight!" But (a voice) cried to her from beneath the (palm-tree): "Grieve not! for thy Lord hath provided

260 Translator's addition from (i.e.) onwards.

261 "Al-Meezan fi Muqaranat al-Adyaan: Facts and Documents", Ibid, p.171.

a rivulet beneath thee; And shake towards thyself the trunk of the palm tree: It will let fall fresh ripe dates upon thee. So eat and drink and cool (thine) eye. And if thou dost see any man, say, 'I have vowed a fast to Allah Most Gracious, and this day will I enter into not talk with any human being'"} (Surat Maryam: 22-26).

a. (She retired with him to a remote place):

This means she went, pregnant, to a distant location farther away from her people so that they would cause her no harm as she feared a scandal, their looks, accusations, astonishment and bewilderment.

Such a behaviour is normal for a virgin, celibate, pure and righteous young girl whose family knows of her traits and purity; yet had she gone to them while pregnant, would they believe it as being a breath from God and that no man had touched her? So, she probably meant to go as far away from her people so that she would save herself from their accusations and doubting looks.[262]

This distant place is towards the east of Bethlehem, where Isa (pbuh) was born, as per the Hadeeth reported by Imam al-Nassaa'i in "*Al-Sunan*" and by al-Bayhaqi in "*Dalaa'il al-Nubuwwah*" of Anas bin Malik regarding the Hadeeth of Prophet Mohammad's Ascension to the Heavens (al-Israa' wa al-Mi'raaj): "And then Jibreel told me to go down and pray, and I did. Do you know where I prayed? I prayed in Bethlehem where Isa son of Maryam was born."[263]

The distant place referenced in the holy verse: (she retired with him to a remote place) is where Maryam gave birth to her son Isa, i.e. Bethlehem, as per the Hadeeth of Prophet Mohammad (pbuh).[264]

Grand scholar Ibn Katheer said, "And this is the most common belief which people have cascaded to one another. Nasraanis have

262 "Al-Qasas al-Qur'ani: Presentation and Analysis of Events", Ibid, 4/240.

263 "Al-Mar'ah fil Qasas al-Qur'ani", Ibid, 2/692.

264 "Al-Qasas al-Qur'ani: Presentation and Analysis of Events", Ibid, 4/242.

no doubt that it is Bethlehem and has been received as such by the masses."[265]

Bethlehem is considered a locale far from Jerusalem as there are approximately 9 miles in between.[266]

On face-value, she gave birth to him in or near that distant location where she was alone.

As for claims that she fled with Yusuf the carpenter to Egypt after her people found out, and that he tried to kill her – having sensed she committed adultery when he saw her pregnant, and that the Holy Spirit came and told him that he had impregnated her – are all events copied from the gospels. Information in the gospels about Yusuf the carpenter is all contradictory, and is testament to its falsehood. When comparing the story of birth in the gospels of Matthew and Luke, we find many discrepancies about whether Yusuf the carpenter was Maryam's fiancée when Isa was born or her husband. Also about when he knew of her pregnancy, his stance on the matter, if the angel appeared and told him the truth of the pregnancy, if the angel did not appear, among other questions that indicate the gospels had been altered and falsified.

What I believe – and God Knows best – is that Yusuf the Carpenter had absolutely nothing to do with Maryam (pbuh), that he was not with her in seclusion, did not travel with her or cater for her as she is the pure, chaste virgin who would in no way have had anything to do with a man who was foreign to her.

The Holy Qur'an and the Hadeeths of Prophet Mohammad (pbuh) did not mention Yusuf the Carpenter whatsoever. The Hadeeths in books of Tafseer are planted ones – dubbed the Israeli ones – and were cited from altered gospels that are in themselves contradictory, proving their falsehood and unreliability.[267]

---

[265] "Tafseer Ibn Katheer", Ibid, 3/114.

[266] "Al-Qasas al-Qur'ani: Presentation and Analysis of Events", Ibid, 4/242.

[267] "Al-Mar'ah fil Qasas al-Qur'ani", Ibid, 2/693.

b. Maryam going into labour:

Having arrived at that distant location in Bethlehem, far from her people, Maryam felt the pains of labour overcoming her. God Says: {And the pains of childbirth drove her to the trunk of a palm-tree: She cried (in her anguish): "Ah! would that I had died before this! would that I had been a thing forgotten and out of sight!"} (Surat Maryam: 23).

Scholars have disagreed on the period of Maryam's pregnancy for if it were a natural one, it would have been for nine months, but if it was a special one, it probably lasted only for hours. Ibn Katheer believes it was the former.[268]

Others believe that her pregnancy was quite fast. Ibn Abbas was referenced by Imams al-Tabari and Ibn Katheer as saying, "She gave birth almost as soon as she became pregnant, without a long time in between."[269]

God Says of Isa (pbuh) in verse 21 of Surat Maryam: {(We wish) to appoint him as a Sign unto men} in a sense that Isa was a miracle in every aspect of the word, including how long he remained in the womb. The miracle is actually in that there was no period of him staying in the womb because otherwise, it would be a natural pregnancy that the mind would accept. But his birth in its entirety was a miracle caused by a Superior action not bound by worldly laws and customs, and hence, it was unlike natural pregnancies. Another argument confirming this opinion is that had Maryam been pregnant for nine months, her people would have probably stoned her to death before having given birth to Isa as her exoneration only came through the words of her new-born child, as stated in the Qur'an.[270]

---

268 "Al-Qasas al-Qur'ani: Presentation and Analysis of Events", Ibid, 4/242.

269 "Tafseer al-Tabari: Taqreeb wa Tahtheeb", Ibid, 5/227.

270 "Tafseer Ibn Katheer", Ibid, 3/114.

Nevertheless, the Holy Qur'an does not state how Isa was conceived nor for how long he remained in the womb. Was it a normal pregnancy where the breath had stimulated the ovary and the foetus grew naturally thereafter?

This is also possible as the breath may have fertilised the ovary and it began its normal cycle for nine lunar months.

Qur'anic text does not state either of the two possibilities, and hence we cannot speak much about a matter that has no confirmed basis.[271]

Dr Salah al-Khalidi agrees with Ibn Abbas that it was merely an hours'-long pregnancy that lasted from when she became pregnant in the Eastern Location till she arrived at the Farther Location of Bethlehem when (The pains of childbirth drove her to the trunk of a palm-tree).

We are more inclined to support this opinion as the Qur'anic wording means that the pains of childbirth forced Maryam to sit by the trunk of a palm-tree, unwillingly. A woman in labour feels sudden jolts of pain and as if a liquid is simmering inside her that violently shakes sideways.[272]

It is as if the foetus starts trembling in the womb's water. The linking of the trunk to the palm-tree is a unique form of Qur'anic imagery that denotes it was a living and full-blown green tree, not a barren severed one that was cast on the ground.[273]

c. Maryam's pains and her wish to die:

While laying there at the palm-tree's trunk, the pains of labour became stronger and Maryam let out a sharp and painful puff of breath as she said ("Ah! would that I had died before this! would that I had been a thing forgotten and out of sight!").

[271] "Fi Thilaal al-Qur'an", Ibid, 4/2306-2307.

[272] Ibn Faris, "Maqaayees al-Lugha", ver. by Abdel-Salam Mohammad Haroun, al-Fikr House, Cairo, 1979, p.977.

[273] "Al-Qasas al-Qur'ani: Presentation and Analysis of Events", Ibid, 4/248.

The virgin Maryam was alone in an area far from her family, with no experience or knowledge of that which she was going through and with nobody by her side to assist her in the delivery of her child. But when she wished for death, it was for fear of being shamed and of the scandal that would ensue as people would accuse her of an act of adultery that she had never committed.[274]

(Would that I had been a thing forgotten and out of sight!): Meaning that she wished she was never born. We can almost imagine her features and sense her conflicting feelings, and the pain she was in, as she wished for death.[275]

It was only for a short period that Maryam suffered from the pains of labour while she was alone, leaning on the palm-tree's trunk. Having delivered Isa (pbuh), she needed only a short while to recuperate, but was still captive of her fears and thoughts, worried and sad. But then she heard a voice from under her calling her.[276]

d. Her son calling her and God's accompanying Blessings:

God Says: {But (a voice) cried to her from beneath the (palm-tree): "Grieve not! for thy Lord hath provided a rivulet beneath thee; And shake towards thyself the trunk of the palm-tree: It will let fall fresh ripe dates upon thee. So eat and drink and cool (thine) eye. And if thou dost see any man, say, 'I have vowed a fast to Allah Most Gracious, and this day will I enter into no talk with any human being'"} (Surat Maryam: 24-26).

While lamenting her situation as she has just given birth alone to a fatherless child, Maryam's fears are quelled through God's Mercy as He grants Isa the ability to speak while just minutes old.[277]

---

274 "Ta'ammulaat fi Surat Maryam", Ibid, p.128-130.

275 "Fi Thilaal al-Qur'an", Ibid, 4/2307.

276 "Al-Qasas al-Qur'ani: Presentation and Analysis of Events", Ibid, 4/250.

277 "Al-Mar'ah fil Qasas al-Qur'ani", Ibid, 2/696.

Isa tells her, as per the Qur'an: ("Grieve not! for thy Lord hath provided a rivulet beneath thee").

The preponderant opinion is that he who called on Maryam from beneath her was Isa and not Jibreel (pbut) as the context is of Isa as well as all preceding pronouns: (So she conceived him, and she retired with him to a remote place. And the pains of childbirth drove her to the trunk of a palm-tree: She cried (in her anguish): "Ah! would that I had died before this! would that I had been a thing forgotten and out of sight!" But (a voice) cried to her from beneath the (palm-tree): "Grieve not!"). Another piece of evidence confirming this opinion is that when she went back to her people with Isa in her arms, she pointed to him when she saw their astonished looks, and only did so because she knew he could speak because he had done so earlier.[278]

The fact that her son was the one who spoke to her only minutes after his birth is a great miracle that could only have occurred by God's Will.[279]

Also, it was God who had inspired Isa (pbuh) to say the content of the words he uttered; otherwise how would Isa be privy to the grand masterplan when only a few moments old? His uttering of (Grieve not!) dispelled Maryam's fears and qualms for God is with her, caring for her, providing her with food and drink – also as a miracle – and Who will also be performing another miracle by having Isa speak in a manner that exonerates her from any wrongdoing when her people realise that it could only have occurred through God's Will.[280]

e. God provides Maryam with a rivulet:

(Thy Lord hath provided a rivulet beneath thee): Isa (pbuh) tells his mother here that God has Willed a (Sarii – Arabic word)

---

[278] "Tafseer al-Tabari: Taqreeb wa Tahtheeb", Ibid, 5/228-229.
[279] "Al-Qasas al-Qur'ani: Presentation and Analysis of Events", Ibid, 4/252.
[280] Ibid, 4/253.

to exist beneath her. Scholars have disagreed on that meant by the word with some stating that Isa is meant by it as the word can mean one whose status is elevated. So the meaning of the Qur'anic verse in this context would be: Fear not for your child, whose locale is currently beneath you, will be of great status when he grows up.[281]

But the majority of scholars believe that the word "creek", which is another derivative of the Arabic base word, is that which is meant here.[282] In this context, the verse would mean that God has Willed the existence of a creek that runs beneath Maryam which had not existed before, and which only came to be when she grasped onto the palm-tree's trunk. This was yet another miracle accompanying the creation of Isa, after those of being pregnant with him and his birth.[283]

f. God Willed the palm-tree to bear fruit out of season:

Having pointed to the creek beneath her, Isa (pbuh) directed her to the palm-tree at which she was resting as per the holy verse: {"And shake towards thyself the trunk of the palm-tree: It will let fall fresh ripe dates upon thee"} (Surat Maryam: 25).

This was a tall, green, living and normal tree, yet its fruit was anything but so as Isa (pbuh) was born in winter, on 25th December, as Nasraanis state; hence, for dates to be ripe at that time of the year was impossible because they only became so in summer.[284]

Having realised that the creation of the creek was a Divine miracle when there was no water before, this confirms that the ripening of the palm-tree's fruit was also a miracle as no fruit,

---

281 Ibid, 4/254.

282 Al-Tabari, "Jaami'a al-Bayan fi Ta'weel al-Qur'an", ver. by Ahmad Mohammad Shakir, al-Risalah Est., Beirut, 1st Ed., 16/24. See also: "Tafseer Ibn Katheer", Ibid, 3/117.

283 "Al-Qasas al-Qur'ani: Presentation and Analysis of Events", Ibid, 4/254.

284 "Dictionary of the Holy Book", Ibid, p.864.

even as seeds thereof, had existed on the tree before God Ordered it to bear them and become ripe all in an instance so that Maryam could have her sustenance from it. The ripe, soft and sweet dates are hence complemented by the water to make a wholesome miraculous meal.[285]

God Says: {And We made the son of Mary and his mother as a sign: We gave them both shelter on high ground, affording rest and security and furnished with springs} (Surat al-Mu'minoun: 50).

"A Sign", as only one, is stated to show greatness as it is one that contains many, and which together indicate Isa's truthfulness.

(We gave them both shelter on high ground) shows God's care for them as He inspired Maryam to seclude herself there when she was about to give birth so that Isa would not be harmed by her people.

A mother's care for her new-born is a matter of instinct that God has bestowed upon mankind since the creation of Adam (pbuh).[286]

g. God's Will in mandating action:

Isa told his mother to shake the palm-tree trunk and pull it towards her so that the ripe dates may fall. God Says: {"And shake towards thyself the trunk of the palm-tree: It will let fall fresh ripe dates upon thee"} (Surat Maryam: 25).

God provided Maryam with many miracles, with very minimal effort on her behalf, like the sustenance she received while at the Mihrab, the water spring which she would have to scoop from and the ripe dates which she had to pull on the trunk to get. God could have let the dates fall upon her without any effort from her but He wanted that Maryam perform some action in order for it to occur.

---

[285] "Al-Qasas al-Qur'ani: Presentation and Analysis of Events", Ibid, 4/256.

[286] "Shri'aat Allah Lil Anbiyaa' fil Qur'an al-Kareem", Ibid, p.608.

In reality, being frail after having just given birth, it was God who had the trunk shake and the dates fall upon Maryam. She merely placed her hands on it, but God was the One who had the dates drop down.

God wanted Maryam to take action so that God's Will may occur. It was a lesson in belief for Maryam so that she may connect between seeking God's aid in all matters while also performing actions thereof. It is also a lesson in belief for us so that we connect between reasons and causes and coordinate between the two while seeking aid from God. Every believer knows for certain that God is the One who takes and who gives, who harms and who benefits others and that what is destined for a person will materialise no matter what. Yet one must always seek God's Guidance and perform actions thereof accordingly so that that which is destined for mankind may come his way. Maryam's movement is proof that action is the means for receiving that which is destined for her.[287]

h. Change in Maryam's psychological state:

Having ordered Maryam to shake the palm-tree trunk, Isa ordered her to eat and drink: (So eat and drink and cool (thine) eye) and fear neither hunger nor thirst.

(Cool (thine) eye) is God letting Maryam know that she should be happy and accepting of God's Will. God specified the eye as it is where one's satisfaction and happiness is reflected; also – in Arabic[288] – it is a metaphor for one who is satisfied. Informing Maryam to be happily satisfied is indicative of the elevated psychological state to which God transformed Maryam as she was a nervous wreck prior to giving birth, when she said: (Ah! would that I had died before this! would that I had been a thing forgotten and out of sight!).

---

[287] "Al-Qasas al-Qur'ani: Presentation and Analysis of Events", Ibid, 4/257.

[288] Translator's addition.

The psychological state of Maryam changed after having safely given birth, hearing her new-born speak to her, seeing God's Signs of caring for her, living in the realm of His miracles, eating ripe dates out of season and drinking water from a Divinely sprung creek. All of this brought her joy, satisfaction and dispelled all her fears – which was accordingly reflected in her eyes.[289]

It was as such that the new-born prophet guided his mother towards proper and fast recognition while still under the palm-tree: That she should not be sad, to pull the trunk towards her, to eat the ripe dates and to drink from the creek below her. Maryam did that which she heard from her new-born and was thus happily satisfied.[290]

i. Benefit of dates for one who just gave birth:

Science has proven that dates contain an agent that strengthens womb muscles in the last months of pregnancy. This assists in childbirth and also reduces afterbirth bleeding. Dates are also an excellent source for sugars that are the best nourishment for muscles. The womb muscle is one of the largest in the body and it exerts much effort during childbirth. When gynaecologists provide pregnant women in child labour with water and sugar, this holy verse has stated to (eat and drink). Dates also reduce blood pressure for a short while in pregnant women, after which it returns to its normal levels, and of course, lower blood pressure minimises bleeding. Dates are also considered laxatives for the colon, which in turn, facilitate easier childbirth.[291]

j. (I have vowed a fast to Allah Most Gracious):

Isa (pbuh) continued to guide Maryam (pbuh) afterwards as well. He told her what to do when confronted by her family: (And if

---

289 "Al-Qasas al-Qur'ani: Presentation and Analysis of Events", Ibid, 4/261.

290 Ibid, 4/262.

291 "Al-Mar'ah fil Qasas al-Qur'ani", Ibid, 2/745.

thou dost see any man, say, 'I have vowed a fast to Allah Most Gracious, and this day will I enter into not talk with any human being'"). Isa told Maryam to do as a mute person would through hand and body gestures that she shall not speak, and that she point to him so that he would do all the talking.

"Vowing" is an action through which one attempts to draw himself closer to God. The mention of a "Vow" in Maryam's story is proof that it was an act of worship known and practised by past believers.

God meant for Maryam's silence as a piece of evidence attesting to her innocence and purity, for as she – the able one to do so – (fasted) from speaking, God Willed her new-born child, Isa (pbuh), to speak in her stead. Isa's ability to do so at such a young age was stronger proof of Maryam's innocence from any accusations.

Fourth: Isa (pbuh) speaks to the people while still an infant:

Maryam (pbuh) followed the instructions of her new-born child, Isa (pbuh), and ate and drank; then after having regained her strength, she carried Isa and headed to her people.

1. Maryam carries her son and heads to her people:

The following holy verses depict some of the astonishment and surprise Maryam's people underwent when she arrived with her child in her arms:

God Says: {At length she brought the (baby) to her people, carrying him (in her arms). They said: "O Mary! truly an amazing thing hast thou brought! O sister of Aaron! Thy father was not a man of evil, nor thy mother a woman unchaste!" But she pointed to the baby. They said: "How can we talk to one who is a child in the cradle?" He said: "I am indeed a servant of Allah. He hath given me revelation and made me a prophet; And He hath made me blessed wheresoever I be, and hath enjoined on me Prayer and Charity as long as I live; (He) hath made me kind to my mother, and not overbearing or miserable; So peace is on me the day I was born, the day that I die, and the day that I shall be raised up to life (again)!"} (Surat Maryam: 27-33).

- (She brought the (baby) to her people, carrying him):

Maryam was strong, brave, calm and reassured as she approached her people while cradling Isa (pbuh) as she was certain that God was standing with her, that she had done no wrong, and that it was God who created Isa.

- (They said: "O Mary! truly an amazing thing hast thou brought!):

Upon meeting Maryam with awe of their chaste and pure daughter carrying a child, they accused her indirectly via this sarcastic sentence.[292] The reason they did not tell her that she had committed adultery is their belief in and piety towards God, and not wanting to commit a sin by saying that their righteous daughter was an adulteress. But they saw this infant with her and were suspicious as to how to correlate between that which they know of her and what they see in her arms.

They sufficed in stating that she had brought forth a grand and awful matter that was inconsistent with that which they knew of her or of the family in which she was raised, among two righteous parents and brother.[293]

The matter to them was of great proportions and they asked her from where she had brought this child?[294]

---

[292] "Al-Qasas al-Qur'ani: Presentation and Analysis of Events", Ibid, 4/268.

[293] Ibid.

[294] "Al-Qasas al-Qur'ani: Presentation and Analysis of Events", Ibid, 4/269.

2. Her family's righteousness and that of her brother Haroun:

Her family referenced the purity of her origin and the chastity of her extended family, brother and parents. They said: {"O sister of Aaron! Thy father was not a man of evil, nor thy mother a woman unchaste!"} (Surat Maryam: 28).

The testament of Maryam's people to her purity and chastity was in negating she was a prostitute through the mention of her mother. This correlates with what Maryam said when Jibreel came to breathe the life of Isa into her: {She said: "How shall I have a son, seeing that no man has touched me, and I am not unchaste?"} (Surat Maryam: 20).

Scholars have disagreed on that meant by (O sister of Aaron!). Some said that real brotherhood was not that meant here, but rather to draw a simile in likening Maryam to Prophet Mousa's brother, Haroun, as both she and he are similar in worship, chastity and righteousness. In this sense, the holy verse would mean: O she who is similar to Haroun, from where have you come to be with this infant?

But the majority of scholars said that it was real brotherhood and that the Haroun mentioned in this verse was Maryam's actual brother, not the brother of Mousa as many centuries separate the two.

We believe the second opinion to be more viable as it was mentioned in a verified hadeeth by Prophet Mohammad (pbuh) reported by Muslim and al-Tirmithi of al-Mugheirah bin Shu'aba – who said: "Prophet Mohammad (pbuh) sent me to Najran. They said: Do you not say (O sister of Haroun)? I said: Yes. They said: And Mousa before Isa with so and so? So when I returned to the Prophet (pbuh) I told him, and he said: Would you have told them that they were named after the prophets and righteous ones before them."[295]

[295] Reported by Muslim, no. 2135.

Hence, this verified Hadeeth makes clear that Haroun was Maryam's brother whose parents named him after Prophet Haroun (pbuh).[296]

3. Maryam's parents' astonishment when she pointed to her baby:

Upon hearing her people's accusations of her, Maryam was upset with their veiled accusation of her, and pointed to her child as she had made a vow not to speak. Having heard Isa speak to her as soon as he was born, she delegated the response to him.

(But she pointed to the baby): She pointed to Isa so that they would ask him, not her. This is the only instance the word "point" is mentioned in such a context in the Qur'an. Pointing can be done either via hand, eyes, head or others so as to convey a certain meaning.

Her people understood that signal and became even more amazed and frustrated as they found her response silly and sarcastic for how could an hours-old baby speak? They asked her in denial: (How can we speak to one who is a child in the cradle?) They supposed that even if they had asked him the question, how would he then be able to respond – being a new-born child?

They saw this child in a cradle – meaning being cradled by his mother, not in an actual manmade cradle. The word was mentioned three times in the Qur'an in the context of speaking about Isa (pbuh).

Despite being only hours old, Isa (pbuh) was fully aware of everything happening around him as a miracle from God. He could hear what Maryam was saying and he understood everything.

Upon hearing their question and knowing that his mother was not going to answer it as it was he who ordered her not to answer

---

[296] "Al-Qasas al-Qur'ani: Presentation and Analysis of Events", Ibid, 4/271.

any questions, Isa (pbuh) volunteered the answer, presented himself to the people and informed them of his future status.

Maryam's people were shocked and mystified at what they had just seen and heard. They were in complete bewilderment as to whether it was real or a figment of their imagination. Did they really just witness an infant speak? Was this truly the voice of an hours'-old child?

It is an absolute truth! The speaking of this infant was a miracle that those believing people had just heard, and it strengthened their faith and belief in The Almighty.[297]

4. New-born Isa's introductory statement of belief:

God says: {He said: "I am indeed a servant of Allah. He hath given me revelation and made me a prophet; And He hath made me blessed wheresoever I be, and hath enjoined on me Prayer and Charity as long as I live; (He) hath made me kind to my mother, and not overbearing or miserable; So peace is on me the day I was born, the day that I die, and the day that I shall be raised up to life (again)"} (Surat Maryam: 30-33).

Isa (pbuh) began by saying that only Allah is the Divine God, partner with none, and that he was a servant of God who created him through a Divine miracle without a father's seed and that he, Isa, was neither God's partner nor son.[298]

Imam Ibn Katheer says: "The first matter he spoke of was confirming that God has no son and that he, Isa, was His servant."[299]

Only Allah is the Divine God and all else are but His servants and subjects. Any confusion between the God and His servants is considered blasphemous. When a group of people elevate one of

[297] "Al-Qasas al-Qur'ani: Presentation and Analysis of Events", Ibid, 4/272.

[298] "Al-Qasas al-Qur'ani: Presentation and Analysis of Events", Ibid, 4/273.

[299] "Tafseer Ibn Katheer", 3/117.

God's servants to His status, they have committed blasphemy and are deemed unbelievers in God.

This belief-based introduction that Isa (pbuh) began with as an infant, in which he acknowledged being God's servant, pre-empted the lies that will be perpetrated by – some people – later when they claimed that Isa was the son of God. Isa then spoke about that which God will be granting him in the future: (He hath given me revelation and made me a prophet). The statement references Isa's future when God will give him the Book, i.e. the Injeel (Bible) which concurs with the Torah before it, and will make him a prophet.

Of course, it was God who inspired Isa to utter such phrases.

Isa's statements (I am indeed a servant of Allah) and (He hath given me revelation and made me a prophet) were pre-emptive denial of what – some Nasraanis – were going to later claim about him as being the son of God for the first phrase, and what the Israelites were going to contest about him for the second. The Israelites were actually planning to kill him as well.

The two statements together (I am indeed a servant of Allah; He hath given me revelation and made me a prophet) are practical affirmation of the promise delivered by the angel Jibreel to Maryam prior to her pregnancy of Isa (pbuh). This occurred when Jibreel was reported in the Qur'an as saying: {Behold! the angels said: "O Mary! Allah giveth thee glad tidings of a Word from Him: his name will be Christ Jesus, the son of Mary, held in honour in this world and the Hereafter and of (the company of) those nearest to Allah. He shall speak to the people in childhood and in maturity. And he shall be (of the company) of the righteous"} (Surat Aal-Imran: 45-46).

Also, the holy verse: {"And Allah will teach him the Book and Wisdom, the *Torah*[300] and the Gospel, And (appoint him) a messenger to the Children of Israel} (Surat Aal-Imran: 48-49).

300 Corrected by Translator. Originally "Law".

a. Meaning of Isa being blessed:

Prophet Isa (pbuh) continues with introducing himself and says: (And He hath made me blessed wheresoever I be), meaning that God has showered me with His Blessings rendering me as such wherever I, Isa, be.

Scholars of past times have differed in their interpretation of the word "blessed". Mujahid said it means one who benefits others. Sufyan al-Thawri said it means one who guides towards righteousness wherever he may be in that he encourages people to do good and warns them from doing evil.[301]

b. (And hath enjoined on me Prayer and Charity as long as I live):

This is what would be occurring in Prophet Isa's future, i.e. God will enjoin him to pray and be charitable for his entire life in a manner where he would uphold all of God's rights – paramount among which is Prayer – and the rights of God's subjects – most important among which is Charity. In saying this, Isa (pbuh) was concurring that he would be upholding and implementing such mandates.

c. Prophet Isa is kind towards his mother:

((He) hath made me kind to my mother), i.e. God made Isa a prophet, blessed and kind to his mother in a manner where he would shower her with goodness, and this was the positive side of the verse.

The verse – no. 32 of Surat Maryam – then goes on to state: (… and not overbearing or miserable) referencing the negative side of man which God had eliminated from Isa's traits.

A person who does not revere and care for his/her parents is deemed overbearing and haughty, and accordingly will not be

[301] "Al-Qasas al-Qur'ani: Presentation and Analysis of Events", Ibid, 4/275.

merciful towards people beyond them either. God Says: {Allah loveth not the arrogant, the vainglorious} (Surat al-Nisaa': 36).

Whenever the word "Mighty" (a synonym of "Overbearing"[302]) is mentioned in the Qur'an as a human trait, it is always intended for denouncement as it is a trait of arrogant and overbearing individuals. When one is righteous, he/she is kind, humble and merciful towards others.

Describing a person as "Mighty" is to denounce him, and accordingly, God elevated Isa above that by Saying: ("(He) hath made me … and not overbearing or miserable). God also elevated Yahya above that by Saying: (And kind to his parents, and he was not overbearing or rebellious.)[303]

d. Granting Isa Peace is a sign of his humanity:

God Says: {"So peace is on me the day I was born, the day that I die, and the day that I shall be raised up to life (again)"!} (Surat Maryam: 33).

Isa (pbuh) informed his mother's people that God has bestowed Peace and Safety upon him in his three most critical life phases: The day he was born, the day he dies and the day he is resurrected on Judgment Day.

The verse means that God has saved Isa from the devil and his proxies the day Isa was born, denying them any hold on him. That He saved him from the great scare the day he dies, and from the greater scare of Judgment Day as that which people shall face on that great day when they exit their graves.[304]

Imam Ibn Katheer said, "This is all proof of Isa's submission to God as one created by Him – who lives, dies and is resurrected

---

302 Translator's addition.

303 "Al-Qasas al-Qur'ani: Presentation and Analysis of Events", Ibid, 4/277.

304 "Al-Qasas al-Qur'ani: Presentation and Analysis of Events", Ibid, 4/278.

like all other creatures. But it is only in these three most difficult phases of human life that he shall fear no harm."[305]

Explaining "Peace" and its specificity in Isa's case when he is reported to say: (So peace is on me) is because God knew that the Israelites will be calling him a liar and not believe in his call. God knew that they would also work towards killing and crucifying him – which they later attempted – but God saved Isa from them and He raised him to the Heavens.[306]

Hence, Isa (pbuh) concluded introducing himself to his mother's people, stated his servitude of The Almighty, stated his prophethood, the Book, his care for his mother, his humility and the peace and safety he will enjoy in his life.

The Qur'an ends the story of Isa (pbuh) with this phrase and does not detail the people's reaction to what he had stated nor does it detail any further information about Maryam (pbuh).[307]

5. The Holy Qur'an's commentary on Isa's birth:

The verses of Surat Maryam then confirm the truth about Isa (pbuh), God's Singularity and refute the claims of Nasraanis. God says: {Such (was) Jesus the son of Mary: (it is) a statement of truth, about which they (vainly) dispute. It is not befitting to (the majesty of) Allah that He should beget a son. Glory be to Him! when He determines a matter, He only says to it, "Be", and it is. Verily Allah is my Lord and your Lord: Him therefore serve ye: this is a Way that is straight. But the sects differ among themselves: and woe to the unbelievers because of the (coming) Judgment of a Momentous Day! How plainly will they see and hear, the Day that they will appear before Us! but the unjust today are in error manifest! But warn them of the Day of Distress, when the matter will be de-

---

[305] Ibid.

[306] Ibid, 4/279.

[307] Ibid.

termined: for (behold,) they are negligent and they do not believe! It is We Who will inherit the earth, and all beings thereon: to Us will they all be returned} (Surat Maryam: 34-40).

This commentary stems from the fact presented before it, i.e. mentioning the pregnancy with Isa, his birth and all he said while an infant.[308]

- God Proclaims the Truth about Isa:

In this follow-up commentary, God informs us that it is the truth about the story of Isa: {Such (was) Jesus the son of Mary: (it is) a statement of truth, about which they (vainly) dispute} (Surat Maryam: 34).

The Israelites claimed that Isa was an illusionist and a liar. Some Nasraanis claimed that Isa was a god, third of three and even son of God, while one group of them remained of the path of righteousness and said he was God's servant and messenger.[309]

God refuted the claim of Nasraanis who said Isa was His son. The Almighty Says: {It is not befitting to (the majesty of) Allah that He should beget a son. Glory be to Him! when He determines a matter, He only says to it, "Be", and it is} (Surat Maryam: 35). So, how then is Isa deemed to be God's son? God has no need for a son! We find nothing strange in the manner in which Isa was created without a father's seed as it was God's Will to do so, and if He Wills something, it Is!

God reports Isa saying the following from verse 36 of Surat Maryam {Verily Allah is my Lord and your Lord: Him therefore serve ye: this is a Way that is straight}.

In the above verse, Isa (pbuh) was telling Nasraanis while he was among them, prior to being raised to the Heavens: "God is my Lord and yours, He is One, has no partner, woman or son, I am

[308] "Al-Qasas al-Qur'ani: Presentation and Analysis of Events", Ibid, 4/180.

[309] Ibid, 4/282.

not His son, I am ordered to worship Him, as should you and this is the path of righteousness." But some Nasraanis did not follow Isa's command and diverged into different sects regarding it. God Says: {But the sects differed among themselves: and woe to the unbelievers because of the (coming) Judgment of a Momentous Day!} (Surat Maryam: 37).[310]

Woe be to them of the horrors they will witness on that Momentous Day. God Says: {How plainly will they see and hear, the Day that they will appear before Us! but the unjust today are in error manifest! But warn them of the Day of Distress, when the matter will be determined: for (behold,) they are negligent and they do not believe!} (Surat Maryam: 38-39). It is a Day of great proportions that shall be witnessed by Jinn, humans and angels all in the presence of The Almighty.

God has warned these people of Judgment Day's punishment: {But warn them of the Day of Distress, when the matter will be determined: for (behold,) they are negligent and they do not believe!} (Surat Maryam: 39).

After being held accountable for their sins, God will make His ruling on their eternal punishment in the fires of Hell, whereby they will feel much remorse. God warns them while they are alive so that they may wake up, stop their non-believing in Him and follow the path of righteousness.[311]

God warns them of that fated Day when all that on Earth shall return to God as He is the Single Inheritor, and it is with this firm truth of belief that God concludes the commentary on Isa's story. God says: {It is We Who will inherit the earth, and all beings thereon: to Us will they all be returned} (Surat Maryam: 40).[312]

---

310 Ibid, 4/283.

311 "Al-Qasas al-Qur'ani: Presentation and Analysis of Events", Ibid, 4/284.

312 "Fi Thilaal al-Qur'an", Ibid, 4/2309.

This emphasises God's Oneness and that none is His partner. God is The Creator and any others are but His creations, as is Isa (pbuh). Only God is The Owner of the Heavens and Earth, life and the afterlife, Inheritor of all of mankind, The One Who makes this world perish and Who brings about Judgment Day, Who resurrects mankind, holds them accountable and rewards or punishes them.[313]

The Holy Qur'an has provided a very minute, delicate and detailed account of Isa's story after it had been marred with much alteration and distortion by people. This is considered a true form of a miraculous historical account and proves that the Qur'an is truly God's Words and that Prophet Mohammad (pbuh) is truly God's Messenger and upon who this Book was descended.[314]

The detailed events told in the Qur'an testify to its Divinity and that it could not have been be manmade. They also stand witness of Prophet Mohammad's truth of prophethood as he could not have drawn any of these facts from either the Old or the New Testaments. The discrepancy between the Qur'an and the Testaments is great as neither of the Testaments is even remotely as precise in its information as that contained in the Qur'an about the righteous Prophet, Isa (pbuh).

Examples on the above are the miracle of Isa speaking while just hours old, his pronouncing of total submission to The Almighty, God elevating Isa above all ill traits, the miracle of the Repast which God descended to the Hawaaris (disciples) from the Heavens in answering their request and that of Isa, and the miracle of saving Isa from crucifixion and torture at the hands of the Israelites – none of which are mentioned in the gospels of Christians nowadays. God has affirmed that He raised Isa to Him[315] - as shall be detailed further down in this book.

---

[313] "Al-Qasas al-Qur'ani: Presentation and Analysis of Events", Ibid, 4/284.

[314] "Al-'Ijaaz al-Tareekhi wal Inbaa'i fil Qur'an al-Kareem", Ibid, 2/.

[315] "Al-'Ijaaz al-Tareekhi wal Inbaa'i fil Qur'an al-Kareem", Ibid, 2/894.

After Isa (pbuh) was raised to the Heavens, there was much disagreement about him throughout the era of Roman oppression. But when Emperor Constantine became Christian and realised the disagreements were so severe, he called for the First Council of Nicaea in 325 AD so as to attain consensus on the matter among the different sects of Christendom.

At that Conference, some participants called for the Singularity of The Almighty and denounced the Trinity while others were blasphemous and claimed the divinity of Isa (pbuh) and of upholding the Trinity. Most prominent among the former group was Arius who was followed by the church of Asyut headed by Miletus, the church of Constantinople headed by Oscanius, and the churches of Antakya, Macedonia, Babel and Palestine, among others. The only patriarch who objected to acknowledging the singularity of The Almighty was that of Alexandria, along with a group of incredulous Christians. At least 2840 patriarchs and bishops of different Christian sects attended the Council, and Emperor Constantine was amazed at that which he saw and heard. Yet he then leaned toward those who claimed the Messiah's divinity due to his pagan background, despite the fact that Arius had acknowledged Prophet Isa's humanity and prophethood. Constantine's opinion was realised with a majority of 700 votes despite the fact that the Church of Arius had received the highest percentage among all others attending the Conference.

Henceforth, from among 70 different gospels presented at the Council, four of those were approved and are the ones revered by Christians nowadays. The 66 others were deemed to have been altered and were ordered burned. This is the disagreement that has endured till this very day and due to which Nasraaniism has splintered into many sects. The Holy Qur'an describes this as follows:

- {Such (was) Jesus the son of Mary: (it is) a statement of truth, about which they (vainly) dispute. It is not befitting to (the majesty of) Allah that He should beget a son. Glory be to Him! when He determines a matter, He only says to it, “Be”, and it is. Verily Allah is my Lord and your Lord: Him therefore serve ye: this is a Way that is straight. But the sects differ among themselves: and woe to the unbelievers because of the (coming) Judgment of a Momentous Day! How plainly will they see and hear, the Day that they will appear before Us! but the unjust today are in error manifest! But warn them of the Day of Distress, when the matter will be determined: for (behold,) they are negligent and they do not believe! It is We Who will inherit the earth, and all beings thereon: to Us will they all be returned} (Surat Maryam: 34-40).

- {When Jesus came with Clear Signs, he said: “Now have I come to you with Wisdom, and in order to make clear to you some of the (points) on which ye dispute: therefore fear Allah and obey me. For Allah, He is my Lord and your Lord: so worship ye Him: this is a Straight Way.” But sects from among themselves fell into disagreement: then woe to the wrongdoers, from the Penalty of a Grievous Day!} (Surat al-Zukhruf: 63-65).

These holy verses are a facet of informative and historical miracles in how the Holy Qur’an details a number of decisive moments in the lives of Prophets Mohammad and Isa (pbut). These events contradict all that mentioned about Isa in the New Testament. There is also a facet of scientific miracles embodied in those abilities granted to Isa by The Almighty to cure the born blind and lepers whose ailments had mystified doctors. The educational miracle is evident in emphasising the reward of beseeching God through prayer and supplication with certainty in God’s absolute Ability to fulfil it. An example on this is the birth of Maryam bint Imran … and how her birth was in response to her mother’s continuous supplication. Believing in God and seeking His guidance in all matters, as worldly life is one of trials and testing, as well as the conflict between good and bad are basic elements of existence. But goodness does not succeed just because it is so; rather, it requires men and women who believe in it and who toil towards upholding it. Such was the life of the Messiah son of Maryam, his mother's, all those who believed in him and those who followed in his footsteps on the path of the great Islam.[316]

6. Al-Najaashi's stance when hearing verses of Surat Maryam:

The following details what occurred when the King of Abyssinia, al-Najaashi, heard verses from Surat Maryam recited to him by Ja'afar bin Abu Talib. Imam Ahmad reported that Um Salama was detailing the story of the migration to Abyssinia and said, " … When Ja'afar bin Abu Talib finished reading his introductory note, al-Najaashi asked if he possessed any of the verses descended upon Prophet Mohammad. Ja'afar answered in the affirmative and recited the beginning of Surat Maryam, upon which al-Najaashi cried until his tears soaked his beard. The patriarchs and bishops also cried until their gospels were also soaked with their tears.

"Al-Najaashi then said, 'This Qur'an that we have just heard, and that which Mousa came with, emanate from the same origin.' He then told Amr bin al-'Aas and Abdullah bin Abu Rabee'aa to leave and that he would never allow them to harm the two Muslim men.

"As the two emissaries from Quraysh left al-Najaashi's court, Amr bin al-'Aas told his colleague, 'I swear that I will come back tomorrow and defame the Muslims to al-Najaashi so that he would be furious with them and I would extract them from his presence.' The calmer Abdullah bin Abu Rabee'aa said, 'Do not do so as Muslims are related to us even if we are not of the same religion.' Then the first said, 'I must do so! I will tell al-Najaashi that Muslims claim Isa son of Maryam to be a servant.

[316] "Al-'Ijaaz al-Tareekhi wal Inbaa'i fil Qur'an al-Kareem", Ibid, 2/896.

"The next day, Amr bin al-'Aas came before al-Najaashi and said, 'O King, those Muslim say an atrocious thing about Isa son of Maryam. So send for them to come here and hear what they have to say about it.'

"So, al-Najaashi called for the Muslim men to attend his council. They were scared upon hearing this and started asking each what they should say.

"Ja'afar bin Abu Talib said, 'We shall say that which we heard from our prophet, Mohammad (pbuh).' Then the next day when the Muslims met with al-Najaashi, he asked them the question.

"Ja'afar said, 'We swear by God that we only state that which our prophet told us, that Isa is a servant of God, His messenger, a Spirit from Him and His Word which He bestowed on the virgin and celibate Maryam.'

"Upon hearing this, al-Najaashi picked up a stick from the ground and said to those around him, 'By God, Isa son of Maryam is no more beyond what the Muslims say than the measure of this stick. Then the patriarchs exhaled heavily as they were angered by what al-Najaashi said, yet none of them dared oppose him. So, al-Najaashi said, 'Express your anger as you wish for what I said is the truth.'"[317]

God descended the following verses upon Prophet Mohammad (pbuh) that speak of al-Najaashi and his likes: {Strongest among men in enmity to the believers wilt thou find the Jews and Pagans; and nearest among them in love to the believers wilt thou find those who say, "We are Christians": because amongst these are men devoted to learning and men who have renounced the world, and they are not arrogant. And when they listen to the revelation received by the Messenger, thou wilt see their eyes overflowing with tears, for they recognise the truth: they pray: "Our Lord! we

---

[317] "Al-Qasas al-Qur'ani: Presentation and Analysis of Events", Ibid, 4/216.

believe; write us down among the witnesses. What cause can we have not to believe in Allah and the truth which has come to us, seeing that we long for our Lord to admit us to the company of the righteous?" And for this their prayer hath Allah rewarded them with gardens, with rivers flowing underneath, their eternal home. Such is the recompense of those who do good} (Surat al-Maa'idah: 82-85).

Al-Najaashi's magnificent stance upon hearing verses of Surat Maryam is proof that true Christians become emotional when hearing the Qur'an, that they believe in the verses and that they consider them evidence of Mohammad's prophethood. This is why God ordered Mohammad (pbuh) to recite these verses to others: (Relate in the Book (the story of) Mary).[318]

7. Maryam (pbuh) and her role in the history of humanity:

Maryam had the most prominent role in aiding and supporting Prophet Isa (pbut) as he set out to deliver God's Message across the land with love, forgiveness and peace. Upon reading the Qur'an, one notices the following about Maryam's life:

- The Holy Qur'an contains no Surah named after a woman except that of Maryam (pbuh). There are none entitled Aminah – Prophet Mohammad's mother, Khadijah – his wife nor Fatima – his daughter.

- Maryam was mentioned 34 times in the Holy Qur'an.[319]

- God ensured Maryam being cared for as per Surat Aal-Imran, verse no. 44: {This is part of the tidings of the things unseen, which We reveal unto thee (O Messenger.) by inspiration: Thou wast not with them when they cast lots with arrows, as to which of

[318] "Al-Qasas al-Qur'ani: Presentation and Analysis of Events", Ibid, 4/216.

[319] Akram Kasaab, "Islam's Relation to Nasraaniism in the Qur'an and Sunnah throughout History", al-Tanweer al-Islami centre for Knowledge Services & Publishing, Cairo, 2007, p.17.

them should be charged with the care of Mary: Nor wast thou with them when they disputed (the point)}.

- Maryam was chosen as the best among women so that she may give birth to Isa as God had purified her of all flaws. God says: {Behold! the angels said: "O Mary! Allah hath chosen thee and purified thee - chosen thee above the women of all nations"} (Surat Aal-Imran: 42).

- Maryam is chaste and honourable. God says: {And Mary the daughter of 'Imran, who guarded her chastity; and We breathed into (her body) of Our spirit; and she testified to the truth of the words of her Lord and of His Revelations, and was one of the devout (Servants)} (Surat al-Tahreem: 12).

God honoured Maryam bint Imran and elevated her to the highest status as she held onto being chaste and pure throughout her life. Hence, we realise that whoever submits to God's Will shall be elevated by Him.[320]

- Maryam and her son Isa are among God's Signs that exemplify His great Ability. God says: {And We made the son of Mary and his mother as a sign: We gave them both shelter on high ground, affording rest and security and furnished with springs} (Surat al-Mu'minoun: 50).

This is also a sign that whoever follows the path of obedience shall be of elevated status, and that whoever follows the path of wrongdoing shall be demeaned.[321]

- Maryam is among the best women on Earth. Prophet Mohammad (pbuh) said, "The best among all women are Maryam bint Imran, Khadijah bint Khuwailid, Fatima bint Mohammad and Pharaoh's woman, Asiya."[322] Another version of the Hadeeth

---

[320] Huda Abdel-Latif 'Aaryan, "Female Persona in Qur'anic Stories", Ghaar Hiraa' Printin & Publishing House, Damascus, Syria, 1st Ed., 2005, p.216.

[321] Ibid, p.216.

[322] "Sunan al-Tirmithi", no. 3888, "Saheeh al-Tirmithi" 53.

states, "The best among all women are four: Maryam bint Imran, Khadijah bint Khuwailid, Fatima bint Mohammad and Pharaoh's woman, Asiya."[323]

- Maryam is among Paradise's best women. Mohammad (pbuh) said, "The best women of Paradise are Khadijah bint Khuwailid, Fatima bint Mohammad, Maryam bint Imran and Pharaoh's woman, Asiya bint Muzahim."[324]

- Maryam is a complete woman. Prophet Mohammad (pbuh) said, "God has made many men complete, but among all women He made only Maryam bint Imran and Pharaoh's woman, Asiya, as such. He has also given Aisha preferential status among women and likened her to al-Thareed among all other foods."[325]

- Maryam was not touched by the devil. Prophet Mohammad (pbuh) said, "Satan imprints his finger on the forehead of all mankind when they are born, except for Isa son of Maryam, for when Satan wanted to do so, it was blocked by the barrier."[326] Another version of the same Hadeeth says, "All mankind are touched by Satan when they born, except for Maryam and her son."[327]

- Maryam was an accepted vow. God Says: {Right graciously did her Lord accept her and He made her grow in purity and beauty} (Surat Aal-Imran: 37).

- Maryam received her sustenance with ease on a daily basis. God Says: {Every time that he entered (Her) chamber to see her, He found her supplied with sustenance. He said: "O Mary! Whence (comes) this to you?" She said: "From Allah. for Allah

---

323 Muslim, "Fi Fadaa'il al-Sahaabah", no. 2430.

324 Al-Albaani, "Silsilat al-Ahaadeeth al-Saheehah wa Shay' min Fiqhiha wa Fawaa'idiha al-Silsilah al-Saheeha", al-Ma'aarif Publishing * Distribution Library, Riyadh, Saudi, 1995, no. 1424.

325 Al-Bukhari, no. 3411; Muslim, no. 2431.

326 Al-Bukhari, no. 3286.

327 Ibid, no. 3431.

Provides sustenance to whom He pleases without measure"} (Surat Aal-Imran: 37).

- Maryam was supported with miracles. God Says: {But (a voice) cried to her from beneath the (palm-tree): "Grieve not! for thy Lord hath provided a rivulet beneath thee; And shake towards thyself the trunk of the palm-tree: It will let fall fresh ripe dates upon thee"} (Surat Maryam: 24-25).

When we Muslims ponder the meanings of Surat Maryam and Surat Aal-Imran, we realise the true worth of Maryam (pbuh) and her great status among the Qur'an's stories of past righteous people; a story of miraculous lessons filled with examples to follow. From her, we have learned the importance of vows, submission to God's Will, always having faith in God and seeking His Guidance in all matters.

From Maryam we have also learned patience, chastity, obedience, bearing responsibility, action and toiling to care for a child who carried forth a Divine Message, which entailed standing up to her people and society, and thus rendering her among the best women of all mankind.[328]

Maryam (pbuh) has taught us how to face psychological traumas through that which we read about her in the Qur'an. The lessons learned from her story are as follows:

- Surrendering to God's Will and Destiny.

- Importance of short isolation.

- Honest patience when faced with difficulties.

- Breaking the cycle of sadness (He called her from beneath her not to be sad).

- Remembering God's countless Graces (He has made a stream beneath thee).

[328] "Female Persona in Qur'anic Stories", Ibid, p.219.

- Not succumbing to weakness (Pull the palm-tree trunk towards you and it shall drop ripe dates onto thee).

- (Eat and drink and cool thine eye) is an example on overcoming psychological shock. In the verse, God directs Maryam towards alleviating the physical and psychological effects that have befallen her so that she may not lose her appetite or her sense of security. (Cool thine eye) is a sign that Maryam should not be sad as her predicament is not a sad ordeal, but rather a good one as she had been chosen from among all mankind.

- Seeking God's assistance through silence and entrusting matters to God.[329]

- Certainty that with difficulty shall come ease for she was the purest woman of mankind, worshipped God to the fullest and was immortalised through the story of her in the Holy Qur'an.

This immortalisation of Maryam's story in the Qur'an has elevated her status, proven her innocence and made her an icon to follow. God then makes her son a righteous and pious prophet and messenger who performs many miracles on God's behalf and who testifies to total submission to God who created him.[330]

Maryam (pbuh) holds special status in the Holy Qur'an as she was chosen to be the vessel for the greatest and most noble matter of maternity in the context of a Divine miracle. Her role was pivotal in the sequence of events regarding her life and that of her family, as well as in the message of those believing in the One God.

Fifth: Isa (pbuh), a Messenger to the Israelites:

Prophet Isa (pbuh) grew up as a pure and pious young man protected by God from Satan and his proxies until God descended

[329] Fawziyah Salih al-Khulaifi, "Facing Psychological Traumas through the Story of Maryam", al-Hadaarah Publishing * Distribution House, Riyadh, Saudi, 2015, p.20-29.

[330] Ibid, p.30.

Revelation and the Injeel upon him, made him prophet and sent him as messenger to the Israelites.

God's sending of Isa as a messenger and descending of the Bible upon him was fulfilment of the glad tidings God sent to Isa's mother before bearing Isa: {"And Allah will teach him the Book and Wisdom, the *Law* [331] and the Gospel, "And (appoint him) a messenger to the Children of Israel"} (Surat Aal-Imran: 48-49).

It is also in fulfilment of what Isa said of himself when he spoke to his mother's people when only hours old: (He said: "I am a servant of God who gave me the Book and made me a prophet).

God sent Isa son of Maryam (pbut) as messenger solely to the Israelites. This is evident as per the following holy verses:

- {"And (appoint him) a messenger to the Children of Israel, (with this message): I have come to you, with a Sign from your Lord} (Surat Aal-Imran: 49).

- {Jesus, the son of Mary, said: "O Children of Israel! I am the messenger of Allah (sent) to you, confirming the *Law* (which came) before me of the Torah, and giving Glad Tidings of a Messenger to come after me, whose name shall be Ahmad"} (Surat al-Saff: 06).

Isa (pbuh) spoke candidly with the Israelites and told them that he was God's messenger to them, that his message confirms that of the Torah and that he brings them glad tidings of the final prophet that shall come after him, i.e. Mohammad bin Abdullah (pbuh).

God sent all messengers as His emissaries, each to his people, except for the final prophet of all, Mohammad (pbuh), who he sent to all mankind. Each prophet would tell his people that God had sent him as a messenger to them. But regarding Prophet Mohammad, God Says: {Say: "O men! I am sent unto you all, as the Messenger of Allah, to Whom belongeth the dominion of the heavens

---

[331] Corrected by Translator.

and the earth: there is no god but He: it is He That giveth both life and death"} (Surat al-A'araaf: 158).

Muslim reported that Jabir bin Abdullah said, "Prophet Mohammad (pbuh) said: 'None before me have been given the five that I have. Each prophet was sent as a messenger only to his people, but I have been sent to people of all colours. War spoils are allowed for me, yet they were not allowed for those before me. The ground has been deemed pure and a place suitable for prayer, so wherever one may be and needs to pray, he may do so right there. I have been granted victory through fear for a month's walk, and was granted the ability to seek forgiveness for others.'"[332]

The Qur'an's choice of words is meticulous, for they are God's. In the Qur'an, Isa (pbuh) delivered God's message to the Israelites by saying (O children of Israel), not (O people). But for Prophet Mousa (pbuh) the Qur'an states that Mousa said (O people).

- God Says: {Moses said to his people: "O my people! why do ye vex and insult me, though ye know that I am the messenger of Allah (sent) to you?"} (Surat al-Saff: 05).

The wisdom behind this is that one is affiliated with his father's people. Hence, one is deemed to be of clan X or Y, and he speaks to them by saying (O my people) as is the case with Mousa (pbuh) who was of the Imran clan and whose father is Imran of the Israelites. But for Prophet Isa it is not so as these were not his people since he has no paternal blood relation with them since he was born through a miracle without a father's seed.[333]

The gist of the matter is that God mandated Isa (pbuh) to deliver His message to the Israelites, and that Isa carried out that task to perfection across the cities and villages of the children of Israel.

---

[332] "Saheeh Muslim", no. 521.

[333] "Al-Qasas al-Qur'ani: Presentation and Analysis of Events", Ibid, 4/286.

The fact that Prophet Isa delivered God's message to only this group of people does not in any manner diminish his importance or that of the message he carried forward, and the same applies to all prophets before Isa as well. But for Prophet Mohammad (pbuh), his message was intended for all mankind for neither does the Qur'an nor Prophet Mohammad's Hadeeths mention or reference any matter that would suggest that other prophets were sent to all mankind as well.[334]

God Says: {We did indeed send, before thee, messengers to their (respective) peoples, and they came to them with Clear Signs: then, to those who transgressed, We meted out Retribution: and it was due from Us to aid those who believed} (Surat al-Roum: 47).

Since the Qur'an stated that prophets were sent as messengers to their respective peoples, we cannot extrapolate or infer any different information or object to God's Words: {Allah knoweth best where (and how) to carry out His mission} (Surat al-An'aam: 124).

God knows best of people's conditions and environments, and accordingly, the messages of prophets, prior to Mohammad (pbuh), including those sent to the Israelites, were in temporal and spatial alignment. Hence, the calling of all their prophets was restricted to the children of Israel and did not go beyond the lands of Iraq, the Levant and Egypt.[335]

This was because God knew that the message of Prophet Mohammad (pbuh) will become the only one He wants mankind to follow. As for Prophet Isa (pbuh), he delivered the message with which he was entrusted and called upon the Israelites to believe in God's Singularity and to not act blasphemously towards Him. God Says: {But said Christ: "O Children of Israel! worship Allah, my Lord and your Lord. Whoever joins other gods with Al-

[334] Faraj-Allah Abdel-Baari, "Naqd Da'awa 'Aalamiyyat al-Nasraaniyah", al-Aafaaq al-Arabiyah House, Cairo, 1st Ed., 2004, p.18.

[335] Ibid.

lah, Allah will forbid him the Paradise, and the Fire will be his abode. There will for the wrong-doers be no one to help} (Surat al-Maa'idah: 72).[336]

1. Obligation to believe that Isa is God's servant and messenger:

Isa (pbuh) is God's servant and messenger and all must believe in his prophethood and message to the Israelites. If one denies the prophethood of the Messiah, he/she is considered having committed blasphemy. Hence, among the reasons for the blasphemy of the Israelites is because they rejected Isa's calling.

God Says: {Say ye: "We believe in Allah, and the revelation given to us, and to Abraham, Ismaeel, Isaac, Jacob, and the Tribes, and that given to Moses and Jesus, and that given to (all) prophets from their Lord: We make no difference between one and another of them: And we bow to Allah (in Islam)"} (Surat al-Baqarah: 136).

God also informed Prophet Mohammad that He took from him his pledge as he did with prophets before him. God Says: {We took from the prophets their Covenant: As (We did) from thee: from Noah, Abraham, Moses, and Jesus the son of Mary: We took from them a solemn covenant} (Surat al-Ahzaab: 07).

This is what Prophet Mohammad called for. Al-Bukhari and Muslim reported that 'Ubadah bin al-Saamit heard the Prophet say: "Whoever testifies that there is no god but Allah, that God has no partners in rule, that Mohammad is God's servant and messenger, that Isa is God's servant and messenger and His Word which He bestowed upon Maryam and a Spirit from Him, that Paradise is a fact and that Hell is a fact, then God will grant him Paradise for whatever good deeds he has performed."[337]

336 "Al-Qasas al-Qur'ani: Presentation and Analysis of Events", Ibid, p.19.

337 "Al-Qasas al-Qur'ani: Presentation and Analysis of Events", Ibid, 4/286.

Believing in the prophethood of Isa (pbuh) must be according to the points mentioned in Prophet Mohammad's Hadeeth, i.e. that Isa is God's servant and messenger, God's Word which He bestowed upon Maryam and a Spirit from God which He created in Maryam's womb.[338]

2. Isa is the last link in the chain of prophets to the Israelites:

The Holy Qur'an has indicated many times that Isa has been sent to follow in the footsteps of other prophets sent before him to the Israelites.

God Says: {We gave Moses the Book and followed him up with a succession of messengers; We gave Jesus the son of Mary Clear (Signs) and strengthened him with the holy spirit} (Surat al-Baqarah: 87).

God says: {And in their footsteps We sent Jesus the son of Mary, confirming the Torah that had come before him} (Surat al-Maa'idah: 46).

God Says: {And We sent Noah and Abraham, and established in their bloodline Prophethood and Revelation: and some of them were on right guidance. But many of them became rebellious transgressors. Then, in their wake, We followed them up with (others of) Our messengers: We sent after them Jesus the son of Mary, and bestowed on him the Bible} (Surat al-Hadeed: 26-27).

So among the prophets that came after Nouh and Ibrahim were Mousa and Haroun who led to the arrival of Isa son of Maryam, who God provided with the Injeel and made him the last prophet to the Israelites. The only prophet sent after Isa (pbuh) was the final and concluding prophet for all mankind, i.e. Prophet Mohammad (pbuh).[339]

---

[338] Ibid.

[339] "Al-Qasas al-Qur'ani: Presentation and Analysis of Events", Ibid, 4/287.

Sixth: Isa's call to Monotheism (Tawheed):

Isa (pbuh) was sent as a prophet and messenger to the Israelites and called upon them to believe only in the One God, that Isa is God's prophet and messenger, that Isa is the son of Maryam and that he is a human being, not a god or son of one.

This was the gist of Prophet Isa's message and is the form of Nasraani monotheism he called for; his disciples believed in him on this basis and the Nasraanis who believed in the same followed in their footsteps.[340]

Since the prophethood of Isa was complementary to that of Mousa, it is only natural that it was based on Tawheed as true Nasraaniism concurs to the existence of only One God. Whatever contradicts with this is considered to deviate from the Messiah's true calling which the Holy Qur'an expressed.[341]

The purpose for which all prophets were sent to mankind had been to call on people to believe in the One God (Tawheed). It was also the main pillar in the calling of Isa (pbuh) as the Qur'an stated that his dogma was exactly that. Hence, only Allah is to be worshipped as He is the Creator of the Heavens and Earth and all that in between. This was pronounced by the Messiah (pbuh) as soon as he was born, and he was not the exception to the rule that was carried forth by the prophets who preceded him. Prophet Isa called on the Israelites to believe in the One God, and was reported by the Qur'an to say once he was born: {"I am indeed a servant of Allah. He hath given me revelation and made me a prophet"} (Surat Maryam: 30).

Prophet Isa's uttering of such words clearly indicates that the only entity worth worshipping is that of the One God; oth-

---

340 Ibid, 4/387.

341 Sireen Mohammad Sa'aeedi, "Fairness towards Islam by non-Muslims and People of the Book who embraced Islam and its Dogma and its Impact of Western Societies", al-Fath Publishing House, Amman, Jordan, 1st Ed., 2017, p.117.

erwise, Isa would not have confessed such a matter. While some people are under the illusion that Isa's speech means that God is One specific to Isa, the Qur'an has dispelled this and reported Prophet Isa's speech as: {Verily Allah is my Lord and your Lord: Him therefore serve ye: this is a Way that is straight} (Surat Maryam: 36).

The Holy Qur'an also emphasises that Isa (pbuh) would always repeat telling this truth to his mother's people. God says: {But said Christ: "O Children of Israel! worship Allah, my Lord and your Lord. Whoever joins other gods with Allah, Allah will forbid him Paradise, and the Fire will be his abode. There will for the wrong-doers be no one to help} (Surat al-Maa'idah: 72).

Sheikh Rasheed Rida's explanation of this holy verse is that Isa (pbuh) ordered them to wholly believe in the One God, called upon them to do so, warned them of being branded sacrilegious if they did not, and warned them of God's retribution if they, or any of God's other creations, joined partners with God in that He will forever forbid them from entering Paradise and that they will burn in Hell for all eternity.[342]

The following matters are evident from the holy verse, above:

- Isa is God's messenger to the Israelites.

- Isa called on them to worship God and warned them from joining others with Him, and that Heaven forbids unbelievers from entering it.

- Isa was sent to follow up on that which came in the Torah.

- God provided Isa with the Injeel (Bible), which contained mercy, wisdom and enlightenment.

- God provided Isa with proof of His existence and supported him through the Holy Spirit.

---

[342] Mohammad Rasheed Rida, "Tafseer al-Manar Tafseer al-Qur'an al-Kareem", Egyptian Public Book Commission, Cairo, 1990, 4/400.

- He showed the Israelites about some of which they had differed.

- He made permissible for them some of which that had been prohibited.

- He brought glad tidings of the arrival of Mohammad (pbuh).

Surat al-Baqarah states: (And We strengthened him with the Holy Spirit), meaning the angel Jibreel (pbuh), who God sent to support Isa (pbuh) in proving to the Israelites that God is One.[343]

Surat Aal-Imran states that God ordered Isa to: (make lawful to you part of what was (Before) forbidden to you). Surat al-Zukhruf states: (and in order to make clear to you some of the (points) on which ye dispute). Their disputes were on matters of their religion and life, so God explained to them their religion and the provisions of the Torah.[344]

1. Prophet Isa's humanity:

The Holy Qur'an gives undisputable evidence on Prophet Isa being human, not divine, and it expressed this to the greatest extent possible, as per the following:

a. God created Isa and Adam in the same manner:

God Says: {The similitude of Jesus before Allah is as that of Adam; He created him from dust, then said to him: "Be". And he was} (Surat Aal-Imran: 59).

The reason for the descending of the above verse was in response to a question posed by Najran's Nasraani emissaries who were arguing with Prophet Mohammad (pbuh) on the nature of Prophet Isa (pbuh). They had asked about Isa's father; so Prophet Mohammad was silent and gave no reply until God descended upon him 80+ verses of Surat Aal-Imran that included the verse,

343 Ahmad al-Ameeri, "Fiqh Da'awat al-Anbiyaa' fi al-Qur'an al-Kareem", al-Salam Printing & Publishing House, Cairo, 1st Ed., 2012, p.508.

344 "Fiqh Da'awat al-Anbiyaa' fi al-Qur'an al-Kareem", p.508.

above. Hence, He who created Adam without the presence of both parents is also able to create Isa without a father's seed. When God is able to create Adam from nothing, then His creation of Isa without only a father is much easier. Such are the facts, but people shall forever be doubtful of that which stares them in the face.[345]

It is true that the creation of Isa (pbuh) in modern day standards is a matter unfamiliar to people, but to what extent is it so outrageous a matter when compared to God's creation of Adam – the father of humanity?! The people who argue and contradict common sense about Prophet Isa's fatherless birth, and spin illusions and myths thereof, are the same people of the Book who concur that Adam was created from dust and that it was the breath from God's Spirit which brought Adam to life! Yet they have spun no illusions and myths about Adam's creation as they do about Prophet Isa's. They do not claim that Adam has a Divine nature despite the fact that the element through which he was created was the same one as that through which Isa was created. It was that element of God's breath in both Adam and Isa, coupled with the Word (Be) through which God creates everything!

Hence, the simplicity of this truth on the creation of Isa and all mankind becomes clear. It is accepted with all ease to the extent that one is amazed how there was any disagreement on this matter in the first place when it mirrors the natural course of life.

This is the language with which the Holy Qur'an speaks to mankind's basic instincts, i.e. through realistic logic about the most complex of matters and renders them easily embraced by all.[346]

b. Be Worshippers:

God Says: {It is not (possible) that a man, to whom is given the Book, and Wisdom, and the prophetic office, should say to

[345] "Tafseer Ibn Katheer", Ibid, 1/357.

[346] "Fi Thilaal al-Qur'an", Ibid, 1/205.

people: "Be ye my worshippers rather than Allah's": on the contrary (He would say) "Be ye worshippers of Him Who is truly the Cherisher of all: For ye have taught the Book and ye have studied it earnestly"} (Surat Aal-Imran: 79).

This verse came in response to Najran's Nasraani emissaries who claimed that Prophet Isa had ordered them to adopt him as a god. The word (worshippers) means that these Nasraanis should be educated scholars as they have persisted in studying and teaching the Book, and that they should not act as being oblivious to the truth He stated of prophet Isa's human nature.[347]

The holy verse also shows that a prophet is a servant and that only God is the Master worshipped by His subjects. So had Isa claimed to be of divine nature and deserving of being worshipped, he would not have said: ("Be ye worshippers of Him Who is truly the Cherisher of all").

The Arabic word in the holy verse for Worshippers, i.e. *Rabbaniyeen* originates from the word (Rabb) which means Master[348]. So its plural means those who are of God and who follow His orders. These are God's servants and subjects, and to Him only do they pray so that they may be deemed (worshippers).[349]

c. Do not be religiously excessive:

God Says: {O People of the Book! Commit no excesses in your religion: Nor say of Allah aught but the truth. Christ Jesus the son of Mary was (no more than) a messenger of Allah, and His Word, which He bestowed on Mary, and a spirit proceeding from Him: so believe in Allah and His messengers. Say not "Trinity": desist: it will be better for you: for Allah is one God. Glory be to Him: (far exalted is He) above having a son. To Him belong all things in the

---

[347] "Zaad al-Muyassar", 1/413. See also: "Tafseer Ibn Katheer", 1/385.

[348] Translator's addition

[349] "Fi Thilaal al-Qur'an", Ibid, 1/419.

heavens and on earth. And enough is Allah as a Disposer of affairs. Christ neither disdaineth nor to serve and worship Allah, nor do the angels, those nearest (to Allah: those who disdain His worship and are arrogant, He will gather them all together unto Himself to (answer)} (Surat al-Nisaa': 171-172).

These two holy verses are directed to Nasraanis of the Book, and in them, God orders Nasraanis to cease from being excessive and crossing their religion's redlines by claiming Isa to be of divine nature versus being Isa the son of Maryam. Isa was a man chosen to carry God's Message; he was created by God's Word (Be) and is from God's Spirit that was conveyed to his mother Maryam via the angel Jibreel (pbuh). After this segment, the Holy Qur'an corrects one of Nasraanis' most important dogmas, i.e. the Trinity.[350]

It is a historically proven fact that the Trinity was not a feature of early Nasraaniism. It seeped into Nasraaniism over varied historical phases along with pagans who embraced it. As ancient paganism had not yet been fully extracted from the beliefs of these new Nasraanis, such as in the existence of multiple gods, the Trinity became a by-product thereof.[351]

The Trinity continues to be a shocking concept to many educated Nasraanis, and church clergy toil to bring them to terms with it through all possible means, including claiming it as one of the unseen matters whose secrets will only be revealed on Judgment Day.[352]

The Trinity is truly a matter that the brain cannot accept, yet Nasraanis attempt to prove that it supersedes it. They say that The Almighty is of a triple nature yet one! That He is three "entities" who share the same nature and status yet who are of one

350 "Fiqh Da'awat al-Anbiyaa' fi al-Qur'an al-Kareem", Ibid, p.477.
351 Ibid.
352 "Fi Thilaal al-Qur'an", 2/815-818.

undividable united self! At the same time, they claim that the son god resulted from the father god and of them came the holy spirit.[353]

The holy verses clarify the truth about God's Singularity where the Divinity of the Creator denotes the servitude of His creations. Isa (pbuh) is accordingly not the son of God, he himself did not claim to be as such nor did he deem himself of a higher order than The Almighty. Isa (pbuh) is the servant of God as are God's close angels and of His other creations. Those who claim otherwise in arrogance shall be hold accountable by The Almighty for such blasphemy.[354]

People of the Book's excessiveness of religion and of crossing boundaries are what cause them to say that which is unbecoming of God. It is because of these that they claim He has a son and that He is divided into three. The notions of prophethood and the trinity have developed within them as per thought's fluctuating decadence, yet as instinct cannot accept a child to be one of God, they were forced to state that the One God embodies three as His traits according to different states. Then when such explanation is not accepted by human intellect, they decree it as a matter of things unseen that will only be unveiled on Judgment Day. But God is more Supreme to have partners as per the holy verse: {Allah is One God. Glory be to Him: (far exalted is He) above having a son. To Him belong all things in the heavens and on earth} (Surat al-Nisaa': 171).

The fact that Prophet Isa was born without the presence of a father is a mindboggling matter to mankind as it contradicts with that which is familiar to humans. But this is not all that exists in the universe as God's Will is boundless and whatever He deems shall be. Of the Messiah (pbuh), God Says: {Christ Jesus the son

353 Ibid, 2/817.

354 Ibid, 2/818.

of Mary was (no more than) a messenger of Allah, and His Word, which He bestowed on Mary, and a spirit proceeding from Him} (Surat al-Nisaa': 171).

- Isa was specifically (God's Messenger) as were all other prophets like Nouh, Ibrahim, Mousa and Mohammad (pbut).

- (And His Word, which He bestowed on Mary): That God ordered the creation of Isa via His Words (Be and it so Was), as mentioned in many other instance in the Qur'an.

God bestowed this Word on Maryam and it subsequently created Isa within her without the seed of a father. The Word that creates everything from nothingness can very easily create Prophet Isa in his mother's womb via (A spirit from Him).

God created Adam from clay by breathing from His Spirit into it and he became a man.

God Says: {Behold, thy Lord said to the angels: "I am about to create man from clay: When I have fashioned him (in due proportion) and breathed into him of My spirit, fall ye down in obeisance unto him"} (Surat Saad: 71-72).

The Spirit in Adam here is the same Spirit in Isa there.

Despite believing in Adam's story and of God's breathing from His Spirit into him, no people of the Book have stated that Adam was a god or part therefrom. Yet they say this about Prophet Isa despite the fact that the creation of both men was via the same manner.[355] Even more so, Adam was created without the presence of any parent or womb while Isa was created with the presence of a mother.

God Says: {The similitude of Jesus before Allah is as that of Adam; He created him from dust, then said to him: "Be". And he was} (Surat Aal-Imran: 59).

---

[355] "Fi Thilaal al-Qur'an", Ibid, 2/817.

The human mind can also conceptualise such a matter and attest to that the God cannot have the same composition as His creations, nor three in one or one in three. Birth is the prelude towards mortality and the attempt towards continued lineage. But God is not so as He is immortal and is the Owner of all that exists, which He created, in the Heavens and on Earth.

- (To Him belong all things in the heavens and on earth):

It suffices that humans connect to God as do subjects towards their Creator as God cares for all mankind without the need for any to assume they are closer to Him through an alleged son of His from among a certain group of them.

- (And enough is Allah as a Disposer of affairs):

The Qur'an states the truth and adds to it the sense of relief as people realise that God caters to their needs.

The Qur'an also corrects the beliefs of Nasraanis and any beliefs of other peoples who claim that the angels are also prophets. God Says: {Christ disdaineth nor to serve and worship Allah, nor do the angels, those nearest (to Allah) those who disdain His worship and are arrogant, He will gather them all together unto Himself to (answer). But to those who believe and do deeds of righteousness, He will give their (due) rewards, and more, out of His bounty: But those who are disdainful and arrogant, He will punish with a grievous penalty; Nor will they find, besides Allah, any to protect or help them} (Surat al-Nisaa': 172-173).

All prophets and messengers of God, including Isa, catered to the determination that God is but One, none is like Him, and none shares any of His qualities or specificities.

This is a truth that all messengers carried forward from Nouh till God's concluding prophet, Mohammad (pbut). Every messenger would say (O' people, worship Allah for He is the only God). Strange enough though, followers of divine religions concur with this firm truth yet some of them claim God to have fathered males and females, or that He had mated with one of His creations as pagans of the times of ignorance believed.[356]

Mankind's emotions will remain turbulent until they ascertain the true connection between them and their God as one in which they are his servants and He their Master; that they are creations and He is the Creator; that all are equal in such status and none are His children or mates. Mankind will only be at peace when piety and good deeds are his path towards redemption; a matter at hand for all who try to do so.

People will be at ease only when they are certain of the truth that they are all servants of One God and that their closeness to Him is dependant upon the piety of each towards Him. Only then will there be equality among mankind.[357]

Islam provides mankind with a new life that frees people from worshipping mortals to that of worshipping the God of all mortals. Islam never witnessed the establishment of a church that demeans mankind by claiming to be the representative of His alleged son or of other entities that draw their authority from that of the claimed son.

Islam has also never witnessed the establishment of a sacred authority that rules and legislates with divine right on the premise that such right to do so is delegated to it by God. Yet the Church has claimed its sacred right of representation on the one hand, and emperors have claimed a similarly equal right.

These so-called *rights* remained rampant in Europe in the name of the son or the Trinity until Crusaders raided the land of Islam, and when they returned home, they took with them the seed of revolting against the Sacred Right. Later came along the so-called reformist revolts that were influenced by Islam such as those of

[356] "Fi Thilaal al-Qur'an", Ibid, 2/818.

[357] "Fi Thilaal al-Qur'an", Ibid, 2/819.

Martin Luther, Calvin and Zingly which denounced the divinity of Man and his alleged delegation to rule. In Islam, the only the ideology that exists is that there is only One God – the Master to be worshipped – and His servants who must worship Him.

The Holy Qur'an provides mankind with the final word on the alleged divinity of Isa (pbuh), his prophethood, the alleged divinity of the Holy Spirit as part of the Trinity, the claim that God has fathered a child and on the claim of God having partners. The Qur'an rules that Isa the son of Maryam is God's servant; that Isa did not forfeit being God's servant; that the angels are God's servants; that all of God's creations will be gathered in His presence on Judgment Day; that those who reject being God's servants shall be severely punished by The Almighty and that those who acknowledge their servitude to The Almighty shall be rewarded immensely[358].

God Says: {Christ disdaineth nor to serve and worship Allah, nor do the angels, those nearest to Allah: those who disdain His worship and are arrogant, He will gather them all together unto Himself to (answer). But to those who believe and do deeds of righteousness, He will give their (due) rewards, and more, out of His bounty: But those who are disdainful and arrogant, He will punish with a grievous penalty; Nor will they find, besides Allah, any to protect or help them} (Surat al-Nisaa': 172-173).

Prophet Isa would never have considered himself more than a servant of God as he was a prophet and messenger of The Almighty and who truly knew the truth about Divinity and servitude being two different and non-merging states. He is the one who knows best that he is but a creation of God and cannot have God's same characteristics. He is also the one who knows best that servitude is to God and that it is only rejected by those who do not believe in creation.

---

358 Ibid.

It is also the status which God describes His messengers, the angels, the Holy Spirit Jibreel, Isa and all other prophets (pbut). Yet a group following the Messiah accept for him that which he rejects for himself.

- (Those who disdain His worship and are arrogant, He will gather them all together unto Himself to answer):

Their disdain and arrogance does not save them from being gathered in God's presence through His Might and Supremacy over mankind as shall those who accept their servitude to God and who surrender to His Will and who shall accordingly be rewarded.[359]

- (But those who are disdainful and arrogant, He will punish with a grievous penalty; Nor will they find, besides Allah, any to protect or help them):

God does not want His servants to express His Greatness and worship Him alone because He needs this, for it neither adds to nor diminishes His supremacy; rather, God wishes that mankind know the truth about divinity and servitude so that their lives may be at ease. Such life can only be attained through this knowledge and the responsibilities it entails.

God wishes that this truth is set in the minds and hearts of mankind so that they may worship Him and not their fellow men. He wishes that they know who is the Master of the universe so that they may succumb to His Will only and raise their foreheads to all except Him. God wants mankind to realise that being close to Him cannot be attained through kinship as is the case in this world we live and mankind's earthly dealings through nepotism and favouritism. Closeness to God can only be attained through piety and righteousness that would build up and populate the Earth.

[359] "Fi Thilaal al-Qur'an", Ibid, 2/820.

All of this is a sum of goodness, dignity, freedom, justice and righteousness that is added to the balance of mankind on Earth and through which they can enjoy a good life. As for that which God rewards these pious men and women with in the Afterlife, it is considered an act of generosity on God's behalf.

Accordingly, we must view belief in God through the bright image that Islam brought forth and which it ordained as the stepping stone for the calling of all messengers, before being reworded by followers and distorted by the generations, as a new birth of mankind. It is one in which exists dignity, freedom, justice, righteousness and an end to worshipping mankind.

Those who shy away from worshipping only God are slaves of all Earthly matters like whims, lusts, myths and other people whose laws, provisions, values and scales of justice they follow blindly when all are equal in front of God. Yet these deceived ones deem their fellow men as gods while on this land. But on Judgment Day (He will punish with a grievous penalty; Nor will they find, besides Allah, any to protect or help them).

This is the grand matter which the holy verse presents to counter Nasraanis deviation during that time in the face of all other deviations throughout time.[360]

2. God is not the Messiah nor is He the third of three:

God Says: {They do blaspheme who say: "(Allah) is Christ the son of Mary." But said Christ: "O Children of Israel! worship Allah, my Lord and your Lord. Whoever joins other gods with Allah, Allah will forbid him the garden, and the Fire will be his abode. There will for the wrong-doers be no one to help. They do blaspheme who say: Allah is one of three in a Trinity: for there is no god except One Allah. If they desist not from their word (of blasphemy), verily a grievous penalty will befall the blasphemers

[360] "Fi Thilaal al-Qur'an", Ibid, 2/936.

among them. Why turn they not to Allah, and seek His forgiveness? For Allah is Oft forgiving, Most Merciful. Christ the son of Mary was no more than a messenger; many were the messengers that passed away before him. His mother was a woman of truth. They had both to eat their (daily) food. See how Allah doth make His signs clear to them; yet see in what ways they are deluded away from the truth! Say: "Will ye worship, besides Allah, something which hath no power either to harm or benefit you? But Allah, He it is that heareth and knoweth all things." Say: "O people of the Book! exceed not in your religion the bounds (of what is proper), trespassing beyond the truth, nor follow the vain desires of people who went wrong in times gone by, who misled many, and strayed (themselves) from the even way} (Surat al-Maa'idah: 72-77).

Many deviations originating from church councils have encroached upon the Nasraaniism which Prophet Isa (pbuh) brought forward, that have adversely influenced the notion of God being but One. The message of Isa echoed those brought forward by all messengers of God before him.

The following is a summary of these councils' conclusions regarding the Trinity, Isa's divinity and the disagreement among them thereafter:

- In the book entitled, "*Sawsanat Suleiman*" by Nomil bin Ni'amah bin Jirjis al-Nasraani, the author states that the dogma of Nasraanis which no church contests – which is the basis of the constitution expressed by the Nicaean Council – is believing in one god: one who controls all; creator of the heavens and earth; all seen and unseen matters; and in one lord and master being Christ, the only son born of the father since eternity of god's light a god of righteousness of the righteous god born and not created, equal to the father in essence which through it all came to be, and who for us humans, and for our sins, has descended from the sky and was embodied in the form of the holy spirit, and from the virgin Mary he took traits, and requested on our behalf during the reign of Pilatus, and who was hurt and buried, then resurrected of the third day as mentioned in the books and ascended to the sky, and sat at the right hand of the lord, and who will gloriously return to judge the living and the dead, and whose reign shall not perish; believing in the holy spirit, the resurrecting god originating from the father who together with the son people prostate to and glorify; the one speaking for prophets. In "*The History of the Bible*", Dr Post states that the nature of god is three equal and coeternal hypostases, i.e. God the Father, God the Son and God the Holy Spirit; to the Father belongs creation through the Son, and to the Son belongs sacrifice, and to the Holy Spirit belongs purification[361].

Due to the difficulty in conceptualising the three hypostases in one and the combining between Unitarianism and the Trinity, Nasraani theology writers have attempted to delay the intellectual understanding of this matter, which the mind rejects anyhow. The thesis entitled, "Al-Usoul and Al-Furoo'a" by Reverend Potter states, "Our understanding of this is limited by the capacity of our minds, and we hope to understand it more clearly in the future when that veil of all that is on Earth and in the heavens is removed. But for now, that which we have understood thus far suffices.[362]"

The Almighty God Says that all such claims are blasphemous as they assume Isa's divinity and that God is one of three.

- God Says: {They do blaspheme who say: "(Allah) is Christ the son of Mary." But said Christ: "O Children of Israel! worship Allah, my Lord and your Lord." Whoever joins other gods with Allah, Allah will forbid him the garden, and the Fire will be his abode. There will for the wrong-doers be no one to help. They do blaspheme who say: Allah is one of three in a Trinity: for there is

361 "Fi Thilaal al-Qur'an", Ibid, 2/944.

362 Ibid.

no god except One Allah. If they desist not from their word (of blasphemy), verily a grievous penalty will befall the blasphemers among them. Why turn they not to Allah, and seek His forgiveness? For Allah is Oft-forgiving, Most Merciful} (Surat al-Maa'idah: 72-74).

This was what Isa (pbuh) warned them from falling into, yet without avail – after God raised him to the Heavens – and which he told them would forbid them from attaining Paradise. But they forgot that which Isa told them (O' children of Israel worship Allah, my God and yours).

The Holy Qur'an refutes their blasphemous statements (They do blaspheme who say: Allah is one of three in a Trinity) and states the truth upon which every creed brought forth by any of God's messengers determines, i.e. that of: (There is no god except One Allah).

God also promises punishment to those who blaspheme in speech and belief (If they desist not from their word (of blasphemy), verily a grievous penalty will befall the blasphemers among them).

After warning and threatening those, God encourages them to change their ways (Why turn they not to Allah, and seek His forgiveness? For Allah is Oft-forgiving, Most Merciful). God Says this so that the doors of repenting remain open for them to seek His forgiveness before it is too late. God then confronts them with realistically sound logic that would revert their instinct towards coherent awareness while also stating bewilderment of their affairs when they deviate from such clarity and explanation.[363]

- {Christ the son of Mary was no more than a messenger; many were the messengers that passed away before him. His mother was a woman of truth. They had both to eat their (daily) food. See how

363 "Fi Thilaal al-Qur'an", Ibid, 2/945.

Allah doth make His signs clear to them; yet see in what ways they are deluded away from the truth!} (Surat al-Maa'idah: 75).

- (Christ the son of Mary was no more than a messenger): To counter the Jews' questioning of his message, and the Nasraanis' claim of Isa being a god.

- (His mother was a woman of truth): To counter those who claimed she had committed debauchery for she was pure, pious and ever worshipping. Also, Isa was born and had a mother; hence how may one who is born be a god?

- (They had both to eat their (daily) food): This is an undeniable tangible physical piece of evidence that he was human in need of food. One in need of food cannot be a god.[364]

The consumption of food was a factual matter in the lives of Isa and his mother, which is a trait of the living and evidence of the pair's humanity. The consumption of food is done to sustain the body's needs so as to sustain its durability; such a need is of humans, not gods. The Almighty Allah is alive within His own, existing within His own, remaining within His own and is in need of nothing. Nothing, such as food, enters God's self nor exits it.

As this logic is undeniable and unquestionable to any human, God decries their decision to disregard it: (See how Allah doth make His signs clear to them; yet see in what ways they are deluded away from the truth!).

This factual human life of Isa (pbuh) was a source of anguish for those who sought to claim him as a god – despite his teachings – as it required much arguing and disagreement among them as to his humanity or divinity.

- {Say: "Will ye worship, besides Allah, that which hath no power either to harm or benefit you? But Allah, He it is that heareth and knoweth all things"} (Surat al-Maa'idah: 76).

[364] "Fiqh Da'awat al-Anbiyaa' fi al-Qur'an al-Kareem", Ibid, p.479.

The choice of the words (that which) instead of (who) is to mean all worshipped creations, including mankind, all in one. Hence, Prophet Isa, his mother Maryam and the Holy Spirit are all included herein and are all unworthy of being worshipped for none of them is God and can neither benefit nor harm others.

(But Allah, He it is that heareth and knoweth all things): God hears all and knows all; He provides goodness and withholds it when He Wills; He hears the supplication and worship of His servants; He knows that which their souls conceal. But all others cannot hear all, know all or answer all prayers.

- {Say: "O people of the Book! exceed not in your religion the bounds (of what is proper), trespassing beyond the truth, nor follow the vain desires of people who went wrong in times gone by, who misled many, and strayed (themselves) from the even way} (Surat al-Maa'idah: 77).

In the above verse, God directs Prophet Mohammad (pbuh) to call on people of the Book not to glorify Prophet Isa (pbuh) or claim his divinity. Doing so has been the source of all deviations in Christianity; that and the inclinations of pagan Roman rulers who later embraced Nasraaniism. This led to the distortion of the call brought forth by Isa, and hence God Says: {"O Children of Israel! worship Allah, my Lord and your Lord." Whoever joins other gods with Allah, Allah will forbid him the garden, and the Fire will be his abode. There will for the wrong-doers be no one to help} (Surat al-Maa'idah: 72).

This new call is one meant to save people of the Book so that they may cease from deviation, whims and desires which caused those before them to be led astray.[365]

The Messiah (pbuh) is God's servant, messenger, creation and was manifested through God's Word "Be". The Messiah and the

[365] "Fi Thilaal al-Qur'an", Ibid, 2/946.

angels never pronounced themselves as any other than God's servants. How could the Messiah then be a god when he was a created servant of The Almighty and who is bound to God's Ability, Will and Authority?!

God Says: {In blasphemy indeed are those that say that Allah is Christ the son of Mary. Say: "Who then hath the least power against Allah, if His will were to destroy Christ the son of Mary, his mother, and all everyone that is on the earth? For to Allah belongeth the dominion of the heavens and the earth, and all that is between. He createth what He pleaseth. For Allah hath power over all things"} (Surat al-Maa'idah: 17).

3. Prophets Dawoud and Isa damn Israelite blasphemers:

God Says: {Curses were pronounced on those among the Children of Israel who rejected Faith, by the tongue of David and of Jesus the son of Mary: because they disobeyed and persisted in excesses. Nor did they (usually) forbid one another the iniquities which they committed: evil indeed were the deeds which they did. Thou seest many of them turning in friendship to the Unbelievers. Evil indeed are (the works) which their souls have sent forward before them (with the result), that Allah's wrath is on them, and in torment will they abide. If only they had believed in Allah, in the Messenger, and in what hath been revealed to him, never would they have taken them for friends and protectors, but most of them are rebellious wrong-doers} (Surat al-Maa'idah: 78-81).

This has been the stance of all prophets that God sent to the children of Israel throughout history. Prophets Dawoud and Isa damned them and God responded to the prayers of His prophets. The children of Israel were insolent, transgressing on the rights of others, socially immoral, allowed wrongdoing and followed in the footsteps of nonbelievers, and accordingly, God decreed they live in endless torture. Thus, it seems that the history of the children of

Israel's damnation – being blaspheming and disobedient – is ancient and that the same prophets who were sent to guide them towards the path of righteousness had themselves damned them too.

- (because they disobeyed and persisted in excesses):

The Holy Qur'an lists many examples on the disobedience and transgression of Israelites as a group, not just on the individual level.

- (Nor did they (usually) forbid one another the iniquities which they committed: evil indeed were the deeds which they did):

Disobedience and aggression may occur in any society where evil people, corruptors or deviant ones reside, yet it is the nature of a righteous society to deter evil and wrongdoing from becoming the norm. When doing evil becomes more difficult than that of good, punishment of evil rendered a deterrent and the majority committing to holding wrongdoers accountable, is when evil will recede and become limited to individuals or groups that society will condemn and hold accountable.[366]

The Holy Qur'an shows the danger of following those who blaspheme through the holy verses: (Thou seest many of them turning in friendship to the Unbelievers. Evil indeed are (the works) which their souls have sent forward before them (with the result), that Allah's wrath is on them, and in torment will they abide. If only they had believed in Allah, in the Messenger, and in what hath been revealed to him, never would they have taken them for friends and protectors, but most of them are rebellious wrong-doers) (Surat al-Maa'idah: 80-81).

4. Allah is far more supreme than to have a son or partner:

- God Says: {No son did Allah beget, nor is there any god along with Him: (if there were many gods), behold, each god would

[366] "Fi Thilaal al-Qur'an", Ibid, 2/948.

have taken away what he had created, and some would have lorded it over others! Glory to Allah. (He is free) from the (sort of) things they attribute to Him! He knows what is hidden and what is open: too high is He for the partners they attribute to Him!} (Surat al-Mu'minoun: 91-92).

Had it been meant to exist more than one god, each would be possessive and tyrannical towards that which he has created and the possessions of each would have been distinct from the other. Then each would quarrel with the rest, and henceforth. This would not contribute towards the universe's cohesiveness – a matter that is contrary to that which exists now. Hence, Allah is The One God who has no partners.[367]

- God Says: {To Him is due the primal origin of the heavens and the earth:(930) How can He have a son when He hath no consort? He created all things, and He hath full knowledge of all things} (Surat al-An'aam: 101).

What need for a son could He Who creates all in this universe from nothingness have?

Mankind are either an extension of the mortal or an aid for the weak. Reproduction is a rule that mandates the presence of a male and a female of equal standing. Hence, how may The Almighty – who is unlike any other – have an equal through which a son is produced? How may there be offspring without intercourse?

A creation can never be partner of the Creator; a truth that speaks to people's understanding and intellect.

He Who is worshipped and obeyed is the Creator of all. God says: {That is Allah, your Lord! there is no god but He, the Creator of all things: then worship ye Him: and He hath power to dispose of all affairs} (Surat al-An'aam: 102).

[367] Omar Ahmad Omar, "Risalat al-Anbiyaa' min Shu'aayb ila Issa", al-Hikmah Printing, Publishing & Distribution House, Cairo, 1997, 2/285.

- God Says: {He to whom belongs the dominion of the heavens and the earth: no son has He begotten, nor has He a partner in His dominion: it is He who created all things, and ordered them in due proportions} (Surat al-Furqan: 2).

God created mankind in their current form so that they may carry out their duties and affairs in both religion and daily life. God designated that each of His creations remains till a time He has determined, and that mankind may have offspring so that life may continue till He decides to end it. It is God who is Omnipresent and immortal and all others obey Him and concur to His Singularity.[368]

God Says: {They say: "(Allah) hath begotten a son": Glory be to Him. Nay, to Him belongs all that is in the heavens and on earth: everything renders worship to Him. To Him is due the primal origin of the heavens and the earth: When He decreeth a matter, He saith to it: "Be," and it is} (Surat al-Baqarah: 116-117).

How can it be that He who has the traits of creating as He wishes, of formulating the heavens and Earth without obstruction or limitation, have a child of His own? It was He, The Almighty, Who was able to create Prophet Isa (pbuh) without the presence of a father![369]

God Says: {They say: "Allah Most Gracious has begotten a son! Indeed ye have put forth a thing most monstrous! At it the skies are ready to burst, the earth to split asunder, and the mountains to fall down in utter ruin, That they should invoke a son for Allah Most Gracious. For it is not consonant with the majesty of Allah Most Gracious that He should beget a son. Not one of the beings in the heavens and the earth but must come to Allah Most Gracious as a servant. He does take an account of them (all), and

[368] "Risalat al-Anbiyaa' min Shu'aayb ila Issa", Ibid, 2/286.

[369] Ibid.

hath numbered them (all) exactly. And everyone of them will come to Him singly on the Day of Judgment} (Surat Maryam: 88-95).

Similar to when a person feels shattered due to injustice that has befallen him/her and a sense of having lost dignity and pride, so does The Almighty state that the heavens, Earth and mountains shudder at (Their claim that God has begotten a boy). God reports the tremor that shook the entire universe due to such false claim and states that those who have claimed so have committed a horrible matter: (Indeed ye have put forth a thing most monstrous! At it the skies are ready to burst, the earth to split asunder, and the mountains to fall down in utter ruin, That they should invoke a son for Allah Most Gracious. For it is not consonant with the majesty of Allah Most Gracious that He should beget a son). Then God issues the standing fact that (Not one of the beings in the heavens and the earth but must come to Allah Most Gracious as a servant. He does take an account of them (all), and hath numbered them (all) exactly. And everyone of them will come to Him singly on the Day of Judgment).

Allah, The All-Knowing, neither needs company, love nor supporters to sustain Him as He is void of such needs due to His Singularity and Might. Yet for those who beseech Him and yearn for His Grace, God Says (On those who believe and work deeds of righteousness, will Allah Most Gracious bestow love).[370]

- God Says: {They say: "Allah hath begotten a son!" Glory be to Him! He is self- sufficient! His are all things in the heavens and on earth! No warrant have ye for this! say ye about Allah what ye know not? Say: "Those who invent a lie against Allah will never prosper." A little enjoyment in this world!- and then, to Us will be their return, then shall We make them taste the severest penalty for their blasphemies} (Surat Yunus: 68-70).

[370] "Fi Thilaal al-Qur'an", Ibid, 3/2321.

The idea that God, The Almighty, had begotten a son is a naïve one emanating from a lack of vision that fails to realise the massive difference between the immortal Godly nature and that of the mortal human creation. It is actually the continuity of mankind through offspring that attests to mankind's shortcomings as this in no way constitutes anything equal to the immortality of the One God.

The only fact for mankind in their lives is death; hence, mankind's offspring are their only means for continuity as we humans get old and frail, and it is our offspring who care for us when we cannot for they are young and strong and through them life perseveres.

But God is Superior to these needs as He neither gets old nor dies. He is in no need of our human urges like continuity through offspring, aid in old age, support, money or any of the like.

God then responds to the claim that (He has begotten a son) by stating that (He is the One of all richness and Owner of all that is on the Earth). He is Owner of all that in the entire universe and is in no need for a son to assist Him in attaining it.

The Holy Qur'an does not delve into theoretical arguing regarding the difference between human and Divine natures, as we see in the writings of philosophers, because the Qur'an speaks to mankind's primal nature. In addition, such philosophers have no physical proof supporting their claims and (They speak of God that of which they possess no proof).

Speaking of a matter without factual knowledge of it is considered a detriment, and more so when it is of a matter concerning The Almighty.

Many priests have throughout time misinterpreted the relationship between the Creator and His subjects. The Church, as well, has created itself as an authority through pagan notions about this relationship and has instated itself as God's proxy and mediary on Earth. This deviant understanding originates from the false pagan claims that the angels were God's daughters, Prophet Isa (pbuh) was the son of God, the tale of sin from which came forth the matter of Confession, and so on and so forth. All the animosity that had and continues to occur between the Church on the one hand and intellectuals and scientists on the other has led to society's rejection of the Church's grip by shrugging off religion itself. And that which is prevalent on Earth nowadays is an episode of wrongful envisaging of the relationship between God and His creations which continues to put humanity at large in harm's way.

But Islam has been keen on clarifying the relationship between mankind and God fully and unambiguously for God is an Immortal Creator, who needs no son, that the relationship between Him and mankind is one of Creator and creations, that the universe and life on it are bound by fixed rules and that whoever heeds them shall be victorious and whoever does not shall stray and lose.

(Say: "Those who invent a lie against Allah will never prosper"):

True prosperity and success is that which originates from heeding God's orders which advocate goodness, human development, social success, enrichment of life and advancing it. It is physical production in destroying human values as we slump into animalistic pitfalls as these are merely temporary successes that deviate from the path of righteousness that guarantees mankind a better life.

(A little enjoyment in this world!- and then, to Us will be their return, then shall We make them taste the severest penalty for their blasphemies):

Enjoyment that is short and disconnected as it is not joined by the aspiration for an Afterlife in Paradise. It is also followed by (Severe punishment) for deviating from God's universal laws.[371]

[371] "Fi Thilaal al-Qur'an", Ibid, 3/1807.

- God Says: {The Jews call 'Uzair a son of Allah, and the Christians call Christ the son of Allah. That is a saying from their mouth; (in this) they but imitate what the unbelievers of old used to say. Allah's curse be on them: how they are deluded away from the Truth! They take their priests and their anchorites to be their lords in derogation of Allah, and (they take as their Lord) Christ the son of Mary; yet they were commanded to worship but One Allah. there is no god but He. Praise and glory to Him: (Far is He) from having the partners they associate (with Him)} (Surat al-Tawbah: 30-31).

(The Jews call 'Uzair a son of Allah): A group of the Jews said this, not their majority and is an indication to their malice and evil which encroaches on God's right and aims to diminish His Greatness.

It has been said that the reason they claimed 'Uzair to be the son of God was that he had preserved the Torah when kings shattered the dominion of the sons of Israel and killed all keepers of the Torah they could find. But they found 'Uzair had memorised it and he dictated it to them, hence attributing to him a heinous claim as being the son of God. Nasraanis have also claimed Isa son of Maryam as the son of God, and God states that such a claim was merely one of words without supporting proof. These Nasraanis were merely echoing olden claims that the angels were female and hence God sent His wrath upon those people.

Although it is unbecoming of a large nation to agree on a matter that is negated by sound thinking and common sense, they did so because they took their priests and hermits as gods beyond The Almighty and followed the lies they spewed. They would permit for their followers that which God has prohibited and vice versa, and the subjects would follow in their priests footsteps.

They also deemed the Messiah son of Maryam as a god beyond The One God and hence went against that which God had ordered them to do: (They were ordered not to worship except one God who has no other). But they reneged on this order and ascribed to Him traits that contradict with His Holy Perfection.[372]

But when they realised they had no proof to that which they claimed, and that they were merely unproven words, God Says (They wish to put out the light of God through their mouths). Those Jews and Nasraanis, and their likes, receive God's answer that: (Allah rejects that His light not be shone). It is Light that all mankind cannot put out even if they toil to do so together. God then adds that His Light shall shine on forever (even if nonbelievers hate that it be so).

God then reveals this Light which He has committed to completing and preserving through: (It is He who sent forth His prophet with guidance), i.e. beneficial knowledge and the (religion of righteousness) through the ushering of Mohammad (pbuh) as prophet and messenger. It is this religion that calls to goodness, righteousness, the singularity of God, good manners, good deeds, useful ethics and the prohibition of all ills that infest the heart of man.

God sent Mohammad (pbuh) with guidance and with the religion of righteousness so that (it would be supreme to all other religions even if nonbelievers hate so) through proof and sword despite the conniving of unbelievers as the promise of God shall be done.[373]

Duty mandates that we worship only one God, follow His Laws, fulfil that which is in His Book, receive from Him values and rules, envisage creation and its rightful truths and worship Him in a manner that is neither extreme nor radical. We should

[372] "Tafseer al-Sa'adi Tayseer al-Kareem al-Rahman fi Tafseer Kalam al-Mannaan", Ibid, 2/648.

[373] "Tafseer al-Sa'adi Tayseer al-Kareem al-Rahman fi Tafseer Kalam al-Mannaan", Ibid, 2/649.

also not go beyond the truth of Isa (pbuh) and ascribe to him that which is not of him. The Qur'an attributed Isa to his mother in 23 instances and determined him to be a man, not a god, born of a woman. He is human, of a human, a messenger of God, not His son and of human not divine nature.[374]

5. God's Great Inquisition of Isa (pbuh) on Judgment Day:

God Says: {And behold! Allah will say: "O Jesus the son of Mary! Didst thou say unto men, worship me and my mother as gods in derogation of Allah?" He will say: "Glory to Thee! never could I say what I had no right (to say). Had I said such a thing, thou wouldst indeed have known it. Thou knowest what is in my heart, Thou I know not what is in Thine. For Thou knowest in full all that is hidden. Never said I to them aught except what Thou didst command me to say, to wit, ´worship Allah, my Lord and your Lord´; and I was a witness over them whilst I dwelt amongst them; when Thou didst take me up Thou wast the Watcher over them, and Thou art a witness to all things. If Thou dost punish them, they are Thy servants: If Thou dost forgive them, Thou art the Exalted in power, the Wise." Allah will say: "This is a day on which the truthful will profit from their truth: theirs are gardens, with rivers flowing beneath, their eternal Home: Allah well-pleased with them, and they with Allah. That is the great salvation, (the fulfilment of all desires). To Allah doth belong the dominion of the heavens and the earth, and all that is therein, and it is He Who hath power over all things} (Surat al-Maa'idah: 116-120).

God knows what Isa said to his people, yet it is the great inquisition on the most feared day. The answers provided by Prophet Isa on that day will strike yet more fear, of the looming punishment, into the hearts of those who ascribed to him that which is

[374] "Risalat al-Anbiyaa' min Shu'aayb ila Issa", Ibid, 2/294.

unbecoming of this honest and righteous servant of God – being man not god.

Such a question would strike horror in the heart of even the strongest of mankind, but to the honest Isa, it will shake him to the very core for he had lived his life for his God in all honesty. Hence, Isa (pbuh) begins his answer with bestowing grace upon The Almighty:[375]

- (He says Glory to Thee): This is Isa (pbuh) exonerating himself of such a blasphemous act. Being so, it is unbecoming of him to have ordered any of his followers to consider him a god.[376]

- (Never could I say what I had no right (to say)): Prophet Isa hurries to completely exonerate himself of such a claim.

- (Had I said such a thing, thou wouldst indeed have known it. Thou knowest what is in my heart, Thou I know not what is in Thine. For Thou knowest in full all that is hidden): The Almighty God who Isa (pbuh) worships has Complete Knowledge of:

- All that lies in the heavens and on Earth.

- All that is within Earth, on it and at sea.

- All evident matters and those of the unforeseen.

- All that lies within the heart of man.

- All that is borne in the womb of every female.

- All matters prior to their occurrence.

- All conditions of His servants: the pious, the sacrilegious, the rich, the poor, etc.

- All secrets within, between and among people.

- All laws He bestows upon His prophets and that which leads to the righteousness of His servants in life and the afterlife.

---

375 "Fi Thilaal al-Qur'an", Ibid, 2/547.

376 Ibrahim Zeid al-Kilani, "Islamic Nation's Civil Qualities as per Surat al-Maa'idah", Preservation of Holy Qur'an Society, Jordan, 1st Ed., 2004, p.187.

All knowledge God has granted mankind of earthly and religious matters is limited to man's ability to comprehend and learn it.

But to God is the knowledge of all unseen matters. He knows that which had occurred, that which will occur and that which were to have occurred but did not.[377]

Prophet Isa (pbuh) infers such matters when he says (For Thou knowest in full all that is hidden).

Prophet Isa then states the truth: (Never said I to them aught except what Thou didst command me to say, to wit, ´worship Allah, my Lord and your Lord´):

"I, Isa, am a servant of Thee and I only commanded them to worship Thee. I did not command them to worship me and my mother as gods beyond Thee. I stated to them that I am a servant of Thee and that Thou are my God as Thou are theirs."

- (And I was a witness over them whilst I dwelt amongst them; when Thou didst take me up Thou wast the Watcher over them, and Thou art a witness to all things):

(When Thou didst take me up Thou wast the Watcher over them): "You knew of that which lay in their hearts and souls (And Thou are capable of all) of knowledge, hearing and seeing. Your knowledge encompasses all information; Your hearing encompasses all words, your sight all visible matters for You weigh the goodness of Your servants through that which You know of evil or goodness that lies within them."

The holy phrase (Thou wast Watcher over them) is indicative of all that lay in the heart of Isa (pbuh) was witnessed by The Almighty, and that he was certain while alive that God is All-Seeing and All-Knowing of his obedience to and worship of God.

[377] Abdel-Aziz Nasser, "Wa Lillah al-Asmaa' al-Husna", Ibid, p.335-341.

(Thou art a witness to all things): God Hears All, Sees All and Knows All.

On Judgment Day, God will present to mankind what each of them has done while alive; a matter rendering the righteous among them fearful of aggressing on the rights of others when they were alive. God Says: {Allah will judge between them on the Day of Judgment: for Allah is witness of all things} (Surat al-Hajj: 17).

Believing that the testimony of God is the greatest of attestations is a human's best point of strength as it is conducted by The Almighty who is Greatest of all, Most Supreme, Most Dignified and Most Knowledgeable – rendering no need for testimonies from any other.

God has testified His Singularity to Himself, as have His angels, prophets and messengers. God Says: {There is no god but He: That is the witness of Allah, His angels, and those endued with knowledge, standing firm on justice. There is no god but He, the Exalted in Power, the Wise} (Surat Aal-Imran: 18).[378]

Prophet Isa concludes his testimony with absolute conceding of his affairs to The Almighty who created both him and all mankind, that God deem whatsoever He wishes regarding Isa's people in either forgiving them or punishing them as He Wills.

- (If Thou dost punish them, they are Thy servants: If Thou dost forgive them, Thou art the Exalted in power, the Wise):

How will those who spewed such a grand lie act, on the most feared day of all, when hearing the man they claimed had ordered them to consider him god beyond The Almighty profess his innocence from such a preposterous accusation?

The context of the holy verses does not answer this question and leaves them to wonder about what shall befall them!

---

[378] "Tafseer al-Sa'adi Tayseer al-Kareem al-Rahman fi Tafseer Kalam al-Mannaan", Ibid, p.635.

- (Allah will say: "This is a day on which the truthful will profit from their truth: theirs are gardens, with rivers flowing beneath, their eternal Home: Allah well-pleased with them, and they with Allah. That is the great salvation, (the fulfilment of all desires)).

This is the proper follow-up to the lies perpetrated against the honourable prophet on the most crucial of all matters, i.e. divinity and servitude. (Allah will say: "This is a day on which the truthful will profit from their truth: theirs are gardens, with rivers flowing beneath, their eternal Home: Allah well-pleased with them, and they with Allah) are God's concluding Words on the matter.[379]

God then pronounces His Individuality in the ownership of the heavens, Earth and all that lies between.

- (To Allah doth belong the dominion of the heavens and the earth, and all that is therein, and it is He Who hath power over all things):

This is a fitting conclusion that suits the grand issue caused by that big lie.[380]

6. Prophet Isa son of Maryam was a blessed servant of God who called for the worship of his Master, the One and Only God:

God says: {When (Jesus) the son of Mary is held up as an example, behold, thy people raise a clamour thereat (in ridicule)! And they say, "Are our gods best, or he?" This they set forth to thee, only by way of disputation: yea, they are a contentious people. He was no more than a servant: We granted Our favour to him, and We made him an example to the Children of Israel. And if it were Our Will, We could make angels from amongst you, succeeding each other on the earth. And (Jesus) shall be a Sign (for the coming of) the Hour (of Judgment): therefore have no doubt

---

[379] "Fi Thilaal al-Qur'an", Ibid, 2/1002.

[380] Ibid.

about the (Hour), but follow ye Me: this is a Straight Way. Let not the Evil One hinder you: for he is to you an enemy avowed. When Jesus came with Clear Signs, he said: "Now have I come to you with Wisdom, and in order to make clear to you some of the (points) on which ye dispute: therefore fear Allah and obey me. "For Allah, He is my Lord and your Lord: so worship ye Him: this is a Straight Way." But sects from among themselves fell into disagreement: then woe to the wrong-doers, from the Penalty of a Grievous Day!} (Surat al-Zukhruf: 57-65).

The Holy Qur'an details in these holy verses that which the unbelievers of Mecca argued with Prophet Mohammad (pbuh) as they defended their feeble doctrines, not to conclude the truth, but rather in stubbornness and blasphemy.

Then they were told that they and the idols they worshipped – which they claimed to be of angels – will be wood for hellfire in the Afterlife. They were also given the example of the same fate awaiting Isa's people who claimed him to be god beyond The Almighty.

The unbelievers of Mecca then claimed that if people of the Book worshipped Isa who was human, then they were more well-guided by worshipping the angels who are God's daughters. But this was a wrongful statement based on a wrong notion. On this occasion, the context states part of Isa's story that reveals his truth and that of his calling, and how his people disagreed on these matters before and after him.

God then warns all those who have deviated from His Guidance with the sudden ushering of Doomsday. The scenery of that feared day is presented as one that grants paradise for the righteous and another that spews painful retribution against blasphemers. On it, God debunks that which they had attributed to the angels and that God is far from their atrocious claims.[381]

[381] "Fi Thilaal al-Qur'an", Ibid, 5/3196.

- (When (Jesus) the son of Mary is held up as an example, behold, thy people raise a clamour thereat (in ridicule)!):

Prophet Mohammad (pbuh) told the people of Quraysh that none shall be worshipped in God's stead, they asked him about Prophet Isa and how his people worshipped him. Therefore, God descended this verse as they equated Isa's people's worship of him to that which they performed to their idols, but with assigning higher importance to their wooden and stone idols as "they were the angel daughters of God". They claimed ("Are our gods best, or he?" This they set forth to thee, only by way of disputation: yea, they are a contentious people).[382]

- (He was no more than a servant: We granted Our favour to him, and We made him an example to the Children of Israel):

Isa was not a god to be worshipped as a group of Nasraanis claimed, but rather a servant of God upon who He bestowed His Grace. God meant for Isa to be an example for them to look up to, yet they deviated from the path of righteousness and lost their way.[383]

God had graced Prophet Isa with prophethood, wisdom, knowledge and labour.[384]

- (And if it were Our Will, We could make angels from amongst you, succeeding each other on the earth):

Meaning: We would replace you with angels to rule the land until We send them angels of their like. As for you, mankind, you cannot bear that angels be sent to you, and God therefore was Merciful towards you that He sent you messengers of your kind so that you may mimic their actions.

---

382 "Fiqh Da'awat al-Anbiyaa' fi al-Qur'an al-Kareem", Ibid, p.497.

383 "Fi Thilaal al-Qur'an", Ibid, 5/3198.

384 "Tafseer al-Sa'adi Tayseer al-Kareem al-Rahman fi Tafseer Kalam al-Mannaan", Ibid, 4/1616.

- (And (Jesus) shall be a Sign (for the coming of) the Hour (of Judgment): therefore have no doubt about the (Hour), but follow ye Me: this is a Straight Way):

Meaning: The coming of Isa (pbuh) is a sign of the encroachment of Doomsday upon you, mankind. That God Who was able to create him without a father is also capable of resurrecting you from the grave, and that Prophet Isa will be lowered from the Heavens at the End of Days as a sign of the soon approaching Day of Judgment.[385]

- (Let not the Evil One hinder you: for he is to you an enemy avowed):

The Holy Qur'an consistently reminds mankind of the immortal battle between them and the devil since the days of their father Adam and the first battle in Heaven. The most ignorant of all is he who knows an enemy awaits him at every turn, yet deliberately takes no precautions not to succumb to his evil doings – and becomes a follower of the devil.[386]

God then reverts to stating the truth about Prophet Isa, the message which he carried forth and how his people disagreed about it before his arrival and after his departure: (When Jesus came with Clear Signs, he said: "Now have I come to you with Wisdom, and in order to make clear to you some of the (points) on which ye dispute: therefore fear Allah and obey me. For Allah, He is my Lord and your Lord: so worship ye Him: this is a Straight Way." But sects from among themselves fell into disagreement: then woe to the wrong-doers, from the Penalty of a Grievous Day!):

God provided the people of Prophet Isa with proofs and clear evidence, be it through the miracles God performed at the hands of Isa or his words of guidance towards righteousness. Isa told his

---

385 Ibid.

386 "Fi Thilaal al-Qur'an", Ibid, 5/3199.

people (I have come forth to you with wisdom) and clarified to them much of which they had argued and disagreed about like the laws brought forth by Prophet Mousa before him. He also called upon them to obey The Almighty and pronounced that God is but One.

("For Allah, He is my Lord and your Lord: so worship ye Him: this is a Straight Way"). Prophet Isa did not say that he was a god, son of God or held any connection to God other than being His servant. But those sects that came after the time of Isa disagreed among them, as did others prior to the coming of Isa. Yet of these who blaspheme without physical proof to their claims, God Says (woe to the wrong-doers, from the Penalty of a Grievous Day!).

The Message of Isa was for the Children of Israel who had awaited his arrival so that he may liberate them of the disgrace they had endured under Roman rule. They waited for him long, yet when he arrived, they denied his calling, stood against him and attempted to crucify him.[387]

Then when Prophet Isa was raised to the Heavens, his followers disagreed among them whereby some held him as a god, others claimed him the son of God and a third group devised the Trinity with Isa at one end and God at another. (But sects from among themselves fell into disagreement: then woe to the wrong-doers, from the Penalty of a Grievous Day!). Thus the message of God's Singularity, brought forth by Prophet Isa, was lost. Afterwards, Arab nonbelievers argued with Prophet Mohammad about Isa and the legends the different sects had adopted after his departure.

Then when the Holy Qur'an speaks of the wrongdoers, it connects those sects after the time of Isa to the ones arguing Prophet Mohammad, and presents what awaits them on Judgment Day along with the rewards that await the pious.

---

[387] "Fi Thilaal al-Qur'an", Ibid, 5/3200.

God Says: {Do they only wait for the Hour - that it should come on them all of a sudden, while they perceive not? Friends on that Day will be foes, one to another, except the Righteous. My devotees! no fear shall be on you that Day, nor shall ye grieve, (Being) those who have believed in Our Signs and bowed (their wills to Ours) in Islam. Enter ye the Garden, ye and your wives, in (beauty and) rejoicing. To them will be passed round, dishes and goblets of gold: there will be there all that the souls could desire, all that their ayes could delight in: and ye shall abide therein (for eye). Such will be the Garden of which ye are made heirs for your (good) deeds (in life). Ye shall have therein abundance of fruit, from which ye shall have satisfaction. The sinners will be in the Punishment of Hell, to dwell therein (for aye): Nowise will the (Punishment) be lightened for them, and in despair will they be there overwhelmed. Nowise shall We be unjust to them: but it is they who have been unjust themselves. They will cry: "O Malik! would that thy Lord put an end to us!" He will say, "Nay, but ye shall abide!" Verily We have brought the Truth to you: but most of you have a hatred for Truth} (Surat al-Zukhruf: 66-78).

The scene begins with the sudden occurrence of Doomsday that takes them by surprise.

- (Do they only wait for the Hour - that it should come on them all of a sudden, while they perceive not?)

This event turns upside-down all that they had been accustomed to in life.[388]

- (Friends on that Day will be foes, one to another, except the Righteous):

During life, friends conspired on evil and each aided the other thereof. Yet on Judgment Day, they allay blame to one another and become foes. But not the righteous, for their affiliation to one an-

[388] "Fi Thilaal al-Qur'an", Ibid, 5/3201.

other remains strong as they had come together in life over goodness. In the midst of all this, a call resonates to all, that:

- (My devotees! no fear shall be on you that Day, nor shall ye grieve, (Being) those who have believed in Our Signs and bowed (their wills to Ours) in Islam. Enter ye the Garden, ye and your wives, in (beauty and) rejoicing. To them will be passed round, dishes and goblets of gold: there will be there all that the souls could desire, all that their ayes could delight in: and ye shall abide therein (for eye). Such will be the Garden of which ye are made heirs for your (good) deeds (in life). Ye shall have therein abundance of fruit, from which ye shall have satisfaction).

But for those who did not abide by God's Commands:

- (The sinners will be in the Punishment of Hell, to dwell therein (for aye):

They shall be cast into hell and receive continuous punishment that neither pauses nor cools, without any hope of redemption for them.

- (Nowise will the (Punishment) be lightened for them, and in despair will they be there overwhelmed).

- (Nowise shall We be unjust to them: but it is they who have been unjust themselves).

Then a shout is heard from far that carries all meanings of despair and misery:

- (They will cry: "O Malik! would that thy Lord put an end to us!" He will say, "Nay, but ye shall abide!"):

It is a cry that comes from behind the closed gates of Hell, emanating from those unjust sinners; one that seeks not salvation, but rather quick death so that they may be relieved of the punishment they are receiving.

Yet the answer comes forth to them that "Nay!" in punishment and torture you shall remain!

In the horrors of such a scene as those who have deviated from righteousness and chose a life of blasphemy comes a Statement by The Almighty:

- (Verily We have brought the Truth to you: but most of you have a hatred for Truth):

Their hatred for the truth is what caused them not to follow it or realise that it was the right path. Had they not hated the truth, they would have followed the calling of Prophet Mohammad (pbuh).

Those who stand against the truth are usually the ones who do not realise that it is so as it contradicts with their whims and prevents them from fulfilling their lusts. And from their weakness in the face of the latter, they draw strength to oppose the truth and attack God's messengers. This is why The Almighty threatens them with that which they fear most so that they may heed His Call.[389]

God Says: {What! have they settled some plan (among themselves)? But it is We Who settle things. Or do they think that We hear not their secrets and their private counsels? Indeed (We do), and Our messengers are by them, to record} (Surat al-Zukhruf: 79-80).

Their insistence on wrongdoing is met by God's decisive Order and Will in enabling the truth as he is aware of all that they conspire publicly and in secret.

Seventh: Isa (pbuh) in the procession of prophets and messengers:

The Holy Qur'an details stories of the blessed processions of messengers from Nouh till Mohammad (pbut). It also details the advent of Prophet Ibrahim and his sons in a non sequential order as the purpose is the procession itself, not its historical timeline.

[389] "Fi Thilaal al-Qur'an", Ibid, 5/3203.

Included in this distinguished procession of pious men is Prophet Isa (pbuh) so that mankind may realise that he was but a prophet like those who came before and after him, and not God or one of three.

God Says: {We gave him Isaac and Jacob: all (three) we guided: and before him, We guided Noah, and among his progeny, David, Solomon, Job, Joseph, Moses, and Aaron: thus do We reward those who do good: And Zakariya and Yahya and Jesus and Elias: all in the ranks of the righteous: And Ismaeel and Elisha, and Jonas, and Lot: and to all We gave favour above the nations: (To them) and to their fathers, and progeny and brethren: We chose them, and we guided them to a straight way. This is the guidance of Allah. He giveth that guidance to whom He pleaseth, of His worshippers. If they were to join other gods with Him, all that they did would be vain for them. These were the men to whom We gave the Book, and authority, and prophethood: if these (their descendants) reject them, Behold! We shall entrust their charge to a new people who reject them not. Those were the (prophets) who received Allah's guidance: Copy the guidance they received; Say: "No reward for this do I ask of you: This is no less than a message for the nations"} (Surat al-An'aam: 84-90).

God's commentary on this remarkable procession is:

- (Thus do We reward those who do good)

- (And to all We gave favour above the nations)

- (We chose them, and we guided them to a straight way)

This was all a prelude to the determinations that followed:

- (This is the guidance of Allah. He giveth that guidance to whom He pleaseth, of His worshippers. If they were to join other gods with Him, all that they did would be vain for them).

Had those "guided" servants deviated from attesting to God's Singularity – from which they draw guidance – their destiny would have been that their deeds be for nothing.

- (These were the men to whom We gave the Book, and authority, and prophethood: if these (their descendants) reject them, Behold! We shall entrust their charge to a new people who reject them not).

This is the second determination: That the prophets He mentioned are the ones He provided with the Book, wisdom, authority and prophethood.

The Arabic word translated as "Authority" can also carry the meaning of "Wisdom". God descended on some of those prophets the Torah, like Mousa, al-Zabour (Psalms), like Dawoud, and the Injeel (Bible), like Isa. God bestowed upon others wisdom, like Dawoud and Suleiman, yet all were given authority that whichever religion God deemed for them to carry forth was His determination. God sent forth messengers so that they may be obeyed and that people are afforded equality and justice. Hence, whence Arab unbelievers (as per the holy verse) reject the Book, its Wisdom and Prophethood, God can do without them.[390]

It is a matter that pacifies all prophets and messengers knowing that they were not alone in being entrusted with God's Will, but rather a link in a continuous chain originating from olden times past. Each felt at ease knowing he was a member of that honourable procession since the advent of history, connected to The Almighty since the most ancient of ages.[391]

- (Those were the (prophets) who received Allah's guidance: Copy the guidance they received; Say: "No reward for this do I ask of you: This is no less than a message for the nations"):

This is the third determination: This group of men leading the procession of faith are the ones who God has guided. It is that which they followed in all their affairs and that which they called

[390] "Fi Thilaal al-Qur'an", Ibid, 2/1144.

[391] Ibid.

on others to follow. God then brings forth glad tidings by saying to those they deliver His Message: (No reward for this do I ask of you: This is no less than a message for the nations).[392]

1. Prophet Isa's teachings emanate from The Almighty:

These teachings include the message of the Messiah and the belief in Divine Revelation. It is only natural that Isa states that he receives revelation from God and that the teachings he pronounces were not of his own. Furthermore, Prophet Isa (pbuh) is mentioned in the Holy Qur'an as one of the prophets who have received Revelations from God.[393]

God Says: {We have sent thee inspiration, as We sent it to Noah and the Messengers after him: we sent inspiration to Abraham, Ismaeel, Isaac, Jacob and the Tribes, to Jesus, Job, Jonah, Aaron, and Solomon, and to David We gave the Psalms. Of some messengers We have already told thee the story; of others We have not; and to Moses Allah spoke direct; Messengers who gave good news as well as warning, that mankind, after (the coming) of the messengers, should have no plea against Allah. For Allah is Exalted in Power, Wise} (Surat al-Nisaa': 163-165).

The Qur'an speaks of one procession of men connected from the onset of human history through one message that calls to righteousness and that warns mankind of falling into doom. A procession that includes a selected elite among mankind like Nouh, Ibrahim, Ismaeel, Ishak, Yacoub, the Tribes, Isa, Ayyub, Yunus, Haroun, Suleiman, Dawoud, Mousa, and others who God detailed their stories in the Qur'an. They encompassed people of different origins and races from all over the world who shared the noble task of carrying forth this Message. Some were sent as messengers

392 Ibid, 2/1145.

393 Mohammad Wasfi, "Temporal and Dogmatic Connection Among Prophets and Messengers", Ibn Hazm House, 1st Ed., 1997, p.315.

to a tribe, others to a city and the last of them to all mankind, i.e. Prophet Mohammad (pbuh).

They all received Revelation from God and none acted nor spoke on his own behalf. God sent forth all messengers so that they may give their people glad tidings of the rewards God has awaiting the believing worshippers among them and the severe punishment for those who do not follow suit. God's reason for this is as per the holy verse: (that mankind, after (the coming) of the messengers, should have no plea against Allah). Although God provided mankind with minds that can lead them towards the path of righteousness if they used them well, He sent forth messengers in case their lusts and whims overcame that which their minds dictated. (For Allah is Exalted in Power, Wise).[394]

As mankind's primal sense is to connect with God and submit to His Will, it is also in man's nature to deviate from the path of righteousness towards that which their lusts take them; hence God sent forth messengers so that they may provide them with the laws and controls required for a life of goodness; and then if they still do not follow that path, they will be deserving of punishment.[395]

No mind, no matter how clever, has reached the same understanding of that of average minds through God's messages. Even Plato and Aristotle, whose minds are claimed to be the most knowledgeable throughout history, were unable to envisage God in His true form as was achieved by minds of Muslims with lesser knowledge who were guided by God's Message.[396]

We, therefore, stand amazed at the Grace of The Almighty who Says: (Messengers who gave good news as well as warning, that mankind, after (the coming) of the messengers, should have no plea against Allah. For Allah is Exalted in Power, Wise).

---

[394] "Fi Thilaal al-Qur'an", Ibid, 2/805-806.

[395] Ibid, 2/811.

[396] Ibid.

2. Isa (pbuh) is among the prophets of Inflexible Purpose:

God Says: {Therefore patiently persevere, as did (all) messengers of inflexible purpose} (Surat al-Ahqaaf: 35).

The prophets of Inflexible Purpose are Nouh, Ibrahim, Mousa, Isa and Mohammad (pbut). The message Isa was ordered by God to heed, as were the other prophets mentioned above, was that stated in Surat al-Shourah, verse 13: {The same religion has He established for you as that which He enjoined on Noah the which We have sent by inspiration to thee and that which We enjoined on Abraham, Moses, and Jesus: Namely, that ye should remain steadfast in religion, and make no divisions therein: to those who worship other things than Allah, hard is the (way) to which thou callest them. Allah chooses to Himself those whom He pleases, and guides to Himself those who turn (to Him)}.

Accordingly, Prophet Isa (pbuh) was among those prophets of Inflexible Purpose who established the religion which God ordered His prophets and messengers to pursue, and it was also a message from God to the nation of Prophet Mohammad (pbuh) to heed the commandments contained within the verse.

That which God has legislated for the prophets of Inflexible Purpose emanates from His perfection of Wisdom and is clear indication that it is of ancient origin from the days of Nouh till the time of Mohammad. It is also meant to give credit to these specific messengers as all concurred to the prophethood of the ones who preceded them and that some were sent to specific peoples, like Prophet Mousa to the Jews and Prophet Isa to the Nasraanis.[397]

God Says: {And remember We took from the prophets their Covenant: As (We did) from thee: from Noah, Abraham, Moses, and Jesus the son of Mary: We took from them a solemn covenant:

[397] Layla Balkheyr, "Qisas Ulu al-'Aazm", Teebah House, Damascus, Syria, 1st Ed., 1432h, p.42.

That (Allah) may question the (custodians) of Truth concerning the Truth they (were charged with): And He has prepared for the unbelievers a grievous penalty} (Surat al-Ahzaab: 7-8):

God took the solemn word of prophets, particularly those of Inflexible Purpose, that they carry forth the path of righteousness with which He entrusted them and that they deliver it to the people so that all bear the responsibility of their actions afterwards.

- (And remember We took from the prophets their Covenant): God first generalises.

- (As (We did) from thee): Then He specifies Prophet Mohammad.

- (From Noah, Abraham, Moses, and Jesus the son of Mary): Then He specifies the other prophets of Inflexible Purpose.

- (We took from them a solemn covenant).

- (That (Allah) may question the (custodians) of Truth concerning the Truth they (were charged with): The truthful are believers who said the word of truth and followed its doctrine. All others are liars as they believe in wrongdoing and pronounce it.

Finally, God's questioning of them regarding their honesty is akin to a teacher asking his/her hardworking student who passed the test with flying colours about their answer that earned them such high award in a graduation ceremony, i.e. Judgment Day. Yet those who followed paths other than that of what God ordered shall be punished.[398]

3. Origin of worship rites:

The uniformity of God's religion is a reality. This has been reflected in the Qur'an: {The same religion has He established for you as that which He enjoined on Noah - the which We have sent by inspiration to thee - and that which We enjoined on Abraham,

[398] "Fi Thilaal al-Qur'an", Ibid, 5/2830.

Moses, and Jesus: Namely, that ye should remain steadfast in religion, and make no divisions therein} (Surat al-Shourah: 13).

As the source of Heavenly Laws are one, God has sent to every nation a messenger with His glad tidings to good doers and warning to wrongdoers, and so as to renew faith and add – by order from God – all that suits each people. God Says: {To each among you have we prescribed a law and an open way} (Surat al-Maa'idah: 48).

God's Words were descended upon Prophet Mohammad (pbuh) as testament to the authenticity of previous Books, but the Qur'an supersedes them all as it embodies all facets of life and that which rectifies mankind till Judgment Day. God Says: {To thee We sent the Book in truth, confirming the scripture that came before it, *and superseding it*[399]} (Surat al-Maa'idah: 48).

Examples on the continuum of rites:

a. Prayer:

- God Says in the stead of Prophet Ibrahim (pbuh): {O my Lord! make me one who establishes regular Prayer, and also (raise such) among my offspring, O our Lord! and accept Thou my Prayer} (Surat Ibrahim: 40).

- God Says: {Allah did aforetime take a covenant from the Children of Israel, and We appointed twelve captains among them. And Allah said: "I am with you: if ye (but) establish regular prayers, practise regular charity, *and*[400] believe in my messengers} (Surat al-Maa'idah: 12).

- God Says in the stead of Isa (pbuh): {And He hath enjoined on me Prayer and Charity as long as I live} (Surat Maryam: 31).

- God Says of Mohammad's nation: {Guard strictly your (habit of) prayers, especially the Middle Prayer; and stand before Allah in a devout (frame of mind)} (Surat al-Baqarah: 238).

---

[399] Correction by translator.

[400] Added by translator.

- God Says: {And We bestowed on him Isaac and, as an additional gift, (a grandson), Jacob, and We made righteous men of every one (of them). And We made them leaders, guiding (men) by Our Command, and We sent them inspiration to do good deeds, to establish regular prayers, and to practise regular charity; and they constantly served Us (and Us only)} (Surat al-Anbiyaa': 72-73).

Accordingly, there is consensus on the legitimacy of prayer, but the discrepancies are in how prayers are performed and their timings.[401]

b. Zakat (Charity):

- God Says: {Nor did the People of the Book make schisms, until after there came to them Clear Evidence. And they have been commanded no more than this: To worship Allah, offering Him sincere devotion, being true (in faith); to establish regular prayer; and to practise regular charity; and that is the Religion Right and Straight} (Surat al-Bayyinah: 4-5).

- God Says: {He used to enjoin on his people Prayer and Charity, and he was most acceptable in the sight of his Lord} (Surat Maryam: 55).

- God Says: {Of their goods, take alms, that so thou mightest purify and sanctify them} (Surat al-Tawbah: 103).

One notes the closeness of Zakat to prayer throughout the Holy Qur'an as the former is fiscal worship and the latter spiritual. The two are a must for connecting God's servants to their Maker and for community support.[402]

c. Fasting:

- God Says: {O ye who believe! Fasting is prescribed to you as it was prescribed to those before you, that ye may (learn) self-re-

---

[401] Zahir bin Awad al-Alma'ai, "Studies in Objective Tafseer of the Holy Qur'an", al-Narjis Printing, Saudi, 2nd Ed., 2001, p.37.

[402] Ibid, p.38.

straint} (Surat al-Baqarah: 183). Hence, as per the holy verse, Fasting is an olden mandate.[403]

d. Law of Equality:

- God Says: {We ordained therein for them: "Life for life, eye for eye, nose or nose, ear for ear, tooth for tooth, and wounds equal for equal"} (Surat al-Maa'idah: 45).

- Upon the advent of Islam, God Says: {O ye who believe! the law of equality (is prescribed to you in cases of murder: the free for the free, the slave for the slave, the woman for the woman. But if any remission is made by the brother of the slain, then grant any reasonable demand, and compensate him with handsome gratitude, this is a concession and a Mercy from your Lord. After this whoever exceeds the limits shall be in grave penalty. In the Law of Equality there is (saving of) Life to you, o ye men of understanding; that ye may restrain yourselves} (Surat al-Baqarah: 178-179).

Accordingly, the law of equal retribution is a penalty that has been mandated in all Divine religions as a necessity for protecting oneself and preventing societies from succumbing to anarchy and lawlessness.[404]

e. Jihad – Exerting an effort:

- God Says: {How many of the prophets fought (in Allah's way), and with them (fought) Large bands of godly men? but they never lost heart if they met with disaster in Allah's way, nor did they weaken (in will) nor give in. And Allah Loves those who are firm and steadfast} (Surat Aal-Imran: 146).

Fighting in self defence or for one's religion is a legitimate matter in all religions according to conditions and realities on the ground.[405]

---

403 "Studies in Objective Tafseer of the Holy Qur'an", Ibid, p.38.

404 Ibid, p.39.

405 Ibid, p.40.

4. Faith fundamentals:

All Heavenly religions have agreed on the foundations of the faith that was brought forward by all messengers. Discrepancies only occurred after they were manipulated and reworded. They are fixed givens that neither evolve nor change, and many verses of the Holy Qur'an affirm this truth.

- God Says: {For We assuredly sent amongst every People a messenger, (with the Command), "Serve Allah, and eschew Evil"} (Surat al-Nahl: 36).

- God Says: {But it has already been revealed to thee, as it was to those before thee, "If thou wert to join (gods with Allah, truly fruitless will be thy work (in life), and thou wilt surely be in the ranks of those who lose (all spiritual good)". Nay, but worship Allah, and be of those who give thanks} (Surat al-Zumar: 65-66).

- God Says: {Not a messenger did We send before thee without this inspiration sent by Us to him: that there is no god but I; therefore worship and serve Me} (Surat al-Anbiyaa': 25).

The Almighty God sent out a public call to all mankind warning them of the devil's doings and reminding them of the singular origin of creation and resurrection: {O ye Children of Adam! Let not Satan seduce you, in the same manner as He got your parents out of the Garden, stripping them of their raiment, to expose their shame: for he and his tribe watch you from a position where ye cannot see them: We made the evil ones friends (only) to those without faith. When they do aught that is shameful, they say: "We found our fathers doing so"; and "(Allah) commanded us thus": Say: "Nay, Allah never commands what is shameful: do ye say of Allah what ye know not?" Say: "My Lord hath commanded justice; and that ye set your whole selves (to Him) at every time and place of prayer, and call upon Him, making your devotion sincere as in His sight: such as He created you in the beginning, so shall ye return"} (Surat al-A'araaf: 27-29).

The dogma of faith which God ordered His prophets and messengers to carry forward and call for contains basic elements that purify the heart from blasphemy and paganism, and which connect it to God. These are:

- That which needs to be believed of God: His existence, creation, destiny, singularity, perfection, and total conviction of all that which He and prophet Mohammad described of Himself.[406]

- The first matter Prophet Isa (pbuh) called for, since he was a child in the cradle, was to believe in the existence of God, His Singularity and in the messages brought forth by God's prophets and messengers. God Says: {He said: "I am indeed a servant of Allah. He hath given me revelation and made me a prophet"} (Surat Maryam: 30).

- Isa would clarify to his mother's people that The Almighty is his God and theirs, and would state that acknowledging such is the rightful path towards redemption. God Says: {When Jesus came with Clear Signs, he said: "Now have I come to you with Wisdom, and in order to make clear to you some of the (points) on which ye dispute: therefore fear Allah and obey me. For Allah, He is my Lord and your Lord: so worship ye Him: this is a Straight Way"} (Surat al-Zukhruf: 63-64).

- Among the miracles that God realised through the Messiah so as to prove his message was one of truth were: resurrecting the dead and curing the blind and the lepers.

Prophet Isa's call was that his people believe, as he did, in the truth of God's messages carried forth by His prophets and messengers like those of Prophets Mousa and Mohammad (pbut). This is evident in the holy verse where God Says: {And in their footsteps We sent Jesus the son of Mary, confirming the Law that had come before him: We sent him the Gospel: therein was guidance and light,

406 "Studies in Objective Tafseer of the Holy Qur'an", Ibid, p.32.

and confirmation of the Law that had come before him: a guidance and an admonition to those who fear Allah} (Surat al-Maa'idah: 46).

a. Believing in Resurrection, Judgment Day, Heaven and Hell:

Resurrection from the dead was contained in the message of the Messiah (pbuh) as it was in the messages of other prophets. Prophet Isa confirmed this fact since he was an infant: {"So peace is on me the day I was born, the day that I die, and the day that I shall be raised up to life (again)"} (Surat Maryam: 33).

This holy verse shows that God generally creates mankind via reproduction and birth, and that the Messiah in particular was created via seedless birth. It also states that the elements of his creation are the same as all mankind and that his ability to talk as an infant was to prove his mother's innocence from being deemed a prostitute. It adds to Prophet Isa's conviction that as he was created in human form, God shall also reap his soul like all others and that he will be resurrected like all mankind. The fact that Prophet Isa's birth was out of the ordinary in no way means he will walk a different path than that which God destined for mankind.

It is also only natural that Prophet Isa's explanation of all that which relates to the dogma of resurrection includes the realities of Heaven and Hell. They who believe in God and follow the guidance of His messengers shall enter Paradise and those who do not heed the call shall enter Hell. Proof that Prophet Isa (pbuh) delivered that message properly is contained in the holy verse: {But said Christ: "O Children of Israel! worship Allah, my Lord and your Lord." Whoever joins other gods with Allah, Allah will forbid him the garden, and the Fire will be his abode. There will for the wrong-doers be no one to help} (Surat al-Maa'idah: 72).

The Holy Qur'an states that both the Torah and Injeel have spoken of Paradise, as later stated in the Holy Qur'an, and that God has promised in them that eternal abode for those who fight for His sake, and that even though they will lose their lives and belongings in this world while doing so, they shall live eternally in Paradise where bounty is abundant.

This is stated in the holy verse: {Allah hath purchased of the believers their persons and their goods; for theirs (in return) is the garden (of Paradise): they fight in His cause, and slay and are slain: a promise binding on Him in truth, through the Torah[407], the Gospel, and the Qur'an: and who is more faithful to his covenant than Allah. then rejoice in the bargain which ye have concluded: that is the achievement supreme} (Surat al-Tawbah: 111).

Prior to his departure, the Messiah had reminded his people of all that which relates to Judgment Day, Heaven and Hell. He also warned them of deviating from worshipping God: {Behold! Allah said: "O Jesus! I will take thee and raise thee to Myself and clear thee (of the falsehoods) of those who blaspheme; I will make those who follow thee superior to those who reject faith, to the Day of Resurrection: Then shall ye all return unto me, and I will judge between you of the matters wherein ye dispute. As to those who reject faith, I will punish them with terrible agony in this world and in the Hereafter, nor will they have anyone to help. As to those who believe and work righteousness, Allah will pay them (in full) their reward; but Allah loveth not those who do wrong"} (Surat Aal-Imran: 55-57).

These holy verses which The Almighty descended upon Prophet Isa were delivered by him to his people and were not kept unpronounced as they pertained to all matters of faith. Hence, we are certain that Prophet Isa (pbuh) relayed these messages to his people once they were revealed to him.[408]

---

[407] Corrected by Translator. Originally "*Law*".

[408] "Studies in Objective Tafseer of the Holy Qur'an", Ibid, p.315.

b. Believing in the Angels:

The Qur'an informs us that the angels are special creatures who do all that God orders them without hesitation or questioning. This is in addition to believing in the existence of Jinn, and that the disobedient among them are the devils.

As for the angels who existed during the calling of Prophet Isa (pbuh), we know that they were the ones who brought glad tidings to his mother, Maryam, of his imminent arrival: {Behold! the angels said: "O Mary! Allah giveth thee glad tidings of a Word from Him: his name will be Christ Jesus, the son of Mary, held in honour in this world and the Hereafter and of (the company of) those nearest to Allah} (Surat Aal-Imran: 45), and in {Behold! the angels said: "O Mary! Allah hath chosen thee and purified thee - chosen thee above the women of all nations} (Surat Aal-Imran: 42).

As for the devil in the Messiah's calling, it is when Imran's woman prayed to The Almighty that He protect her daughter Maryam and her son from the Satan: {When she was delivered, she said: "O my Lord! Behold! I am delivered of a female child!"- and Allah knew best what she brought forth - "And no wise is the male Like the female. I have named her Mary, and I commend her and her offspring to Thy protection from the Evil One, the Rejected"} (Surat Aal-Imran: 36).

The story of Imran's women and the details contained therein are proof that true Christianity believes in the existence of angels and demons and that they are among God's creations.

Believing in angels is a mandatory duty of all as in their absence, nobody would believe in Revelation, the angel of death, the varied tasks performed by angels, or the story of Adam and all angels bowing to him in reverence. Believing in Jinn and demons is also a necessity as when true believers know their enemy, they will take steps to distance themselves from him and ready themselves to stand up to the whims and lusts with which he attempts to corrupt mankind. Followers of all religions surely know the story of Adam and Eve and how Satan went against the order of God and promised to work at misguiding mankind.[409]

5. Basics of ethics and virtues:

All prophets (pbut) were attributed with the best of traits, manners and virtues, and the Holy Qur'an has stated the basics thereof which all religions have agreed upon, like the ten Commandments stated in Surat al-An'aam: {Say: "Come, I will rehearse what Allah hath (really) prohibited you from": Join not anything as equal with Him; be good to your parents; kill not your children on a plea of want; We provide sustenance for you and for them; come not nigh to shameful deeds. Whether open or secret; take not life, which Allah hath made sacred, except by way of justice and law: thus doth He command you, that ye may learn wisdom. And come not nigh to the orphan's property, except to improve it, until he attain the age of full strength; give measure and weight with (full) justice; no burden do We place on any soul, but that which it can bear; whenever ye speak, speak justly, even if a near relative is concerned; and fulfil the covenant of Allah; thus doth He command you, that ye may remember. Verily, this is My way, leading straight: follow it: follow not (other) paths: they will scatter you about from His (great) path: thus doth He command you. that ye may be righteous} (Surat al-An'aam: 151-153).

These ten Commandments are God's Order for the establishment of a perfect human society based on cooperation, goodness, protection from harm and caring for the weak. They are what God ordered His prophet Mohammad (pbuh) to carry out so that equality may reign among all peoples, and is what He ordered all His

[409] "Studies in Objective Tafseer of the Holy Qur'an", Ibid, p.317.

other prophets and messengers of doing although not so eloquently expressed as they are in the Holy Qur'an.[410]

- Commandment I: Not joining any with God

God Says: (Say: "Come, I will rehearse what Allah hath (really) prohibited you from": Join not anything as equal with Him).

This is the grandest of matters as it relates to the Singularity of the Creator of all. It is the source of all legislation that all Divine messages have agreed upon. All wrongdoings may be forgiven except joining partners with God. Believing in this grand matter cleanses the mind and soul from pagan notions and allows one the sense that he/she submits only to the Will of the One God.[411]

- Commandment II: Acting kindly towards parents

God Says: (be good to your parents).

Being good to one's parents means being gracious towards them as it is a tier higher than justice, which includes mercy, loyalty and empathy. God says: {Allah commands justice, the doing of good, and liberality to kith and kin, and He forbids all shameful deeds, and injustice and rebellion: He instructs you, that ye may receive admonition} (Surat al-Nahl: 90), and {Thy Lord hath decreed that ye worship none but Him, and that ye be kind to parents} (Surat al-Israa': 23).

Being kind to one's parents necessitates not being rude to them as God has connected this Commandment with the blasphemous act of joining others with Him throughout many instances in the Holy Qur'an. God says: {Serve Allah, and join not any partners with Him; and do good to parents} (Surat al-Nisaa': 36).

---

[410] "Zahrat al-Tafaaseer", Ibid, 5/2728.

[411] Ibid, 5/2729.

God also connected giving thanks to parents to that of thanking God. God Says: {Show gratitude to Me and to thy parents: to Me is (thy final) Goal. But if they strive to make thee join in worship with Me things of which thou hast no knowledge, obey them not; yet bear them company in this life with justice (and consideration), and follow the way of those who turn to me (in love): in the end the return of you all is to Me, and I will tell you the truth (and meaning) of all that ye did} (Surat Luqman: 14-15).

It also that which God mandated of the children of Israel. God Says: {And remember We took a covenant from the Children of Israel (to this effect): Worship none but Allah, treat with kindness your parents} (Surat al-Baqarah: 83). Hence, whoever does wrong to his/her parents has deviated from God's Will.[412]

- Commandment III: Prohibition of killing children

God Says: (kill not your children on a plea of want; We provide sustenance for you and for them).

As children are the extension of their parents, Islam orders that they be raised well and that their needs, and those of their mothers, be fulfilled, and that they not be buried alive as was the custom of people before the coming of Prophet Mohammad (pbuh). These people would commit such horrible crimes for fear they would be unable to feed their children, yet God forbade it as it is He Who provides sustenance to all mankind. This is also echoed in the holy verse: {There is no moving creature on earth but its sustenance dependeth on Allah. He knoweth the time and place of its definite abode and its temporary deposit: All is in a clear Record} (Surat Houd: 6).

The Academy for Islamic Studies that was held at al-Azhar in 1965 stated that Islam encourages people giving birth as it strengthens the nation socially, politically and militarily. It also de-

[412] "Zahrat al-Tafaaseer", Ibid, 5/2730.

creed that the right to regulate birth is one reserved for the parents which they utilise at necessity, and that they are held responsible for such decision in front of God.[413]

- Commandment IV: Refraining from shameful deeds, whether outwardly or in secret

God Says: (Come not nigh to shameful deeds. Whether open or secret).

All shameful deeds must be refrained from, but especially if conducted out in the open in front of all. That is when punishment is even more than if they were in secret.[414]

Even those shameful deeds which remain unacted upon are considered wrongdoings. It is like one who planned on committing adultery but was unable to do so for some reason when he/she attempted to carry it out. This is still considered a sin as having refrained from it was a matter forced upon the person, and not of his/her own will to cease from committing it. Of this, God Says: {Eschew all sin, open or secret} (Surat al-An'aam: 120).[415]

- Commandment V: Prohibition of killing unjustly

God Says: (Take not life, which Allah hath made sacred, except by way of justice and law).

We all know the story of Cain who killed his brother Abel out of malice and jealousy. God Says: {On that account: We ordained for the Children of Israel that if any one slew a person - unless it be for murder or for spreading mischief in the land - it would be as if he slew the whole people ...} (Surat al-Maa'idah: 32). These are prohibited actions as God has ordained them as such.[416]

413 Ibid, 5/2732.

414 Ibid.

415 Ibid, 5/2733.

416 "Zahrat al-Tafaseer", Ibid, 5/2734.

(Thus doth He command you, that ye may be righteous) is God's concluding statement on either committing the abovementioned wrongdoings or even considering them as viable options. God wishes that mankind observe His Commandments with conviction.[417]

- Commandment VI: Prohibition of plundering orphans' money

God says: (And come not nigh to the orphan's property, except to improve it, until he attain the age of full strength).

As orphans have lost their protective nets of caring parents, God has forbidden any from transgressing on their money except to multiply it for them. Such money is kept in safekeeping by the State or warden till a child becomes of legal age and capable of utilising it properly. God stressed the importance of caring for orphans and their money as they are weak and vulnerable.[418]

- Commandment VII: Being honest in buying and selling

God Says: (Give measure and weight with (full) justice; no burden do We place on any soul, but that which it can bear).

God orders mankind to be fair and honest in measuring quantities on weighing scales to the extent that is humanly possible. As for that beyond their ability, they shall not be questioned about it.

God mandates that weights are measured correctly without any intended deduction as this protects people's rights.[419]

- Commandment VIII: Being Just and speaking the truth

God Says: (Whenever ye speak, speak justly, even if a near relative is concerned).

God orders justice in statements and that they be fair. This necessitates looking into a matter so as to verify its truthfulness.

---

417 Ibid, 5/2735.

418 Ibid, 5/2736.

419 Ibid, 5/2737.

It also covers passing judgment that involves two disputing parties, as per God's Words: {And when ye judge between man and man, that ye judge with justice: Verily how excellent is the teaching which He giveth you!} (Surat al-Nisaa': 58). This includes testimony in that it must be based on what one has personally seen and verified; whether in a game or an exam.

Being the religion of justice, Islam mandates righteousness in all transactions concerning mankind. God Says: {Allah commands justice, the doing of good, and liberality to kith and kin, and He forbids all shameful deeds, and injustice and rebellion: He instructs you, that ye may receive admonition} (Surat al-Nahl: 90).

Even if a party to the conflict is one related to the judge, God mandates that there be no nepotism in passing judgment. Justice is the bond that connects all peoples and fulfilling it is the measure of any nation's worth.[420]

- Commandment IX: Fulfilling the covenant of God

God Says: (Fulfil the covenant of Allah).

This Commandments tells mankind that fulfilling the Covenant of God is more important than fulfilling any others. It is the covenant of primal instinct that God instilled in mankind, as God Says: {When thy Lord drew forth from the Children of Adam - from their loins - their descendants, and made them testify concerning themselves, (saying): "Am I not your Lord (who cherishes and sustains you)?"- They said: "Yea! We do testify!" (This)}.

Covenants among people are the same as if they were with God as people usually strengthen them while adjoining God's Name. God decreed this as per His Saying: {Fulfil the Covenant of Allah when ye have entered into it, and break not your oaths after ye have confirmed them; indeed ye have made Allah your surety; for

[420] "Zahrat al-Tafaaseer", Ibid, 5/2739.

Allah knoweth all that ye do. And be not like a woman who breaks into untwisted strands the yarn which she has spun, after it has become strong. Nor take your oaths to practise deception between yourselves, lest one party should be more numerous than another: for Allah will test you by this; and on the Day of Judgment He will certainly make clear to you (the truth of) that wherein ye disagree}. These two verses indicate three matters:

• First: Whoever strengthen their covenant by adjoining the name of God, have made Him its guarantor, and would have thus let down God Himself if not fulfilled.

• Second: Fulfilling an oath strengthens a nation and allows people to trust it, and that in itself is a strength. Hence God likened those who break their solemn promises to a foolish lady who undoes her strengthened yarn.

• Third: The will to have more land and power cannot be reason for breaking one's oath as this constitutes injustice, anarchy and loss of a power more precious than that of rescinding on an oath. Ibn Abbas was true when saying that whoever breaks their promise will see that God has allowed their enemies to gain power over them.[421]

- Commandment X: Following the path of righteousness

God Says: {Verily, this is My way, leading straight: follow it: follow not (other) paths: they will scatter you about from His (great) path: thus doth He command you. that ye may be righteous}.

This great verse concludes all that preceded it in this selection. As God prohibited these wrongdoings, He warned against following any path other than that which He set out for mankind. All of these Commandments constitute the path towards God, which is a straight and righteous one embodied in Islam.

[421] "Zahrat al-Tafaaseer", Ibid, 5/2740-2741.

(Thus doth He command you. that ye may be righteous) reflects God's hope that the hearts of mankind shall be enlightened with piety towards Him and shall prevent mankind from falling into the pits of hell in the hope that we may yearn for God's forgiveness once fearing His punishment. Surely, God is All-Forgiving of those who repent, believe, perform good deeds and are guided towards the path of righteousness.[422]

These Commandments are shared among religions and constitute the psychological and practical bases for the establishment of righteous groups.[423]

6. Preferential endowment among prophets:

God Says: {Those messengers We endowed with gifts, some above others: To one of them Allah spoke; others He raised to degrees (of honour); to Jesus the son of Mary We gave clear (Signs), and strengthened him with the holy spirit} (Surat al-Baqarah: 253).

It was Prophet Mousa (pbuh) who God spoke to: {Allah Said: "O Moses! I have chosen thee above (other) men, by the mission I (have given thee) and the words I (have spoken to thee)} (Surat al-A'araaf: 144), and in: {And to Moses Allah spoke direct} (Surat al-Nisaa': 164).

Of Prophet Isa (pbuh), God Says: {We gave Jesus the son of Mary Clear (Signs)} (Surat al-Baqarah: 87).

Also: {And strengthened him with the holy spirit} (Surat al-Baqarah: 253).

The Holy Spirit is most likely the Angel Jibreel, as most explanations concur. Hence, whichever prophet of God is supported by the most prominent among angels is deemed better. Some scholars state that the Holy Spirit refers to the spirit of

[422] Ibid, 5/2743.

[423] Ibid, 5/2740.

faith, rendering his spirituality more supreme than others. But the origin for being supported with this spirit is to each believer according to its strength as per the holy verse {And strengthened them with a spirit from Himself} (Surat al-Mujadilah: 22). But for Prophet Isa, the support God provided him with was more supreme.[424]

When God is mentioned as having spoken to a man, we all think of Prophet Mousa (pbuh), and hence he is not mentioned by name in this verse. But Prophet Isa is mentioned as the son of Maryam in most instances in the Holy Qur'an and the wisdom thereof here is clear, as when the Qur'an was descended upon Prophet Mohammad (pbuh), many myths on the prophethood of Isa were already afloat such as being the son of God, having duplicate natures of divinity and humanity, having a purely divine nature that absorbed his human one like the drop that fell into the glass as well as other mythical figments of imagination that drowned churches in non-ending argument. It was these fables that spilt rivers of blood during Roman times, and hence, we see continuous emphasis on the humanity of Prophet Isa by referring him to his mother in most instances.

The clear Signs received by Prophet Isa include the Injeel (Gospel) that was descended upon him and the supernatural acts which God provided mankind through him.[425]

The best among God's messengers are those of Inflexible Purpose who God has praised and singled out from among His other messengers. God ordered Prophet Mohammad (pbuh), who He preferred over all His creations, to follow in their footsteps. Good Says: {Therefore patiently persevere, as did (all) messengers of inflexible purpose} (Surat al-Ahqaaf: 35).

---

[424] "Al-Iman bil Rusul wal Risalaat", Ibid, p.209.

[425] "Fi Thilaal al-Qur'an", Ibid, 1/283.

Those who revere their God the most are His prophets; the best among them are the messengers, and the best messengers are those of Inflexible Purpose. These are five: Mohammad, Nouh, Ibrahim, Mousa and Isa (Peace Be Upon Them). God Says: {And remember We took from the prophets their Covenant: As (We did) from thee: from Noah, Abraham, Moses, and Jesus the son of Mary: We took from them a solemn covenant} (Surat al-Ahzaab: 7).

Also, God Says: {The same religion has He established for you as that which He enjoined on Noah - the which We have sent by inspiration to thee - and that which We enjoined on Abraham, Moses, and Jesus: Namely, that ye should remain steadfast in religion, and make no divisions therein: to those who worship other things than Allah, hard is the (way) to which thou callest them} (Surat al-Shourah: 13). God also specified them when speaking of the grandest of all matters, i.e. the Covenant. God Says: {And we took from them a solemn covenant} (Surat al-Nisaa': 154).

Eighth: Islam is the religion of all prophets, messengers and their true followers:

Islam is the everlasting religion of God which He accepts no other. It is the religion he mandated that all mankind follow, since the beginning or creation, carried forth by Adam, Idrees, Nouh, Ibrahim, the family of Ibrahim and the family of Imran. It was concluded through the last of prophets and is the only one among all religions that calls for the untainted Singularity of The Almighty God, i.e. monotheism.

Islam is the religion that encompasses sound rites and provisions that are unbound by spatial or temporal changes, changes in people's circumstances throughout their life on Earth, colour, race, language, environment, profession or culture.[426]

[426] "Temporal and Dogmatic Connection Among Prophets and Messengers", Ibid, p.318.

Due to God's Grace, He did not wish for mankind to remain in the darkness of ignorance and hence sent us prophets and messengers throughout the times who would strengthen our resolve in the quest towards righteousness that may guide us towards Paradise, instead of that which leads to hell.[427]

1. Nouh and the prophets who preceded him followed Islam:

The fact that Prophet Nouh and prophets who came before him were Muslim is embodied in God's Words to Prophet Mohammad, where God Says: {Relate to them the story of Noah. Behold! he said to his people: "O my people, if it be hard on your (mind) that I should stay (with you) and commemorate the signs of Allah, yet I put my trust in Allah. Get ye then an agreement about your plan and among your partners, so your plan *not*[428] be on to you dark and dubious. Then pass your sentence on me, and give me no respite. But if ye turn back, (consider): no reward have I asked of you: my reward is only due from Allah, and I have been commanded to be of those who submit to Allah's will (in Islam)"} (Surat Yunus: 71-72).

The last phrase in the above is proof that Islam was the religion of those who came before Nouh, which is exactly the same that Mohammad (pbuh) said – reported in the Qur'an by The Almighty: {For me, I have been commanded to serve the Lord of this city, Him Who has sanctified it and to Whom (belong) all things: and I am commanded to be of those who bow in Islam to Allah's Will} (Surat al-Naml: 91).

2. Prophet Ibrahim carried forth Islam's message after Nouh:

Prophet Ibrahim was among those who carried forth the message of Islam after Prophet Nouh. Having mentioned the story of

[427] Ibid, p.219.

[428] Added by Translator.

Nouh is Surat al-Saafaat, God adds: {Verily among those who followed his Way was Abraham} (Surat al-Saafaat: 83).

God then Says: {Him We chose and rendered pure in this world: And he will be in the Hereafter in the ranks of the Righteous. Behold! his Lord said to him: "Bow (thy will to Me)": He said: "I bow (my will) to the Lord and Cherisher of the Universe"} (Surat al-Baqarah: 130-131).

3. Prophets Ismaeel & Ibrahim carried forth the message of Islam:

Ismaeel also carried forth the message of Islam with his father Ibrahim. God Says: {And remember Abraham and Ismaeel raised the foundations of the House (With this prayer): "Our Lord! Accept (this service) from us: For Thou art the All-Hearing, the All-knowing. Our Lord! make of us Muslims, bowing to Thy (Will), and of our progeny a people Muslim, bowing to Thy (will); and show us our place for the celebration of (due) rites; and turn unto us (in Mercy); for Thou art the Oft-Returning, Most Merciful} (Surat al-Baqarah: 127-128).[429]

4. The religion of Prophet Lot was Islam:

The Holy Qur'an states that Prophet Lot (pbuh) followed the same Islam of Ibrahim. God Says: {But Lut had faith in Him} (Surat al-Ankabut: 26). God also Says upon dooming his town: {Then We evacuated those of the Believers who were there. But We found not there any just (Muslim) persons except in one house} (Surat al-Thaariyat: 35-36).

5. Prophets Ishak, Yacoub and the Tribes were Muslim:

God Says: {And this was the legacy that Abraham left to his sons, and so did Jacob; "Oh my sons! Allah hath chosen the Faith

[429] "Temporal and Dogmatic Connection Among Prophets and Messengers", Ibid, p.320.

for you; then die not except in the Faith of Islam." Were ye witnesses when death appeared before Jacob? Behold, he said to his sons: "What will ye worship after me?" They said: "We shall worship Thy Allah and the Allah of thy fathers, of Abraham, Ismaeel and Isaac, the one (True) Allah. To Him we bow (in Islam)"} (Surat al-Baqarah: 132-133).

6. Prophet Yusuf was Muslim:

Prophet Yusuf would always pray to God that he die a Muslim. God Says: {"O my Lord! Thou hast indeed bestowed on me some power, and taught me something of the interpretation of dreams and events,- O Thou Creator of the heavens and the earth! Thou art my Protector in this world and in the Hereafter. Take Thou my soul (at death) as one submitting to Thy will (as a Muslim), and unite me with the righteous"} (Surat Yusuf: 101).

7. Prophet Mousa called on his people to embrace Islam:

God Says: {But none believed in Moses except some children of his People, because of the fear of Pharaoh and his chiefs, lest they should persecute them; and certainly Pharaoh was mighty on the earth and one who transgressed all bounds. Moses said: "O my people! If ye do (really) believe in Allah, then in Him put your trust if ye submit (your will to His) *in Islam*[430]"} (Surat Yunus: 83-84).

The Almighty has also shown how Pharaoh's illusionists also believed in the message of Islam brought forth by God's messenger (pbuh) when they stated the following to Pharaoh after he threatened to kill them: {"For us, We are but sent back unto our Lord: But thou dost wreak thy vengeance on us simply because we believed in the Signs of our Lord when they reached us! Our Lord! pour out on us patience and constan-

[430] Added by Translator.

cy, and take our souls unto thee as Muslims (who bow to Thy Will)!} (Surat al-A'araaf: 125-126).[431]

8. Prophets sent to the Israelites called to Islam:

God Says: {It was We who revealed the *Torah*[432] (to Moses): therein was guidance and light. By its standard have been judged the Jews, by the prophets who bowed (as in Islam) to Allah's will, by the rabbis and the doctors of law: for to them was entrusted the protection of Allah's book, and they were witnesses thereto} (Surat al-Maa'idah: 44). This verse also shows that the rabbis and scribes were also Muslim.

9. Dawoud and Suleiman called to Islam:

God Says: {And Solomon was David's heir} (Surat al-Naml: 16). God also states that Prophet Suleiman (pbuh) sent word to the people of Yemen calling on them to embrace Islam in a message to their queen of Sheba as she and her people were: {"... worshipping the sun besides Allah: Satan has made their deeds seem pleasing in their eyes, and has kept them away from the Path, so they receive no guidance"} (Surat al-Naml: 24).

God states that the queen of Sheba, Balqees, read this invitation to her people: {(The queen) said: "Ye chiefs! here is delivered to me - a letter worthy of respect. It is from Solomon, and is (as follows):´In the name of Allah, Most Gracious, Most Merciful: "Be ye not arrogant against me, but come to me in submission (to the true Religion) *of Islam*[433]'"} (Surat al-Naml: 29-32).

The Almighty states that the queen of Sheba embraced Islam: {She said: "O my Lord! I have indeed wronged my soul: I do (now) submit (in Islam), with Solomon, to the Lord of the Worlds"} (Surat al-Naml: 44).

---

[431] "Temporal and Dogmatic Connection Among Prophets and Messengers", Ibid, p.322.

[432] Corrected by Translator. Originally (Law).

[433] Added by Translator.

10. The Messiah Isa son of Maryam called for embracing Islam:

God sent forth The Messiah Isa son of Maryam with the message of Islam, and he would call on his people to embrace this religion that is founded on concurring to the existence of the Creator and to His Singularity. God Says: {When Jesus found Unbelief on their part He said: "Who will be My helpers to (the work of) Allah?" Said the disciples: "We are Allah's helpers: We believe in Allah, and do thou bear witness that we are Muslims. Our Lord! we believe in what Thou hast revealed, and we follow the Messenger. then write us down among those who bear witness"} (Surat Aal-Imran: 52-53).

God stated that it was He who guided the Hawaaris to embrace Islam. God Says: {"And behold! I inspired the disciples to have faith in Me and Mine Messenger. they said, ´We have faith, and do thou bear witness that we bow to Allah as Muslims´"} (Surat al-Maa'idah: 111).

It is only natural that the disciples of Prophet Isa continued to call on people to embrace Islam after God raised Isa to the Heavens. The believers remained upholding Islam, their religion and believing in The One and Only God. They did not deviate from the true religion of God's Singularity and inherited this true religion generation after another until the times of the last prophet, Mohammad (pbuh).[434]

11. Continuity of Islam till the descending of the Holy Qur'an:

Islam's prevalence persisted until the Holy Qur'an was revealed to Prophet Mohammad (pbuh) and so did the existence of people who believed in it as being the religion Prophet Isa (pbuh) and the Hawaaris called for as indicated in God's Words: {Now

[434] "Temporal and Dogmatic Connection Among Prophets and Messengers", Ibid, p.323.

have We caused the Word to reach them themselves, in order that they may receive admonition. Those to whom We sent the Book before this,- they do believe in this (revelation): And when it is recited to them, they say: "We believe therein, for it is the Truth from our Lord: indeed we have been Muslims (bowing to Allah's Will) from before this"} (Surat al-Qasas: 51-53).

Also, God Says: {Twice will they be given their reward, for that they have persevered, that they avert Evil with Good, and that they spend (in charity) out of what We have given them. And when they hear vain talk, they turn away therefrom and say: "To us our deeds, and to you yours; peace be to you: we seek not the ignorant"} (Surat al-Qasas: 54-55).

12. Prophet Mohammad (pbuh) called to Islam:

The Holy Qur'an was revealed to the bearer of Islam's banner, Prophet Mohammad (pbuh), who was the first to believe in its message. God Says: {The Messenger believeth in what hath been revealed to him from his Lord} (Surat al-Baqarah: 285).

It is only natural that the Prophet believed in that which was descended upon him before he called on the people to believe in it. Hence, God ordered him that he first believe in it and then call on the people to do the same. God Says: {Say: "Verily, I am commanded to serve Allah with sincere devotion; And I am commanded to be the first of those who bow to Allah in Islam"} (Surat al-Zumar: 11-12). Also, God Says: {Say: "Shall I take for my protector any other than Allah, the Maker of the heavens and the earth? And He it is that feedeth but is not fed?" Say: "Nay! but I am commanded to be the first of those who bow to Allah (in Islam), and be not thou of the company of those who join gods with Allah"} (Surat al-An'aam: 14).

Prophet Mohammad (pbuh) was the first of Muslims in relation to the time he was delegated to carry forth the message of

Islam, but as for Islam itself being prevalent prior to him, other prophets and messengers who came before him had that honour earlier. Mohammad pronounced the same phrase which Nouh (pbuh) uttered, as previously mentioned, i.e. {... and I am commanded to be of those who bow in Islam to Allah's Will} (Surat al-Naml: 91).

Despite being the first Muslim of his people, Prophet Mohammad (pbuh) believed in the same religion in which his grandfather Ibrahim believed. God Says: {Abraham was indeed a model, devoutly obedient to Allah, (and) true in Faith, and he joined not gods with Allah. He showed his gratitude for the favours of Allah, who chose him, and guided him to a Straight Way. And We gave him Good in this world, and he will be, in the Hereafter, in the ranks of the Righteous. So We have taught thee the inspired (Message), "Follow the ways of Abraham the True in Faith, and he joined not gods with Allah"} (Surat al-Nahl: 120-123).

Also, God Says: {Say: "Verily, my Lord hath guided me to a way that is straight,- a religion of right,- the path (trod) by Abraham the true in Faith, and he (certainly) joined not gods with Allah." Say: "Truly, my prayer and my service of sacrifice, my life and my death, are (all) for Allah, the Cherisher of the Worlds: No partner hath He: this am I commanded, and I am the first of those who bow to His will *(in Islam)*[435]} (Surat al-An'aam: 161-163).[436]

Being the concluding prophet through who God completed Islam, Mohammad (pbuh) was the last among all prophets and messengers before him to carry its banner and call on the masses to embrace it. Accordingly, God tells Prophet Mohammad: {Say: "We believe in Allah, and in what has been revealed to us and what was revealed to Abraham, Ismaeel, Isaac, Jacob, and the Tribes, and in (the Books) given to Moses, Jesus, and the

435 Added by Translator.

436 "Temporal and Dogmatic Connection Among Prophets and Messengers", Ibid, p.325.

prophets, from their Lord: We make no distinction between one and another among them, and to Allah do we bow our will (in Islam)"} (Surat Aal-Imran: 84).[437]

The Almighty informs the followers of Prophet Mohammad's message that they were named Muslim ever since the time of Ibrahim. God Says: {And strive in His cause as ye ought to strive, (with sincerity and under discipline). He has chosen you, and has imposed no difficulties on you in religion; it is the cult of your father Abraham. It is He Who has named you Muslims, both before and in this (Revelation); that the Messenger may be a witness for you, and ye be witnesses for mankind! So establish regular Prayer, give regular Charity, and hold fast to Allah. He is your Protector - the Best to protect and the Best to help!} (Surat al-Hajj: 78).

The followers of the religion Prophet Mohammad called to are dubbed Muslims as the word *Islam* (Surrender and Submittal)[438] is an utterance that encompasses all dogmas brought forth by all messengers and prophets throughout history. They are called such so that the notion of the concluded religion may resonate throughout time. God Says: {Say ye: "We believe in Allah, and the revelation given to us, and to Abraham, Ismaeel, Isaac, Jacob, and the Tribes, and that given to Moses and Jesus, and that given to (all) prophets from their Lord: We make no difference between one and another of them: And we bow to Allah (in Islam)"} (Surat al-Baqarah: 136).

One act of God's Grace towards mankind is that He sent them messengers throughout human history, in consecutive and complementary order, who carried forth the message of Islam and who reminded people of this religion. God Says: {Messengers who gave good news as well as warning, that mankind, after (the com-

[437] Ibid, p.326.

[438] Added by Translator.

ing) of the messengers, should have no plea against Allah. For Allah is Exalted in Power, Wise} (Surat al-Nisaa': 165).[439]

Ninth: Prophet Isa's confirmation of the Torah:

In many instances throughout the Holy Qur'an, God states that Prophet Isa (pbuh) confirms the authenticity of the Torah. God Says: {And in their footsteps We sent Jesus the son of Mary, confirming the *Torah*[440] that had come before him} (Surat al-Maa'idah: 46). Also, God Says: {When Jesus came with Clear Signs, he said: "Now have I come to you with Wisdom, and in order to make clear to you some of the (points) on which ye dispute: therefore fear Allah and obey me} (Surat al-Zukhruf: 63).

Accordingly, the message of Isa complemented that of Mousa (pbut) and explained and corrected the deviations that occurred to it through time. Prophet Isa was also ordered to lessen some of its duties so to make it easier for the Israelites to fulfil its mandates. God Says of Prophet Isa: {"(I have come to you), to attest the *Torah*[441] which was before me. And to make lawful to you part of what was (Before) forbidden to you"} (Surat Aal-Imran: 50). Thus, the natural conception for Nasraaniism was that it upholds the Torah's provisions while taking into consideration the corrections thereof stated in the Injeel.[442]

1. The Torah:

It is the Book that God descended upon Prophet Mousa (pbuh), which most likely includes the scrolls He descended upon him. The Holy Qur'an refers to these scrolls: {The Books of Abraham} (Surat al-A'ala: 19). Also: {Nay, is he not acquainted with what is in the books of Moses?} (Surat al-Najm: 36). It also includes the tablets

439 "Temporal and Dogmatic Connection Among Prophets and Messengers", Ibid, p.328.

440 Corrected by Translator.

441 Corrected by Translator.

442 "Sources of Nasraaniism: Study and Critique", Ibid, 1/61.

which Mousa brought forth after praying to God near Mt. Sinai: {And We ordained laws for him in the tablets in all matters, both commanding and explaining all things: "Take and hold these with firmness"} (Surat al-A'araaf: 145).

The word *Torah* is Hebrew and means (education or law). The Holy Qur'an came as one that acknowledges past Holy Books, but which supersedes all, including the Torah and Injeel. God Says: {A. L. M. Allah. There is no god but He,-the Living, the Self-Subsisting, Eternal. It is He Who sent down to thee (step by step), in truth, the Book, confirming what went before it; and He sent down the *Torah*[443] (of Moses) and the Gospel (of Jesus) before this, as a guide to mankind, and He sent down the criterion (of judgment between right and wrong). Then those who reject Faith in the Signs of Allah will suffer the severest penalty, and Allah is Exalted in Might, Lord of Retribution} (Surat Aal-Imran: 1-4).

Hence, believing in the Torah which God descended upon Mousa is a pillar of faith as it was mentioned in the Holy Qur'an and we were ordered to believe in it.[444]

2. The Torah's description in the Holy Qur'an:

Naturally speaking, the Holy Qur'an described the untainted Torah positively, commended it and acknowledged its goodness for as the Holy Qur'an is from God, so was the Torah.

a. The Torah in Surat al-A'araaf:

In verse 145, God Says: {And We ordained laws for him in the tablets in all matters, both commanding and explaining all things, (and said): "Take and hold these with firmness, and enjoin thy people to hold fast by the best in the precepts: soon shall I show you the homes of the wicked "}.

443 Corrected by Translator.

444 "Studies in Objective Tafseer of the Holy Qur'an", Ibid, p.262.

This verse commends the Torah and demands that the people of Mousa adopt its best principles.[445]

b. The Torah in Surat al-Anbiyaa':

In verses 48-49, God Says: {In the past We granted to Moses and Aaron the criterion (for judgment), and a Light and a *Reminder* [446]for those who would do right, Those who fear their Lord in their most secret thoughts, and who hold the Hour (of Judgment) in awe}.

God described the Torah here as:

• **First:** A Criterion for discriminating between right and wrong, as all of God's Books possess such a trait.

• **Second:** A Light that guides the enlightened through the darkness that surrounds them.

• **Third:** A Reminder for the believers of the duties God has mandated of them, that they may remember when delving into the Torah, and abide by.[447]

c. The Torah in Surat al-An'aam:

In verse 91, God Says: {No just estimate of Allah do they make when they say: "Nothing doth Allah send down to man (by way of revelation)" Say: "Who then sent down the Book which Moses brought? - a light and guidance to man: But ye make it into (separate) sheets for show, while ye conceal much (of its contents): therein were ye taught that which ye knew not - neither ye nor your fathers." Say: "(Allah) (sent it down)": Then leave them to plunge in vain discourse and trifling}.

God described the Torah here as:

---

445 Salah Eddine al-Khalidi, "Hadeeth al-Qur'an 'an al-Tawraah wal Injeel", al-Nafaa'is House, Amman, Jordan, 1st Ed., 2017, p.61.

446 Corrected by Translator.

447 "Hadeeth al-Qur'an 'an al-Tawraah wal Injeel", Ibid, p.63.

• **First:** A Book that God wrote on tablets and descended upon Prophet Mousa (pbuh). It was one of the four Holy Books in which one must believe, i.e. The Torah, the Zabour, the Injeel and the Qur'an.

• **Second:** A Light that shows the Israelites the way of righteousness followed by those who believed in Mousa.

• **Third:** Guidance towards righteousness that leads people towards the goodness which pleases God.[448]

d. The Torah was complete, detailed, a guide and a mercy:

God Says: {Moreover, We gave Moses the Book, completing (Our favour) to those who would do right, and explaining all things in detail,- and a guide and a mercy, that they might believe in the meeting with their Lord} (Surat al-An'aam: 154).

The Torah was complete in its provisions and laws, fulfilled the needs of the Israelites and sufficed them in this regard. It was complete and detailed all that the Israelites needed for their life, and it guided them towards goodness and brought mercy to them as it included laws.[449]

e. The Torah was a guide and mercy:

God Says: {And before this, was the Book of Moses as a guide and a mercy: And this Book confirms (it) in the Arabic tongue; to admonish the unjust, and as Glad Tidings to those who do right} (Surat al-Ahqaaf: 12).

The Arabic word in the Qur'an for *Guide* is *Imam,* i.e. the point to which people refer, adjudicate at, abide by and follow. He/she could also be one who is followed, like a ruler of good example, one who leads prayer, or an intangible leader like a book people uphold as the law and abide by its provisions.

---

[448] "Hadeeth al-Qur'an 'an al-Tawraah wal Injeel", Ibid, p.67.

[449] Ibid.

The above are the traits of all Holy Books.[450]

f. The Torah is a Book of rule:

God Says: {It was We who revealed the *Torah*[451] (to Moses): therein was guidance and light. By its standard have been judged the Jews, by the prophets who bowed (as in Islam) to Allah's will, by the rabbis and the doctors of law: for to them was entrusted the protection of Allah's book, and they were witnesses thereto} (Surat al-Maa'idah: 44).

This holy verse shows that God ordered the prophets who He sent to the Israelites to abide by the Torah and implement its provisions as God had ordered of Mousa when He descended the Torah upon him before them. This means that the Israelites had been demanded for centuries to uphold the Torah, and that it was the message of every prophet God had sent to them from the time of Mousa till that of Isa (pbut).[452]

g. The Qur'an's Confirmation of the Divine Torah:

The traits of exalting and commending stated in the Holy Qur'an are of the Torah descended by God, not the altered one, which we believe to be His Words.

God Says of Isa's confirmation of His Torah: {"(I have come to you), to attest the *Torah*[453] which was before me. And to make lawful to you part of what was (Before) forbidden to you; I have come to you with a Sign from your Lord. So fear Allah, and obey me} (Surat Aal-Imran: 50).

Also, God Says: {And in their footsteps We sent Jesus the son of Mary, confirming the *Torah*[454] that had come before him: We sent him the Gospel: therein was guidance and light, and confir-

[450] Ibid, p.69.

[451] Corrected by Translator.

[452] "Hadeeth al-Qur'an 'an al-Tawraah wal Injeel", p.71.

[453] Corrected by Translator.

[454] Corrected by Translator.

mation of the *Torah*[455] that had come before him: a guidance and an admonition to those who fear Allah} (Surat al-Maa'idah: 46).

We note how the base word *confirm* is stated twice in the above verse:

• First, of Isa the Messenger having been sent to confirm that which was before him.

• Second, of the Injeel having been descended as confirmation of the Torah.

Hence, Prophet Isa (pbuh) confirmed the authenticity of the Divine Torah, that the Injeel was descended upon him from God – which also confirms the Torah's authenticity – and that Prophet Mohammad (pbuh) also confirms the Divine Torah.

God Says: {And when there came to them a messenger from Allah, confirming what was with them, a party of the people of the Book threw away the Book of Allah behind their backs, as if (it had been something) they did not know!} (Surat al-Baqarah: 101).

God took a covenant from prophets that they encourage their followers to believe in the final messenger, Prophet Mohammad (pbuh). God Says: {Behold! Allah took the covenant of the prophets, saying: "I give you a Book and Wisdom; then comes to you a messenger, confirming what is with you; do ye believe in him and render him help." Allah said: "Do ye agree, and take this my Covenant as binding on you?" They said: "We agree." He said: "Then bear witness, and I am with you among the witnesses"} (Surat Aal-Imran: 81).

The Holy Qur'an is confirmatory of the Divine Torah's topics, facts, laws and bases, ethics, virtues, history, stories, directives, determinations and others.[456]

---

[455] Corrected by Translator.

[456] "Hadeeth al-Qur'an 'an al-Tawraah wal Injeel", Ibid, p.135-137.

h. Torah Definition:

God states that Jewish rabbis altered the wording of the Torah by adding and subtracting much to and from it. But God exposed their actions in many instances throughout the Holy Qur'an:

- God Says: {Can ye (o ye men of Faith) entertain the hope that they will believe in you? Seeing that a party of them heard the Word of Allah, and perverted it knowingly after they understood it} (Surat al-Baqarah: 75).

- God Says: {And there are among them illiterates, who know not the Book, but (see therein their own) desires, and they do nothing but conjecture. Then woe to those who write the Book with their own hands, and then say: "This is from Allah," to traffic with it for miserable price!- Woe to them for what their hands do write, and for the gain they make thereby} (Surat al-Baqarah: 78-79).

- God Says: {Of the Jews there are those who displace words from their (right) places} (Surat al-Nisaa': 46).

- God Says: {They change the words from their (right) places and forget a good part of the message that was sent them} (Surat al-Maa'idah: 13).

- God Says: {Or it be among the Jews,- men who will listen to any lie,- will listen even to others who have never so much as come to thee. They change the words from their (right) times and places: they say, "If ye are given this, take it, but if not, beware!" If any one´s trial is intended by Allah, thou hast no authority in the least for him against Allah. For such - it is not Allah's will to purify their hearts. For them there is disgrace in this world, and in the Hereafter a heavy punishment. (They are fond of) listening to falsehood, of devouring anything forbidden} (Surat al-Maa'idah: 41-42).

Some scholars have specified the type of alterations conducted by Israelite holy to the Torah:

- Alteration through change

- Alteration through addition

- Alteration through removal

- Alteration through changing meaning while keeping pronunciation the same.[457]

These are manifested in different forms:

• Covering Truth with falsehood and concealing the Truth so that the masses would believe in the latter:

God Says: {Ye People of the Book! Why do ye clothe Truth with falsehood, and conceal the Truth, while ye have knowledge?} (Surat Aal-Imran: 71). An example on this is that they accused Haroun (pbuh) of placing the calf for them and that he ordered them to worship it.

• Concealing the truth:

This is evident in the same verse, above, and in: {And cover not Truth with falsehood, nor conceal the Truth when ye know (what it is)} (Surat al-Baqarah: 42).

One of the examples on concealing the truth of Prophet Mohammad's arrival in the Torah, which they know for fact, is that told by Safiyya bint Huyay bin Akhtab, the leader of Jews, and who later married Prophet Mohammad after having embraced Islam. She said that her uncle asked her father about Prophet Mohammad when he came to Medina as whether or not he was the awaited prophet. Huyay bin Akhtab said Mohammad was, but that they shall not believe in him. They also concealed God's mandate that adulterers be stoned to death, but God exposed them at the hands of their past rabbi, the Sahabi Abdullah bin Islam who revealed that the Torah did mandate it.

---

[457] Mohammad al-Baar, "Introduction to Studying the Torah and the Old Testament", al-Qalam House, Damascus, 2nd Ed., 2011, p.120.

• **Hiding the Truth:**

This is very similar to its concealment but scholars distinguish between the two and consider the latter conducted for a grave matter like the prophethood of Mohammad (pbuh), while the former is to that which brought them shame. God Says: {O people of the Book! There hath come to you our Messenger, revealing to you much that ye used to hide in the Book, and passing over much (that is now unnecessary)} (Surat al-Maa'idah: 15).

• **Shifting words from their original places:**

Replacing a word for another or a sentence for another. This is alteration through change of word or phrase location in order to change the meaning. God Says: {They change the words from their (right) places and forget a good part of the message that was sent them} and {They change the words from their (right) times and places} (Surat al-Maa'idah: 13 & 41 respectively).

• Twisting their tongues: This was done when they read the Torah and would add words from their heads instead of the Words of God. God Says: {There is among them a section who distort the Book with their tongues: (As they read) you would think it is a part of the Book, but it is no part of the Book; and they say, "That is from Allah," but it is not from Allah. It is they who tell a lie against Allah, and (well) they know it!} (Surat Aal-Imran: 78).[458]

With these alterations of the Holy Book that was descended upon Prophet Mousa (pbuh), and along the passage of time, the original Torah was lost through wars and destitution in the land and due to Jews' relinquishing their faith many times. Tribes among them – like the Bal'aim, Ashtaron, Malkum and others – began worshipping idols, slaughtered livestock in their name and erected grand temples for them.[459]

[458] "Introduction to Studying the Torah and the Old Testament", Ibid, p.12-122.

[459] Ibid, p.122.

The Old Testament is rife with such examples where in the Era of Judges (140 years) they renounced their faith seven times, worshipped idols instead, slaughtered their own children as sacrificial gifts and falsely claimed that Mousa (pbuh) was a servant of such idols for who he himself had erected temples!

Only a few verses of the lost Holy Torah remained and thus, the messengers sent forth to them by God would remind them of it so that the Israelites may cease from their wrongdoing and blasphemy. Yet many messengers have died at the hands of the Israelites after having branded them liars. God Says: {Some ye called impostors, and others ye slay} (Surat al-Baqarah: 87).

As only glimpses of the Divine Torah survived, their rabbis collected those and added to them that which Satan inspired them, phrased the outcome in books and presented them to their people as being the Torah descended from God. But modern research in the past three centuries has proven that the current Torah was written along the passage of 1000 years by hundreds of writers. Scholars add that this began once the Jews began returning after the Babylonian Captivity period, in the fifth and fourth centuries BC, i.e. almost 10 centuries after the death of Prophet Mousa (pbuh).[460]

All books of the Torah were written after that Exile, as were others of the Old Testament – a matter evidenced through the high volume of Babylonian words contained therein.

Nasraani theologians have admitted to the loss of the Torah of Mousa – which establishes that religion's bases. The author of the book "*Summary of Sunni Proofs to the truth of Christian Origins*"[461] states that: "It is impossible that the original version of Mousa's Torah still exists, and we do not know what

[460] "Introduction to Studying the Torah and the Old Testament", Ibid, p.123.

[461] Translated by Translator from (Khulasat al-Adillah al-Sunniyah 'aala Sidq 'Usool al-Masihiyyah).

happened to it. It was most likely lost with the coffin when Nebuchadnezzar II ruined the temple; hence the discourse among Jews that the holy books were lost and that the writer Ezra – who was a prophet – consolidated all the different books, fixed their mistakes and returned them to their original form." Grand scholar Mohammad Rasheed Rida said: "We know their answer when they are asked from where Ezra brought about those books after they had been lost, and on what he relied in correcting their mistakes. They say he wrote it through that which was inspired to him. But where is the proof of such inspiration? Had there truly existed (inspiration), why would the writer need to collect the books from people who may have altered their contents? We would have wished he had jotted down only the alleged divine laws he claimed, void of the historical events that were added to it."

The news contained in these versions was the most prominent testament to their falsehood – news like Prophet Nouh being a man who consumes alcohol till he passes out or of Prophet Lott being a man who also becomes intoxicated so that he may have sex with his two daughters over the course of two consecutive nights so that they may bear children and grandchildren! Many falsehoods about a number of God's chosen prophets exist in this new collection of books that denounces them. Is such an accepted practise?[462]

i. The Holy Qur'an does not acknowledge the authenticity of the altered Torah:

The so-called *Old Testament* is marred with mistakes and lies, and only a small portion of it carries an amount of truth. It is this Torah that the Holy Qur'an holds in contempt. The scattered miniscule examples of the Divine Torah contained within the books

[462] Mohammad al-Ghazaali, "Sayhat Tahtheer min Du'aat al-Tanseer", al-Qalam House, Damascus, 1st Ed., 2000, p.116.

of the Old Testament are but a drop in the ocean of alterations and lies committed therein by their rabbis.[463]

The Holy Qur'an details God's repudiation of the claims contained in this altered version:

- God's repudiation of their claim that He tires:

Writers of the Torah claim that when God created the Heavens and Earth, he became tired and hence had to relax on the seventh day; a day that coincided with Saturday. This is stated in the second chapter of the book of Genesis: (Thus the heavens and the earth were completed in all their vast array. By the seventh day God had finished the work he had been doing; so on the seventh day he rested from all his work. Then God blessed the seventh day and made it holy, because on it he rested from all the work of creating that he had done.) [Genesis 2:3].[464]

Attributing a break time to The Almighty is blasphemous and sacrilegious as it denotes a limitation, tiredness and fatigue – all of which are attributed to mankind who are creations of The Almighty Who does not tire! God Says: {We created the heavens and the earth and all between them in Six Days, nor did any sense of weariness touch Us} (Surat Qaaf: 38).

God created the Heavens and Earth in six days though He could have created them in an instant as when He Wills any matter, He orders it to be and it is. This short but concise holy verse is clear repudiation of the claims perpetrated by the authors of the Torah.

- Repudiating their claim that God had searched for Adam:

Rabbis who authored the Torah claim that when Adam and Eve ate from the tree, they became naked, heard the footsteps of God as he strolled in paradise and were embarrassed of Him, so Adam hid behind one of its trees and God began searching for Adam, but

[463] "Hadeeth al-Qur'an 'an al-Tawraah wal Injeel", Ibid, p.142.

[464] Ibid, p.144.

could not see him nor did God know that he had eaten from the tree.

Rabbis wrote in the book of Genesis: "And they heard the sound of the Lord God walking in the garden in the cool of the day, and the man and his wife hid themselves from the presence of the Lord God among the trees of the garden. But the Lord God called to the man, 'Where are you?' He answered 'I heard you in the garden but I was afraid because I was naked; so I hid.' And he said, 'Who told you that you were naked? Have you eaten from the tree that I commanded you not to eat from?' The man said, 'The woman you put here with me gave me some fruit from the tree and I ate it.'" [Genesis 3: 8-12].[465]

A number of untruths and lies exist in the above text:

- Describing God's physical appearance as possessing two legs that walk and make audible sound as does any human. God Says: {There is nothing whatever like unto Him, and He is the One that hears and sees (all things)} (Surat al-Shourah: 11).

- Describing God as ignorant, unknowledgeable and unaware of hidden matters.

This concealment and dialogue between God and Adam is akin of the Hide and Seek game played by children. God refutes all these falsehoods: {When they tasted of the tree, their shame became manifest to them, and they began to sew together the leaves of the garden over their bodies. And their Lord called unto them: "Did I not forbid you that tree, and tell you that Satan was an avowed enemy unto you?"} (Surat al-A'araaf: 22).

- Repudiating their claim that Prophet Haroun made the golden calf:

The fake Torah claims that Prophet Haroun (pbuh) took the jewellery of the Israelites and from it he shaped the golden calf and

465 "Hadeeth al-Qur'an 'an al-Tawraah wal Injeel", Ibid, p.145.

called on them to worship it. The book of Exodus claims: "When the people saw that Moses was so long in coming down from the mountain, they gathered around Aaron and said, 'Come make us gods who will go before us. As for this fellow Moses who brought us up out of Egypt, we know not what has happened to him.' Aaron answered them, 'Take off the gold earrings that your wives, your sons and your daughters are wearing, and bring them to me.' So all the people took off their earrings and brought them to Aaron. He took what they handed him and made it into an idol cast in the shape of a calf, fashioning it with a tool. Then they said, 'These are your gods, Israel, who brought you up out of Egypt.' When Aaron saw this, he built an altar in front of the calf and announced, 'Tomorrow there will be a festival to the Lord … So the next day the people rose early and sacrificed burnt offerings . Afterward they sat down to eat and drink and got up to indulge in revelry …" [Exodus: 32/ 1-6].[466]

Rabbis here attribute blasphemy to Prophet Haroun (pbuh), but the Holy Qur'an repudiated them by stating that the calf was crafted by the rogue Samiri:

- God Says: {(Allah) said: "We have tested thy people in thy absence: the Samiri has led them astray"} (Surat Ta Ha: 85).

- God Says: {They said: "We broke not the promise to thee, as far as lay in our power: but we were made to carry the weight of the ornaments of the (whole) people, and we threw them (into the fire), and that was what the Samiri suggested. "Then he brought out (of the fire) before the (people) the image of a calf: It seemed to low: so they said: This is your god, and the god of Moses, but (Moses) has forgotten!"} (Surat Ta Ha: 87-88).

God Says: {Aaron had already, before this said to them: "O my people! ye are being tested in this: for verily your Lord is Allah

466 Ibid, p.147

Most Gracious; so follow me and obey my command." They had said: "We will not abandon this cult, but we will devote ourselves to it until Moses returns to us"} (Surat Ta Ha 90-91).

- Repudiating their claim of being God's children and beloved ones:

Rabbis spin lies of God, are selfish, racist and have deceived the majority of Jews into believing that they are God's children and loved ones, that God had chosen and supported them, that He shall not forsake them, that they are the guided ones and that Paradise is an abode only for them. The Holy Qur'an has refuted their claims. God Says: {(Both) the Jews and the Christians say: "We are sons of Allah, and his beloved." Say: "Why then doth He punish you for your sins? Nay, ye are but men,- of the men he hath created: He forgiveth whom He pleaseth, and He punisheth whom He pleaseth: and to Allah belongeth the dominion of the heavens and the earth, and all that is between: and unto Him is the final goal (of all)"} (Surat al-Maa'idah: 18).

They lie in their claim that they are the children of God and His beloved ones as they are creations like all other human beings and are not distinct from others in shape or figure. God gives preferential treatment on the basis of piety towards Him and for man's good deeds. Yet God knows no favouritism as He forgives whomever He Wills and punishes whomever He Wills.[467]

- Repudiating their claim of being God's friends:

God Says: {Say: "O ye that stand on Judaism! If ye think that ye are friends to Allah, to the exclusion of (other) men, then express your desire for Death, if ye are truthful!" But never will they express their desire (for Death), because of the (deeds) their hands have sent on before them! and Allah knows well those that do wrong! Say: "The Death from which ye flee will truly overtake

[467] "Hadeeth al-Qur'an 'an al-Tawraah wal Injeel", Ibid, p.148.

you: then will ye be sent back to the Knower of things secret and open: and He will tell you (the truth of) the things that ye did!"} (Surat al-Jumu'aah: 6-8).

Naturally, those Jews did not wish for death nor did they succeed in the challenge. They preferred to be dubbed 'Cowards' as they knew they were liars, that Prophet Mohammad (pbuh) was truthful, that God would have taken their lives had they wished for death and that they would have consequently wound up in Hell. This meaning was emphasised in the Holy Qur'an: {Say: "If the last Home, with Allah, be for you specially, and not for anyone else, then seek ye for death, if ye are sincere." But they will never seek for death, on account of the (sins) which their hands have sent on before them, and Allah is well-acquainted with the wrong-doers. Thou wilt indeed find them, of all people, most greedy of life,-even more than the idolaters: Each one of them wishes He could be given a life of a thousand years: But the grant of such life will not save him from (due) punishment. For Allah sees well all that they do} (Surat al-Baqarah: 94-96).

The dossier of Jews' deeds in the Heavens is a black one and severe punishment awaits them when their lives are taken. Such people will never wish for death as their aim is to revel in this life while enjoying drinking, eating and pursuing debauchery. Being humiliated or ruled over by others are matters for which they have no regard as they do not consider their worldly actions in preparation for Judgment Day.[468]

- Repudiating their claim that Prophet Ibrahim was Jewish:

Jews claimed that Prophet Ibrahim (pbuh) was of their religion, while Nasraanis claimed he was of theirs. God refuted both claims: {Ye People of the Book! Why dispute ye about Abraham, when the *Torah*[469] and the Gospel Were not revealed Till after him? Have ye

[468] Al-Khalidi, Ibid, p.151.

[469] Corrected by Translator.

no understanding? Ah! Ye are those who fell to disputing (Even) in matters of which ye had some knowledge! but why dispute ye in matters of which ye have no knowledge? It is Allah Who knows, and ye who know not! Abraham was not a Jew nor yet a Christian; but he was true in Faith, and bowed his will to Allah's Which is Islam, and he joined not gods with Allah. Without doubt, among men, the nearest of kin to Abraham, are those who follow him, as are also this Messenger and those who believe: And Allah is the Protector of those who have faith} (Surat Aal-Imran: 65-68).

The above examples suffice as proof of the lies perpetrated in the altered Jewish Torah of the Old Testament that is infested with untruths created by evil rabbis.[470]

Tenth: The Injeel (Bible) and the gospels

The word "Injeel", i.e. Bible, is stated 12 times in the Holy Qur'an. The following holy verses are some examples:

God Says: {It is He Who sent down to thee (step by step), in truth, the Book, confirming what went before it; and He sent down the *Torah*[471] (of Moses) and the Gospel (of Jesus) before this, as a guide to mankind, and He sent down the criterion (of judgment between right and wrong). Then those who reject Faith in the Signs of Allah will suffer the severest penalty, and Allah is Exalted in Might, Lord of Retribution} (Surat Aal-Imran: 3-4).

- God Says: {Ye People of the Book! Why dispute ye about Abraham, when the *Torah*[472] and the Gospel Were not revealed Till after him? Have ye no understanding?} (Surat Aal-Imran: 65).

- God Says: {If only they had stood fast by the *Torah*[473], the Gospel, and all the revelation that was sent to them from their

[470] Al-Khalidi, Ibid, p.151.

[471] Corrected by Translator.

[472] Corrected by Translator.

[473] Corrected by Translator.

Lord, they would have enjoyed happiness from every side. There is from among them a party on the right course: but many of them follow a course that is evil} (Surat al-Maa'idah: 66).

- God Says: {Say: "O People of the Book! ye have no ground to stand upon unless ye stand fast by the *Torah*[474], the Gospel, and all the revelation that has come to you from your Lord." It is the revelation that cometh to thee from thy Lord, that increaseth in most of them their obstinate rebellion and blasphemy. But sorrow thou not over (these) people without Faith} (Surat al-Maa'idah: 68).

The word *Injeel* is the Arabic version of the transliterated original Greek *Inhelius*, meaning glad tidings and education.[475] The Injeel is the Book that God descended upon His Prophet Isa son of Maryam as light and guidance for the Israelites, as reported in the Holy Qur'an. Nowadays, the word *Injeel* refers to the four gospels of Nasraanis, i.e. Matthew, Mark, Luke and John. It can also refer to the gospels of the New Testament.[476]

None of the existing gospels nowadays is known to be rightly connected to Prophet Isa – most of which should actually not be related to him at all. The best way to describe these gospels is that they are historical classifications of the life of the Messiah, along with some of his commandments, advices and miracles.[477]

The Injeel had no better luck in preserving its original scripture than did the Torah. After the raising of Isa to the Heavens, the pages of the Book descended upon him also disappeared till this very day. Due to Roman rule and the influence the Jews had among the

474 Corrected by Translator.

475 Rahmatullah al-Hindi al-'Uthmani, "Ithhar al-Haq", ver. by Ahmad Hijazi al-Saqqa, al-Turaath print, Qatari Print, 1/79-80.

476 Sarah al-Abbaadi, "Al-Tahreef wal Tanaaqud fi al-Anaajeel", Teeba al-Khadra House, Mecca, 1st Ed., 2003, p.23.

477 "Studies in Objective Tafseer of the Holy Qur'an", Ibid, p.267.

masses, the two parties colluded in chasing down all who believed in Prophet Isa and in confiscating any materials that referenced his teachings. This persecution lasted for more than three centuries through which Christians have disagreed much among themselves; a matter reflected in the books whose disciples have been reported to have marred.

All these books were dubbed "gospels" as their authors had explained the life of Isa and registered in them his sermons and teachings that they remembered. There was a wide discrepancy among the contents of these gospels as it is reported that they numbered around 70.[478]

Others believe these gospels numbered around 100,[479] and were based either on Unitarianism or the Trinity. This division remained in full force till the First Council of Nicaea in 320 AD when Constantine upheld the Trinity and paved they way for the Messiah to become the son of God – despite being the opinion of the minority of attendees. Another Council then sanctified the Holy Spirit, all Unitarian gospels were deemed false and were accordingly confiscated on a mass scale.

Sheikh Mohammad Rasheed, author of "Al-Manar", relays the opinion of some church historians that the number of false gospels is 35. He also relays the opinion of the Maronite author of "Thakheerat al-Albaab" , who denies the large number of gospels and limits them to no more than 20 on the premise that a single gospel was given different names. He counted them all, stated that some names were repeated and that the gospel of Barnabas was among the main twenty. But let us presume that they truly were only 20 gospels; so where are those beyond the four prevalent ones nowadays?

---

478 "Sayhat Tahtheer min Du'aat al-Tanseer", Ibid, p.119

479 Mahmoud Abdel-Hameed, "Ma'a al-Anbiyaa' wa Jihaadihim", al-Fikr House, Damascus, 1st Ed., 2003, p.349.

In truth, the gospels that upheld Unitarianism were the majority, and it is only destiny that preserved that of Barnabas as an example thereof. But it was the tyranny of the Roman Empire that led to the discontinuation of those. The four adopted ones do not depict the truth as their origins and translations are obscure.

If we were to suppose that some of that contained within them is based on goodness, they are definitely not of the quality of the Injeel – which was mentioned as being both that of God and that of Isa at times – which told the masses to repent and believe in it. The author of "Al-Manar" stated that a Holy Book is attributed to God because it was He Who descended it, and to God's messenger as it was he who received it from God. Hence we say the Injeel of Isa and the Torah of Mousa.[480]

God Says: {From those, too, who call themselves Christians, We did take a Covenant, but they forgot a good part of the message that was sent them: so we estranged them, with enmity and hatred between the one and the other, to the day of judgment. And soon will Allah show them what it is they have done} (Surat al-Maa'idah: 14).

Nasraanis are far from having followed that which Prophet Isa commanded them. "Al-Manar" states that the Jews became rabid in aggression and pursuit of monotheist Nasraanis who possessed no civil entity of power or knowledge that would preserve in writing that of the Messiah's Injeel which they remembered.

Nasraanis' history and sacred books show that most of their preachers would disseminate faulty teachings concerning the Messiah, and some of them have written that down to the extent that they dubbed these writings 'gospels.' These four gospels have only appeared three centuries after the time of Prophet Isa when Nasraanis proclaimed a state as King Constantine became Nasraani

480 "Sayhat Tahtheer min Du'aat al-Tanseer", Ibid, p.120.

and ushered Nasraaniism into a new phase of paganism. These gospels are no more than a redacted history of the Messiah (pbuh), are contradictory, are of obscure origin and history, are contentious and comprise of different languages.[481]

In his book entitled, "Ithhaar al-Haq" (Exposing the Truth), Sheikh Rahmatullah al-Hindi gives 100 examples from the holy books of Jews and Nasraanis on pronunciation and moral alterations thereof. Past and contemporary Islamic scholars specialised in comparative theology have critiqued all bases of current Nasraaniism and exposed many questionable matters. Nowadays in the 21st century since the birth of Isa, we refer Christian authenticators to that which confirms our opinion: Ahmad Abdul-Wahhab's "Ikhtilaf fi Tarajim al-Kitaab al-Muqaddas" (Discrepancies in the translations of the Holy Book) studied documents authenticated by Christian scholars that show a vast discrepancy among the holy book's translations that touch upon the core of Christianity's integrity.[482]

The cascaded dogmas that have been inherited among Nasraanis sprouted from this land, and were not descended by God. They are the products of human councils supervised over by pagan authorities; yet if we were to suppose their foundations were sound, they still defy logic and intellect and ascribe to a religion that is akin of myths. This is the essence of the struggle between religion and science, the vast divide between sought civilisations and that for which clergymen aim. The suppression of the true religion has paved the way for myths and fables.[483]

None of the four gospels was written while Prophet Isa (pbuh) was on Earth[484]; these gospels are:

---

[481] Ibid.

[482] Ibid, p.122.

[483] "Sayhat Tahtheer min Du'aat al-Tanseer", Ibid, p.122-123.

[484] Ibid

1. The gospel of Matthew:

This is Nasraanis' first and oldest gospel and was written four years after the Messiah. It was originally written in Hebrew and then translated, as it exists now, but who translated it and where is the original document so that a comparison between the two may occur? There are no answers to any of the above. Hence, what scientific value can there be for a document whose origin and translator are unknown, and one that is neither directly connected to the Messiah nor to any of his disciples?

2. The gospel of Mark:

It was written in Greek 23 years after Prophet Isa was raised to the Heavens. Nasraanis have disagreed on its actual dating with some saying it was written by Peter (the chief of Hawaaris) and by others who claimed Mark had authored it after the death of Peter and Paul. "*Musrshid al-Taalibeen*" (Beacon of Seekers) states that it was written by authority of Peter in 61 AD so that it may benefit the nations who embraced Nasraaniism through him. This gospel renounces Isa's divinity. So why do we notice doubt among Nasraaniism historians in specifically identifying who wrote this gospel?

3. The gospel of Luke:

Nasraaniism historians agree that it was written twenty years after Isa (pbuh) was raised to the Heavens. He was not a disciple of Isa but rather one of Paul's who was actually a fanatic Jew anti-Christian. Paul had never laid eyes on the Messiah and would insult Nasraanis gravely. But when he realised that persecuting Nasraaniism was reaping him no rewards, he claimed having had an epileptic episode in which the Messiah touched him and ordered him to stop causing his followers harm. From that time onwards, he became a believers and claimed that the Messiah had sent him to promote his Injeel. The Church fell for the ruse and he removed the prohibition on eating dead animals and drinking alcohol. The gospel of Luke makes many previously unknown additions to those of Matthew and Mark that cause nothing but suspicion.[485]

4. The gospel of John:

It was written 32 years after Prophet Isa was raised to the Heavens. The Church claims it was written by (John bin Zabdi), a disciple of Prophet Isa. But the majority of Nasraaniism scholars have denied this claim and stated it was classified by a student at Alexandria School in the 2nd century AD. Five-hundred Nasraani scholars at the British council of culture wrote that (the gospel of John is undoubtedly a forged book whose writer wished to oppose two of Prophet Isa's disciples, i.e. Saints John and Matthew, and claimed in the book's margin that he was the one the Messiah loved most among all Hawaaris…}.[486]

This gospel was distinct in containing previously unheard of examples indicating the divinity of the Messiah. Astonishingly enough, the Church relies on it in its belief that is contrary to the religion God descended upon Isa, all the while knowing that this gospel was not written by John, a disciple of the Messiah. Sheikh al-Najjar states in "*Qasas al-Anbiyaa*'" (Prophets' Stories) contradictions among these current gospels which you may refer to if you wish as it is an accurate and precious work.[487]

It has to be clear to any intellectual that all existing gospels are altered versions of that which truly descended upon Prophet Isa (pbuh). This reluctance in believing the information they contain should suffice that they be deemed untrustworthy.[488]

[485] Abdul-Wahhaab al-Najjaar, "Qasas al-Anbiyaa'", al-Jeel Printing, Publishing & Distribution House, Beirut, 1st Ed., 2009, p.400.

[486] "Ma'a al-Anbiyaa' wa Jihaadihim", Ibid, p.352.

[487] "Qasas al-Anbiyaa'", p.402.

[488] "Ma'a al-Anbiyaa' wa Jihaadihim", Ibid, p.352.

• Dr Sarah Hamid Mohammad al-Abbaadi carried out an exhaustive study detailed in her book "*Alterations and Contradictions among the Four Gospels*", and came out with the following conclusions:

- Much doubt mars the most prominent points in the adopted gospels of Nasraanis regarding their authors and their dates of writing.

- Adopting these and not others among Nasraanis' many gospels was conducted by a pagan Roman ruler (Constantine) who was able to force his will on Unitarians, and who burnt all other gospels.

- These gospels are not at all connected in time sequencing to the days of their authors.

- Honest researchers concur that the original Injeel of the Messiah (pbuh) exists, as mentioned in the Qur'an, but that it is missing.

- There is clear presence of three types of alterations in the four gospels, i.e. of replacing, adding and deducting as stated in the Holy Qur'an.

- Zealot Christians' absolutely reject Barnabas's gospel as it exposes the alterations present in the four gospels, particularly that regarding faith.

- Clear contradictions exist in each gospel and among all four.

- The four gospel mention inaccurate historical events; they are more fictitious than real.

- The four gospels are unworthy of being the argument for Nasraanis in carrying out their faith as they are altered, contradictory and provide no evidence that their writers were *inspired* when they authored them[489].

---

489 "Al-Tahreef wal Tanaaqud fi al-Anaajeel", Ibid, p.308-309.

In his same book, mentioned above, grand scholar Rahmatullah al-Hindi details 100 examples from Jewish and Nasraani holy books regarding such alterations.[490]

• Dr Azziyyah Ali Taha presented a comprehensive study on the methodology of collecting the Sunnah of Prophet Mohammad (pbuh) and that of the gospels in her book entitled, "*Methodology of Collecting the Sunnah and the Gospels*". She concluded the following:

- Nasraanis of the New Testament did not follow a fixed and well-established method for collecting these gospels.

- The gospels were written in a language different from the original that was prevalent in Palestine when the Injeel was descended upon Prophet Isa (pbuh).

- All authors of the New Testament did not meet Prophet Isa in person and some claimed to be of his disciples and wrote in their stead without clarifying this. Also, the authors and the timing of writing these gospels are contentious matters.

- Many gospels had existed but they were burnt. People were also in conflict regarding the truth about the Messiah (pbuh).

- Politics played a major role in the shaping of Christianity in the fourth century AD and in presenting it in its current form. Emperor Constantine tried uniting Nasraanis under his rule for fear that his empire may be divided, and so he brought together all priests at the Council of Nicaea, colluded with the bishop of Alexandria that there are three gods and punished all who stated otherwise. Having been pagan prior to becoming Christian, it is no wonder he supported the claim of the Trinity.

- Storytellers of the different gospels contradicted with one another on the main matter that concerns the heart of Nasraaniism, i.e. the crucifixion and its aftermath: trial, burial and resurrection.

490 "Sayhat Tahtheer min Du'aat al-Tanseer", Ibid, p.121.

- They also disagreed on the truth of the god yet stated that Isa was ignorant, a liar, abusive of his mother and that she was an adulteress, as they relate Isa to Yusuf the carpenter who was not married to Maryam (pbuh) when she bore Isa, but who was rather her fiancé, as they claim.[491]

- Christian clergymen struggled with experimental sciences at the onset of the scientific renaissance in Europe and the Church fought against its scientists. Philosophers from among the clergymen emerged and attempted to bridge the gap between science and Christianity, yet a tremor occurred when the clergymen themselves attempted implementing modern scientific theories to their faith. Schools of German criticism were established as a result, as well as for searching for the historical Isa in Europe.

- Samuel Remoras was the first to look into the historical Isa although the result he reached almost entirely toppled Christianity.

She added, "Thus, we witnessed how 19th century scholars concluded the same notions in agreeing that the statements upon which Christianity is founded nowadays – as per the New Testament gospels – are in no way or form related to the historical Isa. There was no acknowledged and fixed methodology followed at the Council of Nicaea for adopting those particular gospels, and uncertainty continued throughout the 20th century and reached its peak when some Nasraanis claimed that the god had died. Also when members of the advanced theology school claimed the god had shortcomings, was imperfect and needed humans to complement himself. But The Almighty is far above that as He is Ultimately The Supreme One![492]

[491] Azziyyah Ali Taha, "Manhajiyyat Jam'a al-Sunnah wa Jam'a al-Anaajeel", al-Risaalah Est., Lebanon, 2nd Ed., 1996, p.552.

[492] Ibid, p.553.

God Says: {Say: He is Allah, the One and Only; Allah, the Eternal, Absolute; He begetteth not, nor is He begotten; And there is none like unto Him} (Surat al-Ikhlaas).

• Dr Abdul-Razzak Abdul-Hameed conducted an exquisite study for his M.A. thesis (Sources of Nasraaniism – study and critique) and concluded a number of matters. The following are examples:

- The Holy Qur'an and the correct Hadeeths are the most reliable sources for revealing the truth about Prophet Isa (pbuh).

- Most of the actual roots for most of that which Nasraanis follow today are principles of Plato's modern philosophy and pagan traditions and beliefs. Hence, the level to which Nasraanis are actually connected to their original holy gospels is miniscule.

- There is a difference between saying (The Torah and the Injeel) and (The Old and New Testaments) as the Old Testament comprises a number of gospels (39 or 46), five of which are attributed to Mousa (pbuh), and are dubbed the Torah or the Pentateuch. The New Testament comprises 27 books, four are gospels of Matthew, Mark, Luke and John, but are not the true Injeel descended from God upon Prophet Isa (pbuh).

- Some Nasraani sources are general, like that dubbed the holy book's Old and New testaments and councils' decisions; while others are sect-specific like Papal decrees.

- Attributing the books of the Old and New Testaments to Prophet Isa is usually conducted for promotional reasons as most of these books were composed after the time of Prophet Isa.

- Although the Injeel that was descended upon Prophet Isa (pbuh) has now been lost, some references of it remain in some paragraphs of the New Testament.

- Not a single action or statement attributed to Prophet Isa in any of the gospels can be considered true as none of those works possesses an authentic and connected chain of narrators.

- Each of the Old and New Testaments has sources it branched off from, verbal stories, traditions and customs of different people and nations, some human temporary laws, some statements by men of wisdom, and the like.

- There exist many contradiction in every gospel and among all whose errors are both in matters of faith and in historical and scientific accounts.

- The holy gospels of Nasraanis, particularly the Old Testament, are living proof to the worst kind of secularism as they attack The Almighty through His Names and Traits and attack and demean His prophets and messengers.[493]

- That which is infamously known of some interpreters regarding the story of the enemy who encircled the altar of Dawoud (pbuh) speaks ill of his wives: "99 sheep for only one woman and just one sheep for (Oria al-Hathi) …" is one of the Israeli stories, due to the influence of the story in the Old Testament, and none of this was proven of the Prophet.

- The four gospels adopted by Nasraanis were chosen from among scores of others as they were closest to what Nasraaniism settled on after being influenced by paganism, philosophies and gradual departure from Divine Inspiration.

- All that which was attributed to Prophet Isa or his disciples regarding gospels and messages remains hearsay.

- There was most likely a relationship of apprenticeship or the like of the composer of the third gospel and that of the messengers' actions to the Jewish Paul Saul.

- Paul pretended to shift to Nasraaniism for personal reasons like fulfilling his desire for presidency and leadership. He then spoke openly of opposing all of the Messiah's disciples who knew more about their Prophet (pbuh) than anyone else.

[493] "Sources of Nasraaniism: Study and Critique", Ibid, 2/977-979.

- On the basis of the principles Paul pronounced and called for in comparison with that followed by Nasraanis today, we are right in stating that Paul is the true father of current Nasraaniism.

- There exists a difference between the Hawaari disciple John and the theologian philosopher John – who were alive during the same time - and the latter is most likely the author of the fourth gospel.

- The gospel of Luke – as stated by its author – represented a personal letter from a friend to another, and was not meant to inspire or infer any favouritism. It was merely a collection, formulation, and arrangement of oral accounts which the writer felt he had what it took to undertake such a task.[494]

- The Arabic translation of Nasraanis' holy book possesses a number of scientific and technical problems, most prominent among which are the weak style, numerous grammatical and spelling mistakes, lack of unity in text or joining together repetitive pieces of information.

- The discrepancy between copies and publications or prints and translations, conducting many modifications to the text every once in a while on the pretence of reviewing, editing or correcting …

- Nasraani councils are considered of great importance to altered Nasraaniism as they assist in building and instilling its dogmas and laws. They also play a role in dividing Nasraanis into sects and parties.

- All councils that convened after the Seventh Ecumenical Council of Nicaea in 787 AD are considered private or spatial ones despite their curators deeming them international or general.

- The Messiah (pbuh) neither established a church nor considered establishing one, and any unfounded statements to the contrary cannot be used as evidence.

---

494 "Sources of Nasraaniism: Study and Critique", Ibid, 2/980.

- The flourishing of the Western Church during the Middle Ages in Europe is deemed its greatest source of authority and that of its popes over the masses – who then hijacked religion to serve their personal interests.

- The Middle Ages is also considered the period during which this authority began gaining momentum.

- The claim that the Pope can do no wrong and is sinless is a falsehood and is unsupported by any historical evidence.

- Popes of the Middle ages and others have added a number of commitments and duties requested of their Nasraani followers – some of which still exist till this very day – while others have been forfeited due to changing circumstances and shortage of means.[495]

Eleventh: Prophet Isa brings glad tidings of Prophet Mohammad (pbut):

Prophet Mohammad (pbuh) is the last and final of God's prophets and messengers. God informed all prophets and messengers of this fact and took upon them a solemn oath that they believe in him:

- God Says: {Behold! Allah took the covenant of the prophets, saying: "I give you a Book and Wisdom; then comes to you a messenger, confirming what is with you; do ye believe in him and render him help." Allah said: "Do ye agree, and take this my Covenant as binding on you?" They said: "We agree." He said: "Then bear witness, and I am with you among the witnesses." If any turn back after this, they are perverted transgressors} (Surat Aal-Imran: 81-82).

God has showed that every prophet complements the prophet who preceded him and that they continue to do so until the arrival of the final prophet, Mohammad (pbuh). Hence, in accordance with

[495] "Sources of Nasraaniism: Study and Critique", Ibid, 2/981-982.

the oath which the prophets promised God, Jews and Nasraanis must believe in Prophet Mohammad for had they not done so, they would not be true followers of Prophets Mousa and Isa (pbut). Jabir reported Prophet Mohammad telling him: (Had Mousa been alive now among you, he would do nothing but follow me).[496]

All prophets have ushered glad tidings of the arrival of the final prophet. Prophet Ibrahim (pbuh) was among those. He prayed, as reported in the Holy Qur'an: {"Our Lord! send amongst them a Messenger of their own, who shall rehearse Thy Signs to them and instruct them in scripture and wisdom, and sanctify them: For Thou art the Exalted in Might, the Wise"} (Surat al-Baqarah: 129).

The glad tidings were stated more emphatically by Prophets Mousa and Isa (pbut). Also, God mentioned some of Prophet Mohammad's traits in both the Torah and Injeel, which means that Jews and Nasraanis knew that God was going to send forth a messenger. Yet when God sent forth Mohammad (pbuh), they denounced him and called him a liar.[497] God Says: {The people of the Book know this as they know their own sons; but some of them conceal the truth which they themselves know} (Surat al-Baqarah: 146).

Had Prophet Mohammad's description not existed, they would not have been able to recognise him as they do their own children; therefore, it was definitely written in their books despite the alterations Jews and Nasraanis conducted on them. God Says: {Say: "Whether ye believe in it or not, it is true that those who were given knowledge beforehand, when it is recited to them, fall down on their faces in humble prostration, And they say: ´Glory to our Lord! Truly has the promise of our Lord been fulfilled!'" They fall down on their faces in tears, and it increases their (earnest) humility} (Surat al-Israa': 107-109).

---

[496] Reported by Ahmad, no. 14104.

[497] "Al-Qasas al-Qur'ani: Presentation and Analysis of Events", Ibid, 4/335.

Having falling to their knees crying and in prayer can in no way denote that they returned to their monasteries and churches with the Cross drawn on their chests![498]

1. Traits of Mohammad (pbuh) in the Torah and Injeel:

God Says: {"Those who follow the messenger, the unlettered Prophet, whom they find mentioned in their own (scriptures), in the *Torah*[499] and the Gospel; for he commands them what is just and forbids them what is evil; he allows them as lawful what is good (and pure) and prohibits them from what is bad (and impure); He releases them from their heavy burdens and from the yokes that are upon them. So it is those who believe in him, honour him, help him, and follow the light which is sent down with him,- it is they who will prosper." Say: "O men! I am sent unto you all, as the Messenger of Allah, to Whom belongeth the dominion of the heavens and the earth: there is no god but He: it is He That giveth both life and death. So believe in Allah and His Messenger, the Unlettered Prophet, who believeth in Allah and His words: follow him that (so) ye may be guided"} (Surat al-A'araaf: 157-158).

This is great news that testifies to the children of Israel, brought to them by their Prophets Mousa and Isa (pbut) from long ago, that a prophet will be sent to them with known traits and message.

- He is the unlettered prophet.

- He calls for righteousness and denounces evil doing.

- He permits for them good things and prohibits them from the bad.

- He removes a load and chains off the chests of those Israelites who believe in him as, otherwise, they would be burdened by their weight in punishment for their disbelief in him. Prophet Moham-

---

498 Mohammad Saleem al-Faadili, "Al-Nasraaniyah fi Meezan al-'Aaql wal Islam", al-Kitaab al-Thaqaafi House, Jordan, 1st Ed., 2003, p.210.

499 Corrected by Translator.

mad does this so that they believe in him, revere God, pay Zakat and believe in God's Signs.[500]

A number of Jews who embraced Islam, like Abdullah bin Sallaam, encouraged their people to believe in Mohammad as it is well-documented through historical accounts that the Jews of the Arabian peninsula and Nasraani priests, had been anticipating the arrival of a messenger from God. But the Jews expected the final prophet to be from among them; yet as he was of Ismaeel's lineage, they opposed his calling, annulled all their oaths and treaties with him, caused rifts between him and pagan tribes and attempted to poison and kill him. But The Almighty protected him from their ill intentions and gave him victory over them.[501]

Despite all alterations and additions, many references to Prophet Mohammad still exist in the books of Nasraanis and Jews nowadays.

Al-Bukhari reported of Ataa' bin Yasaar, "I met Abdullah bin Amr bin al-'Aas and asked him if the Torah mentions any trait of Prophet Mohammad. He said he was mentioned therein exactly as per the holy verse (O prophet We have sent you as witness, bringing glad tidings and warning of matters) … Then I asked Ka'ab al-Ahbaar about what Amr had said to me and he concurred."[502]

This dialogue is evidence that the traits of Prophet Mohammad (pbuh) mentioned in the Qur'an are the same ones mentioned in the Torah and Injeel.[503]

2. Isa (pbuh) brings glad tidings of Mohammad (pbuh):

God Says: {And remember, Jesus, the son of Mary, said: "O Children of Israel! I am the messenger of Allah (sent) to you,

[500] "Fi Thilaal al-Qur'an", Ibid, 3/1378.
[501] "Al-'Ijaaz al-Tareekhi wal Inbaa'i fil Qur'an al-Kareem", Ibid, 2/301.
[502] "Saheeh al-Bukhari", no. 2125.
[503] "Al-Qasas al-Qur'ani: Presentation and Analysis of Events", Ibid, 4/337.

confirming the *Torah*[504] (which came) before me, and giving Glad Tidings of a Messenger to come after me, whose name shall be Ahmad." But when he came to them with Clear Signs, they said, "This is evident sorcery!" Who doth greater wrong than one who invents falsehood against Allah, even as he is being invited to Islam? And Allah guides not those who do wrong} (Surat al-Saff: 6-7).

Prophet Isa (pbuh) told the Israelites (I am God's messenger to you), not that he was a god, son of God, or one of three. (Confirming the Torah which came before me and ushering glad tidings of a prophet who comes after me named Ahmad). This was the connected sequence of God's Message where one hands the baton to the next.

The glad tidings of Mohammad brought forth by Isa in the verse above is firm proof, whether included in current gospels as the circumstances surrounding their writing and disconnected chain of reporters renders them inconsequential of being a reference point. The Holy Qur'an was read to the Jews and Nasraanis of the Arabian peninsula and many of their faithful scholars believed in the truth that Mohammad (pbuh) was truly the awaited messenger.[505]

Nasraanis who were alive at the time of Prophet Mohammad (pbuh) forfeited the oath they gave to Prophet Isa and called Mohammad a liar. Then when they witnessed his proofs, the majority among them claimed them to be sorcery. But a few, like Al-Najaashi, King of Abyssinia, believed in Prophet Mohammad – as previously stated. Roman king Hercules also bore witness in his letter when receiving the Prophet's messenger. In his message he asked Rome for news of this concluding prophet, and upon receiving their response, he told his people: O Romans, I have gathered you for good news. I have received a message from this man call-

[504] Corrected by Translator.

[505] "Fi Thilaal al-Qur'an", Ibid, 3/1378.

ing upon me to embrace his religion, any by God, he is the prophet we have been awaiting; we find him in our Book; so let us go and believe in him so that we may win both in this life and in the Hereafter.

Since Prophet Isa (pbuh) brought forth glad tidings of him, Prophet Mohammad (pbuh) used that testimony and stated that he was (The glad tidings of Isa).

a- Correlating between his two names (Ahmad) and (Mohammad):

The glad tidings brought forth by Isa of Mohammad (pbut) state his name as Ahmad although in reality it is Mohammad. But there exists no difference between the two as both originate from the same source word in Arabic. Also, Prophet Mohammad was known to go by both names.

The holy verse: (And ushering in glad tidings of a prophet who comes after me named Ahmad) refers to Mohammad (pbuh) in character as one whose manners and actions are blessed and as one who thanks God much as the word originates from (thankfulness).[506]

As both Mohammad and Ahmad originate from the same source word, there is no contradiction between the two names.

The usage of the word Ahmad by Prophet Isa shows his wisdom in acknowledging the grace of Prophet Mohammad towards him and all who preceded him. Prophet Isa used to say: The concluding prophet who shall come after me is more *thankful* of God than I am, more *thankful* of God than all who came before me, and the most among us who prays, *thanks*, extolls and praises God. This was Prophet Isa exhibiting humility towards Prophet Mohammad (pbut).[507]

506 "Al-Mufradaat fi Ghareeb al-Qur'an", Ibid, p.256.

507 "Al-Qasas al-Qur'ani: Presentation and Analysis of Events", Ibid, 4/339.

Prophet Mohammad has informed us that he goes by many names. Al-Bukhari and Muslim reported of Jubayr bin Mit'im that the Prophet (pbuh) said: (I go by five names: I am Mohammad, Ahmad, the Eraser with who God erases blasphemy, al-Haashir who people are gathered on Judgment Day at my feet, and al-'Aaqib who no prophets shall come after.)[508]

Hence, there is no discrepancy between the two names. Prophet Mohammad (pbuh) said: (I and the prophets who came before me are like the man who built a beautiful house yet left out a block at its corner, and people would go around it and admire it and say, 'Would you put this block in place?'"

b- Glad tidings of Mohammad (pbuh) gleam in holy Books:

The news of Prophet Mohammad's arrival led scores of honest people of the Book to believe in him. These included individuals like al-Hassan bin Ayyub, al-Turjuman, Ziyadah al-Nasab al-Rasi, priest Abdul-Ahad Dawoud, Ibrahim Khalil, Maurice Bokkay, and many others.[509]

The proofs and books that argued with people of the Book indicate that the name Mohammad was expressly stated in the scriptures of people of the Book till late ages. Among those were:

- Ibn Qutaybah (died 627h.)
- Al-Maawirdi (died 450h.)
- Al-Fakhr al-Raazi (died 606h.)
- Al-Qaraafi (died 684h.)
- Ibn Taymiyah (died 728h.)
- Ibn al-Qayyim al-Jawziyah (died 751h.)

Ibn Taymiyah said: (I personally saw a copy of al-Zabour that expressly stated the prophethood of Mohammad (pbuh) by his

[508] Al-Bukhari, no. 3532; Muslim, no. 2354.

[509] Munqith Mahmoud al-Saqqaar, "Hal Bashar al-Kitaab al-Muqaddas bi Mohammad (pbuh)?", p.7.

name, and saw another copy of al-Zabour without it. Hence, some of the copies contain within them traits of the Prophet while others do not.)[510]

Ibn Taymiyah also reported a text from the gospel of Daniel regarding Prophet Mohammad, who also stated him as being a prophet: (They ‘the children of Israel’ shall remain damned, humiliated and weak until I send forth the prophet of Ismail’s lineage who Hajar brought glad tidings about, and to who I sent my angel carrying forth the glad tidings, to inspire that prophet, teach him the names, adorn him with piety, make goodness his motto, piety his conscience, truth his words, fidelity his nature, righteousness his means, and give him a specific Book that concurs with those that preceded it, that cancels some notions contained in them, who I shall raise to me through a holy journey, elevate him from one heaven to the next until he rises above all, draw him close to me, bid him greeting, inspire him, then send him back to me servants happy and content, preserving that which I entrusted him with, obedient to my orders, who calls on his people to worship me in My Singularity, informs them of what he saw of My miracles, who they would call him a liar and hurt him, then Daniel reported the story of Prophet Mohammad as the angel informed him, until he connects the last days of his nation to the End of Days.)[511]

Also, the gospel of Isaiah also outwardly states the name of the Prophet (pbuh): (We heard from mountains afar the voice of Mohammad) thus stating his name outright.[512]

Daniel (pbuh) said: (Arrows will be departing from bows and will be quenched with blood at your order, O Mohammad.) This

---

510 Ibn Taymiyah, “Al-Jawaab al-Saheeh Liman Baddal Deen al-Maseeh”, ver. by Safar al-Hawaali, al-Bayan Magazine, 1st Ed., 1432h, 2/27.

511 Fadil al-Saamirraa’i, “Nubuwwat Mohammad Bayn al-Shakki wal Yaqeen”, al-Quds Library – Baghdad, al-Bashaa’ir House, Amman, 1971, p.301.

512 Al-Qaraafi, “Al-Ajwibah al-Faakhirah ‘aan al-As’ilah al-Faajirah”, Saeed Ra’fat Printing Co., 2nd Ed., 1987, p.255.

text was reported by al-Fakhr al-Raazi, Imam al-Qaraafi, Ibn Taymiyah and Ibn al-Qayyim al-Jawziyah, among other texts which show that the name of Prophet Mohammad (pbuh) existed in some copies till very late eras.

On page 63 of his Urdu book entitled, "*Khulaasat Sayf al-Muslimeen*", honourable Haydar Ali al-Qurashi states that the priest Oskan the Armenian translated the gospel of Isiah into Armenian in 1666 and printed it in 1733 AD. The following paragraph is from Chapter 42: (Praise God anew as the sign of His Might cometh and his name is Ahmad). Armenians possess this translation which you would need to seek.

In his book entitled, "*Mohammad's Prophethood between Doubt and Certainty*", Dr Faadil Salih al-Samirraa'i reports many glad tidings from people of the Book regarding the prophethood of Mohammad (pbuh). They number 23 instances and whoever wishes to learn more should refer to that book.[513]

c- Glad tidings of Mohammad (pbuh) in the gospel of Barnabas:

Barnabas is considered a saint who the Church glorifies and who is mentioned in "*The Acts of the Apostles*". This saint wrote a gospel that was among those prohibited to be seen prior to Islam's onset and was mentioned in the book entitled, "*Mohammad in The Torah, Injeel and Qur'an*" – the Gospel of Barnabas.

It is said that Pope Gelasius prohibited the reading of this gospel in 429 AD. In his book entitled, "*The Lost Years of Jesus*", Dr Charles Francis Potter stated that the gospel of Barnabas was set aside by the Church during its first era, and that the recently discovered Dead Sea scrolls have agreed with this gospel.

Many other discoveries which many of people never heard of then began occurring. The sources that mention these matters, all

---

[513] "Nubuwwat Mohammad Bayn al-Shakki wal Yaqeen", Ibid, p.305-372.

of which are foreign, have stated that there exist two other scrolls in al-Fayyoum and Upper Egypt.[514]

It states that: The Papal decree issued by Pope Gelasius who was Pontiff in 492 AD detailed the gospels prohibited to be viewed, and among them was the Gospel of Barnabas. Hence, this is clear proof that this gospel existed before Islam and was well-known among elite scholars.[515]

A copy of Barnabas's Gospel was found in a purely Christian setting, as the only copy in the world nowadays known to be of this gospel is an Italian one that exists in the Imperial Library of Vienna … and the first who found the Italian version, who history did not erase, was an advisor of the king of Russia named Cramer … then it went to Cramer Tholand who gifted it to Prince Eugene Francis of Savoy. The Italian copy was found by a Latin monk named Maurino who had found the letters of Larinayus which included a letter in which he denounced St. Paul the Messenger as it was a point also stated in the Gospel of St. Barnabas. This caused the aforementioned monk much anxiousness to locate this gospel.

He stated that he had become at a certain time close to Pope Xystus V and on one day had entered the papal library together with him where the Pope had fallen asleep, so Maurino decided to kill time by reading some books till the Pope woke up. The first book he laid hands on was the very gospel itself he had been seeking and was ecstatic at such a discovery. He hid the book on his body and the Pope woke up soon after, upon which Maurino excused himself along with that treasure. Then when he was alone, he read it with great passion and embraced Islam afterwards.

---

[514] Ibrahim Khalil Ahmad, "Mohammad fi al-Tawraah wal Injeel wal Qur'an", al-Manar House, 1989, p.93.

[515] Ibid, p.145.

This gospel was not mentioned in the writings of famous Muslim writers, whether old or new, and not even in the writings of religious scholars despite the fact that the Gospel of Barnabas can support them greatly in their debates. In addition, it was not even mentioned in old Arab, foreign or Orientalist books that wrote volumes on the rarest of books, both past and present.[516]

The Church prohibits the reading of this gospel and does not acknowledge its authenticity as it is based on principles that totally contravene with those of the Church because it denies the divinity of Isa or of him being the son of God. It also states that Isa was God's servant and messenger, rejects the Cross and openly states the name of Prophet Mohammad throughout. The following are examples:

- 14:39 – Adam, having sprung up upon his feet, saw in the air a writing that shone like the sun, which said: There is only one God, and Mohammad is the messenger of God.

- 41:29 – God hid himself and the angel Michael drove them forth from paradise (30) whereupon Adam, turning him round, saw written above the gate: There is only One God, and Mohammad is the messenger of God.

- 54 – Speaks of Judgment Day then states: Next shall God give life to all the elect, who shall cry out: O Mohammad, be mindful of us!

- 97:14 – Jesus answered: The name of the Messiah is admirable… God said: Wait Mohammad … (17) Mohammad is his blessed name.

- 163:7 – The disciples answered, 'O Master, who shall that man be of whom thou speakest, who shall come into the world?'

[516] Dr Khalil Sa'aadah's introduction of Barnabas's Gospel, … not present in the print.

- 163:8 – Jesus answered with joy of heart: 'He is Mohammad, messenger of God.' As well as other glad tidings of Mohammad (pbuh) mentioned in this gospel.[517]

d- Abdul-Ahad Dawoud's book *"Mohammad in the Holy Book"*:

Professor Abdul-Ahad was a grand Chaldean priest of the Roman Catholic church. His name was David Benjamin Kildani and had carefully studied both the Old and New Testaments. From these Testaments, he extracted the glad tidings of Prophet Mohammad (pbuh) that were stated by the prophets sent to the Israelites, as well as that of Prophet Isa in his favour. He also pointed out Nasraanis' alterations of these glad tidings – a matter which led him to believe that Prophet Mohammad was truly God's messenger and the concluding prophet. Dr Dawoud renounced Christianity and embraced Islam. He also authored an English book on his research outcomes and it was translated into Arabic by Fahmi Shamma and printed by the Supreme Shariah Councils in Qatar in 1985.

Prof. Dawoud states that Isa's glad tidings of Ahmad (pbut) were stated in the gospel of John: 14, 15 and 16. That which is truly of importance in these three chapters is a single sentence stated in Chapter 14 that exactly mirrors the holy verse: (And bringing forth glad tidings of a messenger after me named Ahmad).

The exact phrase in the gospel of John, as explained by prof. Dawoud is: (I shall seek the Father and He shall send you a messenger named the *Periklytos* who shall remain with forever) actually refers to Ahmad. But Nasraanis have altered this phrase to state the same but replacing the italicised word with *Another Parakletos*.

There is a big difference, as states Dr Dawoud, between the original word and the altered one as the latter infers that Isa (pbuh)

[517] "Nubuwwat Mohammad Bayn al-Shakki wal Yaqeen", p. 305, 376.

had a number of *Paracleti*. The phrase *Another Parakletos* means consoler, mediary or assistant, not the concluding Prophet.[518]

Periklytos is a Greek word that specifically means (the most exalted and most famous) derived from exaltation and praise, being (*Ahmad*) as mentioned in the Qur'an. The Aramaic version thereof, which Isa (pbuh) spoke, mentioned in his glad tidings on the arrival of Prophet Mohammad is (Muhaamedan or Hameedan) which exactly correlates with the Arabic (Mohammad) or (Ahmad).[519]

The outcome reached by Dr Dawoud in this research was that: The Qur'anic Words that state Isa son of Maryam (pbut) announced to the Israelites were that he came as (one bringing forth glad tidings of a messenger who shall come after me named Ahmad).

He could only have known through Divine Inspiration that the word *Periklytos* meant (Ahmad). Noteworthy is that this unique name had never been given to anyone before and was "reserved" in miracle form for the most famous and commendable messengers of God. Not a single Greek person was named Periklytos at the time, nor was any Arab named (Ahmad).[520]

The following are two examples on the altered versions of the holy book and John's Gospel:

First: That of "*The Holy Book*" of Middle East Publishing House, printed in Jerusalem in 1984 where (*Periklytos*) was translated as (*Consoler*): "If you love me, memorise my commandments, and I shall ask the Lord, and he shall give you another consoler, so as to remain with you forever."

Second: "*The Holy Book: A Book of Life: Interpretive Translation*", printed in Egypt in 1988: "If you love me carry out my

---

[518] Abdel-Ahad Dawoud, "Mohammad fil Kitaab al-Muqaddas", Ministry of Awqaf and Islamic Affairs, Qatar, 4th Ed., 2000, p.219-220.

[519] Ibid, 222-223.

[520] Ibid, 223.

commandments, and I shall request the Lord for another assistant, who shall remain with you forever."[521]

Referencing the Aramaic origin of John's Gospel, as well as the original Greek translation of Prophet Isa's glad tidings, provide correlation, cohesion and alignment among the three words: Aramaic (Muhaamedan), Greek (Periklytos) and Qur'anic Arabic (Ahmad).[522]

e- Theologians admit that the Periklytos is Ahmad:

The fair among Nasraani theologians admit that the original Greek word in the Gospel of John is the Arabic equivalent of the Qur'anic *Ahmad*.

Sheikh Abdul-Wahhab al-Najjar, author of "*Stories of the Prophets*" told of an incident that occurred between him and Italian orientalist Dr Carlo Nelino that confirms this truth. The two were students at the faculty of science where the author studied from 1839 till 1846. Dr Nelino had a PhD in ancient Greek literature, in which language the gospels were written, and had come to Cairo to learn Arabic where the two became friends.

One day, al-Najjar asked Nelino about the meaning of *Periklytos* and he responded that priests deem it to mean *Consoler*. The author said, "I am asking Dr Carlo Nelino who has a PhD in ancient Greek language, not a priest." The professor said, "It means he who thanks a lot." So al-Najjar asked him if it correlates to *Ahmad*, and Nelino responded in the affirmative. When Aa-Najjar said that our Prophet goes by that name, Nelino said, "O brother, you memorise a great deal."[523]

As such did the original gospels agree on the text that was Prophet Isa's glad tidings of the arrival of Mohammad (pbuh),

[521] Salah al-Khalidi, Ibid, 4/344.

[522] Al-Khalidi, Ibid, 4/345.

[523] Ibid, 4/346.

and many fair Nasraanis have acknowledged this fact despite the alteration conducted by translators and authors unto later gospels.[524]

3. Some traits of believers in Mohammad (pbuh) from the Torah and Injeel:

God Says: {Mohammad is the messenger of Allah, and those who are with him are strong against Unbelievers, (but) compassionate amongst each other. Thou wilt see them bow and prostrate themselves (in prayer), seeking Grace from Allah and (His) Good Pleasure. On their faces are their marks, (being) the traces of their prostration. This is their similitude in the Tawrah; and their similitude in the Gospel is: like a seed which sends forth its blade, then makes it strong; it then becomes thick, and it stands on its own stem, (filling) the sowers with wonder and delight. As a result, it fills the Unbelievers with rage at them. Allah has promised those among them who believe and do righteous deeds forgiveness, and a great Reward} (Surat al-Fat.h: 29).

The holy verse starts with proving the trait of Mohammad (pbuh) in a graceful and eloquent style; one that consists of many images of this select group:

- An image of their dealings with unbelievers and then among themselves: (strong against Unbelievers, (but) compassionate amongst each other).

- An image of their worship: (Thou wilt see them bow and prostrate themselves 'in prayer').

- An image of that which occupies their hearts: (seeking Grace from Allah and (His) Good Pleasure).

- An image of how worshiping God influences their looks: (On their faces are their marks, (being) the traces of their prostration),

[524] Salah al-Khalidi, Ibid, 4/346.

(This is their similitude in the Tawrah) and such is how they are described there.

- Other sequenced images of how they are described in the Injeel: (like a seed which sends forth its blade, then makes it strong; it then becomes thick, etc.)[525]

This bright image is not a novelty as it was inscribed in the panel of destiny and hence older than the Torah and the Injeel in which it was stated. It is what God described of them in the Books of Mousa and Isa who brought glad tidings of those men before their birth.[526]

God also spoke of those who toil towards goodness in His three Holy Books and stated that He bought from them that which they had forsaken their selves and belongings for, and granted them Paradise as the price thereof via believing in Him and fighting in His Sake. When they fight, they will kill some of the enemies and some of them will die as martyrs who will enter His Paradise. This was God's solemn promise that was stated in the Torah, Injeel and Qur'an, and is also proof that the Divine Injeel contained Jihadist notions and directives.[527]

God Says: {Allah hath purchased of the believers their persons and their goods; for theirs (in return) is the garden (of Paradise): they fight in His cause, and slay and are slain: a promise binding on Him in truth, through the *Torah*[528], the Gospel, and the Qur´an: and who is more faithful to his covenant than Allah. then rejoice in the bargain which ye have concluded: that is the achievement supreme} (Surat al-Tawbah: 111).

God's promise of Paradise to those who fight in His Name, and who kill and are killed, is a given in the Torah, Injeel and Qur'an.

---

525 "Fi Thilaal al-Qur'an", Ibid, 6/3331.

526 Ibid, 6/3333.

527 "Al-Qasas al-Qur'ani: Presentation and Analysis of Events", Ibid, 4/293.

528 Corrected by Translator.

It is the responsibility of every person who believes in the prophets and in God's Way.[529]

4. False priesthood:

God Says: {We sent after them Jesus the son of Mary, and bestowed on him the Gospel; and We ordained in the hearts of those who followed him Compassion and Mercy. But the Monasticism which they invented for themselves, We did not prescribe for them: (We commanded) only the seeking for the Good Pleasure of Allah. but that they did not foster as they should have done. Yet We bestowed, on those among them who believed, their (due) reward, but many of them are rebellious transgressors} (Surat al-Hadeed: 27).

God sent forth Isa son of Maryam (pbut) as a messenger, descended upon him the Injeel and many good people among the children of Israel and others believed in him.

- (We ordained in the hearts of those who followed him Compassion and Mercy): The natural fruit of Prophet Isa's message is its compassion and mercy which are reflected in those who believed in him and followed his commandments. Other verses in the Holy Qur'an have also stated this, as well as historical images told by historians of al-Najaashi and the emissaries from Najran, and others whose ancestors had righteously followed Isa and who in turn embraced Islam when it became known to them.

- (But the Monasticism which they invented for themselves, We did not prescribe for them: (We commanded) only the seeking for the Good Pleasure of Allah): The majority of Qur'an interpreters agree this means that the priesthood known in Christianity was a choice made by some of Prophet Isa's followers which they had invented for themselves, that it may please The Almighty and remove them from worldly matters. But God had not prescribed it to Isa (pbuh).

529 "Fi Thilaal al-Qur'an", Ibid, 3/1719.

But when they chose to do so and deemed it a duty, they became responsible to God that they preserve its sanctity in prayer and worship which would allow them to achieve that state of devotion they sought.

But the priesthood ended up as rites and rituals void of spirit and a disguise by others: (But that they did not foster as they should have done. Yet We bestowed, on those among them who believed, their (due) reward, but many of them are rebellious transgressors).

They inhabited monasteries, kept themselves distant from people and remained as such until a group of them changed course, renounced the religion with which God entrusted them and adopted heresies instead.[530]

[530] "Al-Qasas al-Qur'ani: Presentation and Analysis of Events", Ibid, 4/391; "Tafseer al-Tabari: Taqreeb wa Tahtheeb", 7/239.

CHAPTER III

The Miracles of Prophet Isa (pbuh) and Raising him to the Heavens

First: Miracles and conditions thereof:

1. Miracle definition:

A miracle is a matter out of the ordinary, coupled with challenge, void of contradiction, that is revealed by God at the hands of His messengers.[531] It contravenes with universal norms, is not subject to reasons or causes, nobody can attain it via personal effort or gain, and is a gift from God Who chooses its type and time so as to prove to the followers of His prophets that they is truthful.

Magic and other actions performed by physical or spiritual craftsmen do not fall under the umbrella of Supernatural as they are matters that can be learned, practised and mastered.[532]

2. Miracle conditions:

A miracle as per the above definition must be:

- Supernatural
- Of God's doing
- Uncontested
- Unchallengeable
- Attributed to The Almighty
- After having received God's Message[533]

---

[531] Mustafa Muslim, "Mabaahith fi I'ajaaz al-Qur'an", al-Qalam House, Damascus, 1st Ed., 1989, p.14.

[532] Ibid.

[533] Ibid, p.17-18.

3. Miracles support the Message:

Had it not been for miracles, people would not know who to believe nor who was a true or false prophet. Supporting the calling of a prophet through a miracle of truth is the norm with all prophets of God. The Holy Qur'an states this norm in the stories of prophets and past nations. God did not hold it against the people who demanded their prophets provide them with miracles proving their truthfulness. God only condemned them when they demanded certain types of miracles out of obstinance and ignorance that they inherited from their forefathers.[534]

4. God's Wisdom in choosing prophets' miracles:

When considering the miracles of past prophets, and that of the concluding prophet, Mohammad (pbuh), we notice that they are chosen to support the environment in which that messenger will be delivering his message, i.e. that which is famous in the people's era, that aligns with their intellectual level and civilisation so that the argument may be stronger.

a- The prophets who lived in Arab countries were aided with miracles that correlated with their desert environment; hence the miracle of Salih (pbuh) was a she-camel of strange origin and birth that stunned the Bedouins.

b- Magic was rife among Egyptians and the Pharaoh used it as a means to terrorise people; hence the miracle of Mousa (pbuh) was the stick and the hand that performed miracles whose outward appearance was no different than that used by Pharaoh's magicians.[535] Yet those who knew magic well were able to distinguish between that which was magical and that which was Supernatural, i.e. of God's doing, and hence they were the first to believe in Mousa's call.[536]

---

[534] Ibid, p.24.

[535] Mohammad Abu Zahra, "Al-Mu'ajizah al-Kubra al-Qur'an", al-Fikr al-Arabi House, Egypt, Cairo, D.T. p.437.

[536] "Al-Iman bil Rusul wal Risalaat", Ibid, p.243.

c- Roman philosophy based on reason spread after the times of Mousa (pbuh) so the miracles of prophets sent to the Israelites defied reason so as to prove that the entire universe follows the Laws of the One God Who does whatever He pleases.[537] The miracles of Suleiman (pbuh), for example, came in opposition of the theory that says all creations originated from the first who existed, and hence he (pbuh) harnessed the Jinn, birds and wind to obey him and understood the tongue of birds and animals.[538]

d- In the age when medicine and Roman philosophy was also based on reason, the miracles of Isa (pbuh) were that he was born from one parent, not two as is the norm. Isa (pbuh) also spoke to the people words of wisdom while a new-born, created birdlike figurines from clay and breathed life into them through God's Will and cured the born-blind and the lepers.

e- In the era of Prophet Mohammad (pbuh), linguistic eloquence and articulateness was at its height and the meticulous use of words was sacred and revered to an extent higher than anything else. Word usage was so important to them that they hung the seven Mu'allaqat inside the Kaaba, which was considered the holiest structure for Arabs during the Time of Ignorance. Hence came God's miracle in the form of language that was highly regarded among Prophet Mohammad's people at the time.[539]

5. Difference between Miracles and Graces:

- Graces are of a lesser degree of extraordinariness.

- Graces correlate to the mind, but Miracles are superhuman.

- Graces follow Miracles as they are granted to those who have followed their prophets well.

---

[537] Ibid.

[538] Ibid.

[539] Ibid, p.244.

- Graces are granted to the righteous as a result of their piety, but miracles are granted without action to warrant them.[540]

- God may give Graces to whomever He wishes of His righteous followers of prophets.[541]

- Graces are not of equal importance to miracles; they are usually concealed, unlike miracles which must be presented to the masses as attestation to the honesty of the sent prophet.[542]

- In some cases, graces may be granted by God to one who doesn't fully fulfil his/her religious duties so as to strengthen their commitment, or when in need so as to fulfil it for them. Hence, graces are more akin of those who came after the companions of the prophets.[543]

6. Difference between Graces and Magic:

Any superhuman act at the hands of one who is not a prophet is considered magic and they shall be exposed as such through their words or actions.[544]

Graces granted to the righteous are caused by belief and piety; whereas demonic acts are due to that which a prophet has prohibited.[545]

Second: The Miracles of Prophet Isa son of Maryam (pbuh):

God Willed that Prophet Isa be, in himself, a Sign to the people and hence He granted him many miracles. Among those were his mother bearing him without the seed of a father, Isa speaking as he

540 Mohammad bin Abdel-Aziz al-Shaayi'a, "Aaraa' Ibn Hajar al-Haythami al-I'atiqaadiyah", Dar al-Manaahij Library, 1st Ed., 1427h, p.473.

541 "Al-Iman bil Rusul wal Risalaat", Ibid, p.256.

542 Ibid.

543 Ibid.

544 Ibid.

545 Ibid, p.257.

exited his mother's womb, and Isa speaking to his mother's people as a new-born.[546]

Then as a young man and a prophet and messenger, God provided Isa with a number of miracles. Also, when the Israelites were determined to crucify and kill Isa, God protected him from them by raising him to the Heavens where he currently lives in body and soul in an unseen life whose parameters we do not know – and this in itself is also a miracle. Then when God brings Isa back on Earth at the End of Days, that too shall be a miracle.

God Says: {And (remember) her who guarded her chastity: We breathed into her of Our Spirit, and We made her and her son a sign for all peoples} (Surat al-Anbiyaa': 91).

The two together, Isa and his mother, were one miracle as they are inseparable. Also, the miracles God effected in Maryam were a prelude for the arrival of Isa (pbut), and hence the two are considered one as recipients of said miracles.[547]

God also supported Isa with the Holy Spirit, i.e. the angel Jibreel (pbut). God Says: {To Jesus the son of Mary We gave clear (Signs), and strengthened him with the holy spirit} (Surat al-Baqarah: 253).

God Says as a reminder to Isa of His Grace towards him: {Then will Allah say: "O Jesus the son of Mary! Recount My favour to thee and to thy mother. Behold! I strengthened thee with the holy spirit, so that thou didst speak to the people in childhood and in maturity} (Surat al-Maa'idah: 110).

The moral spirit is that which gives life to hearts and souls; not the Divine Spirit as it is of God's secrets and preserved for Him only. As a moral spirit, Jibreel was given the same status as that of the Holy Qur'an as per the following holy verse: {And thus have

546 "Al-Qasas al-Qur'ani: Presentation and Analysis of Events", Ibid, 4/295.

547 "Al-Qasas al-Qur'ani: Presentation and Analysis of Events", Ibid, 4/297.

We, by Our Command, sent inspiration to thee: thou knewest not (before) what was Revelation, and what was Faith; but We have made the (Qur'an) a Light, wherewith We guide such of Our servants as We will; and verily thou dost guide (men) to the Straight Way} (Surat al-Shourah: 52). God added (Spirit) to (Holy), meaning Jibreel, i.e. the pure and blessed one.[548]

God created Jibreel from untainted purity, hence he is an angel who God created from light. It is said he was named as such as he descends from God while carrying that which purifies the spirits of God's servants through Qur'an, Wisdom and God's Grace.[549]

But the Holy Spirit, Jibreel, is not an angel specific to Prophet Isa as the Holy Qur'an states that he also descended upon Prophet Mohammad (pbut).

God Says: {When We substitute one revelation for another,- and Allah knows best what He reveals (in stages),- they say, "Thou art but a forger": but most of them understand not. Say, the Holy Spirit has brought the revelation from thy Lord in Truth, in order to strengthen those who believe, and as a Guide and Glad Tidings to Muslims} (Surat al-Nahl: 101-102). Hence, it was Jibreel – the Holy Spirit – through who God descended the Qur'an upon Mohammad.

As he was carrying out the mandates of his calling, God sent Jibreel to Prophet Isa so as to strengthen him. God did the same with all prophets throughout their time as he did for Prophet Mohammad. Jibreel descended upon our Prophet many times, not just to reveal to him God's Words, but also to teach and guide him. Jibreel also aided Mohammad (pbuh) by leading angels to fight with Prophet Mohammad in the battles of Badr, Uhud and al-Ahzaab.[550]

548 Mahmoud Saafi, "Al-Jadwal fi I'araab al-Qur'an wa Sarfihi wa Bayaanih", al-Rasheed House, Beirut, 1st Ed., 1990, 1/192.

549 "Al-Qasas al-Qur'ani: Presentation and Analysis of Events", Ibid, 4/298.

550 "Al-Qasas al-Qur'ani: Presentation and Analysis of Events", Ibid, 4/298.

The miracles of Prophet Isa (pbuh) are as follows:

1. Born fatherless of only a mother:

God Says: {The similitude of Jesus before Allah is as that of Adam; He created him from dust, then said to him: "Be". And he was} (Surat Aal-Imran: 59).

God Says: {He said: "So (it will be): Thy Lord saith, ´that is easy for Me: and (We wish) to appoint him as a Sign unto men and a Mercy from Us´: It is a matter (so) decreed"} (Surat Maryam: 21).

2. Strengthening him with the Holy Spirit:

The Holy Spirit is the angel Jibreel (pbuh) and Prophet Isa speaks of him with exact words while he was still an infant in the cradle:

God Says: {He said: "I am indeed a servant of Allah. He hath given me revelation and made me a prophet; And He hath made me blessed wheresoever I be, and hath enjoined on me Prayer and Charity as long as I live; (He) hath made me kind to my mother, and not overbearing or miserable; So peace is on me the day I was born, the day that I die, and the day that I shall be raised up to life (again)"!} (Surat Maryam: 30-33).

3. Teaching him the Book, Wisdom, the Torah and the Injeel:

Prophet Isa (pbuh) was taught that which was descended from God in all past Holy Books, like the Torah and the Zabour which were lost due to time and alteration.[551]

4. Curing the born blind and the lepers with God's Permission:

As those born able-sighted but lost this ability at a later stage have the possibility of being cured, God Willed that His Mira-

[551] "Al-'Ijaaz al-Tareekhi wal Inbaa'i fil Qur'an al-Kareem", Ibid, 2/872.

cle of curing the born blind be utilised by Prophet Isa as a Sign of God's Ability since it is impossible for the born blind to be cured. This was at a time when medicine was prominent among Isa's people, and when he, himself, was not a doctor. Leprosy was also, and it remains to be, a hard to cure disfiguration of the skin, yet through God's Miracle, Prophet Isa was the vessel for doing just that.[552]

Yet even if science were to reach solutions for curing the two abovementioned ailments through whatever its may devise for that purpose, it will never be able to do so with a simple wipe of hand as was God's miracle to Isa (pbuh).[553]

God Says: {And I heal those born blind, and the lepers} (Surat Aal-Imran: 49) and {And thou didst heal those born blind, and the lepers, by My leave} (Surat al-Maa'idah: 110).

5. Resurrecting the dead with God's Permission:

God Says: {And I quicken the dead, by Allah's leave; and I declare to you what ye eat, and what ye store in your houses. Surely therein is a Sign for you if ye did believe} (Surat Aal-Imran: 49) and {And behold! thou didst bring forth the dead by My leave} (Surat al-Maa'idah: 110).

Prophet Isa (pbuh) would pass by the dead and pray to God that He resurrects them, upon which God would accept Isa's prayer and have them come out of their graves alive.[554]

As no human can resurrect the dead, the fact that Prophet Isa was able to do so through God's Permission, and act as the vessel

552 Khalid Abdel-Aleem, "Waqafaat fi Hayaat al-Anbiyaa'", Ibn Katheer House, Beirut, 1st Ed., 2004, p.203.

553 Abdul-Majeed al-'Aarabli, "Uhibbuka Ayyuha al-Maseeh", Arwa Print, Jordan, 2nd Ed., 2006, p.166.

554 Mohammad Abu Zahra, "Muhadaraat fil Nasraaniyah", General Headquarters for Scientific, Fatwa, Da'awa & Irshaad Research Administrations, Kingdom of Saudi Arabic, Riyadh, 4th Ed., 1404h, p.20.

through which God's Commands were transferred, was proof to his people that he was a messenger sent by The Almighty.

The miracle of Isa resurrecting the dead came in steps and stages:

- In Surat Aal-Imran, Isa says to the Israelites: (And I quicken the dead by Allah's leave).

- In Surat al-Maa'idah, God Signals His Grace to Isa: (And behold! thou didst bring forth the dead by My leave).

So they were first brought to life through Isa, and then exited their graves alive with God's Permission when Isa called upon them to do so.

The miracles of Isa were many so that God may prove to his people who had forgotten about spirituality and God that Isa was a true prophet who was bringing forth glad tidings to the pious, and warning the wrongdoers of punishment. Prophet Isa (pbuh) formed clay in the shape of birds which then acquired life by him blowing into them – through God's Grace. Then, through Isa, God resurrects the dead whose bodies had already decomposed, and the like.

During the time of Prophet Isa (pbuh), Jews did not believe in Judgment Day or the Afterlife – if not through words, then through actions – so God ordained Isa as His vessel through which He resurrected the dead as a Sign so as to force them to believe in Him. Yet against God's Signs they have rebelled.[555]

6. Breathing life into clay figurines with God's Permission:

God Says: {I make for you out of clay, as it were, the figure of a bird, and breathe into it, and it becomes a bird by Allah's leave: And I heal those born blind, and the lepers, and I quicken the dead, by Allah's leave; and I declare to you what ye eat, and what ye

[555] "Muhadaraat fil Nasraaniyah", Ibid, p.22.

store in your houses. Surely therein is a Sign for you if ye did believe} (Surat Aal-Imran: 49).

Prophet Isa would make bird figurines of clay, then when they dried he would breathe into them and they would become real living birds, all through God's Permission and Will.

This same miracle was expressed differently in Surat al-Maa'idah – verse 110: {Behold! thou didst *make*[556] out of clay, the figure of a bird, by My leave, and thou didst breathe into it and it becometh a bird by My leave}.

God Says: {Praise be to Allah, Who created the heavens and the earth, and made the darkness and the light} (Surat al-An'aam: 01). God Says: {To Him is due the primal origin of the heavens and the earth} (Surat al-An'aam: 101). This is proof that God created these without them having had an origin. The same applies in the usage of the word (create) regarding the birds of clay Prophet Isa breathed life into as they, too, had no prior similarity.

- God Says: {Is then He Who creates like one that creates not? Will ye not receive admonition?} (Surat al-Nahl: 17). Creation also occurs when creating something out of another, as per the following: {He has created man from a sperm-drop; and behold this same (man) becomes an open disputer!} (Surat al-Nahl: 04).

- God Says: {He created man from sounding clay like unto pottery, And He created Jinns from fire free of smoke} (Surat al-Rahman: 14-15). This is creation via transformation which God decreed for other forms of life. Another example is: {And behold! thou didst make out of clay, the figure of a bird, by My leave, and thou didst breathe into it and it becometh a bird by My leave, and thou didst heal those born blind, and the lepers, by My leave. And behold! thou didst bring forth the dead by My leave. And behold! I did restrain the Children of Israel from (violence

[556] Translator's note: The Arabic version of the word (make) in the above verse is actually (create), but the Qur'an translator, Yusuf Ali, used the former instead.

to) thee when thou didst show them the clear Signs, and the unbelievers among them said: ´This is nothing but evident magic'} (Surat al-Maa'idah: 110).

Accordingly, the creation performed by Prophet Isa was one of transformation, not innovation as it was God who aided him in doing so from clay then into the life form of a bird.[557]

This was also the explanation provided by Imam Ibn Katheer.[558]

- What was it that Isa (pbuh) created?

Prophet Isa took dirt, made it into clay, crafted from the clay the shape of a bird, breathed into it and it came to life with God's Leave.

This was not an act of creation from nothingness, but rather the transformation of matter which God had created of nothingness and placed on Earth. Isa took that and transformed it via mixing two of God's creations, i.e. sand and water into a clay figurine. But Prophet Isa did not create anything from a void.

The so-called creation attributed to Prophet Isa – transformational creation – was possible only through God's Leave. Hence, God is the Causer and Creator, while Prophet Isa was the vessel through which God enacted His Will.[559]

The Qur'an specifically states this matter: {… I make for you out of clay …} (Surat Aal-Imran: 49).

Also, God Says, stating the clay from which birds were created: {And behold! thou didst make out of clay, the figure of a bird, by My leave, and thou didst breathe into it and it becometh a bird by My leave} (Surat al-Maa'idah: 110).

Prophet Isa's saying that he creates from clay bird shapes is to indicate that he was skilled at crafting such figurines.

---

557 "Al-Qasas al-Qur'ani: Presentation and Analysis of Events", Ibid, 4/302.

558 "Tafseer Ibn Katheer", 3/109.

559 "Al-Qasas al-Qur'ani: Presentation and Analysis of Events", Ibid, 4/302.

- It was God Who permitted Isa (pbuh) to breathe into the figurine.

- It was God Who Willed that the figurine come to life.

- It was God who gave life to the bird figurine, while Isa was merely the conduit.

That breath of air into the figurine that was performed by Prophet Isa was the physical reason through which God created that life. The Holy Qur'an is explicit in emphasising the truth that God was the Creator by twice stating the phrase (with God's Leave) as per: {And behold! thou didst make out of clay, the figure of a bird, by My leave, and thou didst breathe into it and it becometh a bird by My leave} (Surat al-Maa'idah: 110).

This miracle was a sign of proof attesting to Prophet Isa's truth of being God's messenger as he would not have been able to do so had he not been a true prophet at whose hands God performed such a miracle.[560]

7. Reporting matters unseen through God's Revelation:

Prophet Isa (pbuh) was able to speak of many matters which he could not have been physically aware of or had witnessed in person. An example on this is stating to his people about that which was in their households. God Says: {And I declare to you what ye eat, and what ye store in your houses} (Surat Aal-Imran: 49).

The Holy Qur'an was meticulous in stating that all miracles that Prophet Isa performed were but a *Sign* from God. This word is repeated throughout the holy text which speaks of these miracles.

The word *Sign* is repeated three time in the following holy verses; in the beginning, middle and end. God Says: {And (appoint him) a messenger to the Children of Israel, (with this message): "I have come to you, with a Sign from your Lord, in that

[560] "Al-Qasas al-Qur'ani: Presentation and Analysis of Events", Ibid, 4/305.

I make for you out of clay, as it were, the figure of a bird, and breathe into it, and it becomes a bird by Allah's leave: And I heal those born blind, and the lepers, and I quicken the dead, by Allah's leave; and I declare to you what ye eat, and what ye store in your houses. Surely therein is a Sign for you if ye did believe; (I have come to you), to attest the *Torah*[561] which was before me. And to make lawful to you part of what was (Before) forbidden to you; I have come to you with a Sign from your Lord. So fear Allah, and obey me. It is Allah Who is my Lord and your Lord; then worship Him. This is a Way that is straight"} (Surat Aal-Imran: 49-51).

Prophet Isa was keen on emphasising the separation between divinity and servitude, that he was God's servant and messenger, that The Almighty was his God and the God of the universe, and that he said this to the Israelites. This is why he concluded his statement by calling on the Israelites: {It is Allah Who is my Lord and your Lord; then worship Him. This is a Way that is straight} (Surat Aal-Imran: 51).

This contravenes the claims of Nasraanis that Prophet Isa (pbuh) was a god as he had informed them that God is his Lord and theirs, that He sent him forth, that they are mandated to worship and obey The Almighty, and that this was the path of righteousness to follow: (Allah is my God and yours, this is the path of righteousness).[562]

8. God Descends a table from the Heavens in answering Hawaaris' request:

God Says: {Behold! the disciples, said: "O Jesus the son of Mary! can thy Lord send down to us a table set (with viands) from heaven?" Said Jesus: "Fear Allah, if ye have faith." They said: "We only wish to eat thereof and satisfy our hearts, and to know

[561] Corrected by Translator.

[562] "Al-Qasas al-Qur'ani: Presentation and Analysis of Events", Ibid, 4/312.

that thou hast indeed told us the truth; and that we ourselves may be witnesses to the miracle." Said Jesus the son of Mary: "O Allah our Lord! Send us from heaven a table set (with viands), that there may be for us - for the first and the last of us - a solemn festival and a sign from thee; and provide for our sustenance, for thou art the best Sustainer (of our needs)." Allah said: "I will send it down unto you: But if any of you after that resisteth faith, I will punish him with a penalty such as I have not inflicted on any one among all the peoples"} (Surat al-Maa'idah: 112-115).

We note that all miracles of the Messiah which the Holy Qur'an states are physical ones so that they may be proof of his prophethood as well as being suiting of the time of his people whose life was dominated by lust for the physical. Therefore, the signs presented to them were testament that they could not have originated except from one who God supported.[563]

The role a miracle plays is to emphasise the honesty of the messenger bearing it and; subsequently, people believing in it by worshipping and obeying God. It is neither meant to impress nor astonish, but rather to transform the heart of mankind so that people would repent from their wrongdoings when they witness it.

Third: Isa (pbuh), his Hawaaris and the Repast:

1. The Hawaaris – Disciples:

The word *Hawaaris* was stated five times in the Holy Qur'an, all in plural form. The word is a descriptor of Prophet Isa's believing followers and there have been many interpretations as to from where they acquired such a name. These men were said to be hunters/fishermen while others claimed them to have held

563 Abdel-Qadir Najoush, "Adyan al-'Aalam al-Muqarin", al-Diyaa' House, Kuwait, 2014, p.198.

such title as they would purify people's hearts through religion and knowledge. Others said they were hunters/fishermen as they would capture the hearts of the wondering and lead them towards righteousness.[564]

Imam al-Tabari cited three likely reasons for this name and gave preference to the first:

- Their clothes were white.

- They whitened people's clothes.

- They were the purest among prophets' followers.[565]

Imam Ibn Katheer stated that they were most likely named as such because they believed in Isa (pbuh), supported and stood up for him. He explained that the singular form of the name *Hawaari*, meant Champion of others.[566]

The most likely explanation is that stated by Ibn Katheer, attested with that reported by al-Bukhari and Muslim of Jabir bin Abdullah who said, "Prophet Mohammad (pbuh) asked who would bring him news of the people on the day of al-Ahzaab and Zubair said he would. The Prophet repeated the question and al-Zubair repeated his answer. So the Prophet said: Every prophet has a Hawaari, and my Hawaari is al-Zubair."[567]

The Prophet wanted one of his companions to go and see what the unbelievers were doing on the day of al-Ahzaab and it was al-Zubair bin Al-Awaam who said he would do so three times – hence the meaning of the above Hadeeth. This does not mean that al-Zubair was the only one among the Prophet's companions who championed him, but rather that he was the most prominent of his Hawaaris on that occasion.

---

564 "Al-Mufradaat fi Ghareeb al-Qur'an", Ibid, p.236; "Al-Qasas al-Qur'ani: Presentation and Analysis of Events", Ibid, 4/313.

565 "Tafseer al-Tabari, Taqreeb wa Tahtheeb", Ibid, 2/279-280.

566 "Tafseer Ibn Katheer", Ibid, 1/345.

567 Al-Bukhari, no. 2847; Muslim, no. 2415.

Thus the term *Hawaaris* was not used as a distinct descriptor of only Prophet Isa's companions; rather of all followers of prophets including Mohammad (pbut).[568]

a- Isa (pbuh) calls on the Hawaaris to attest to his honesty:

Upon witnessing the denial of the majority of Israelites, Prophet Isa called on his Hawaaris to stand up for him. God Says: {When Jesus found Unbelief on their part He said: "Who will be My helpers to (the work of) Allah." Said the disciples: "We are Allah's helpers: We believe in Allah, and do thou bear witness that we are Muslims. Our Lord! we believe in what Thou hast revealed, and we follow the Messenger. then write us down among those who bear witness"} (Surat Aal-Imran: 52-53).

Despite the fact that Prophet Isa was sent to the Israelites as God's messenger to them, supported with all the aforementioned miracles, so as to alleviate some of the restraints and duties that were set upon them through the Torah, they still refused to believe in him.

- (Who will be My helpers to (the work of) Allah): Who will stand by me and attest to the truthfulness of the message that God sent me so that people would follow His Way?[569] In giving his Hawaaris the choice of response there exists reference to three matters:

- First: The majority were unbelievers; thus Isa's statement (When Jesus found Unbelief on their part). As such, Prophet Isa's wished to know who among the larger group were those who believed in him.

- Second: As referenced by the holy verse, Prophet Isa (pbuh) sensed that he was to be targeted with harm and that his true calling is also being attacked by that majority. Hence, he sought aid from those who would champion him in his calling.

[568] Ibid, no. 2847.

[569] "Fi Thilaal al-Qur'an", Ibid, 1/401.

- Third: The holy verse also infers that true championing in such a situation is based on sincerity of intention to God and seeking His aid in all matters. Although numbering but few, they were many with God as their supporter. God Says: {Allah will certainly aid those who aid his (cause); for verily Allah is full of Strength, Exalted in Might, (able to enforce His Will)} (Surat al-Hajj: 40).

- (Said the disciples: "We are Allah's helpers"): Isa's disciples were faithful to him, stood by him and aided him in calling for righteousness after God aided Isa with His Light. They were men whose hearts became pure and free of earthly want due to being in the presence of the Messiah (pbuh).

- (We are helpers): This denotes two matters:

1) They realised he was speaking of The Almighty and that he was a faithful messenger. Thus, they considered responding to his calling as that of responding favourably to God's. So if they were his helpers, then in turn they are God's. This is why they said: (We are God's helpers) and did not say (Yours).

2) They understood that aiding Prophet Isa was through purity of intention towards The Almighty and cleansing their hearts of any matters that taint them. This is why they said:[570]

- (We believe in Allah, and do thou bear witness that we are Muslims): This shows their awareness of what it means to be supporters of Isa and of God. They said (We believe in Allah) the One and Only.

They professed their belief in God out loud and publicly, requesting from their prophet to attest to this on their behalf when in the presence of The Almighty. (And do thou bear witness that we are Muslims): They said so for having believed in Isa (pbuh), embraced his religion and hence submitted to God's Will. Submis-

[570] Mohammad Abu Zahra, "Zahrat al-Tafaaseer", 3/1237.

sion is the total surrender of oneself to God's Will, and as such, is proof that every prophet sent by The Almighty was carrying the message of Islam, i.e. Submission, just as Prophet Isa's Hawaaris professed theirs.[571]

They then prayed to The Almighty:

- (Our Lord! we believe in what Thou hast revealed, and we follow the Messenger): They pronounced their total belief in God and that He is the One and Only Creator. They announced they submitted to Him in totality as submission to His Will can only be attained through it. They believed in that which God had descended upon Prophet Isa and that they would toil to spread his message and way of life.[572]

They then prayed that God strengthens their faith and transforms them from a state of believing in the unseen to that which brings them closer to being witnesses of events, and said:

- (… then write us down among those who bear witness): Meaning that as their hearts have been filled with the knowledge and certainty of God's Might, that God may elevate them to a higher status by being among those who witness. This last word (witness) denotes those whose hearts are filled with knowledge to the extent akin to physically witnessing matters as if they were occurring right in front of them. Of this group of people, Prophet Mohammad (pbuh) said: "Worship God as if you see Him, but if you do not, then be certain that He does."[573] Hence, this is a tier of faith and knowledge higher than mere faith on its own. The text denotes the presence of a group of honest and pure servants of God who have attained the highest levels of certainty.

---

571 "Al-Qasas al-Qur'ani: Presentation and Analysis of Events", Ibid, 4/319.

572 Mohammad Abu Zahra, "Zahrat al-Tafaaseer", 3/1239.

573 Ibid.

Prophet Isa (pbuh) sensed the ill-intentions of the Jews as his message of light and righteousness began spreading throughout the land. Despite having proven to them through the miracles with which God endowed him, the Israelites still did not believe in Prophet Isa and pursued their well-known treacherous natures, which were a distinct sign of their past and remain as such nowadays, by planning to kill him. As the calling of righteousness reached its epoch and danger loomed, God Says:

- (And (the unbelievers) plotted and planned, and Allah too planned, and the best of planners is Allah): As Isa sensed that the unbelievers were conniving to kill him, having also witnessed their treacherous nature in person after he succeeded in forming a group of followers from among them, The All-Seeing God knew of what they were plotting in their effort to end the calling of Isa. They connived and God planned. They connived because they were treacherous and such is what they do, but The Almighty is all Goodness and conniving is not of His Pure nature. So God planned and protected Isa from their harm.[574]

The holy verses inform us that the most important traits of the Hawaaris are:

- Believing in God and His messenger.

- Acknowledging Islam as religion and message to people.

- They were Muslims who submitted to God's Commandments.

- They requested that Isa (pbuh) testify for them of such on Judgment Day.

This elite group of men learned from Isa (pbuh) about the provisions of the Torah which was descended upon Mousa (pbuh), details of the Injeel which was descended upon him, piety, perseverance, altruism and resolve and they spread among the masses to cascade those principles.

---

[574] Mohammad Abu Zahra, "Zahrat al-Tafaaseer", Ibid, 3/1241.

All prophets before and after Isa (pbuh) formed such an elite group of men who would aid them in carrying forth the Message of God. Success can only be attained if we adopt this same notion and follow in the footsteps of the prophets (pbut) so as to achieve righteousness.[575]

b- Following in the footsteps of Hawaaris:

God Says: {O ye who believe! Be ye helpers of Allah: As said Jesus the son of Mary, to the Disciples, "Who will be my helpers to (the work of) Allah." Said the disciples, "We are Allah's helpers!" then a portion of the Children of Israel believed, and a portion disbelieved: But We gave power to those who believed, against their enemies, and they became the ones that prevailed} (Surat al-Saff: 14).

The Hawaaris were the Messiah's disciples – deemed to be 12 men – who shadowed him and were eager to learn from him as much as they could. They were the ones who spread his teachings and memorised his commandments.

- (O ye who believe! Be ye helpers of Allah): God, here, is calling upon the believers of Prophet Mohammad's nation to follow in the footsteps of the Hawaaris who beseeched The Almighty to be His helpers, and Demands of them to champion His religion and assistant His prophet as did the Hawaaris with Prophet Isa.[576] They said (We are God's helpers).

- (… then a portion of the Children of Israel believed, and a portion disbelieved: But We gave power to those who believed, against their enemies, and they became the ones that prevailed): Those who believed were the ones who embraced the calling of Isa (pbuh) and through his Hawaaris. God strengthened those against their enemies of unbelievers, and through such aid from God, they

---

[575] Abboud al-Raadi, "Fi Rihaab Qasas al-Anbiyaa' wal Rusul", 2/556-558.

[576] "Al-Qasas al-Qur'ani: Presentation and Analysis of Events", Ibid, 4/318.

prevailed over them. This is God telling the nation of Prophet Mohammad (pbuh) to follow suit of those Hawaaris and that, in return, He will grant them victory over their enemies.[577]

2. God Speaks of the Table He Descended and of the Blessings He will Bestow upon Isa on Judgment Day:

God Says: {One day will Allah gather the messengers together, and ask: "What was the response ye received (from men to your teaching)?" They will say: "We have no knowledge: it is Thou Who knowest in full all that is hidden." Then will Allah say: "O Jesus the son of Mary! Recount My favour to thee and to thy mother. Behold! I strengthened thee with the holy spirit, so that thou didst speak to the people in childhood and in maturity. Behold! I taught thee the Book and Wisdom, the *Torah*[578] and the Gospel and behold! thou didst make out of clay, the figure of a bird, by My leave, and thou didst breathe into it and it becometh a bird by My leave, and thou didst heal those born blind, and the lepers, by My leave. And behold! thou didst bring forth the dead by My leave. And behold! I did restrain the Children of Israel from (violence to) thee when thou didst show them the clear Signs, and the unbelievers among them said: 'This is nothing but evident magic'} (Surat al-Maa'idah: 109-110).

In the above, God Speaks about the great tests and horrors of Judgment Day in which God assembles all prophets and asks them about how their nations received their respective messages. They answer that they know not such answers as God is the All-Knowing of that which mankind conceal in their hearts.

- God then tells Isa son of Maryam to (Recount My favour) through his heart and tongue by thanking Him for the blessings He

---

[577] "Tafseer al-Sa'adi Tayseer al-Kareem al-Rahman fi Tafseer Kalam al-Mannaan", Ibid, 4/1826.

[578] Corrected by Translator.

Bestowed upon Isa and his mother, of which He had not Bestowed on any others.

- Examples on the blessings God Bestowed upon Isa (pbuh) were as follows:

• Strengthening him with the Holy Spirit (the angel Jibreel) who delivered God's Message to Isa and supported him in strengthening his resolve

• Speaking to people with words of wisdom while an infant and as a young man – words of such wisdom that cannot be naturally attained by a person at that early age. Prophet Isa stated while merely a new-born, as per the Holy Qur'an: {He said: "I am indeed a servant of Allah. He hath given me revelation and made me a prophet; And He hath made me blessed wheresoever I be, and hath enjoined on me Prayer and Charity as long as I live} (Surat Maryam: 31-32).

• Teaching Isa about all past Holy Books, particularly the Torah, and hence rendering him the most knowledgeable prophet sent to the Israelites after Prophet Mousa (pbuh) – as well as teaching him about the Injeel.

• Permitting him to be the vessel through which God gave life to clay figurines of birds by Isa breathing into them.

• Permitting him to be the vessel through which God cured the born blind, lepers and resurrected the dead. Such miracles that doctors and others cannot achieve even with latest technologies nowadays.

• Saving Isa from the ill intentions of Jews who connived to kill him.

- The Hawaaris, Table and the grand inquisition on Judgment Day:

God Says: {"And behold! I inspired the disciples to have faith in Me and Mine Messenger. they said, ´We have faith, and do thou bear witness that we bow to Allah as Muslims´". Behold! the disciples, said: "O Jesus the son of Mary! can thy Lord send down to us a table set (with viands) from heaven?" Said Jesus: "Fear Allah, if ye have faith." They said: "We only wish to eat thereof and satisfy our hearts, and to know that thou hast indeed told us the truth; and that we ourselves may be witnesses to the miracle." Said Jesus the son of Mary: "O Allah our Lord! Send us from heaven a table set (with viands), that there may be for us - for the first and the last of us - a solemn festival and a sign from thee; and provide for our sustenance, for thou art the best Sustainer (of our needs)." Allah said: "I will send it down unto you: But if any of you after that resisteth faith, I will punish him with a penalty such as I have not inflicted on any one among all the peoples."} (Surat al-Maa'idah: 111-115).

Through the above holy verses, God tells Isa (pbuh) to speak of His Blessings having provided for him the means to have helpers and followers, and who God had ordered – through the revelation He sent to Isa – that they embrace his message. Accordingly, Prophet Isa's helpers said that:

- They believed and attested to embracing Islam, i.e. Submission to the Will of The Almighty.

- They requested God descend upon them a Table of food (Repast); not that they doubted in God's ability to do so, but rather as a means of being polite in their request. But as such a request seemed to be anti-belief, Prophet Isa told them to be fearful of The Almighty for having requested such an earthly matter.

- The Hawaaris then stated that they made this request because they wished to eat off it – a sign that they are in need.

- Also, that they needed to put their hearts at ease through physically seeing a Sign of God's Greatness and Power – matters which lead to increased conviction in any human being.

- They also needed to have the conviction that Prophet Isa was truly a messenger through a Sign that only his God could provide.

- Their final reason for requesting this Table be descended upon them was so that they could personally testify that they saw and witnessed it first-hand, and relay the same incident to others after him.

Upon hearing their reasoning, Prophet Isa (pbuh) requested from The Almighty that He Descend this Table upon them so that its time of descending be a celebration commemorating such a great event. Similarly, God Decreed Muslims' celebrations and rites as reminders of His Miracles and Blessings which He has Bestowed upon mankind.

Prophet Isa then states that God is the Best Provider, i.e. that the Table be a Sign attesting to God's Greatness for eternity, and one that sustains their hunger on Earth.[579]

God responded favourably to their request for a miracle, yet The Almighty warns them that if they disbelieved in Him after He descends it, He will punish them severely. God states this so that all know that requesting such a miracle is not a matter they should take lightly as if it were something that occurred everyday. God has punished and even doomed all those who disbelieved in Him after having provided them with miracles attesting to His Greatness; yet in the verses, above, punishment may be awaiting those who did so in the case of Prophet Isa either in this life or in the Hereafter.[580]

The Holy Qur'an then speaks of the alleged divinity attributed by Nasraanis to Prophet Isa and his mother (pbut) through an inquisition of Isa. God does so in order for those who attributed this to

579 "Tafseer al-Sa'adi Tayseer al-Kareem al-Rahman fi Tafseer Kalam al-Mannaan", Ibid, 1/457.

580 "Fi Thilaal al-Qur'an", Ibid, 2/100.

Isa, as they will all be present on Judgment Day and witnessing the event, that they hear Isa clear himself of such falsehood – a matter that will cause them great alarm for having perpetrated such a lie against him:[581]

God Says: {And behold! Allah will say: "O Jesus the son of Mary! Didst thou say unto men, worship me and my mother as gods in derogation of Allah?" He will say: "Glory to Thee! never could I say what I had no right (to say). Had I said such a thing, thou wouldst indeed have known it. Thou knowest what is in my heart, Thou I know not what is in Thine. For Thou knowest in full all that is hidden. Never said I to them aught except what Thou didst command me to say, to wit, ´worship Allah, my Lord and your Lord´; and I was a witness over them whilst I dwelt amongst them; when Thou didst take me up Thou wast the Watcher over them, and Thou art a witness to all things. If Thou dost punish them, they are Thy servants: If Thou dost forgive them, Thou art the Exalted in power, the Wise." Allah will say: "This is a day on which the truthful will profit from their truth: theirs are gardens, with rivers flowing beneath,- their eternal Home: Allah well-pleased with them, and they with Allah." That is the great salvation, (the fulfilment of all desires). To Allah doth belong the dominion of the heavens and the earth, and all that is therein, and it is He Who hath power over all things} (Surat al-Maa'idah: 116-120).

- (And behold! Allah will say: "O Jesus the son of Mary! Didst thou say unto men, worship me and my mother as gods in derogation of Allah?"):

Here, God scolds Nasraanis who claimed Him to be one of three personas. God states this to Isa who distances himself from it by saying: (Glory to Thee! never could I say what I had no right (to say).

[581] Ibid.

- (Had I said such a thing, thou wouldst indeed have known it. Thou knowest what is in my heart, Thou I know not what is in Thine): This is a reflection of Prophet Isa's humility in speaking to his Master. Prophet Isa then states that which he told the Israelites: (Never said I to them aught except what Thou didst command me to say) as he is an honest and faithful servant of God. Prophet Isa then adds he told them to: (worship Allah, my Lord and your Lord) as he and his mother, Maryam, are servants of The Almighty.

- Prophet Isa then bears witness to the actions of the Israelites while he was among them, but as God had raised him to the Heavens, he says: (when Thou didst take me up Thou wast the Watcher over them), i.e. the One who knew that which lay in their hearts and minds.

- Prophet Isa then states the ultimate truth: (Thou art a witness to all things), and adds that it is God's choice whether He punishes them or not.

- God then Speaks of the rewards that await the truthful, pious and righteous: (This is a day on which the truthful will profit from their truth: theirs are gardens, with rivers flowing beneath, their eternal Home: Allah well-pleased with them, and they with Allah." That is the great salvation, (the fulfilment of all desires).

- (To Allah doth belong the dominion of the heavens and the earth, and all that is therein, and it is He Who hath power over all things): God is the Creator and the One Able to carry out whatever He Wishes. He is Unbound by any restraints and all of His creations heed His Will.[582]

[582] "Tafseer al-Sa'adi Tayseer al-Kareem al-Rahman fi Tafseer Kalam al-Mannaan", Ibid, 1/459.

Fourth: Conspiring to Kill Isa (pbuh) and raising him to the Heavens:

Many of the Jews to who Prophet Isa (pbuh) was sent did not like his teachings. Of these people God Says: {Curses were pronounced on those among the Children of Israel who rejected Faith, by the tongue of David and of Jesus the son of Mary: because they disobeyed and persisted in excesses. Nor did they (usually) forbid one another the iniquities which they committed: evil indeed were the deeds which they did} (Surat al-Maa'idah: 78-79).

The Jews' rabbis and the Pharisees deemed the calling a threat to their interests and wealth and their priests were disturbed by the notion of worshipping God rightfully by acknowledging His Singularity. They also dreaded forsaking usury, bribery, corruption and injustice so they said ill matters of Prophet Isa and ratted him out to the ruler.[583]

They claimed to be of a higher order unequal to any, who all lay beneath them, and transformed the religion brought forth to them by Mousa (pbuh) into a religious aristocracy. They even treated a group among them called al-Saamirah as outcasts, and then when Isa (pbuh) came and ordained all mankind as equals, they antagonised and attacked him. But seeing the weak, poor and marginalised embracing the calling of Isa, the Jews began conspiring against him and instigating the Romans to cause him harm so that they and their rabbis may continue to enjoy their unchallenged status of falsely believing they were God's chosen ones.

They told the ruler that there was a man who was misguiding the people, telling them not to obey the king, corrupting the masses, separating between father and child, that he was the son of an adulteress, among other lies they spun against him. Accordingly, the ruler ordered Prophet Isa be arrested and crucified till death, so

583 "Risalat al-Anbiyaa' min Shu'aayb ila Issa", Ibid, 2/311.

he sent his soldiers to capture him. When they located Isa (pbuh), they surrounded and stormed his house but God saved him by raising him to the Heavens. God then cast the similitude of Prophet Isa on the first among them who had pursued him, and the soldiers captured that person – believing he was Prophet Isa – and they abused, crucified and placed thorns on that man's head. But this was what God Willed that they think, that it was Prophet Isa who they crucified when in reality it was not.[584]

God Says: {And (the unbelievers) plotted and planned, and Allah too planned, and the best of planners is Allah. Behold! Allah said: "O Jesus! I will take thee and raise thee to Myself and clear thee (of the falsehoods) of those who blaspheme; I will make those who follow thee superior to those who reject faith, to the Day of Resurrection: Then shall ye all return unto me, and I will judge between you of the matters wherein ye dispute. As to those who reject faith, I will punish them with terrible agony in this world and in the Hereafter, nor will they have anyone to help. As to those who believe and work righteousness, Allah will pay them (in full) their reward; but Allah loveth not those who do wrong. This is what we rehearse unto thee of the Signs and the Message of Wisdom."} (Surat Aal-Imran: 54-58).

The holy verse has assigned a wicked form of plotting against the prophet they aimed to kill, but God made plans in a kind and benevolent manner to undo their evil and save Isa (pbuh) from them.

- God Says: {And behold! I did restrain the Children of Israel from (violence to) thee when thou didst show them the clear Signs, and the unbelievers among them said: ´This is nothing but evident magic'} (Surat al-Maa'idah: 110). This holy verse summarises all the above.[585]

---

[584] "Risalat al-Anbiyaa' min Shu'aayb ila Issa", Ibid, 2/311.

[585] Ibid, 4/348.

1. (I will take thee and raise thee to Myself and clear thee (of the falsehoods) of those who blaspheme; I will make those who follow thee superior to those who reject faith, to the Day of Resurrection):

God undid the Jews' plotting against Isa (pbuh) by taking him, raising him the Heavens and purifying him of them. Muslim scholars have all agreed that Isa was saved from being killed and crucified, yet they disagreed on the meaning of (I am *taking you*[586] and raising you to Me).

- Some said it meant that God raised Prophet Isa to the Heavens and that at a later time, after Isa is sent back to Earth, God will end his life. In this sense, the word in question means (death).

- Some said it meant that God shall (take hold) of Prophet Isa by removing him from Earth. This meaning is echoed in an Arabic term meaning that one (collects) all debt that is due to him/her from another. In this sense, the phrase is meant to state that God shall "collect" Prophet Isa from Earth and raise him to His side in a non-death form. This opinion is the preferred one to Imam al-Tabari.[587]

- Some said it referred to actual death as we know it by taking the text on face-value. Hence, God had saved Prophet Isa from the Jews when they aimed to kill him, then God took his soul and caused him death, and then raised him to the Heavens afterwards.[588]

- The final group of scholars state that that intended by (death) in the holy verse meant (sleeping). Accordingly, God caused Prophet Isa to fall asleep, then raised him to the Heavens while

---

[586] Translator's note: The Arabic scripture states the word (taking your life) originating from the base Arabic word (death).

[587] "Al-Qasas al-Qur'ani: Presentation and Analysis of Events", Ibid, 4/350; "Tafseer al-Tabari Taqreeb wa Tahtheeb", p456.

[588] "Al-Qasas al-Qur'ani: Presentation and Analysis of Events", 4/350.

asleep. This is the favoured explanation to Ibn Katheer who stated, "God raised him to the Heavens after having caused him a death-like sleep and saved him from the Jews who had aimed to harm him by ratting on him to unbelieving kings of that time."[589]

2. The two meanings of "Death" in the Qur'an, i.e. Actual Death & Sleep:

a- The word "Death" in the Qur'an sometimes refers to the actual matter we all know, of a life having ended. This is stated twice in the Qur'an:

First, in the holy verse: {Say: "O ye men! If ye are in doubt as to my religion, (behold!) I worship not what ye worship, other than Allah. But I worship Allah - *Who will take your souls (at death)* ..."} (Surat Yunus: 104). Second, in the holy verse: {It is Allah who creates you *and takes your souls at death*; and of you there are some who are sent back to a feeble age, so that they know nothing after having known (much): for Allah is All-Knowing, All-Powerful} (Surat al-Nahl: 70).

b- The word "Death" in the Qur'an sometimes refers to "Sleep". This is also stated twice in the Qur'an:

First, in the holy verse: {It is He who doth *take your souls* by night, and hath knowledge of all that ye have done by day: by day doth He raise you up again; that a term appointed be fulfilled} (Surat al-An'aam: 70): Meaning that God makes people sleep at night whereby He collects their souls during that sleep, and then returns them to our bodies when we awaken. Second, as in the holy verse: {It is Allah that takes the souls (of men) at death; and *those that die not (He takes) during their sleep*: those on whom He has passed the decree of death, He keeps back (from returning to life), but *the rest He sends (to their bodies)* for a term appointed; verily in this are Signs for those who reflect} (Surat al-Zumar: 42). This verse has

[589] Ibn Katheer, "Al-Bidaayah wal Nihaayah", Ibid, 12/91.

deemed “sleep” to be “death” and has divided people after that sleep into two categories:

- Those who sleep and die while asleep as God had destined their lives to end at that moment, whereby He holds onto their souls and does not return them to their bodies.

- Those who sleep and God grabs hold of their souls while asleep but whose lives have not been destined to end yet, whereby He returns their souls to their bodies upon waking up from that sleep.

The two holy verses (al-An’aam: 60 & al-Zumar: 42) clarify that sleeping is considered a Minor Death whereby souls are returned to the bodies of those destined to still have years left to live. Prophet Mohammad (pbuh) emphasised that sleep was considered death, and waking up resurrection, in the prayers he used to say once going to bed: “In Your Name I awaken and in Your Name I die.” Then upon waking up, he would say, “All gratitude be to Allah who has resurrected us after having captured our souls, and to Him we shall all be resurrected on Judgment Day.”[590]

3. God Captures Isa’s soul twice, i.e. in Sleep & in Death:

Having stated the instances where the Holy Qur’an mentioned “Death” other than in the case of Prophet Isa (pbuh), the following two examples are statements from the Qur’an concerning only Prophet Isa:

- First: When the Jews aimed to crucify and kill Prophet Isa but God told him (I will take thee and raise thee to Myself) – after which God caused him death of sleep and then raised him to the Heavens.

- Second: When God returns Prophet Isa in the days preceding Judgment Day so that he may complete the rest of his age which

[590] Al-Bukhari, no. 6312. Also see: Muslim, no. 2711.

God has destined him, and then God will capture his soul as He does to all mankind in actual death (when Thou didst take me up Thou wast the Watcher over them).

It cannot be that the death stated in the Arabic version of the holy verse (I will take thee and raise thee to Myself) meant the end of life as there exist many corroborated texts on the descending of Prophet Isa at the End of Days – which are mentioned further down. Had God taken the life of Isa at that time, He would not be descending him later as God does not permit that Isa (pbuh) die twice.[591]

4. God Cast sleep on Isa then Raised him:

The gist of the holy verse in Surat Aal-Imran: (O Jesus! I will take thee and raise thee to Myself and clear thee (of the falsehoods) of those who blaspheme) was God telling Prophet Isa He will cast sleep upon him when the Jews come to kill him and then raise him to the Heavens. This was God's promise to Isa so as to save him from the Jews' mischief.

The Qur'an and the Sunnah have informed us that The Almighty raised two honourable prophets to the Heavens while they were alive, i.e. Prophet Isa, and Prophet Mohammad (pbut) on the night of Ascension to the Heavens. While that of Prophet Mohammad lasted only hours, upon which God returned him to Mecca before dawn, God chose to keep Isa (pbuh) there until just before the End of Days.[592]

Fifth: (But they killed him not, nor crucified him, but so it was made to appear to them):

The Holy Qur'an speaks of the Jews' attempt to kill Isa (pbuh) in three different instances:

---

591 "Al-Qasas al-Qur'ani: Presentation and Analysis of Events", Ibid, 4/357; "Tafseer al-Tabari Taqreeb wa Tahtheeb", 2/283.

592 Ibid, 4/358.

- In a passing remark in Surat al-Maa'idah (110): {And behold! I did restrain the Children of Israel from (violence to) thee when thou didst show them the clear Signs, and the unbelievers among them said: 'This is nothing but evident magic'}.

- In Surat Aal-Imran (55): {Allah said: "O Jesus! I will take thee and raise thee to Myself and clear thee (of the falsehoods) of those who blaspheme}.

- In Surat al-Nisaa' (153-159): {The people of the Book ask thee to cause a book to descend to them from heaven: Indeed they asked Moses for an even greater (miracle), for they said: "Show us Allah in public," but they were dazed for their presumption, with thunder and lightning. Yet they worshipped the calf even after clear signs had come to them; even so we forgave them; and gave Moses manifest proofs of authority. And for their covenant we raised over them (the towering height) of Mount (Sinai); and (on another occasion) we said: "Enter the gate with humility"; and (once again) we commanded them: "Transgress not in the matter of the sabbath." And we took from them a solemn covenant. (They have incurred divine displeasure): In that they broke their covenant; that they rejected the signs of Allah. that they slew the Messengers in defiance of right; that they said, "Our hearts are the wrappings (which preserve Allah's Word; We need no more)";- Nay, Allah hath set the seal on their hearts for their blasphemy, and little is it they believe;- That they rejected Faith; that they uttered against Mary a grave false charge; That they said (in boast), "We killed Christ Jesus the son of Mary, the Messenger of Allah.; but they killed him not, nor crucified him, but so it was made to appear to them, and those who differ therein are full of doubts, with no (certain) knowledge, but only conjecture to follow, for of a surety they killed him not: Nay, Allah raised him up unto Himself; and Allah is Exalted in Power, Wise; And there is none of the People of the Book but must believe in him before his death; and on the Day of Judgment he will be a witness against them}.

1. Some of the Jews' crimes:

The first two of the above eight verses detail some of the Jews' crimes against Prophet Mohammad (pbuh), as well as their disobeying of Prophet Mousa (pbuh).

- God states to Prophet Mohammad (pbuh) the mistreatment of prophets at the hands of the Jews as they asked him to descend Divine books to them (The people of the Book ask thee to cause a book to descend to them from heaven). God consoles the Prophet due to their mischievous acts against him and States that their ancestors had asked Prophet Mousa before him an even greater and more horrible matter, i.e. that of seeing God in person, that He stand before them and proclaim He is God: (Indeed they asked Moses for an even greater (miracle), for they said: "Show us Allah in public"). God punished them for their horrid request: (They were dazed for their presumption, with thunder and lightning).

- They adopted the calf as a god when Mousa went to Mt. al-Toor (Mt. Sinai) to pray to God: (Yet they worshipped the calf even after clear signs had come to them; even so we forgave them; and gave Moses manifest proofs of authority). God took from them a solemn covenant during the life of Mousa: (And for their covenant we raised over them (the towering height) of Mount Sinai). God took the same from them after the death of Prophet Mousa when He ordered them to enter the Holy Land's gate: (We said: "Enter the gate with humility"). Then a third time when God prohibited them from transgressing on the sanctity of the Sabbath and fishing on it: (We commanded them: "Transgress not in the matter of the sabbath"). Yet, again, they did not adhere to their word at Mt. Sinai, nor did they enter the gate as they were ordered. Instead, they entered it crawling and did not adhere to the sanctity of the Sabbath, so God transformed them into humiliated monkeys.[593]

- Verses (155: 159) then state the Jews' crimes which resulted in being damned by God; most horrid among which was their insistence on killing and crucifying Isa (pbuh). Yet God saved him by raising him to Himself. The holy verses began with stating how they broke their solemn covenant: {But because of their breach of their covenant, We cursed them, and made their hearts grow hard} (Surat al-Maa'idah: 13).

2. Some reasons for God Damning the Jews:

As stated in the above holy verses:

a- They reneged on the solemn covenant they gave God.

b- They blasphemously rejected the Signs they received.

c- They killed God's prophets without any cause.

d- They rejected embracing the path of righteousness brought forth to them by Prophet Mohammad (pbuh), claimed their hearts to be thick and unaccepting of any goodness.

e- For being unbelievers as a whole, not just in the signs they received as per the 2nd point above. They were unbelievers and they conspired to kill Prophet Isa.

f- For their stance against the virtuous virgin Maryam (pbuh).[594] They claimed Maryam was an adulteress and that Isa (pbuh) was her bastard son.

g- For publicly gloating that they killed Prophet Isa son of Maryam (pbut) having believed it was actually him they crucified. But in reality, they killed a lookalike. But God damned them for this public boasting of having assumed they killed one of His messengers as they referred to him in the four names he was known by,

593 "Al-Qasas al-Qur'ani: Presentation and Analysis of Events", Ibid, 4/362.

594 Ibid, 4/365.

i.e. the Messiah, Isa, son of Maryam, God's messenger. They did not state these four names out of belief in Isa; rather, they were being sarcastic.[595]

Imam Ibn Katheer said, "In stating that they killed (The Messiah, Isa, son of Maryam, God's messenger), the Jews meant to say that this man (Isa) who claimed to be of such status is the one they killed, out of pure sarcasm and gloating. The same applies to the statements of the unbelievers who claimed of Prophet Mohammad (pbuh): {They say: O thou to whom the Message is being revealed! truly thou art mad (or possessed)!} (Surat al-Hijr: 06).[596]

3. The Jews neither killed nor crucified Isa (pbuh):

God imputed the false claim of the Jews as having killed Isa (pbuh). God Says: {They killed him not, nor crucified him, but so it was made to appear to them, and those who differ therein are full of doubts, with no (certain) knowledge, but only conjecture to follow, for of a surety they killed him not: Nay, Allah raised him up unto Himself; and Allah is Exalted in Power, Wise; And there is none of the People of the Book but must believe in him before his death; and on the Day of Judgment he will be a witness against them} (Surat al-Nisaa': 157-159).

4. Sequence of events on night when lookalike was captured:

Both Jews and Nasraanis err on the matter of Prophet Isa's alleged death and crucifixion with the former stating they killed him and the latter believing he was crucified and buried but was resurrected three days later.

Yet neither party is certain on the matter as events occurred rapidly and the stories intertwined and contradicted with one another during that period to an extent that ascertaining the truth

595 Ibid.

596 "Tafseer Ibn Katheer", Ibid, 1/543.

became very difficult, except through that which God reports in the Holy Qur'an.

The four gospels, all of which were composed after the age of the Messiah, speak of the night he was captured, crucified, died, was buried and resurrected. They were all meant to oppress his religion and his disciples to an extent through which it was impossible to verify the validity of any of the events in an air of secrecy, fear and dispersal that prevailed at the time. Other gospels were also written in that period, yet these four were chosen to be the most valid by the end of the 2nd Century AD. They were deemed official and recognised for reasons that are not all beyond doubt.[597]

Accordingly, researchers cannot ascertain the events of that incident which occurred in late night nor can they rely on a solid source that gives strength to one over another. God Says of them: (Those who differ therein are full of doubts, with no (certain) knowledge, but only conjecture to follow). God provides the ultimate truth: (But they killed him not, nor crucified him, but so it was made to appear to them) and (For of a surety they killed him not: Nay, Allah raised him up unto Himself; and Allah is Exalted in Power, Wise).[598]

Islam historians paid much interest to this incident, like Imam Ibn Katheer who detailed the following on this incident: "Of the news on the Jews – may God curse and punish them – that when God sent forth Prophet Isa with clear Signs and proofs, they envied him for the gifts God bestowed upon him of prophethood and miracles through which God implemented His Will like curing the born blind and the lepers and resurrecting the dead, among others. The Jews still called him a liar and pursued all means of hurting him to the extent that he did not stay among them in the

[597] Abu Zahra, "Muhadaraat fil Nasraaniyah – Naqlan 'Aan (Fi Thilaal al-Qur'an)", Ibid, 2/802.

[598] "Fi Thilaal al-Qur'an", Ibid, 2/802.

same town. Instead, Isa and his mother would travel as much as possible, but the Jews were unconvinced and went to the king of Damascus at the time. This king was an unbelieving planet worshipper whose people were called the Greeks. The Jews told him that in the Holy Land was a man who was inciting the people and corrupting them from heeding the king's wishes. The king was angered by this, sent a message to his deputy in Jerusalem to arrest this man, ordered he be crucified and thorns be placed on his head, and that his harm no longer affects the masses. When his deputy received that letter, he set off to carry out the orders.

He and a number of Jews went to the house of Isa (pbuh) as he was among a group of his companions – 12, 13 or 17 of them – on Friday night. When Isa sensed their presence and that there was no way for him to evade them, he asked his companions who among them would accept to be cast his same appearance and that that person would be his companion in Heaven. One of them said he would but it was as if Prophet Isa felt he was too young for the task. So Prophet Isa repeated the same question two more times and the same young man was the only one to accept the task. So Prophet Isa told him it was done and that he would be that person, upon which The Almighty cast the same looks of Prophet Isa on that volunteer. Then, part of the ceiling opened up, Prophet Isa was cast to sleep and he was raised to the Heavens in that state. It is as God Says: (Behold! Allah said: "O Jesus! I will take thee and raise thee to Myself …).

"When Isa was raised through the ceiling, his companions exited the house and the Jews and soldiers believed the young man among them to be Prophet Isa (pbuh). They took him, crucified him and placed thorns on his head. The Jews happily expressed that they were the ones who sought this fate for him and some Nasraanis joined them in doing so out of ignorance, except those who were with him in the house as they had witnessed him being raised. All the others believed as did the Jews that the crucified person was the Messiah son of Maryam to the extent that they stated Maryam had sat under the crucified person and cried. This is all of God's tests for his servants, yet He clarified everything in the Holy Qur'an he descended upon His prophet Mohammad (pbuh).

God states to those who have conflicting stories of Prophet Isa that the Jews claimed they caused his death and that the Nasraanis concurred to this matter out of ignorance. But God Says they killed a man who He made to look like Prophet Isa and that He raised him to the Heavens."[599]

Ibn Abbas's version of events is as follows: "When God wished to raise Isa to the Heavens, Isa came out from a waterway with his head dripping wet and said: Some of you will disbelieve in me 12 times after having believed in me. He then said: Who among you would agree to become my lookalike, be killed in my stead and join my rank in Heaven? The youngest among them said he would. Prophet Isa told him to sit down, repeated the question twice, received the same answer twice and said to the young man: It is done; you are the one. Then God cast upon that young man Prophet Isa's looks and Isa was raised to the Heavens from an opening in the ceiling. Then the Jews took his lookalike, killed him and crucified him. Then some of them disbelieved in Isa 12 times as he had told them they would."

- Nasraanis split into three groups:

First, the Jacobians, who stated that God was among them and then ascended to the Heavens. Second, the Nestorians, who stated that the son of god was among them then God raised him to Himself. Third, the Muslims, who stated that God's servant and messenger was among them then God raised him to Himself. The two blasphemous groups colluded against the Muslim one and killed

[599] "Al-Qasas al-Qur'ani: Presentation and Analysis of Events", 4/372 from "Tafseer Ibn Katheer", 1/543-544.

its members. Islam remained obscure from that time onwards till God sent forth Prophet Mohammad (pbuh), and this is a statement with a verified chain of reporters of Ibn Abbas.[600]

5. Sequence of that night's events:

Steps of the events that took place on that night are as follows:

- The Jews succeeded in convincing the Roman ruler to order the arrest and death of Isa.

- A band of Roman soldiers and Jews went to where Isa (pbuh) was to carry out the ruler's orders.

- Isa's domicile was in the Holy land, as per the sequence of events regarding the killing, crucifixion and Via Dolorosa.

- Isa (pbuh) was in a house in Jerusalem that night with 12 of his Hawaaris, as stated by Ibn Abbas.

- Isa (pbuh) knew of the impending arrival of the band to arrest, kill and crucify him. He was neither scared, worried nor sad as he knew God was there with him.

- God informed Isa that they will neither capture nor harm him and the He will cast Isa's looks on one of his Hawaaris then raise him unto Himself. God told Isa to ask who among his Hawaaris would volunteer and be the crucified martyr.

- Isa (pbuh) relayed God's glad tidings that He will protect him so as to pacify them.

- Isa (pbuh) asked his Hawaaris who would volunteer himself for the task and receive the reward of accompanying him in Heaven.

- A youth among the Hawaaris volunteered and was granted the honour.

- The name of that volunteer was not mentioned.

---

[600] "Al-Qasas al-Qur'ani: Presentation and Analysis of Events", 4/373. See: "Tafseer Ibn Katheer", 1/544-545.

- Through His Might and Ability, God cast the exact looks of Prophet Isa on that young man.

- The Hawaaris who were there looked at the young man afterwards and he appeared to them to have completely mirrored Prophet Isa's appearance and looks, but they knew it was not him.

- When the band of soldiers and Jews arrived at the house, Prophet Isa and his lookalike were both there, and were witnessed there together by the other Hawaaris.

- As the mob embarked on entering the house, God performed a miracle by making an opening in the ceiling.

- God cast sleep onto Prophet Isa while among his Hawaaris as they witnessed this miracle and were pacified to know that God had saved him.[601]

- The band of aggressors entered the house and saw Prophet Isa's lookalike, not doubting for a second that it was the real Isa.

- The band took the lookalike and it seems he neither spoke to them, denied being the real Isa, said that the real Isa had been raised to the Heavens nor that they had failed to capture him. He was ready to be killed and become a martyr.

- We do not know what happened to the other 11 Hawaaris who were in the house.

- The band took Prophet Isa's lookalike, crucified him on a stick, killed him on the cross and he died a martyr; all the while as Prophet Isa was in the Heavens.

- People who looked at the crucified youth did not doubt for a second that he was not Prophet Isa as they were unaware of the miracle God had performed on him earlier. Some of them gloated happily while others were sad, then after a while they lowered the body of the martyr lookalike and buried him.

[601] "Al-Qasas al-Qur'ani: Presentation and Analysis of Events", Ibid, 4/375.

- The Jews were gloating happily for having thought they had caused death and crucifixion to the real Isa as they pronounced this openly: We have killed the Messiah Isa son of Maryam the Messenger of God.

- Nasraanis were not aware of God's miracles of that night and were convinced that that they saw on the cross was their prophet, Isa son of Maryam. They believed the Jews' gloating of his death, and they said: They killed and crucified our prophet Isa.[602]

- The Jews and Romans punished all who believed in Isa (pbuh). They killed, crucified, imprisoned and expelled many of them to the extent that Nasraanis were so overwhelmed with the events of the night that they had no time to consider the matter with clear heads. Many Nasraanis severely disagreed among each other on the events of that night to the extent that they believed the Jews' claim. This false belief permitted idolatry to encroach on Nasraaniism where some deemed Isa a god and others considered him the son of God.

- The real events that transpired on that night remained concealed from the Jews and Nasraanis as they both believed the one who was crucified to be Isa son of Maryam, God's messenger. Then when God sent forth Prophet Mohammad (pbuh), He descended upon him the Holy Qur'an that clarified all ambiguities.[603]

6. Holy Verses on the killing of the lookalike:

Having stated the sequence of events, above, we are better able to understand the meaning of the holy verses: {They killed him not, nor crucified him, but so it was made to appear to them, and those who differ therein are full of doubts, with no (certain) knowledge, but only conjecture to follow, for of a surety they killed him

[602] "Al-Qasas al-Qur'ani: Presentation and Analysis of Events", Ibid, 4/376.

[603] Ibid, 4/377.

not: Nay, Allah raised him up unto Himself; and Allah is Exalted in Power, Wise; And there is none of the People of the Book but must believe in him before his death; and on the Day of Judgment he will be a witness against them} (Surat al-Nisaa': 157-159).

- (But so it was made to appear to them): God cast Prophet Isa's looks on that man and it was he, not Prophet Isa, who the Jews and soldiers killed and crucified.

- (And those who differ therein are full of doubts): A man who looked exactly like Prophet Isa was killed and crucified, but who was he? The real Isa or his lookalike?

- (And those who differ): Applies to the Jews who gloated of having killed Isa son of Maryam God's messenger, and the Nasraanis who said, "Our Prophet Isa was killed and crucified by the Jews."

- (With no (certain) knowledge): Neither the Nasraanis nor the Jews were certain about who it was that was crucified.

- (But only conjecture to follow): As neither the Jews nor the Nasraanis had ascertained the identity of the deceased, they were perplexed for having succumbed to conjecture which only leads to doubt.[604]

- (For of a surety they killed him not): The did not kill Isa having verified it was truly him.

They killed someone they thought was Prophet Isa, but certainly not Isa. So, where did Prophet Isa end up in since that was the case? What happened to him on that night?

The answer is in verse 158 of Surat al-Nisaa': {Nay, Allah raised him up unto Himself; and Allah is Exalted in Power, Wise}.

- (Nay, Allah raised him up unto Himself): "Nay" undid the previous claim of the Jews alleged killing of Isa. (Allah raised him

---

604 "Al-Qasas al-Qur'ani: Presentation and Analysis of Events", Ibid, 4/378.

up unto Himself): This annuls the Jews' claim: (We have killed the Messiah Isa son of Maryam God's Messenger). It is also clear to mean that God raised Isa in body and soul while he was alive from the opening in the ceiling.

Prior to that incident, God had promised Isa to take him unto Himself so as to save him from harm by casting sleep on him: (Behold! Allah said: "O Jesus! I will take thee and raise thee to Myself).

- (And Allah is Exalted in Power, Wise): God states this to show His Might and Wisdom as He is Strong and Able and protects His helpers from harm. He saved His prophet in such a miraculous manner and left his enemies in doubt and delusion.[605]

As the Jews did not kill Prophet Isa, he shall be sent back at the End of Days and live out the rest of his destined age. People of the Book who are alive at that time shall believe in him as being God's servant and messenger. To this end, God Says: {And there is none of the People of the Book but must believe in him before his death; and on the Day of Judgment he will be a witness against them} (Surat al-Nisaa': 159). This verse will be discussed in detail when we speak of the descending of Prophet Isa (pbuh) at the End of Days, further below.

7. Gospels disagree on events of that night, closest is Barnabas's:

The four gospels acknowledged by Nasraanis, i.e. Matthew, Luke, Mark and John, have conflicted among each other on the events of that night to an extent that has caused confusion among Nasraanis who believe in them.

As previously stated, the closest gospel to Qur'anic truth is that of Barnabas which Nasraanis neither believe in nor acknowledge. Barnabas, a disciple of Prophet Isa, states that an-

605 Ibid, 4/381.

other of the Prophet's Hawaaris, Judas Iscariot, betrayed Isa and conspired with the Jews to arrest him. God then cast the similitude of Isa on Judas and they crucified him believing he was Isa. This, of course, contradicts with that mentioned above of Ibn Abbas's version of events and that of the majority of Muslim scholars.

Chapter 211 of Barnabas's gospel states that Prophet Isa had informed them a few days prior to the event that his time to leave this world has ushered: "Jesus being in the house of Nicodemus beyond the brook Cedron, comforted his disciples, saying: "The hour is near that I must depart from the world; console yourselves and be not sad, seeing that where I go I shall not feel any tribulation."[606]

Chapter 213 of Barnabas gospel details a dialogue between prophet Isa and the Hawaaris, including Judas Iscariot: "Jesus said again: 'Verily I say unto you, that one of you shall betray me, insomuch that I shall be sold like a sheep; but woe unto him, for he shall fulfil all that our father David said of such a one, that "he shall fall into the pit which he had prepared for others.' Whereupon the disciples looked one upon another, saying with sorrow: 'Who shall be the traitor?' Judas then said: 'Shall it be I, O Master?' Jesus answered: 'Thou hast told me who it shall be that shall betray me.'"[607]

Chapters 215, 216 and 217 detailed the night Prophet Isa was raised to the Heavens and the arrest of the traitor: "When the soldiers with Judas drew near to the place where Jesus was, Jesus heard the approach of many people, wherefore in fear he withdrew into the house. And the eleven were sleeping. Then God, seeing the danger of his servant, commanded Gabriel, Michael, Rafael,

[606] "Gospel of Barnabas", ver. by Sayf Eddine Ahmad Faadil, al-Qalam House, 1st Ed., Damascus, 1973, p.284.

[607] Ibid.

and Uriel; his ministers, to take Jesus out of the world. The holy angels came and took Jesus out by the window that looks toward the South;. They bare him and placed him in the third heaven in the company of angels blessing God for evermore. Judas entered impetuously before all into the chamber whence Jesus had been taken up. And the disciples were sleeping. Whereupon the wonderful God acted wonderfully, insomuch that Judas was so changed in speech and in face to be like Jesus that we believed him to be Jesus. And he, having awakened us, was seeking where the Master was. Whereupon we marvelled, and answered: 'You, Lord, are our master; have you now forgotten us?'

"And he, smiling, said: 'Now are you foolish, that know not me to be Judas Iscariot!' And as he was saying this the soldiery entered, and laid their hands upon Judas, because he was in every way like to Jesus. We having heard Judas' saying, and seeing the multitude of soldiers, fled as beside ourselves. And John, who was wrapped in a linen cloth, awoke and fled, and when a soldier seized him by the linen cloth he left the linen cloth and fled naked. For God heard the prayer of Jesus, and saved the eleven from evil. The soldiers took Judas ;and bound him, not without derision. For he truthfully denied that he was Jesus; and the soldiers, mocking him, said: 'Sir, fear not, for we are come to make you king of Israel, and we have bound you because we know that you do refuse the kingdom.' Judas answered: 'Now have you lost your senses! You are come to take Jesus of Nazareth;, with arms and lanterns as [against] a robber; and you have bound me that have guided you?'"[608]

Barnabas continues reciting the story till the crucifixion of Judas Iscariot and his burial, as being Isa, as God had cast the similitude of Isa onto him.[609]

608 "Gospel of Barnabas", Ibid, p.288-289.

609 Ibid, p.289-293.

Barnabas's eyewitness version of events correlates with the holy verse: (But they killed him not, nor crucified him, but so it was made to appear to them).[610]

8. Meaning of Crucifixion and Sacrifice to Nasraanis:

Nasraanis believe Prophet Isa was crucified in redemption for mankind's sins and this is the second pillar of belief to Nasraanis. They also believe that matters of prophethood and divinity are causalities of the crucifixion.

This dogma – as per Christianity – is based on the premise that the entire human race is branded sinful due to Adam eating from the forbidden tree, through the coaxing of the serpent, and hence became deserving of God's damnation and sentenced to eternal doom in Hell.[611]

Christianity adds that God's Mercy wished to rid this world of this primal guilt it had inherited and thus mandated suitable compensation. As a death sentence needed to be carried out in person or from a substitute who volunteers for it instead, God permitted that His son be sacrificed on the cross so as to redeem mankind since Adam's sin remained in his offspring until the arrival of Isa who was both human and divine. In Christianity, Isa is the son of God and the son of Maryam; his human body was crucified so as to wipe away Adam's sin from his descendants. Despite this, they state that even if one believes in this claim and adopts it as religion, he/she shall not be saved.[612]

Accordingly, "Sacrifice" to Nasraanis means being relieved of death due to the primal sin of mankind inherited from Adam.[613]

---

[610] "Al-Qasas al-Qur'ani: Presentation and Analysis of Events", Ibid, 4/386.

[611] "Paganism in People of the Book's Dogmas", Ibid, p.536.

[612] Mohammad Wasfi, "Al-Maseeh wal Tathleeth", al-Rahmaaniyah Print, Egypt, 1st Ed., 1937, p.148.

[613] "Paganism in People of the Book's Dogmas", Ibid, p.537.

They believe that Isa wholeheartedly accepted being crucified so as to overcome that sin, was buried afterwards, beat death three days later by being resurrected and was raised to the Heavens. To Nasraanis, whoever does not believe in the crucifixion is not considered from among them and hence they enshrined it in their dogma. To this end, they claim that God descended from the Heavens, was embodied in the Holy Spirit and the Virgin Mary, became human and was crucified so that His blood would redeem mankind from Adam's sin.[614]

The Crucifixion is an utter falsehood throughout. Isa (pbuh) was God's messenger and prophet and was not crucified; rather, he was raised to God. The Messiah (pbuh) did not attribute Redemption to himself, nor did the Hawaaris to him. This was attributed to Prophet Isa by Paul who was among Christianity's fiercest enemies; who then all of a sudden spun 180 degrees, without warning, and embraced Christianity and became its intellectual and ardent keeper. Paul's first declaration was that the Messiah was the son of God and that he was named as such because he was the embodied god who descended so as to be crucified to redeem mankind – as per pagan saviour gods.

Paul's Redemption Theory was embraced by the masses due to the style he pursued in delivering it. He aimed to extract Christianity from its closed circle of the Holy Land to the wider arena among non-Jewish environments. In order for his calling to suit this new envisioned society, Paul decided to enact certain modifications onto the dogmas which this new society would be pleased with.

Christianity's Redemption Theory – brought forth by Paul – is based on the false premise that Adam (pbuh) committed a mistake which transcended to his descendants and that the only path to-

[614] Abu Ubaydah al-Khazraji, "Bayn al-Islam wal Maseehiyah", ver. by Dr Mohammad Shaamah, Wahbeh Library, Cairo, 2nd Ed., p.72.

wards redemption was that which they claimed of God descending from the Heavens for the sake of mankind.[615]

We reject these falsehoods that have been perpetrated against our beloved prophet, Isa (pbuh). The unfounded fabrications stated in Nasraani gospels on Prophet Isa being crucified and insulted are far too beneath the Messiah's status as he is among God's select messengers who He chose from among all mankind. Woe to those who claim Prophet Isa underwent any form of degradation like that which they spew for God has reported of Prophet Isa: {And He hath made me blessed wheresoever I be} (Surat Maryam: 31).

Nasraanis have based their claim of crucifixion on the gospels, yet we have shown that they were altered and contradictory through undeniable proof, that they were not carried forth through an unbroken chain of narrators, that they are singular pieces of events that are temporally disconnected from the Messiah, and accordingly, all that is mentioned within them is untrustworthy, doubtful, and in no way at par with truth or certainty.

Nasraani Trinity sects have agreed that the Messiah (pbuh) was crucified in atonement of Adam's sin that was inherited by his children and their descendants. They concur that in order for the sin to be quelled, the god must become man, be killed, enter hell, punish himself severely, and become damned by that cross only so that he may dispel Adam's sin! How can such lies be regurgitated against The Almighty?![616]

The above belief is clearly misguided and ignorant to say the least. It is one that proper minds and sound instincts can only reject. The following are some scholars' responses on this matter:

---

[615] Ahmad Ali Ajeenah, "Al-Khalaas al-Maseehi wa Nathrat al-Islam Ilayhi", al-Aafaaq al-Arabiyah House, Cairo, 2006, p.755.

[616] "Paganism in People of the Book's Dogmas", Ibid, p.545.

a- God does not hold an inherited sin against mankind:

God holds no sins that require atonement through forfeiting the life of a prophet or an alleged son. Muslims believe that every human being is responsible for his/her actions and shall be judged accordingly. Mankind is born innocent of any sin and is by instinct inclined towards accepting truth. No human is born bearing the brunt of wrongs perpetrated by those before him/her.

- God Says: {Every soul draws the meed of its acts on none but itself: no bearer of burdens can bear the burden of another} (Surat al-An'aam: 164).

All Divine religions agree on this principle.

- God Says: {Nay, is he not acquainted with what is in the books of Moses; And of Abraham who fulfilled his engagements? Namely, that no bearer of burdens can bear the burden of another; That man can have nothing but what he strives for; That (the fruit of) his striving will soon come in sight: Then will he be rewarded with a reward complete} (Surat al-Najm: 36-41).

This holy verse states that holding one accountable for the error of another is prohibited in Islam and does not concur with the basic notion of human justice.[617] God Says: {He said: "(Allah) forbid that we take other than him with whom we found our property: Indeed (if we did so), we should be acting wrongfully} (Surat Yusuf: 79).

b- If Adam had erred, why should his descendants bear his guilt?:

This is a principle which all religions have forbidden. How is it just that all mankind bear the guilt of a sin committed by Adam (pbuh) and how could God accept that Prophets Mousa, Ibrahim and all others be punished in Hell forever due to this sin?

[617] "Al-Khalaas al-Maseehi wa Nathrat al-Islam Ilayhi", Ibid, p.757.

Furthermore, what did the Messiah do that was so horrible for him to bear Adam's sin, as per Nasraanis claims, be tortured as such to the extent his screams could be heard from afar? Had Nasraanis only claimed this to have been of the human Messiah, it would have been erroneous, but to claim it of the Messiah they claim as god?! Blasphemous! How could it be that the god was being tortured so horribly and so mercilessly?![618]

Adam's eating from the tree was not considered a sin requiring punishment as he was among the prophets who can do no wrong. Adam ate from the tree having forgotten God's order not to do so, and accordingly, it was an error not mandating punishment. Also, God is too Merciful to hold such a matter against any of His servants when they commit such an act forgetfully.

In addition, Adam (pbuh) repented and God accepted that from him. This denies Adam's guilt and it absolves his descendants of any related to it. Furthermore, God ordering Adam to descend to Earth was not a punishment, as Nasraanis think; rather, it was bestowing on him the honour of viceregency there.

It is as God had promised: (I will create a vicegerent on earth). God did not Say He will make Adam a viceregent in Paradise nor in the Heavens, but rather on Earth. Adam was worshipping God while he was in Paradise to honour Him, so God descended him to Earth so as to worship Him as a duty. With the two forms of worship present in Adam, he thus became worthy of viceregency.[619]

The Holy Qur'an also indicates that God's descending of Adam to Earth came after his repentance: {But his Lord chose him (for His Grace): He turned to him, and gave him Guidance. He said: "Get ye down, both of you"} (Surat Ta Ha : 122-123). As repentance absolves guilt, the descending of Adam to Earth was meant as an honour and a privilege, not a punishment. Sending Adam down

618 "Paganism in People of the Book's Dogmas", Ibid, p.547.

619 "Al-Khalaas al-Maseehi wa Nathrat al-Islam Ilayhi", Ibid, p.756.

to Earth mandated hard work so as to sustain a living, and this in itself is a means for receiving more reward for such good deeds. It was an act of God's Wisdom so that mankind may reign on Earth and build up that which He created.[620]

c- Gospels' contradictory accounts of the Crucifixion:

The gospels' recounting of the story of the "alleged" crucifixion of Prophet Isa (pbuh) differ immensely from one another. Was Isa the bearer of the cross or someone else? Was the wine which the crucified man drank normal or mixed with bitterness?[621] Were the two thieves crucified next to him ones who taunted him, or was it only one who did so?[622] Did the crucifixion occur at three or six in the afternoon?[623] Did the crucified man wail or did he surrender his soul peacefully?[624] Were there countless women who saw the crucified man or was their number limited?[625]

The gospels have contradicted with one another on every detail of the crucifixion. Such contradictory accounts should suffice to reject all that which they contain as holding one correct would mean all others are not, and vice versa. Not only have Nasraanis disagreed on this matter alone, but also on the shape of the cross itself, on which the crucified man was hung. The Holy Book Dictionary gives three shapes of the cross: X, T, +.[626] This denotes that they are unsure about any matter concerning the crucifixion and that the truth has escaped them. God is All-Truthful on this matter, and on all others: {But they killed him not, nor crucified him, but so it was made to appear to them} (al-Nisaa': 157).[627]

---

620 Ibid.

621 Mark (15/23), p.59. Luke (23/36), p.35-36.

622 Mark (15/27), p.59. Luke (23/39-43), p.35-26.

623 Mark, p.138. "Paganism in People of the Book's Dogmas", Ibid, p.549.

624 "Paganism in People of the Book's Dogmas", Ibid, p.549.

625 Ibid.

626 Ibid.

627 Ibid, p.553.

On this same point, God also Says: {And those who differ therein are full of doubts, with no (certain) knowledge, but only conjecture to follow, for of a surety they killed him not: Nay, Allah raised him up unto Himself; and Allah is Exalted in Power, Wise} (Surat al-Nisaa': 157-158).

When the notion of Crucifixion to Nasraanis is baseless, then whatever is based upon it is also so, and this includes the Messiah's resurrection from the grave. Both the Crucifixion the Resurrection are deemed the main pillars of faith to Nasraanis, and the latter in particular has been the basis for many important matters. Reason for this is that the resurrection denotes the divinity of Isa and entrenches Christian philosophies of the Church that were unknown during the life of the Messiah (pbuh). This notion has been the basis for a number of worship rites in Christianity like the Passover, Last Supper, sanctity of the cross and carrying it.[628]

Christian redemption was influenced by pagan beliefs as the incarnation of gods into human form for means of redemption is a notion that was widespread among the Greeks, and then the Romans, for centuries prior to the arrival of the Messiah (pbuh). The prevalence of these beliefs in these countries greatly influenced those who passed on the teachings of Christianity. Also, the crucifixion and torture of the god as well as the resurrection of the saviour were other pagan notions that prevailed in such societies prior to the arrival of Isa. Hence, the theory of Redemption was a pagan notion that entered Christianity from Paul and his followers who did nothing but attribute the name of Isa to it.[629]

- The teachings of Isa remained pure of contamination until Paul became Nasraani and obliterated them. Paul then rephrased these teachings in his inherited pagan mould, including his letters which constitute more than 50% of the New Testament deemed

[628] "Paganism in People of the Book's Dogmas", Ibid, p.609.

[629] "Al-Khalaas al-Maseehi wa Nathrat al-Islam Ilayhi", Ibid, p.758.

holy by Nasraanis. Paul introduced the dogmas of Crucifixion, Sacrifice and Sin; abolished circumcision and permitted the consumption of pork. One may say that the Christianity of today is that of Paul, not Isa (pbuh).

- Pagans embracing Christianity, like Emperor Constantine, greatly influenced Nasraaniism by infusing it with pagan beliefs. Researchers like Dr Mohammad Ali Abdul-Muti[630] and theology professor Ahmad Ali Ajeenah[631] have made many parallels between many Nasraani dogmas and their counterparts in pagan religions like Buddhism, Zoroastrianism and Ancient Egyptian.[632]

- The Trinity notion was born from the decrees of the many councils throughout varied eras. The Nicaean Council of 325 AD, for example, decreed the divinity of Prophet Isa, while the First Constantinople Council in 381 AD decreed the divinity of the Holy Spirit. Also, the First Council of Ephesus of 431 AD decreed there were three gods: the father, the son and the holy spirit. They also disagreed on the nature of the Messiah; whether he was of one nature, of two natures or detached from the father alone or from the father and the holy spirit together.

The above is proof that the Trinity in which Nasraanis believe was not brought forth by Prophet Isa (pbuh) nor did he order any such matter of any of his disciples.[633]

As evidenced in the Holy Qur'an, Prophet Isa was merely the human messenger of God and called on his people to worship God as the Only Ruler of the universe: {He said: "I am indeed a servant of Allah. He hath given me revelation and made me a prophet} (Surat Maryam: 30), and {But said Christ: "O Children of Israel! worship Allah, my Lord and your Lord"} (Surat al-Maa'idah: 72).

630 "Paganism in People of the Book's Dogmas", Ibid, p.607.
631 See: "Al-Khalaas al-Maseehi wa Nathrat al-Islam Ilayhi".
632 "Paganism in People of the Book's Dogmas", Ibid, p.607.
633 "Paganism in People of the Book's Dogmas", Ibid, p.608.

The Holy Qur'an also states that Prophet Isa will absolve himself on Judgment Day of Nasraanis' current beliefs when he responds to God's question: {And behold! Allah will say: "O Jesus the son of Mary! Didst thou say unto men, worship me and my mother as gods in derogation of Allah?" He will say: "Glory to Thee! never could I say what I had no right (to say). Had I said such a thing, thou wouldst indeed have known it. Thou knowest what is in my heart, Thou I know not what is in Thine. For Thou knowest in full all that is hidden. Never said I to them aught except what Thou didst command me to say, to wit, 'worship Allah, my Lord and your Lord'"} (Surat al-Maa'idah: 116-117). God's forgiveness of sins is not based on sacrifice, rather, on correct belief in The Almighty, worshipping Him, repenting, performing good deeds and ceasing from wrongdoing.[634]

Achieving salvation from God's punishment is conducted via honest repentance and intent.

- God Says: {But if the thief repents after his crime, and amends his conduct, Allah turneth to him in forgiveness; for Allah is Oft-forgiving, Most Merciful} (Surat al-Maa'idah: 39).

- God Says: {Except those who repent and believe, and work righteousness: for these will enter the Garden and will not be wronged in the least} (Surat Maryam: 60).

- God Says: {But, without doubt, I am (also) He that forgives again and again, to those who repent, believe, and do right} (Surat Ta Ha : 82).

- God Says: {Unless he repents, believes, and works righteous deeds, for Allah will change the evil of such persons into good, and Allah is Oft-Forgiving, Most Merciful} (Surat al-Furqan: 70).

The meaning of the holy verse (Allah turneth to him in forgiveness) is that all past bad deeds shall transform into good ones

[634] "Al-Khalaas al-Maseehi wa Nathrat al-Islam Ilayhi", Ibid, p.758.

whenever a servant of God realises that these deeds were bad and repents from repeating them.[635]

- As for Faith, God Says: {The Messenger believeth in what hath been revealed to him from his Lord, as do the men of faith. Each one (of them) believeth in Allah, His angels, His books, and His Messengers. "We make no distinction (they say) between one and another of His messengers"} (Surat al-Baqarah: 285).

- Speaking to the believers, God Says: {O ye who believe! Believe in Allah and His Messenger, and the scripture which He hath sent to His Messenger and the scripture which He sent to those before (him). Any who denieth Allah, His angels, His Books, His Messenger, and the Day of Judgment, hath gone far, far astray} (Surat al-Nisaa': 136).

Hence, Belief in God encompasses believing in Him, His angels, His books, His messengers and the Day of Judgment. Belief (Faith) is the second step towards salvation as per the Holy Qur'an as all believers must embrace every single step thereof – as referenced in the above verses – so that on Judgment Day, the believers may be rewarded and the unbelievers punished.[636]

- God Says: {If there is any good (done), He doubleth it, and giveth from His own presence a great reward} (Surat al-Nisaa': 40). God's Grace does not stop at this end as He also multiplies a good deed ten fold, while every bad deed is weighed as just one. God Says: {He that doeth good shall have ten times as much to his credit: He that doeth evil shall only be recompensed according to his evil: no wrong shall be done unto (any of) them} (Surat al-An'aam: 160).

- As for those who spend their money to seek God's favour, their good deeds are doubled 700 fold. God Says: {The parable

635 Salah Abu al-Saud, "Izhaaq al-Baatil wal Rad 'Aala Shubuhaat al-Qiss Zakariya Boutrus", al-Nafithah Library, Egypt, 1st Ed., 2009, p.286.

636 "Izhaaq al-Baatil wal Rad 'Aala Shubuhaat al-Qiss Zakariya Boutrus", Ibid, p.286.

of those who spend their substance in the way of Allah is that of a grain of corn: it groweth seven ears, and each ear Hath a hundred grains. Allah giveth manifold increase to whom He pleaseth: And Allah careth for all and He knoweth all things} (Surat al-Baqarah: 261).

- As per the Holy Qur'an, the path leading to Paradise is via correct belief in Him, God's six pillars of Faith, Judgment Day, Books, Messengers, Angels, Destiny (good and bad), righteous deeds like prayer and Zakat, Hajj, Fasting, reading the Qur'an, giving charity, etc. This is all done so that one's scales of goodness on Judgment Day will tip the balance and be worthy of God's Mercy. God Says: {Then, he whose balance (of good deeds) will be (found) heavy, will be in a life of good pleasure and Satisfaction} (Surat al-Qaari'aa: 06-07).

- The good deeds which will tip one's scales on Judgment Day are those conducted in obeying God's Orders and ceasing from that which He Prohibited. God Says: {Those who obey Allah and His Messenger will be admitted to Gardens with rivers flowing beneath, to abide therein (for ever) and that will be the supreme achievement} (Surat al-Nisaa': 13).[637]

Sixth: Prophet Isa's Descending at the End of Days:

God raised Isa (pbuh) unto Himself; he is now enjoying a good life in the Heavens and had met our Prophet Mohammad (pbuh) on the latter's Journey to the Heavens where he first met him at al-Masjid al-Aqsa when our Prophet Mohammad led all other prophets in prayer, including Isa, and a second time when Prophet Mohammad was ushered up to the Heavens. Prophet Mohammad told us that he met Isa (pbuh) on the second level of the Heavens. He reports:

[637] "Izhaaq al-Baatil wal Rad 'Aala Shubuhaat al-Qiss Zakariya Boutrus", Ibid, p.286.

"A voice asked: 'Who is this?' Jibreel said it was him. 'Who is with you?' Jibreel said it was Mohammad (pbuh). 'Has he been sent for?' Jibreel said he had. So the voice said: 'Welcome be to him then.' Then I came upon Isa and Yahia who said: 'Welcome to you from a brother and a prophet.[638]'"

1. Appearance of Isa (pbuh):

Prophet Mohammad (pbuh) informed us of some of Prophet Isa's physique and outward appearance. Abu Hurayrah reported that the Prophet (pbuh) said, "On the night I was ushered up to the Heavens, I saw Mousa who was tall and stout, and I saw Isa who was of medium height, thin, with rosy cheeks as if he had just had a hot bath …"[639]

Many Hadeeths with verified chains of narrators summarise the description of Prophet Isa as one who was of medium build, light skinned to reddish and had long shiny black hair that looked healthy.[640]

2. Evidence from the Holy Qur'an attesting to the descending of Isa:

- God Says: {When (Jesus) the son of Mary is held up as an example, behold, thy people raise a clamour thereat (in ridicule)! And they say, "Are our gods best, or he?" This they set forth to thee, only by way of disputation: yea, they are a contentious people. He was no more than a servant: We granted Our favour to him, and We made him an example to the Children of Israel. And if it were Our Will, We could make angels from amongst you, succeeding each other on the earth. And (Jesus) shall be a Sign (for the coming of) the Hour (of Judgment): therefore have no doubt

[638] Al-Bukhari, no. 3207. Muslim, no. 164. "Al-Qasas al-Qur'ani: Presentation and Analysis of Events", 4/399.

[639] Al-Bukhari, no. 3394. Muslim, no. 168.

[640] "Al-Qasas al-Qur'ani: Presentation and Analysis of Events", Ibid, 4/401.

about the (Hour), but follow ye Me: this is a Straight Way. Let not the Evil One hinder you: for he is to you an enemy avowed} (Surat al-Zukhruf: 57-62).

The phrase (And (Jesus) shall be a Sign (for the coming of) the Hour (of Judgment): therefore, have no doubt about the Hour) indicates that Prophet Isa shall descend to Earth at the End of Days and that he shall be a sign of its ushering.[641]

- God Says: {And there is none of the People of the Book but must believe in him before his death; and on the Day of Judgment he will be a witness against them} (Surat al-Nisaa': 159).

It is at this time that Prophet Isa will kill the false Messiah, break the cross and accept none other but Islam from all people.

3. Evidence from the Sunnah attesting to the descending of Isa:

Many of Prophet Mohammad's Hadeeths have spoken of Prophet Isa's descending. Imam al-Kashmiri dedicated a book for these Hadeeths which he titled "*Al-Tasreeh Fima Tawatara fi Nuzool al-Maseeh*". The following are examples:

- That reported by al-Bukhari and Muslim of Abu Hurayrah who reported that Prophet Mohammad (pbuh) said: "I swear by He who holds the reign of my life that the son of Maryam shall descend to you as a fair judge who will break the cross, kill the pig, impose taxes on lands of non-Muslims (Jizyah), and that money will be so much in surplus that none would accept it so that one prostration may be better than that of the world and all in it." Abu Hurayrah then said, "And read if you wish: (And there is none of the people of the Book but must believe in him before his death; and on the Day of Judgment he will be a witness against them.)[642]

---

[641] "Al-Qasas al-Qur'ani: Presentation and Analysis of Events", Ibid, 4/403.

[642] "Saheeh al-Bukhari Ahaadeeth al-Anbiyaa'", Ibid, 6/490.

- Muslim reported that Jabir said, "I heard the Prophet (pbuh) say: 'A group from among my nation shall still defend the truth and shall be successful in this endeavour until Judgment Day. Isa son of Maryam will then descend and their leader will ask Isa to pray for them, but Isa will say: No, as each of you is a leader of the other for God Has Blessed this nation."[643]

- Sheikh Mohammad Nassereddine al-Albaani said: "I realise that the Hadeeths on the false prophet and on the descending of Isa (pbuh) are of verified chains of narrators. They must be believed in regardless of what some people, who are ignorant in this field, claim. Had any of these traced their sequencing, they would have found them solid, as has been attested to by the leading figures of this science like al-Haafeth Ibn Hajar."[644]

- Judge Ayaad said: "The descending of Isa and his killing of the imposter are true and verified matters for people who follow the Sunnah of verified Hadeeths. No intellectual nor legislative matters oppose it; hence it must be considered true.[645]"

4. Wisdom behind descending Prophet Isa, not another:

The following are some reasons for the descending of Prophet Isa (pbuh), specifically, and not another prophet:

First: So as to counter the Jews' claim of having gloated about killing and crucifying prophet Isa (pbuh): (That they said (in boast), "We killed Christ Jesus the son of Mary, the Messenger of Allah"). It is he who will kill them and their imposter ruler, the false Messiah.

Second: So as to complete that which remains of his life which God has destined him, die and be buried on Earth for he is a cre-

[643] Muslim, "Baab Nuzool Isa bin Matyam Haakiman", 2/194, Sharh al-Nawawi.

[644] Al-Albani, "Tamaam al-Minnah fil Ta'aleeq 'Aala Fiqh al-Sunnah", al-Rayah House, Riyadh, 3rd Ed., 1409h, p.79.

[645] "Sharh Saheeh Muslim", 18/75.

ation of God who has been in the Heavens for centuries now, but who must eventually die. It is only God who does not die. Yet Prophet Isa cannot die in the Heavens and be buried there as it is not the locale where humans die. God created mankind from earth, buries them in earth and will resurrect them from earth. God Says: {From the (earth) did We create you, and into it shall We return you, and from it shall We bring you out once again} (Surat Ta Ha : 55).

Third: So as to dispel the lies of Nasraanis about him. Prophet Isa will call upon them to worship the One God, and he will renounce all the lies upon which Nasraaniism had been based. He will break the cross and kill the swine. It is also meant to dispel their falsehoods of Isa having been killed, crucified and his soul having left his body while he was on the cross.[646]

Fourth: His testament that Prophet Mohammad (pbut) was the concluding prophet and that Islam is the religion to follow as it annuls all previous religions like Judaism and Nasraaniism.

5. By what shall Isa (pbuh) rule?:

Prophet Isa (pbuh) will rule by the law descended upon Prophet Mohammad and will be one of his followers. He will not be given a new message to uphold as Islam is the concluding religion till Judgment Day. Prophet Isa will thus be a ruler in the Nation of Islam and one who renews faith in it as there shall exist no new prophet after Mohammad (pbuh).[647]

6. Security and Blessings shall abound:

Al-Nawaas bin Sam'aan reported a long Hadeeth on the false prophet, the descending of Isa, the insurgence of Gog and Magog

---

[646] Mohammad Anwar Shah al-Kashmeeri, "Al-Tasreeh bima Tawaatara fi Nuzool al-Maseeh", ver. by Abdel-Fattah Abu Ghudda, al-Matboo'aat al-Islamiyah Office, Aleppo, 4th Ed., 1982, p.93-94.

[647] Yusuf Abdullah al-Waabil, "Ashraat al-Sa'aah", p.358.

during the time of Isa and how he prays for their doom and that they are so doomed.[648] Included in it is this statement by Prophet Mohammad: "Then God sends rain that engulfs all and washes all of Earth until it shines like a mirror. Then the Earth is ordered to bear fruit and blessings. People then eat from a pomegranate and hide in its shade due to its vastness. Milk is blessed and one milking of camel suffices many people; that of cow suffices a whole tribe; that of sheep suffices a family."[649]

Other manifestations of blessings after the descending of Prophet Isa include that people will no longer envy or hold hatred in their hearts for one another. There will no longer be animosity among animals as sheep and wolves will graze together, and that peace, security and wealth shall spread throughout the land.[650]

7. Prophet Isa's most important actions after his descending:

From the same Hadeeth, above, which was reported in *Saheeh Muslim* and in other books of Hadeeth and Sunnah,[651] the following is a summary of the most prominent matters concerning Prophet Isa (pbuh):

- He shall descend at the height of the false prophet's reign.

- He shall descend at the white minaret East of Damascus.

- Upon descending, he will be wearing two pieces of beautiful light yellow garb.

- Two angels will accompany him as he descends, with him placing his palms on their wings.

- His head will be dripping wet with water from the Heavens that will fall generously in big drops when he lowers his head and slower when he raises it.

---

648 Ibid, p.361.

649 "Saheeh Muslim Ma'a Sharh al-Nawawi", 18/63-70.

650 "Al-Qasas al-Qur'ani: Presentation and Analysis of Events", Ibid, 4/427.

651 Reported by Muslim, no. 937. "Sunan al-Tirmithi", no. 2341.

- His descending with water dripping from his head mirrors his state when God raised him to the Heavens.

- He will have more resolve and influence, and his breath will reach as far as his sight and will kill any unbeliever in its path. This is a miracle that God will perform through Isa (pbuh).

- This same breath that Prophet Isa breathed life into clay birds rendering them alive, while among the Israelites, shall at the End of Days kill the living unbelievers – all through God's Will.

- He will pursue the Imposter Messiah who escapes to Palestine, and will catch up with him in Lod – a Palestinian city near al-Ramleh and close to the Holy Land – where Isa (pbuh) will kill him. The sedition of the false Messiah shall end there.

- He will then be surrounded by the righteous believers, who God had saved from the false Messiah's sedition, and they will voice their pleasure of having been done with him. They will be pleased with life by Prophet Isa who will wipe on their faces and inform them of their statuses in Paradise.

- As they are in this happy mode, Gog and Magog[652] will rise from the East and head towards Palestine.

- God tells Prophet Isa that no man has the power to overcome Gog and Magog as they are the strongest on Earth. God orders Isa to hold out with his believing followers at Mt. Sinai (al-Toor) where Mousa (pbuh) had sought God's Grace, and that God shall protect them there.

- Gog and Magog will invade Earth in huge numbers. The first among them will be drinking at Lake Tiberias and the mob will leave it dry by the time their last arrives at it. They would say: We knew of a lake here, but where has all its water gone?

- Gog and Magog and their mob encircle Isa (pbuh) and his followers at Mt. Sinai and lay siege to the mountain.

---

[652] "Al-Qasas al-Qur'ani: Presentation and Analysis of Events", Ibid, 4/410.

- The siege takes its toll on the believers until they can no longer find any source of food.

- Prophet Isa and his followers beseech aid from The Almighty and pray for the demise of Gog and Magog.

- God responds favourably to their prayers and casts disease and plague against the mob with worms, found in the nostrils of cattle, infesting their necks. The plague annihilates the entire mob overnight through the tiny worm that brings them tumbling down.

- Isa (pbuh) and his followers descend Mt. Sinai and find swarms of corpses. They are unable to breathe due to the stench and pray to The Almighty that He relieves them of it.

- God responds favourably and sends camel-sized birds from the Heavens that carry away the corpses.

- God then sends strong rain that engulfs the entire area and washes away the filth of the unbelievers.

- Isa (pbuh) and the believers live on the Holy Land and thank God for all His Graces. They then spend on Earth the happiest time known to mankind since the days of Adam.

- God orders the Earth to bear fruit as the forces of evil are no longer present to the extent that a piece of pomegranate suffices a group and its skin is large enough for people to lie under.

- God then blesses the produce of cattle to suffice entire tribes of people.[653]

- Prophet Isa and his followers live peacefully and plentifully. Then when Prophet Isa dies of natural causes, the believers bury him. A while later, God ends the life of the followers, sends upon them a blessed gust of air and they all die quietly and peacefully.

- Only the evil remain alive; they are overtaken by Satan; they become slaves to their lusts and mate as donkeys do with both

653 "Al-Qasas al-Qur'ani: Presentation and Analysis of Events", Ibid, 4/411-412.

men and women walking naked and indulging in outward sex witnessed by all. It is then that God orders all life to end and for the Apocalypse to occur.[654]

8. Prophet Isa remains 40 years on Earth after descending to it:

Prophet Mohammad (pbuh) has informed us that righteous Muslims shall enjoy the company of Prophet Isa for 40 years once he descends to Earth. Abu Dawoud and Ahmad reported of Abu Hurayrah that Prophet Mohammad said, "There shall be no prophet between me and Isa, and he will be descending. If you see him, you will know him by his looks as he is of medium build with light reddish skin. He will be wearing two yellowish pieces of clothing and his head will be as if it is dripping water although not wet. He will call for Islam, break the cross, kill the pig and apply Jizyah. In his time, God will end the life of all sects who are not Muslim. Isa will also kill the false Messiah, remain on Earth for 40 years and then die, whereupon Muslims will pray on his corpse."[655]

The above Hadeeth does not contradict with others that specify the period to seven years. In *Saheeh Muslim*, its author reports that Abdullah reported of bin Amr bin al-'Aas that Prophet Mohammad (pbuh) said, "God will send forth Isa son of Maryam as if he were Orwah bin Mas'oud, who would seek and kill him, then people will live seven years without any animosity. God will then send a cool gust of wind from the Levant that would collect the souls of all who have a miniscule of belief or goodness within them even if they were in the belly of a mountain."[656]

---

654 Ibid, 4/412.

655 Ibid. See also: "Sunan Abu Dawoud, Kitaab al-Malaahim", no. 4324.

656 "Saheeh Muslim", no. 2940.

Orwah bin Mas'oud was one of Prophet Mohammad's companions and was the master of the Thaqeef clan. The seven years mentioned in the Hadeeth are those which people will live on Earth without any animosity. But Prophet Isa shall remain alive for 40 years as stated above.

It also appears that the mentioning of seven years is stated for showing plentifulness. A similar usage is stated in the Holy Qur'an: {And if all the trees on earth were pens and the ocean (were ink), with seven oceans behind it to add to its (supply), yet would not the Words of Allah be exhausted (in the writing)} (Surat Luqman: 27).

Chapter IV

Najran's Nasraanis – from Arguing to Mubahala

Books on Prophet Mohammad's life report that a delegation of Nasraanis from Najran came to Prophet Mohammad to argue with him about the Messiah and his alleged divinity.

First: Najraanis' stance on Prophet Mohammad's calling:

When Prophet Mohammad's message to Najraanis calling on them to embrace Islam reached their archbishop, he was extremely frightened and requested that a man from Najran come to see him. This man was Sharhabeel bin Wada'aa, from Hamdan, and was always the first to be summoned whenever a problem would occur. The archbishop showed him Prophet Mohammad's letter and asked his opinion about it. Sharhabeel said it seemed legitimate that Mohammad (pbuh) was truly a prophet as God had promised Ibrahim (pbuh) that from among Ismaeel's descendants will come a prophet. The archbishop then called on two other men – Abdullah bin Sharhabeel and Jabbar bin Fayyad – who gave him the same answer. He then called on the clans to gather, numbering over 120 thousand, to take their opinion on the matter and they agreed that he send these three men to bring him news of Mohammad (pbuh).[657] This was the consensus reached by Najran's Nasraani leaders after much consultation and discussion.[658]

---

[657] Al-Bayhaqi, "Dalaa'il al-Nubuwwah", 5/385-386. See: Ibn Qayyim al-Jawziyah, "Zad al-Mu'aad fi Huda Khayr al-'Ibaad", ver. by Shu'aayb al-Arna'out, al-Risalah Est., al-Manar Islamic Library, Beirut, 27th Ed., 1994, 3/631-632. Ahmad Ali Ajeenah, "Nasaara Najraan bayn al-Mujaadalah wal Mubaahalah", p.21.

[658] "Nasaara Najraan bayn al-Mujaadalah wal Mubaahalah", Ibid, p.21.

• Some Najran Nasraanis travel to Prophet Mohammad and acknowledge the truth of his prophethood:

Two men named Abu Harithah[659] and Kouz bin ‘Alqamah were riding to see Prophet Mohammad when the former stated he believed Prophet Mohammad was the true unlettered prophet they had been awaiting. Kouz then asked him why did he not follow him if he believed so, and Abu Harithah said it was out of respect for the Romans who had given them money and honoured them, but also for fear of their reprisal. He then embraced Islam.[660]

The chieftains of Najran had the habit of inheriting the book of each passing ruler before them. Each book would be read by the new ruler and then sealed with wax. As the ruler at the time of Prophet Mohammad was walking with his son he stumbled and his son cursed Prophet Mohammad. His father told him not to as he was the true awaited prophet and that his name was mentioned in the sealed books. Then when he died, his son broke the seals and found the name of Prophet Mohammad written therein, upon which he embraced Islam and performed Hajj.[661]

A number of matters beckon attention here:

- **First:** Jews and Nasraanis had prior knowledge of Mohammad's calling, knew of him through his description and verified this information through their books. It was God's Wisdom that His prophets speak of the glad tidings on the impending arrival of Prophet Mohammad (pbuh) and that he is a true messenger of God.[662]

659 Their high priest and rabbi. Nasraani Roman kings honoured, financed and supported him as they heard of his vast religious knowledge.

660 Al-Bayhaqi, “Dalaa’il al-Nubuwwah”, 5/383. See: Ahmad Ajeenah, “Nasaara Najraan Bayn al-Mujaadalah wal Mubaahalah”, Ibid, p.23.

661 Ibn Hisham, “Al-Seerah al-Nabawiyyah”, ver. by Dr Ahmad Hijazi al-Saqqa, al-Turaath al-Arabi House, Cairo, 1979, 2/376-377.

662 “Nasaara Najraan Bayn al-Mujaadalah wal Mubaahalah”, Ibid, p.24.

Hercules had acknowledged the truthfulness of Prophet Mohammad's calling, yet he died an infidel. When Dihiyyah al-kalbi approached Hercules with the letter from the Prophet, Hercules acknowledged him and that his name was mentioned in their books. But Hercules feared for his life from the Romans if he admitted to this. In order to prove his point, Hercules asked Dihiyyah to go and say the same to the high priest and report back to him what happens. Upon viewing the letter, the high priest took off his black garb, put on white clothes and stood in front of the Romans while they were at church, pronounced his belief in Mohammad, and was beaten to death by them for renouncing their faith. Upon reporting this to Hercules, he said he could not embrace Islam for fear of receiving the same fate.[663]

Al-Bukhari and Muslim reported another Hadeeth concerning Hercules when he called upon Abu Sufyan – who was still an unbeliever at the time – and asked him about Prophet Mohammad. After hearing his answers, Hercules said that this sounded like the traits of the true prophet he knew was coming, and at whose feet he wished to stay and wash.[664]

Ibn Ishak reports that when Hercules read the letter from Prophet Mohammad and verified the information in it from a man who was knowledgeable in old Hebrew scripture, Hercules called on elite Romans to inform them that Mohammad was the awaited messenger who he and the others should follow. Yet when he saw them angered by his words to the extent that they sought to kill him, he said he was only joking with them and wished to see how strong against an enemy their resolve was.[665]

[663] Ibid, p.27.

[664] Al-Bukhari, no. 2941.

[665] "Dalaa'il al-Nubuwwah", Ibid, 5/384.

Roman political and religious leaders knew the truth of Prophet Mohammad's calling, yet they cared more about their mortal interests and posts.

- **Second:** The acknowledgement by people of the Book regarding the truthfulness of Prophet Mohammad's calling does not in itself suffice as they needed to believe all that which he spoke about, embrace Islam and follow it.[666]

The mighty Roman Hercules had concurred to Mohammad's prophethood, yet he did not embrace Islam. The same applies to the Prophet's uncle, Abu Talib, who testified that Islam was the truest of religions, yet he did not embrace it either.

Ibn al-Qayyim said that when viewing history books and news of testimonies by many people of the Book as well as unbelievers of the time, we notice that they knew of Prophet Mohammad's honesty and of the truth of his calling. But such testimony has not rendered them Muslim for this was only them reporting their knowledge of the matter, not their acceptance and embracing of it.[667]

- **Third:** The feeble reasons people gave for not embracing Islam despite their knowledge of its truthfulness for fear of appearing unappreciative of those who funded and honoured them – as stated above of Kouz and Abu Harithah – or for fear of their reprisal reveals that they favour wealth and power over righteousness. Such, too, was the stance expressed by Hercules who – as stated by al-Khafaji – knew of Prophet Mohammad from the Books, but who favoured his personal worldly interest over that of his eternal one.[668] Many Jews and Nasraanis knew of the same and admitted

666 "Nasaara Najraan Bayn al-Mujaadalah wal Mubaahalah", Ibid, p.30.

667 "Zaad al-Mu'aad fi Huda Khayr al-'Ibaad", 3/638-639.

668 Ahmad Shihaab Eddine al-Khafaaji, "Naseem al-Riyaad fi Sharh al-Shifaa'", Azhari Print, Cairo, 2nd Ed., 3/267.

it, but those among them who did not embrace Islam did so out of envy and stubbornness, to which many have admitted.[669]

Second: Appearance of Najran's emissaries:

Najran's emissaries to Prophet Mohammad (pbuh) entered his masjid as he prayed Asr and were wearing priests' clothes. Companions of Prophet Mohammad said they had never seen such emissaries dressed up like them before; then, when it was time for their prayers, they performed them in the Prophet's masjid. Prophet Mohammad told his companions to let them be and they prayed toward the East.[670]

In al-Bayhaqi's version of events, they headed to perform their prayers in the masjid and Muslims aimed to prevent them, but the Prophet (pbuh) told his companions to let them be and they faced the East and conducted their prayers.[671] Then they approached Prophet Mohammad who turned away and did not speak to them. Uthman bin Affan told them it was because of their clothing, so they departed that day and returned after they had removed their ornaments and rings and wore clothes of hermits. They greeted the Prophet (pbuh) who greeted them back. The Prophet then said, "I swear by He Who sent me with righteousness that when they approached me the first time, Satan was among them."[672] Prophet Mohammad turned away from them the first time as he sensed their overt pride through the jewellery they adorned, yet when they returned in humble garb, he responded to their greetings and began speaking with them.[673]

---

669 "Nasaara Najraan Bayn al-Mujaadalah wal Mubaahalah", Ibid, p.37.

670 "Dalaa'il al-Nubuwwah", Ibid, 5/382. "Al-Bidaayah wal Nihaayah", Ibid, 5/51.

671 "Dalaa'il al-Nubuwwah", Ibid, 5/382.

672 "Dalaa'il al-Nubuwwah", Ibid, 5/386-387.

673 "Nasaara Najraan Bayn al-Mujaadalah wal Mubaahalah", Ibid, p.43.

Third: Councils of arguing and debate:

1. God's Order that Prophet Mohammad argue people of the Book:

Prophet Mohammad (pbuh) called people to believing in the One God and not adjoining any partners to Him. He called on them to believe in his calling that upheld God's religion and Law all the while stating that he was the final and concluding of prophets and that his message overrode all previous ones.

Faith denotes believing in all prophets and messengers, and that he/she who distinguishes between one or another has become an unbeliever. This is the reason for which Prophet Mohammad called upon people of the Book to believe in him, and it is why he debated with people of the Book. The Jews were swift to argue with Prophet Mohammad as well as with all other Muslims. At first, as stated by Sheikh Abu Zahra – the discussions were calm and purely religious. Then they took a turn with them calling the Prophet bad names, ridiculing him and betraying his trust to the extent that he had to remove some of them by force and quarrel with others. The arguments took many dimensions as the Prophet was speaking with people who concurred to the authenticity of a Book and believed in messengers, and he would ask them about matters that came from those very Books. He also denounced them for rejecting to follow that which their Books ordained. In turn, they too would ask meticulously phrased questions as they knew that which existed in their Books, yet they deviated from righteousness.[674]

The Almighty had ordered Prophet Mohammad to argue with people of the Book with kindness. God Says: {Invite (all) to the Way of thy Lord with wisdom and beautiful preaching; and argue

---

[674] Mohammad Abu Zahra, "Tareekh al-Jadal", al-Fikr al-Arabi House, Cairo, 2nd Ed., 1980, p. 89.

with them in ways that are best and most gracious} (Surat al-Nahl: 125), and {And dispute ye not with the People of the Book, except with means better than mere disputation} (Surat al-'Ankabut: 46).[675]

2. Many parties attended the debate councils:

The debate councils were out in the open and were witnessed by many Muslims, Jews and Nasraanis. They were also attended by members of delegations, many prominent Muslims and some Jewish inhabitants of Medina who argued with Nasraanis on matters of faith.[676]

Ibn Ishak said, "When Najran's Nasraanis came to Prophet Mohammad (pbuh), the Jews' rabbis met them there and began arguing. A man named Rafi' bin Harmalah told the Nasraanis they were liars and denounced Isa and the Injeel. Then a man from the Nasraanis told the Jews they were liars and denounced Mousa and the Torah. At that moment, God descended the following on Prophet Mohammad: {The Jews say: "The Christians have naught (to stand) upon; and the Christians say: "The Jews have naught (To stand) upon." Yet they (Profess to) study the (same) Book. Like unto their word is what those say who know not; but Allah will judge between them in their quarrel on the Day of Judgment} (Surat al-Baqarah: 113).[677]

They also argued on the matter of Ibrahim (pbuh) with the Jews claiming he was Jewish and the Nasraanis claiming he was of them. So God descended the following on Prophet Mohammad: {Ye People of the Book! Why dispute ye about Abraham, when the *Torah*[678] and the Gospel Were not revealed Till after him? Have ye no understanding? Ah! Ye are those who fell to disputing (Even) in matters of which ye had some knowledge!

[675] "Nasaara Najraan Bayn al-Mujaadalah wal Mubaahalah", Ibid, p.66.

[676] Ibid, p.70.

[677] "Al-Seerah al-Nabawiyyah", Ibid, 2/356.

[678] Corrected by Translator.

but why dispute ye in matters of which ye have no knowledge? It is Allah Who knows, and ye who know not! Abraham was not a Jew nor yet a Christian; but he was true in Faith, and bowed his will to Allah's (Which is Islam), and he joined not gods with Allah. Without doubt, among men, the nearest of kin to Abraham, are those who follow him, as are also this Messenger and those who believe: And Allah is the Protector of those who have faith} (Surat Aal-Imran: 65-68).

It seems also that the Jews interfered in the debates between the Prophet (pbuh) and Najran's Nasraanis. When Jewish rabbis and Nasraani priests were gathered in the presence of the Prophet, Abu Rafi' al-Qarthi said: "Do you wish, O Mohammad, that we worship you as Nasraanis worship Isa son of Maryam?" So a Nasraani named al-Rabees said: "Is this what you seek O Mohammad and to it you are calling on us?" The Prophet said: "God forbid that we order the worship of any other but Him. This is not what He sent me with nor what He ordered me of." So God descended the following holy verses: {It is not (possible) that a man, to whom is given the Book, and Wisdom, and the prophetic office, should say to people: "Be ye my worshippers rather than Allah's": on the contrary (He would say) "Be ye worshippers of Him Who is truly the Cherisher of all: For ye have taught the Book and ye have studied it earnestly." Nor would he instruct you to take angels and prophets for Lords and patrons. What! would he bid you to unbelief after ye have bowed your will (To Allah in Islam)?} (Surat Aal-Imran: 79-80).[679]

Fourth: Arguing topics:

Najran's Nasraanis argued with Prophet Mohammad (pbuh) about a number of topics related to Nasraaniism, most important of which were the following:

[679] "Nasaara Najraan Bayn al-Mujaadalah wal Mubaahalah", Ibid, p.72.

1. Their claim of the Messiah's divinity for being born without a father's seed:

Many versions of events have been told regarding the debates that occurred between the two parties on this topic. The following is but one:

- Ibn Jareer al-Tabari reported that al-Rabee'a said the Nasraanis argued with Prophet Mohammad over Prophet Isa and asked the former about the father of the latter. They also made many false claims and spewed lies about The Almighty who had neither a mistress nor a son. Al-Rabee'a reports:

"Prophet Mohammad asked them, 'Do you not know that every boy looks like his father?' They said, 'We do.'

"The Prophet asked, 'Do you not know that God is Ever-Present and Immortal, and that Isa shall die?' They said, 'We do.'

"The Prophet asked, 'Do you not know that Our God Sees All, Invigorates All, Protects All and Sustains All?' They said, 'We do.'

"The Prophet asked, 'Could Isa do any of this?' They said, 'No.'

"The Prophet asked, 'Do you not know then that The Almighty is aware of All that occurs on Earth and in the Heavens?' They said, 'We do.'

"The Prophet asked, 'Did Isa know anything other than what he was taught?' They said, 'No.'

"The Prophet asked, 'Do you not know that God created Isa in the womb through His Will?' They said, 'We do.'

"The Prophet asked, 'Do you not know that Our God needs neither food nor drink nor does he excrete?' They said, 'We do.'

"The Prophet asked, 'Do you not know that Isa's mother bore him as does any woman, gave birth to him as does any woman, breastfed him as does any woman and that he ate, drank and excreted?' They said, 'We do.'

"The Prophet then said, 'As such, how do you claim of Isa otherwise?'

"Al-Rabee'a said they knew yet refused to concur out of pride. Therefore God descended this verse on Prophet Mohammad: {A.L.M. Allah. There is no god but He, the Living, the Self-Subsisting, the Eternal}" (Surat Aal-Imran: 1-2).[680]

As Nasraaniism is based on Isa's alleged divinity, it is evident that many questions in those debates revolved around this topic. Yet, Prophet Mohammad (pbuh) was able to disprove their claims every time through undisputed facts.

Approximately 80 verses of Surat Aal-Imran are dedicated to dispelling these claims.[681]

2. Claiming the Messiah's divinity due to the miracles he performed:

Regarding the holy verse: {The similitude of Jesus before Allah is as that of Adam; He created him from dust, then said to him: "Be". And he was.} (Aal-Imran: 59), Ibn Jareer al-Tabari reported of Ibn Jareer that 'Ekremah said,

"Ibn Juraij said that they heard that the Nasraani emissaries of Najran had met Prophet Mohammad, and that among the delegation members were al-Sayyid and al-'Aaqib who were Najran's lords at the time. They said, 'Why do you, O Mohammad, curse our man?' Prophet Mohammad asked, 'Who is your man?' They said, 'Isa son of Maryam; you claim he is a servant.' Prophet Mohammad said, 'True. He is the servant of God and His Word which He cast upon Maryam and a Spirit from Him.' They became angry

680 Al-Tabari, "Jaami'a al-Bayan fi Ta'weel al-Qur'an", ver. by Mahmoud Shaakir, al-Kutub al-'Ilmiyyah House, Beirut, 1st Ed., 1992, 6/154.

681 "Nasaara Najraan bayn al-Mujaadalah wal Mubaahalah", Ibid, p.78.

and said, 'If you say the truth, then show us a servant who can resurrect the dead, cure the born blind, breathe life into birdlike clay figurines; he is God, not a servant.' So prophet Mohammad remained silent until Jibreel descended upon him and delivered God's Words: {They do blaspheme who say: "(Allah) is Christ the son of Mary…"} (Surat al-Maa'idah: 72).[682]

The Holy Qur'an descended upon Mohammad (pbuh) at every instance to dispel Nasraanis' claims of Prophet Isa's divinity and to clarify the truth about the nature of these miracles. In the holy verses, mentioned above, Prophet Isa attributes the miracles to The Almighty by saying (With God's Leave). It is God, therefore, Who is The Creator and the Giver of life.[683]

The miracles performed by God at the hands of Prophet Isa were meant to prove to the Israelites that Isa was truly a prophet sent by God to deliver His Message. Yet, they are in no way evidence of Isa's divinity.

3. Misconstruing Isa's description in being God's Word and a Spirit from Him:

The Nasraanis argued with Prophet Mohammad (pbuh) regarding Prophet Isa's description as being God's Word and a Spirit from Him. They said, "Do you not claim Isa is God's Word and a Spirit from Him?" Prophet Mohammad said, "I do." They said, "This suffices us" and they read into it much blasphemy.[684]

So God descended the following verses: {But those in whose hearts is perversity follow the part thereof that is allegorical, seeking discord} (Surat Aal-Imran: 07). God also descended the following: {The similitude of Jesus before Allah is as that of Adam} (Surat Aal-Imran: 59).

682 Ibid, p.81.

683 "Nasaara Najraan bayn al-Mujaadalah wal Mubaahalah", Ibid, p.83

684 Ibid.

The first holy verse shows that their question included wrongs which were refuted. Prophet Mohammad (pbuh) then recited to them inconspicuous holy verses that carry no ambiguities and which clearly concur to God's Singularity whereby He cannot be demeaned by claiming Him to be a father, have partners, be divided nor separated. The Holy Qur'an's stating that Isa was God's Word and a Spirit from Him refer to the Divine miracle of Isa being born without a father's seed. God's Singularity is a fixed and given matter that does not carry any discussion or misinterpretation.[685]

Prophet Isa (pbuh) is a born creature as per: {Behold! the angels said: "O Mary! Allah giveth thee glad tidings of a Word from Him: his name will be Christ Jesus, the son of Mary, held in honour in this world and the Hereafter and of (the company of) those nearest to Allah. He shall speak to the people in childhood and in maturity. And he shall be (of the company) of the righteous." She said: "O my Lord! How shall I have a son when no man hath touched me?" He said: "Even so: Allah createth what He willeth: When He hath decreed a plan, He but saith to it, 'Be', and it is!} (Surat Aal-Imran: 45-47).

The verses show that Prophet Isa is (a Word from God) and not all of God's Words. God expressed His intention regarding this phrase (a Word from God) in the following:

- God Says: {Even so: Allah createth what He willeth: When He hath decreed a plan, He but saith to it, 'Be,' and it is!} (Surat Aal-Imran: 47).

- God Says: {The similitude of Jesus before Allah is as that of Adam; He created him from dust, then said to him: "Be". And he was} (Surat Aal-Imran: 59).

[685] Mohammad Izzat Darwazeh, "Seerat al-Rasool (pbuh)", International Conference on Seerah, Doha Printing, 3rd Ed., 1400h, 2/243.

- God Says: {Such (was) Jesus the son of Mary: (it is) a statement of truth, about which they (vainly) dispute. It is not befitting to (the majesty of) Allah that He should beget a son. Glory be to Him! when He determines a matter, He only says to it, "Be", and it is} (Surat Maryam: 34-35).

These holy verses are evidence that God said "Be!" and that what He Willed occurred, and as such was Prophet Isa created! Accordingly, this is the interpretation of (a Word from Him).[686]

As for God's Words about the Messiah: {Christ Jesus the son of Mary was (no more than) a messenger of Allah, and His Word, which He bestowed on Mary, and a spirit proceeding from Him} (Surat al-Nisaa': 171). As with everything He creates, God said (Be!) and Isa (Was!); accordingly, Isa is but a creation of God.[687]

The description of the Messiah as being (a Spirit from Him) is not detached from God's self:

- God Says: {And He has subjected to you, as from Him, all that is in the heavens and on earth} (Surat al-Jaathiyah: 13).

- God Says: {And ye have no good thing but is from Allah} (Surat al-Nahl: 53).

- God Says: {Whatever good, (O man!) happens to thee, is from Allah} (Surat al-Nisaa': 79).

- God Says: {Those who reject (Truth), among the People of the Book and among the Polytheists, were not going to depart (from their ways) until there should come to them Clear Evidence, A messenger from Allah, rehearsing scriptures kept pure and Holy} (Surat al-Bayyinah: 1-2).

---

[686] Ibn Taymiyyah, "Daqaa'iq al-Tafseer al-Jaami'a", compiled, presented, verified by Mohammad al-sayyid al-Jaleend, Silsilat al-Turaath al-Falsafi, al-Ansaar House, Cairo, 1st Ed., 1978, 2/82-83.

[687] "Fi Thilaal al-Qur'an", Ibid, 2/817.

Hence, all these matters are from God and they are of His creations; foremost of these was a Spirit from God which he sent to Maryam who was also created.[688] A (Spirit from Him) is not meant to show *partialism* as God's Spirit cannot be divided into *parts* nor sections or divisions.

(A Spirit from Him) is adding a creation to its Creator, not as an adjective, but rather so as to show specificity and honour that gives it more prominence over others as being a charitable spirit that obeys God.[689]

Prophet Isa (pbuh) was not distinct among all other mankind in receiving this honour as God gave others the same:

- The spirit of Adam (pbuh) when God informed the angels of him: {Behold! thy Lord said to the angels: "I am about to create man, from sounding clay from mud moulded into shape; When I have fashioned him (in due proportion) and breathed into him of My spirit, fall ye down in obeisance unto him"} (Surat al-Hijr: 28-29).

- The she-camel which was Prophet Salih's miracle to his people of Thamud: {The Thamud (people) rejected (their prophet) through their inordinate wrongdoing, Behold, the most wicked man among them was deputed (for impiety). But the Messenger of Allah said to them: "It is a She-camel of Allah. And (bar her not from) having her drink!"} (Surat al-Shams: 11-13).

Hence, what is meant by *Word* and *Spirit* is different from that claimed by Nasraanis.

4. The Holy Qur'an's discussion of Argued topics:

The Qur'anic verses that were descended upon Prophet Mohammad as a result of Najran's Nasraani delegation – from the

[688] "Nasaara Najraan bayn al-Mujaadalah wal Mubaahalah", Ibid, p.83.

[689] "Al-Meezan fi Muqaranat al-Adyaan: facts and Documents", p.184-186

beginning of Surat Aal-Imran till its 80th verse or so – covered many topics like their faith, refuting their claims and dispelling their falsehoods with proofs.[690]

God Says: {Allah. There is no god but He} (Surat Aal-Imran: 02). God is telling mankind that Divinity is a matter of His alone, that worship of any kind can only be of Him as He is the Only God in the universe and that any other than Him is a creation of His who neither shares nor partners with Him in His Dominion.[691] God States that none other than Him is deserving of being worshipped, and in saying so, God responds to Nasraanis' claims of worshipping Prophet Isa (pbuh).[692]

In saying {Allah. The Living, the Self-Subsisting} (Surat Aal-Imran: 02), God Refutes their claim that the Messiah is the son of God as it is impossible for The Living and The Self-Subsisting to have a son. Fakhreddine al-Raazi says, "God shows us that he is The Living and The Self-Subsistent whereas Isa is not as he was born, and ate, drank and excreted. Nasraanis claim Isa was killed and was defenceless in preventing his own death. This proves he was neither All-Living nor Self-Subsistent; hence, Isa was not a god and this dispels Nasraanis' claim regarding the Trinity."[693]

Having Stated such undisputable proofs, God then warns them of severe torture and retribution: {Then those who reject Faith in the Signs of Allah will suffer the severest penalty, and Allah is Exalted in Might, Lord of Retribution} (Surat Aal-Imran: 04).

Afterwards, God Says: {From Allah, verily nothing is hidden on earth or in the heavens} (Surat Aal-Imran: 05). This means that God Knows that which the Nasraanis aimed to achieve, what they

---

690 "Nasaara Najraan bayn al-Mujaadalah wal Mubaahalah", Ibid, p.88.

691 Ibid.

692 Ibid.

693 Fakhr Eddine al-Raazi, "Mafateeh al-Ghayb", 7/129.

connived to do and how they have claimed Isa to be a god – all in blasphemous accusations against The Almighty.[694]

Having dispelled through proofs the lies of Nasraaniism by Decreeing Isa never to have been divine, God Embarks on refuting their claim regarding Isa's divinity for being borne without the seed of a father.

God Says: {He it is Who shapes you in the wombs as He pleases. There is no god but He, the Exalted in Might, the Wise} (Surat Aal-Imran: 06). It is God who decides if a child is male, female, dark, red or the like. God shaped Isa in his mother's womb as He Wished. Had Isa been a god, he would not have been borne by a womb or through one, and was therefore a creation of God.

Nasraanis do not contest that Isa (pbuh) was born from a womb as was Adam (pbuh); hence, how could he have been a god?[695]

The holy verses of Surat Aal-Imran have stated that their love for that which they lusted for of monies, children and power prevented them from following and embracing righteousness after having realised it as being so.

Fifth: Mubahala is the final resort:

God then ordered Prophet Mohammad to perform an act known as Mubahala against those who remain stubborn on the matter of Prophet Isa (pbuh) after having shown them proofs that dispelled their claims.

Mubahala is a term that refers to an act performed by a group of people who disagree on a matter, whereby they would say in earnest: "May God curse the liar(s) among us concerning this matter."[696]

694 "Nasaara Najraan bayn al-Mujaadalah wal Mubaahalah", Ibid, p.89.

695 "Tafseer al-Tabari: Taqreeb wa Tahtheeb" as from "Nasaara Najraan bayn al-Mujaadalah wal Mubaahalah", p.101.

696 "Nasaara Najraan bayn al-Mujaadalah wal Mubaahalah", Ibid, p.114.

God Said to Prophet Mohammad: {If any one disputes in this matter with thee, now after (full) knowledge Hath come to thee, say: "Come! let us gather together, our sons and your sons, our women and your women, ourselves and yourselves: Then let us earnestly pray, and invoke the curse of Allah on those who lie!"} (Surat Aal-Imran: 61).

The verse means that if anyone still argues with Prophet Mohammad about Isa son of Maryam who God has shown to be His servant and messenger, the Prophet must call upon them to perform Mubahala.[697]

This is why Prophet Mohammad then told them, "God has ordered me that you either accept this or that I call upon you to perform Mubahala." They said, "We will return to our people and think about the matter then return to see you."[698]

Najran's Nasraanis held their internal consultations and decided to reject performing Mubahala at any cost. They travelled to meet with Prophet Mohammad and told him, "We have decided not to perform Mubahala with you and leave you to follow your religion and us to follow ours."[699]

1. Reason they abstained from Mubahala:

They feared God's retribution as they knew Prophet Mohammad was honest and that his prophethood was true. They admitted in many statements they made that he was the prophet of who Books had brought glad tidings.

- Abdul-Maseeh al-'Aaqib is reported to have told the Nasraani gathering, "You know that if any prophet conducted Mubahala, all members of the other group would be annihilated. You will be

[697] Mohammad al-Taahir Asour, "Tahreer al-Ma'ana al-Sadeed wa Tanweer al-'Aaql al-Jadeed min Tafseer al-Kitaab al-Majeed", 3/264.

[698] "Rouh al-Ma'aani fi Tafseer al-Qur'an al-'Atheem wal Sab'a al-Muthaani", Ibid, 3/188.

[699] Ibn al-Atheer, "Al-Kaamil fil Tareekh", 2/162.

a matter of the past if you do so. As you know that this man is a prophet sent from God, do not perform Mubahala with him."

- When the emissaries from Najran saw Prophet Mohammad (pbuh) accompanied by Fatima, al-Hassan, al-Hussein and Ali, they said, "These are faces who if they swore to God to remove mountains, He would do so, without them even having to perform Mubahala."[700]

Abstaining from performing Mubahala attests to the truth of Prophet Mohammad and that they knew this, as otherwise, they would have performed it. As such, it is also proof that that which the Nasraanis claimed of Isa being a god or son of a god was not true.

2. Najran's delegation requests a truce:

Having refused to perform Mubahala, Najran's delegation requested a truce be forged with Prophet Mohammad through which they would pay Jizyah. Prophet Mohammad accepted their request, mandated to them the amount of Jizyah, told them how to pay it and explained to them rights, duties and terms of dealings between them and Muslims.[701]

They said to Prophet Mohammad, "We shall give you that which you demanded, and send forth with us a man who you truly trust." Prophet Mohammad said, "I will send with you a very trustworthy man. Stand up O Abu Obaidah bin al-Jarrah. He is the trusted one of this nation."[702]

The amount of Jizyah was 1000 ounces of silver to be paid in the month of Rajab and 1000 ounces of the same to be paid in the month of Safar.[703]

---

[700] "Nasaara Najraan bayn al-Mujaadalah wal Mubaahalah", Ibid, p.139.

[701] "Nasaara Najraan bayn al-Mujaadalah wal Mubaahalah", Ibid, p.152.

[702] Al-Bukhari, "Kitaab al-Maghaazi", no. 4380.

[703] "Fath al-Baari Sharh Saheeh al-Bukhari", Ibid, 7/118.

The letter which Prophet Mohammad (pbuh) sent to Najraanis detailed Islam's justice and benevolence in dealing with non-Muslims, emphasised their rights, the Islamic State's commitment to protecting them, not interfering in their religious affairs, not imposing on any of their rights or sovereignty and that they too would protect the Prophet and not expose him to any threats as long as the truce was valid.[704]

3. Calling on Najraanis to believe in The Almighty:

As God dispelled their claims about Prophet Isa (pbuh), and seeing that they have exhausted all their excuses in refusing to perform Mubahala, The Almighty orders Prophet Mohammad to call upon them to embrace Islam – the religion which all prophets and messengers had called for.[705]

God tells Prophet Mohammad: {Say: "O People of the Book! come to common terms as between us and you: That we worship none but Allah. that we associate no partners with him; that we erect not, from among ourselves, Lords and patrons other than Allah." If then they turn back, say ye: "Bear witness that we (at least) are Muslims (bowing to Allah's Will)} (Surat Aal-Imran: 64).

Believing in the One God Who has no partner has always been the essence of all Divine messages. This is why Prophet Mohammad (pbuh) called upon them to meet at this common principle in which all followers of messengers believe: {Come to common terms as between us and you: That we worship none but Allah. that we associate no partners with him; that we erect not, from among ourselves, Lords and patrons other than Allah} (Surat Aal-Imran: 64).

Prophet Mohammad would always refer to this holy verse when sending letters to rulers, like those he sent to Hercules,

[704] "Nasaara Najraan bayn al-Mujaadalah wal Mubaahalah", Ibid, p.168.

[705] "Tafseer al-Manar Tafseer al-Qur'an al-Kareem", Ibid, 3/267-268.

al-Muqawqis and other leaders, as it is the foundation on which Islam is based.[706]

Sixth: All messengers called for attesting to the Singularity of God:

All prophets and messengers (pbut) called for attesting to God's Singularity in the universe and to worshipping and obeying Him. They informed their peoples of who their Creator is, facts of the universe like life, death, heaven, hell, demons, angels and about man's nature, all through the revelations they received from The Almighty.

The Holy Qur'an has preserved for us the life stories of these prophets among who is Isa (pbuh). This book, between your hands at the moment, has detailed the story of this great prophet and that of his blessed mother from the Qur'an's true and incontestable point of view.

[706] "Nasaara Najraan bayn al-Mujaadalah wal Mubaahalah", Ibid, p.179.

Conclusion

1. Isa (pbuh) was born in the land of Galilee from the territories of Palestine or (Galilee of the Nations), as the Israelis later called it, because it was an open territory for all eastern and western nations - in the city of Bethlehem - about 10 km to the south of Jerusalem.

2. The life of the Israelites in Palestine went through three eras: the reign of judges, the reign of kings and the reign of division.

3.The children of Israel were invaded by Bakhtanasr (Chaldean ruler of Babylon) who occupied the Levant and Palestine, expelled the Pharaohs and marched on the state of Judah which had rebelled against him, destroyed it and the Temple of Jerusalem and drove its people into slave-like exile to Babylon in what is known as the Babylonian Captivity.

4. The Babylonian state fell into the hands of the Persians during the reign of their king Cyrus in 538 BC, who allowed the Jews to return to Jerusalem and build their temple. He also appointed a ruler from among them.

5. Alexander the Great of Macedonia marched on the Levant and Palestine, conquered them, ended Persians' rule, and Jews' area became under the rule of the Greeks from the end of the fourth century BC till the middle of the first century BC.

6. In mid first century BC, Roman commander Pompey marched on the Levant and Palestine in 64 BC and ended the rule of the Greeks there, and the Jews came under the rule and control of the Romans, and it is in their time that the Messiah was born.

7. Palestine was subjected to Roman policy, initially adopted a system of protection and allowed a local Jewish king to be the shell ruler so as to secure his loyalty.

8. In the era of Augustus Emperor of Rome (died: 14 AD) the Roman Empire encircled the entire Mediterranean, European

countries located west of the Rhine and till the Black Sea. It also ruled over Anatolia (Turkey), Mesopotamia, the Levant, Egypt and the entire North African region. Hence, Nasraani society was born into a place where two worlds met: East and West, Semites and Romans, Greeks, Jews and non-Jews.

9. A Jewish man, Herod the Elder, ruled from 40-37 BC, and then in the year 6 AD, Rome brought the whole country under direct rule, annexing the Jewish provinces of the south and Samaria in the middle within one state.

10. The political situation in the era of the Messiah (pbuh) was the worst ever, and the social situation was even worse than that. Rulers' absolute power confiscated all laws and liberties. This led to great disparity between rulers and subjects. The former were tyrannical, possessed wealth and led luxurious lives, while the latter were destitute and lived in humiliation. This was in addition to the taxes that were levied on behalf of Rome, with the sole responsibility of the clergy rendered to collecting money. The society was void of interdependence and cohesion, nationalism spread among the masses and social classes emerged.

11. The Divine teachings carried forth by Isa (pbuh) were suitable for this environment, and came as a remedy for its problems. As the love for money and power dominated that society, the spiritual teachings of Isa allowed people to transcend beyond those physical wants.

12. The prevailing ideas and beliefs in and around this environment influenced Christianity into taking on varied forms after Isa was raised to the Heavens. Three players conflicted among one another during this age: the Greek civilisation that shaped the human mind, the Roman state which ascribed for it its institutions and Judaism which Christianity had come to reform after it became a factor of destruction of mind and life's parameters.

13. The Romans then left behind the same which the Greeks did, i.e. the notion of "deification of man". The institutions, structures and organisations left behind by the Greeks, which in turn regulated Roman religious life, seeped into Christian religious life with great and serious deviation from the Nasraaniism brought forth by Isa (pbuh).

14. Among the most important groups of Jews in this period were the Samarians, Sadducees, Pharisees, Qumranians, and Asanians. Except for the Samarians, all others emerged in the period after the Babylonian Captivity.

15. The Temple was demolished by the Babylonians and then Persian Cyrus ordered it rebuilt. Then came King Herod who rebuilt it again during the time of Isa.

16. The most reliable book we have today is the Holy Qur'an and it is why we adopted it for this grave matter of the truth about the Messiah (pbuh). It has been preserved by The Almighty's Will (Falsehood does not seep into it as it is in His Care nor does it do so from behind Him as He is All-Seeing). The Holy Qur'an is The Validator of all previous Books of God, and which supersedes them.

17. Historically speaking, confirmed information about the call of Isa is not readily available as it was a long period ago and was one that witnessed much disruption of historical narratives rendering filtering the right from the wrong extremely difficult.

18. The Injeel descended upon Isa (pbuh) does not exist today even in Nasraani circles. How may we then deviate from Heavenly Revelation, i.e. the Holy Qur'an, and embrace human compositions dubbed "gospels"?

19. The Qur'an, together with the true Sunnah, are the only sources, scientifically and historically speaking, that accurately depict the history of all divine messages, from Adam (pbuh) to the concluding prophet: Mohammad (pbuh).

20. The Qur'an holds scientific worth even among Nasraanis, and they concur, despite not believing in it, the quality of its sources, accuracy of its news, its unprecedented sequencing of trustworthy chains of narration, and the absence of that characterised by their gospels of contradictions, errors, replacements, additions and omissions.

21. There is no book on Earth better than the Qur'an that has assigned to Isa (pbuh), his virgin mother and his generous family greater honour and veneration.

22. The Holy Qur'an's honouring of Isa (pbuh), his mother and his family surpasses beyond any doubt those of the currently existing Torah and Injeel. In addition, the Holy Qur'an corrects the mistakes and false accusations that were directed at Isa (pbuh) and his pure mother by Jews and Christians themselves.

23. The Holy Qur'an contains Surat Aal-Imran, which is the name of the family of Isa (pbuh), and the word (Aal) is one ascribed to venerable families. This is the second longest Surah of the Qur'an. There is also a Surah entitled (Maryam), the name of the Virgin mother of the Messiah (pbut). But the Qur'an contains no Surahs named after the family of Prophet Mohammad (pbuh), Bani Hashim or Bani Abdul-Mutallib, nor is there one named after his mother, Amna bint Wahab.

24. The Holy Qur'an is the only truthful historical document that contains no ambiguity or distortion, and which enjoys absolute 100% credibility in providing the true story of Isa (pbuh), his mother, his family, his calling, his supporters, his people and his truth.

25. The Qur'an's reporting of Prophet Isa's life is evidence of historical marvel which testifies that the Qur'an cannot be of human making, but rather the Word of God the Creator. It also stands as testament to Prophet Mohammad's truthfulness as

these facts could not have been deducted by him from the Old and New Testaments because of the great discrepancy between the two. It suffices to state that there are facts in the Qur'an not mentioned in either Testament such as the miracle of Isa (pbuh) speaking while just a new-born and confessing his complete servitude to The Almighty.

26. The name of Isa (pbuh) was mentioned 25 times in the Qur'an. The name of his mother Maryam (pbuh) was stated 34 times: 23 times coupled with the name Isa son of Maryam, and 11 times on its own.

27. The Holy Qur'an details Isa's family from his mother's parents' side, and shows the greatness of this family's righteousness, piety and worship.

28. God states that Prophet Isa (pbuh) was born from his mother so as to refute that which Nasraanis claim about him being the son of God. Isa had a mother who had parents, and who they in turn also had theirs, all the way back till Adam (pbuh).

29. God mentions the circumstances surrounding the conceiving of Maryam, her birth and her upbringing. She was surrounded by worship and piety as a foetus in her mother's womb all the way through till she became an adult. God selected her for a grave matter as her mother had vowed that Maryam – while still in her womb – would be dedicated once born to the worship of God and the servitude of the Holy Land.

30. The supplication of Imran's woman was proof of her sincerity, the strength of her faith and of her good worship for her Lord. Therefore, she was steadfast in her vow and asked God to save Maryam and her offspring from the doings of Satan.

31. God embraced Maryam (pbuh) with good acceptance, rooted her well and granted her Prophet Zakariya (pbuh) to cater to her needs and righteousness.

32. Maryam lived her childhood and youth in Zakariya's care, learned the sciences from him, followed him in prayer and adopted his good Islamic manners. She was worshipping of God, prayed to Him constantly, was altruistic and connected to The Almighty.

33. Maryam (pbuh) was the reason for Zakariya's prayers to God to be granted good offspring as he saw the virtues and dignity God had bestowed on Maryam, and because she reminded him that her sustenance was all from God.

34. God answered the prayer of Zakaria and granted him a child although his wife had been infertile. This was a miracle from God that went beyond all reasoning of mankind and science.

35. Zakariya and Yahya (pbut) were the last prophets sent to the Israelites before God sent forth Isa son of Maryam (pbut).

36. Having told the story of the birth of Yahya, son of Zakariya, from a barren old woman and an elderly man – a true miracle in itself – God then speaks of an even greater miracle He performed, that being of Isa's birth from a mother without the seed of a father.

37. God blessed Maryam by selecting her from among all women on Earth after her mother vowed she would be dedicated to God's worship and servitude, provided her with good upbringing under the watchful eyes of Zakariya, provided her with all forms of sustenance while she was praying at the Mihrab, purified her of all impurities and distinguished her from among all other women to be the bearer of His miracle of Isa (pbuh) without the seed of a father.

38. Maryam (pbuh) possessed perfection of devotion and obedience to God, The Almighty, both innately and outwardly. She was described as an *Attestor to Truth* due to believing in God's signs and in that which her parents had told her regarding her own conception.

39. The life of Maryam (pbuh) was distinguished with obedience, worship, reverence and prayer to God in preparation for the great matter of bearing Isa (pbuh) without a father.

40. The verses that speak about Imran's family, Maryam and Zakaria (pbut) in Surat Aal-Imran are news of the unseen and a clear indication of the prophethood of Mohammad (pbuh). As Jews and Nasraanis knew that Prophet Mohammad was unlettered and could neither read nor write, such information could have only be revealed to him by The Almighty as it was known by only a handful of priests who Mohammad was never in touch with; hence, it is testament to his honesty and the truth of his message.

41. The gospels make contradictory statements on Isa and Maryam (pbut) that are far from the truth. Even interpreters of the gospels have been confused in explaining each.

42. The angels heralded news of Isa to Maryam and stated a number of his descriptions which were later realised, e.g. a leader in life and in the Hereafter, dear to God, speaks to people as an infant and a young man and among the righteous.

43. The Holy Qur'an mentions the dialogue between Jibreel and Maryam in a very meticulous manner; a precision found only there.

44. The meaning of Isa being a (Word from God) in (A Word from Him which He cast upon Maryam) is the same Word with which God creates everything, i.e. (Be). Hence, God created Isa through His Order for the matter to occur, as others have occurred, as is stated in the Holy Qur'an. God cast this word upon Maryam and created Isa in her womb without a father's seed – contrary to what is customary in human life formulation. God created Adam through uttering the same Word and he became a man from nothingness. Prophet Isa came to exist through the Word (Be!), but he is not The Word.

45. A (Spirit from Him) is not meant to show partialism as God's Spirit cannot be divided into parts nor sections or divisions. (A Spirit from Him) is adding a creation to its Creator, not as an adjective, but rather so as to show specificity and honour that gives it more prominence over others as being a charitable spirit that obeys God. It is similar to the holy verse (When I have fashioned him (in due proportion) and breathed into him of My spirit, fall ye down in obeisance unto him). Therefore, the Spirit is of God's creations.

46. Surat Maryam details Isa's birth with precise accuracy, descriptions of the place and the psychological state experienced by Maryam, starting from going to the far place, going into labour and the pain she suffered during childbirth to the extent that she wished for her own death. This is in addition to her son calling on her from under her and the accompanying blessings.

47. God decreed Maryam not to speak to her people so that the new-born Isa would do the talking as a miracle from God, and so as to prove to all that Maryam was still the virgin and had committed no wrong.

48. When Isa (pbuh) spoke while just a new-born, he dispelled all lies perpetrated against his mother and voiced that his birth was a miracle from The Almighty God. Isa spoke to his mother's people about his birth without the seed of a father, the message God has entrusted him with, the Book that he shall bear, his prophethood, God's order to him that he pray and fast, be good to his mother, among others. The Holy Qur'an at this point ceases from stating more about the birth of Prophet Isa (pbuh).

49. After having spoken of Maryam's and her son's (pbut) life story with high transparency and unparalleled credibility, God Says: (Such (was) Jesus the son of Mary: (it is) a statement of truth, about which they (vainly) dispute. It is not befitting to (the majesty of) Allah that He should beget a son. Glory be to

Him! when He determines a matter, He only says to it, "Be", and it is).

50. The Holy Qur'an details the story of the Messiah with tremendous precision after both his honourable life and his generous call had been marred by much distortion and alteration. This is truly one of the historical miracles in the Qur'an that testifies It is the Word of God the Creator and that Prophet Mohammad was sent by God.

51. The King of Abyssinia, al-Najaashi, was touched after Ja'afar bin Abu Talib recited Surat Maryam, and he eventually embraced Islam.

52. There is no Surah in the name of a woman except Surat Maryam (pbuh) neither in the name of Aminah, Prophet Mohammad's mother, nor Khadijah his wife or his daughter Fatima.

53. Prophet Isa (pbuh) lived his life as a pure and pious young man protected by The Almighty who kept Satan at bay from him. Then God descended his Revelation upon Isa and made him a prophet and messenger who He sent forth to the Israelites along with His Book, the Injeel. The coming of Isa and the Injeel were in fulfilling the glad tidings God sent Isa's mother before she bore him: {And Allah will teach him the Book and Wisdom, the *Torah*[707] and the Gospel, And (appoint him) a messenger to the Children of Israel} (Surat Aal-Imran: 48-49). It is also confirmation of what Isa said when he spoke to the Israelites as an infant: (He said: I am indeed a servant of Allah. He hath given me revelation and made me a prophet).

54. Isa (pbuh) addressed the Israelites, proved that he was the Messenger of God to them, and invited them to worship God, attest to God's Singularity and abide by His Law.

[707] Corrected by Translator.

55. Qur'anic verses express Isa's humanity and that his creation was similar to that of Adam who God created from dust via the Word (Be!). These verses state that Isa is not a god or the son of God, but rather His servant and messenger, and that God is of Higher Order than to beget a son, partner or mistress.

56. The Qur'an details God's great interrogation, in front of all mankind, of Isa (pbuh) on the Day of Resurrection.

57. Qur'anic verses show that Isa (pbuh) is a servant who God had blessed and who called for monotheism and worshiping The Almighty.

58. The Qur'an showcases the procession of great faith led by Nouh, to Ibrahim, to the concluding Prophet Mohammad (pbut). Among these is Isa (pbuh) so that all would know that he was a prophet like all others before and after him, not that he was God, the son of God or one of three.

59. The message of Isa (pbuh) also included faith in revelation, and that the teachings he communicated were not from him but were inspired to him from The Almighty, as was the case with all other prophets.

60. The Holy Qur'an states that Isa, Nouh, Ibrahim, Mousa and Mohammad (pbut) are messengers of Inflexible Purpose.

61. The Holy Qur'an shows that all laws and religions emanate from the same source as evidenced through worship rites like prayer, Zakat, fasting, retribution, toiling towards righteousness, etc.

62. The Holy Qur'an shows that all Divine messages agree on the origins of faith throughout the calls of all prophets (pbut) whose messages did not differ in determining the origins of faith before they were distorted and altered.

63. The concern of Isa (pbuh) was to call on people to obey God, to worship Him exclusively, and to achieve true monotheism that

is based on deep faith and solid knowledge. The foundations of Isa's calling were belief in God, Judgment Day, angels, Heavenly Books, prophets, messengers and destiny.

64. The prophets (pbut) possessed the best qualities and noblest morals and virtues, particularly truth, honesty, discernment, speech, etc. The Holy Qur'an spwaks about the origins of religion and its universal morals followed by all messengers – like the ten commandments mentioned in Surat al-An'aam.

65. Islam is the eternal religion of God, which He accepts no other in its stead. It is the religion God ordained for mankind since their creation and which was brought forth to them via Adam, Idrees, Nouh, Ibrahim, Ibrahim's descendants, Imran's descendants and which was concluded with the message brought forth by Mohammad (pbut). It is the religion that calls for pure monotheism and which contains correct rites and provisions that change neither temporally nor spatially.

66. God sent Isa (pbuh) the son of Maryam with the message of Islam. Isa called on the children of Israel to embrace this religion based on the recognition of the Creator and his Oneness.

67. God informed us that Isa (pbuh) concurred to the untainted Torah in various verses in the Qur'an and that his call was complementary to that of Mousa's (pbuh). Prophet Isa also brought some relief to the Israelites from some provisions in the Torah. Therefore, the natural notion for Nasraaniism was that it follows the Torah while taking into consideration the amendments contained in the Injeel.

68. The Qur'an describes the Divine Torah with positive attributes, praises and commends it and acknowledges its virtues. This is only natural as both the Qur'an and the Torah are from God, and hence the latter – which God originally descended – is dubbed guidance, mercy, light, brightness and law.

69. God has stated that Jewish rabbis altered the Torah by adding much and deducting more. The Qur'an has exposed their deception throughout many holy verses.

70. The Qur'an does not recognise the distorted Torah written by the rabbis throughout the long course of Jewish history, which they dubbed the Old Testament.

71. The luck of the Injeel was no better than that of the Torah as after Prophet Isa was raised to the Heavens, the scripture that came with him has vanished till this very day.

72. The widespread mayhem that followed the absence of Isa (pbuh) was due to the power of the Romans and to the Jews' meddling. Both parties colluded in persecuting those who had believed in Isa and confiscated all that eluded to his teachings. This persecution continued for three centuries during which Christians had many disagreements.

73. Many discrepancies and even contradictions appeared among the gospels said to have been composed by Isa's disciples. Some estimate them to number 70 or more gospels.

74. The current gospels are historical works on the life of Maryam and her son Isa and what happened to him from birth until the end of his life on Earth, according to their beliefs. None of these gospels was written while Prophet Isa was alive.

75. The existence of alteration in the four gospels is clearly evident in its three types: Alteration via switching, alteration via addition and alteration via deduction – also, as evidenced by the Holy Qur'an.

76. Political factors in the fourth century AD influenced the formulation and construction of Christianity into the manner it is known today. Emperor Constantine attempted to harness Nasraaniism to serve him for fear that his empire may become divided. Therefore, he brought together all priests at the Nica-

ean Council and conspired with Alexandria's archbishop to agree on the existence of three gods. The Emperor combatted all those who said otherwise. Also, prior to becoming Christian, Constantine followed paganism which concurred to the existence of more than one god. It is, therefore, no wonder that he would agree with claiming the existence of three deities in Christianity.

77. Isa heralded the coming of Prophet Mohammad (pbuh), and his qualities were stated in the Torah and the Injeel. This has been proven by Nasraani scholars, most famous among which is Abdul-Ahad Dawoud in his book entitled, "*Mohammad in the Holy Book*".

78. God decreed that Prophet Isa be a Sign of His Greatness and thus granted him many miracles. In addition to those mentioned above, Isa could cure the born blind and the lepers, resurrect the dead, create life from clay – all through God's Permission – was informed of matters unseen and the Table that was descended upon him from Heaven.

79. The Hawaaris were supporters of Isa (pbuh) who responded to his call and became helpers of The Almighty in Who they believed.

80. Isa was subjected to the deception of the Jews who tried to kill him, but God protected him and raised him unto Himself.

81. The Arabic word "Death" – as stated in the Holy Qur'an – can mean both actual death and sleep.

82. God *Took* Isa once and will *Take* him again: First of sleep and Second of actual death:

- First Time: Death of sleep when the Jews attempted to crucify and kill him but God saved him by casting sleep on him and then raised him unto Himself, as in: (O Jesus! I will take thee and raise thee to Myself).

- Second Time: When God will descend Isa to Earth at the End of Days so as to complete the rest of his life which God has set for him and then die as all human beings. That death will be of Isa's life ending: (When Thou didst take me up Thou wast the Watcher over them, and Thou art a witness to all things), i.e. when You took my life and I died.

83. The Qur'an speaks of the Jews' attempt to kill Isa (pbuh) in three different Surahs:

- A quick reference to saving him from the children of Israel when he showed them the proofs, in Surat al-Maa'idah (110): (And behold! I did restrain the Children of Israel from (violence to) thee when thou didst show them the clear Signs).

- In the self-explanatory verse of Surat Aal-Imran: (Behold! Allah said: "O Jesus! I will take thee and raise thee to Myself and clear thee ...).

- In the self-explanatory verses of Surat al-Nisaa' (157-158): (That they said (in boast), "We killed Christ Jesus the son of Mary, the Messenger of Allah"; but they killed him not, nor crucified him, but so it was made to appear to them, and those who differ therein are full of doubts, with no (certain) knowledge, but only conjecture to follow, for of a surety they killed him not: Nay, Allah raised him up unto Himself; and Allah is Exalted in Power, Wise).

84. The four gospels (Matthew, Luke, Mark, and John), accredited by Nasraanis nowadays, give conflicting and contradictory accounts of the events of the last night of Isa's life on Earth.

85. The Christian doctrine of Salvation, which was falsely established by Paul, is that Adam (pbuh) sinned, that this sin passed by inheritance to all his children and that the only way to salvation from it is that which they claimed that God came down and incarnated Himself in the form of man in order for Him to be cru-

cified, overcome death and be resurrected so that mankind will be redeemed.

86. Nasraanis base their belief of Isa's crucifixion on that which was written in the gospels, which we have already dispelled as being distorted, altered and contradictory.

87. God holds no sins against mankind that require atonement through forfeiting the life of a prophet or crucifying an alleged son. No human is born bearing the brunt of wrongs perpetrated by those before him/her: (No bearer of burdens can bear the burden of another) (Surat al-An'aam: 164).

88. Christian Salvation was influenced by pagan doctrines as divine incarnation for salvation was among pagan beliefs that were widespread in Greek and Roman countries hundreds of years before the advent of the Messiah (pbuh). Another pagan image that prevailed in pre-Christian pagan societies was crucifying and punishing the god for means of redemption. The resurrection of the redeemer for salvation was a third pagan image that emerged among pre-Christian pagans thanks to Paul and his followers who merely wrote the name of Isa (pbuh) in the place of these saviour pagan gods.

89. The entry of pagans into Nasraaniism, like Emperor Constantine, had the greatest effect on impregnating Christianity with pagan teachings, which led to the emergence of Trinitarianism due to the decisions of the various ecclesiastical councils at different times:

- Council of Nicaea in 325 AD decreed the divinity of Isa (pbuh).

- The First Council of Constantinople in 381 AD decreed the divinity of the Holy Spirit.

- The Council of Ephesus I in 431 AD decreed the three gods: Father, Son and Holy Spirit.

Then they disagreed on the nature of the Messiah. Was he of: one nature? Or of two natures? Did he: emanate from the Father alone, or from both the Father and the Holy Spirit? Thus, it is clear that the doctrine of the Trinitarian faith that Christians believe in was not brought by Isa (pbuh) nor did he order it of his followers, because Isa (pbuh) as shown in this book, called on people to only worship God alone Who has no partners. Prophet Isa did not claim for himself a status other than being God's servant: (He said: "I am indeed a servant of Allah. He hath given me revelation) (Surat Maryam: 30).

90. Christianity which believed in the prophethood of Isa and in his humanity continued since the earliest times of Christianity and has been persecuted by religious and political authorities which claim the sonship of Isa. These Unitarian Christians have been murdered, torched and imprisoned.

91. One of the most famous proponents of Isa's humanity was Arius who was born in Libya. His call was accepted by large masses in Alexandria and even by a group of deacons and priests. Also, during periods of Orthodox control, Arianism had a clear presence in Egypt and in other countries of the Byzantine Empire.

92. Many Unitarian Christians exist nowadays, evidenced by their many churches and their growing numbers in Europe, America and some Asian countries. Many intellectuals have embraced the Christian doctrine of monotheism, including a significant number of Christian clergy. Prophet Mohammad (pbuh) was keen on calling on the Arians to follow his message, and he mentioned them in his letter to Hercules when he called on him to do the same.

93. God raised Isa (pbuh) unto Himself; he is now enjoying a good life in the Heavens and had met our Prophet Mohammad (pbuh) on the latter's Journey to the Heavens where he first met

him at al-Masjid al-Aqsa when Prophet Mohammad led all other prophets in prayer, including Isa, and a second time when Prophet Mohammad was ushered up to the Heavens. Prophet Mohammad told us that he also met Isa (pbuh) on the second level of the Heavens.

94. The Holy Qur'an and the purified Sunnah indicate the arrival of Isa (pbuh) at the End of Days, and that his descension is among the Greater Signs of Judgment Day which include: the exit of Gog and Magog, the three eclipses, the smoke, the sun rising from the West and the fire that forces people to huddle together.

95. Isa (pbuh) will govern with the same law brought forth by Prophet Mohammad and will be among his followers and one leading the nation of Islam's renewal after Mohammad (pbuh). Islam is the concluding religion that shall never be substituted with another.

96. Surat Aal-Imran describes a great debate that occurred between Prophet Mohammad (pbuh) and Najran's Nasraanis. The most important topic therein is the Qur'an's annulment of Prophet Isa's divinity through incontestable evidence.

97. Najran's Nasraanis refused to perform Mubahala for fear of God's retribution as they were certain of Prophet Mohammad's honesty and that of his prophethood. Reports of them have proven they acknowledged Mohammad as the Prophet which Holy Books had heralded. They requested a truce with the Prophet and he granted them one.

98. European intellectualism revolted against the teachings of the Church that were far from the revelation of Heaven, irrational and illogical. Protestant reformists led the revolt against the Church, opposed manifestations of religious rites and the monopoly of the Church and that of the Pope as the supreme Christian authorities. They also deemed distorted Christianity

a religion that limited the mind and hindered technological advancement that was based on reason. This led to forfeiting Christian doctrines.

99. Qur'anic discourse is the closest to the liberated European mind and to its eagerness for truths on faith facts and logic which have been lost in the world of material lusts.

100. The Qur'an shows the truth of Isa (pbuh) and the fact that he is merely a messenger of Inflexible Purpose and a servant of the One and Only Almighty God.

Dr. Ali Mohammad al-Sallabi

• Dr. Ali Mohammad al-Sallabi was born in Benghazi in Libya in 1963.

• A writer, historian and an Islamic thinker.

• The deputy secretary general of the International Union of Muslim Scholars.

• Gained licentiate from Dawa and Fundamentals of Religion College in Madina El Monawara in 1993.

• By his book "Moderation in Holy Qur'an", he gained master degree from Fundamentals of Religion College in Omdurman Islamic University in 1996.

• By his book "Jurisprudence of Empowerment in Holy Qur'an", he gained PHD degree in the Islamic studies from Omdurman Islamic University in Sudan in 1999.

• In his scholar march, he got disciplined by a group of scholars like Sheikh al Qaradawi, Sheikh Akram Dhiya' al Omeri, Dr. Yasin al Khateeb, Salman al Awdah, Yasin Abdel Aziz, Mohammad Buhairi, Mubarak Ahmad Rahma, Ahmad Mohammad Jeeli, Sheikh Rashid al Ghannouci, Sheikh Mohammad al Harathi and other scholars.

• Since his early scholar formation, Dr. Ali al-Sallabi was interested in Holy Qur'an interpretation, Islamic history, jurisprudence of divine established ways (sunnah) and cultures rules.

• Famous for his books and concerns in Holy Qur'an science, jurisprudence, history and Islamic thought.

• A member in the historical review committee and texts auditing committee for many drama actions like Omar Bin al Khattab, Abu Jaafar al Mansour, Imam al Hassan series and Others.

• He waged national initiatives politically and socially in Libya and was interested in national reconciliation project that lasted in writing his book titled “Justice and National Reconciliation; a Religious and Human Necessity”.

• Participated in the (national) reform project: Libya the Futuristic from 2005-2010.

• He interfered to release the political prisoners by leading negotiations with Saif al-Islam Gaddafi and supervised the intellectual dialogues that were complemented by his book titled “Corrective Studies in Jihad, Numeracy and Judging People Concepts”.

• Writings of Dr. Sallabi exceeded seventy in history and Islamic thought with those following translated into English:

-Prophetic Biography

-Abu Bakr al-Seddiq

-Omar Bin al-Khattab

-Othman Bin-Affan

-Ali Bin Abi Talib

-Al-Hassan Bin Ali Bin Abi Talib

-Omar Bin Abdel Aziz

-Salahuddin al-Ayoubi

-Mohammad al-Fateh

-Isa Ibn Maryam (the Whole Truth)